# Microwave
# VEGETARIAN

**Compiled by Judith Ferguson**
**Photography by Peter Barry**
**Designed by Philip Clucas**
**Produced by Ted Smart and David Gibbon**

© 1987 Illustrations and text: Colour Library Books Ltd.,
    Guildford, Surrey, England.
Text filmsetting by Focus Photoset Ltd., London, England.
All rights reserved.
Printed and bound in Barcelona, Spain by Cronión, S.A.
1987 edition published by Crescent Books, distributed by Crown Publishers, Inc.
ISBN 0 517 64079 1
h g f e d c b a

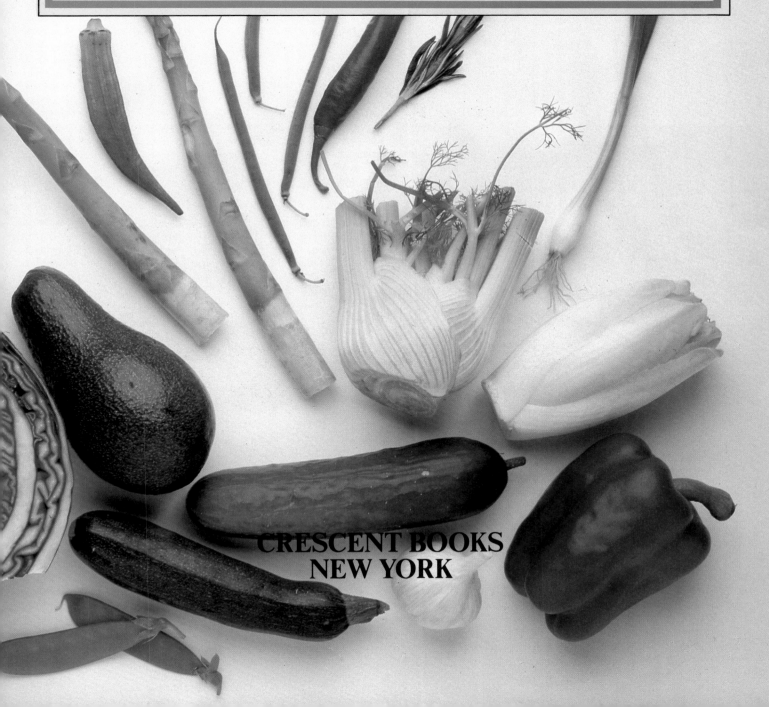

# Microwave
# VEGETARIAN
## COOKING

**CRESCENT BOOKS**
**NEW YORK**

4

# Contents

# INTRODUCTION

The microwave oven has a brilliant way with vegetables. Fast cooking times mean vegetables keep their fresh color and crisp texture. Low evaporation means vegetables need very little water to cook, so they retain their nutritional value. Fresh vegetables cook as quickly as frozen vegetables do by conventional methods, and frozen vegetables are cooked beautifully in almost the blink of an eye.

Vegetarian diets are losing their "cranky" image as more people turn to that way of eating because of weight and nutrition consciousness. The humble dried bean or lentil has an abundant supply of protein to add to our diets, with the added plus of more fibre than many other protein foods.

The microwave method of rehydrating pulses – dried peas, beans and lentils – eliminates overnight soaking. Just cover the dried pulses with water and bring them to the boil, which usually takes about 10 minutes on the highest setting. After that, allow the pulses to boil for 2 minutes. Leave them standing, covered, in the hot water for 1 hour and they will be ready to cook according to your recipe. Dried pulses usually take about an hour to cook. If that doesn't seem like convenience cooking, remember that conventional methods would take twice as long. It is essential, though, that dried peas, beans and lentils are thoroughly cooked. Eating insufficiently cooked pulses can be dangerous.

Vegetarian menus have suffered from the image that they are composed solely of nut cutlets. I have always found that unfair, since well seasoned cutlets are a delicious alternative to meat and a good addition to a healthy diet. Nut cutlets, escalopes and croquettes are very easy to cook in a microwave oven with the use of a browning dish. Be creative with shapes, too, because nut mixtures hold up better in a microwave oven than they do when fried or baked conventionally.

When organizing the recipes into chapters, I was amazed to find just how many recipes could fit easily in several different categories. Pulses can be used in salads, appetizers or entrées. Main courses can be cut down and used as appetizers, and appetizers can be expanded into main-meal-sized portions. Even desserts can be based on vegetables. Which all goes to prove that, vegetarian or not, we can all enjoy more creative meals thanks to the versatility of vegetables.

# Microwave
## VEGETARIAN
# APPETIZERS

## Tomato and Tarragon Creams with Corn Salad

**PREPARATION TIME:** 25 minutes

**MICROWAVE COOKING TIME:** 9-10 minutes

**SERVES:** 4 people

14oz plum tomatoes, canned
2 tbsps tomato paste
1 onion, finely chopped
1 tsp chopped tarragon
1 bay leaf
Salt and pepper
8oz low fat or cream cheese
2 eggs
1 cup whipped cream
1 tbsp gelatin or agar-agar
3 tbsps water and lemon juice mixed
Salt and pepper

**SALAD**
8oz baby corn-on-the-cob
1 green pepper, cut in thin strips
4-6 tomatoes, peeled, seeded and cut in
    strips
4-6 green onions, shredded
3 tbsps salad oil
1 tbsp white wine vinegar
1 tsp white wine vinegar
1 tsp Dijon mustard
1 tsp chopped fresh tarragon
Lettuce leaves

**GARNISH**
Whole tarragon leaves

Sprinkle the gelatin on top of the water and lemon juice in a small custard cup. If using agar-agar in leaf form, dissolve with the water or lemon juice in a small cup. Combine the tomatoes, onion, tarragon, bay leaf, tomato paste, salt and pepper in a deep bowl. Cook, uncovered, 5 minutes on HIGH. Push the pulp through a strainer and set it aside to cool. Beat the eggs and cheese together until smooth. Add the cooled tomato pulp. Melt the gelatin or agar-agar for 30 seconds on

This page: Tomato and Tarragon Creams with Corn Salad. Facing Page: Danish Egg Salad (top) and Pasta and Asparagus Salad (bottom).

HIGH. Pour into the tomato mixture and stir well. Set briefly over ice and stir constantly until beginning to thicken. Fold in the cream and adjust the seasoning. Brush 4 custard cups lightly with oil and spoon in the tomato mixture. Chill until firm. Put the corn into a large bowl with enough hot water to cover. Cover loosely and cook for 3-4 minutes on HIGH until tender. After 2-3 minutes add the pepper strips. Remove the vegetables with a slotted spoon and rinse under cold water. Set aside to drain. Put the tomatoes into the same water and cook 30 seconds on HIGH. Put into cold water immediately. Remove the skins, cut in half and scoop out the seeds. Slice the flesh into thin strips. Mix the oil, vinegar, tarragon, salt and pepper and combine with the vegetables. Add the green onions just before serving. Arrange lettuce leaves on serving plates and carefully turn out the tomato creams. It may be necessary to dip the molds briefly into hot water to loosen. Decorate the creams with whole tarragon leaves and serve surrounded with the corn salad.

## Danish Egg Salad

**PREPARATION TIME:** 20 minutes
**MICROWAVE COOKING TIME:**
7 minutes
**SERVES:** 4 people

4 eggs
2 tbsps cream
2 tbsps butter or margarine
1 cup frozen peas, thawed
1 cucumber, cut into ½ inch dice
6 sticks of celery, diced
3 green onions, chopped
2 tbsps chopped dill
1 cup diced cheese
1 cup sour cream
¼ cup mayonnaise
Paprika
Salt and pepper
1 head Chinese cabbage, shredded

Beat the eggs and cream together with salt and pepper. Heat a browning dish 5 minutes on HIGH, melt the butter or margarine for 1 minute on HIGH. Pour in half the egg mixture and cook the omelet on one side for 1 minute on HIGH. Turn over and cook a further 1 minute. Cook the egg in two batches. Cook the peas for 1 minute on HIGH with 2 tbsps water. Rinse under cold water and drain to dry. Mix the sour cream, mayonnaise, dill, salt and pepper together. Reserve 2 tbsps dressing and mix the remaining dressing with the peas, celery, cheese and cucumber. Arrange the Chinese cabbage on serving plates. Pile on the salad. Cut the omelets into strips and arrange on top. Drizzle the remaining dressing over the omelet strips and sprinkle with paprika.

## Warm Salad with Avocado, Grapes, Blue Cheese and Walnuts

**PREPARATION TIME:** 20 minutes
**MICROWAVE COOKING TIME:**
1-2 minutes
**SERVES:** 4 people

1 head curly endive
1 head Belgian endive (chicory)
1 head radicchio
1 small bunch lambs lettuce or watercress
1 head Chinese cabbage
1 head leaf or iceberg lettuce
4 tbsps chopped fresh herbs
1 cup walnuts
1 cup blue cheese crumbled
1 large or 2 small avocados
1 small bunch black grapes

**DRESSING**
6 tbsps walnut oil and grapeseed oil mixed
2 tbsps lemon vinegar or white wine vinegar and lemon juice mixed
Pinch sugar

Tear the curly endive, Belgian endive, radicchio and lettuce into small pieces. If using lambs lettuce separate the leaves. If using watercress remove any thick stalks. Shred the Chinese cabbage and peel and slice the avocado. Cut the grapes in half and remove any seeds. Combine all the salad ingredients in a large bowl. Mix the salad dressing ingredients and toss with the salad. Arrange on individual salad plates and heat each plate for 1-2 minutes on HIGH before serving.

## Pasta and Asparagus Salad

**PREPARATION TIME:** 15 minutes
**MICROWAVE COOKING TIME:**
11 minutes plus 8 minutes standing time
**SERVES:** 4 people

4oz tagliatelle/fettuccine
1lb asparagus, trimmed and cut into 2 inch pieces
2 zucchini, cut into 2 inch sticks
1 lemon, peeled and segmented
2 tbsps chopped parsley
2 tbsps chopped marjoram
Grated rind and juice of 1 lemon
⅓ cup salad oil
Pinch sugar (optional)
Salt and pepper
1 head lettuce
1 head Belgian endive (chicory)

Put the pasta into a large bowl with 2 cups hot water, a pinch of salt and 1 tsp oil. Cook 6 minutes on HIGH and leave to stand in the water for 8 minutes. Drain and leave to cool completely. Cook the asparagus in ½ cup water for 5 minutes on HIGH or until tender. Add the zucchini after 3 minutes cooking time. Rinse under cold water and drain. Combine the pasta, asparagus, zucchini, parsley, marjoram and lemon segments in a large bowl. Mix the lemon rind, juice, oil, salt and pepper together to blend well. Pour over the combined ingredients and toss to coat. Arrange lettuce and endive on serving plates and pile on the salad to serve.

**Facing page: Warm Salad with Avocado, Grapes, Blue Cheese and Walnuts.**

cook the onion, pepper, and chili pepper for 2 minutes on HIGH. Add to the puréed potato along with the corn and milk. Cook 2 minutes on HIGH and adjust the seasoning. Garnish with chopped parsley.

## Purée of Asparagus Soup

**PREPARATION TIME:** 15 minutes

**MICROWAVE COOKING TIME:** 11 minutes plus 5 minutes standing time

**SERVES:** 4 people

*3lbs asparagus*
*3½ cups vegetable stock*
*¼ tsp ground mace*
*1 cup light cream*
*Salt and pepper*

**GARNISH**
*½ cup whipped cream, unsweetened*
*Ground mace*

Trim the thick ends of the asparagus and chop the spears to even-sized pieces. Place in a large bowl with the stock, mace, salt and pepper. Partially cover and cook 10 minutes on HIGH or until the asparagus is soft. Leave to stand for 5 minutes. Purée in a food processor and strain if desired. Add the cream and heat 1 minute on HIGH. Garnish each serving with a spoonful of whipped cream and sprinkle with mace.

## Fresh Pea Soup with Thyme

**PREPARATION TIME:** 20 minutes

**MICROWAVE COOKING TIME:** 7-13 minutes

**SERVES:** 4 people

*4lbs fresh peas, shelled (3lbs frozen peas may be substituted)*
*3½ cups vegetable stock*
*2 sprigs fresh thyme*
*1 cup light cream*
*Salt and pepper*

**GARNISH**
*½ cup heavy cream*
*Reserved peas*

Place the peas in a large bowl with the stock, thyme, salt and pepper. Partially cover and cook for 10 minutes on HIGH or until the peas are soft. If using frozen peas, cook for 5 minutes on HIGH. Leave to stand for 5 minutes. Remove the thyme and discard. Remove about 4 tbsps peas to reserve for garnish. Purée the remaining peas and stock in a food processor until smooth. Strain the soup if desired. Stir in the cream and adjust the seasoning. Add the reserved peas and re-heat 2-3 minutes on HIGH. Before serving, swirl a spoonful of cream through each bowl.

## Beet and Sour Cream Soup with Horseradish

**PREPARATION TIME:** 20 minutes

**MICROWAVE COOKING TIME:** 22-23 minutes plus 10 minutes standing time

**SERVES:** 4 people

*8oz turnips, peeled and cut in even-size pieces*
*1lb beets*
*3½ cups vegetable stock*
*1 bay leaf*
*Salt and pepper*
*1 cup sour cream*
*1 tbsp grated fresh or bottled horseradish*

**GARNISH**
*Chopped chives*
*Reserved sour cream*

Cook unpeeled beets in a large bowl, covered, with ¼ cup stock for 10 minutes on HIGH. Leave to stand for 10 minutes before peeling. Pre-cooked or canned beetroot may be substituted. Cut into small pieces and return to the bowl with the turnips, remaining stock, bay leaf, salt and pepper. Partially cover the bowl and cook for a further 10 minutes on HIGH. Remove the bay leaf and

purée the soup in a food processor until smooth. Reserve 4 tbsps sour cream and add the rest to the soup along with the horseradish. Heat 2-3 minutes on MEDIUM. Do not allow the soup to boil. Serve topped with sour cream and chopped chives.

## Lettuce Cream Soup with Coriander

**PREPARATION TIME:** 20 minutes

**MICROWAVE COOKING TIME:** 15-16 minutes plus 5 minutes standing time

**SERVES:** 4 people

*2 medium-sized potatoes, cut into even-size pieces*
*3½ cups vegetable stock*
*2 small heads lettuce, washed and shredded*
*½ tsp ground coriander*
*1-1½ cups light cream*
*Salt and pepper*

**GARNISH**
*Reserved shredded lettuce*
*Chopped parsley*

Place the potatoes, stock and a pinch of salt in a large bowl. Partially cover the bowl and cook 10 minutes on HIGH or until the potatoes are tender. Add the lettuce, reserving about a quarter for garnish. Add the coriander and pepper and cook a further 3 minutes on HIGH. Leave to stand 5 minutes before blending in a food processor until smooth. Add 1 cup cream (add more cream if the soup is too thick). The soup should be the consistency of lightly-whipped cream. Add the reserved shredded lettuce and parsley and re-heat for 2-3 minutes on HIGH.

**Facing page: Lettuce Cream Soup with Coriander (top) and Purée of Asparagus Soup (bottom).**

## Mushroom and Sherry Cream Soup

**PREPARATION TIME:** 20 minutes

**MICROWAVE COOKING TIME:**
9-11 minutes plus 5 minutes standing time

**SERVES:** 4 people

2lbs mushrooms, chopped
5-6 slices bread, crusts removed
2½ cups vegetable stock
1 sprig fresh thyme
1 bay leaf
½ clove garlic, crushed (optional)
1½ cups light cream
¼ cup sherry
Salt and pepper

**GARNISH**
½ cup whipped cream
Grated nutmeg

Combine the mushrooms, bread, stock, thyme, bay leaf, salt, pepper and garlic (if using) in a large bowl. Partially cover and cook on HIGH for 7-8 minutes. Leave to stand for 5 minutes. Remove the thyme and the bay leaf and purée in a food processor until smooth. If the soup is not thick enough, add 1-2 slices more bread with the crusts removed. Add the sherry and process once more. Re-heat 2-3 minutes on HIGH. Garnish each bowl with a spoonful of whipped cream and a sprinkling of nutmeg.

## Purée of Leek and Potato Soup

**PREPARATION TIME:** 20 minutes

**MICROWAVE COOKING TIME:**
12 minutes plus 5 minutes standing time

**SERVES:** 4 people

3 medium-size potatoes, cut in even-size pieces
4 leeks, depending on size
3½ cups vegetable stock
1 bay leaf
2 sprigs thyme
¼ tsp ground nutmeg

Salt and pepper
1-1½ cups light cream

Wash leeks well and shred the light green portion of 1 of the leeks and reserve. Slice the remaining leeks and combine with the potatoes in a large bowl. Pour on the stock and add the bay leaf, thyme and a pinch of salt. Partially cover the bowl and cook on HIGH for 10 minutes or until the potatoes and leeks are tender. Leave to stand for 5 minutes. Remove the bay leaf and thyme and purée the soup in a food processor until smooth. Add the nutmeg, pepper and 1 cup cream. Process again and

**This page: Purée of Leek and Potato Soup (top) and Mushroom and Sherry Cream Soup (bottom). Facing page: Spring Vegetable Soup.**

add more cream if the soup is too thick. It should be the consistency of lightly whipped cream. Put the reserved leek into a small dish with 2 tbsps water and cook for 2 minutes on HIGH. Drain and garnish the soup with a spoonful of sour cream and the reserved leek strips.

## Purée of Carrot Soup

**PREPARATION TIME:** 20 minutes

**MICROWAVE COOKING TIME:** 16-17 minutes

**SERVES:** 4 people

*3lbs carrots, scraped and grated*
*3½ cups vegetable stock*
*2-3 sprigs rosemary*
*1 cup milk or light cream*
*Salt and pepper*

**GARNISH**
*½ cup unsweetened whipped cream*
*Chopped parsley*

Combine the carrots, rosemary, salt, pepper and stock in a large bowl. Partially cover and cook 15 minutes on HIGH or until the carrots are very tender. Remove the rosemary and purée the soup in a food processor. Add the milk or cream and process until smooth. Adjust the seasoning and re-heat 1-2 minutes on HIGH before serving. Top with spoonfuls of whipped cream and chopped parsley.

This page: Purée of Carrot Soup.
Facing page: Green Beans with Lemon Herb Sauce (top) and Asparagus Tied with Fresh Herbs (bottom).

## Spring Vegetable Soup

**PREPARATION TIME:** 25 minutes

**MICROWAVE COOKING TIME:** 30 minutes plus 15-20 minutes standing time

**SERVES:** 4-6 people

**VEGETABLE STOCK**
*8oz carrots, roughly chopped*
*6 sticks celery, roughly chopped*
*1 turnip, roughly chopped (optional)*
*3 onions, chopped and the peel of 1 reserved for color*
*1 tomato, quartered and seeded*
*3 parsley stalks*
*1 whole clove*
*1 bay leaf*
*1 blade mace*
*2 sprigs thyme or other fresh herbs*
*6 black peppercorns*
*Pinch salt*
*4 cups water*

**SOUP**
*3½ cups vegetable stock*
*1 head green cabbage, shredded*
*4oz asparagus cut in 1 inch pieces*
*4oz green beans cut in 1 inch pieces*
*3 carrots, cut in 2 inch strips*
*4oz fresh or frozen peas*
*1 large red pepper, thinly sliced*
*3 green onions, sliced*
*¼ cup white wine, optional*
*Salt and pepper*

Combine all the ingredients for the stock in a large bowl. Half cover the bowl with plastic wrap and cook 15 minutes on HIGH. The stock will boil, so the bowl must be deep enough to contain it. Allow to stand for 15-20 minutes before straining. The stock will keep up to 3 days in the refrigerator or frozen in ice cube trays for convenience. To prepare the soup, pour the measured stock into a large bowl. If using fresh peas add them to the stock and partially cover the bowl. Cook the peas for 5 minutes on HIGH. Add the carrots and cook a further 5 minutes on HIGH. Add the beans, asparagus and cabbage and cook for 5 minutes further on HIGH. Add the onions, peppers and wine after 2 minutes cooking time. If using frozen peas, add them with the onions and peppers. Season with salt and pepper to taste before serving. If preparing the soup in advance, re-heat it for 5-6 minutes on HIGH before serving.

# SIDE DISHES

## Green Beans with Lemon Herb Sauce

**PREPARATION TIME:** 10 minutes

**MICROWAVE COOKING TIME:**
7 minutes

**SERVES:** 4 people

1lb green beans
¼ cup water
Salt

**SAUCE**
1 cup low fat soft cheese or fromage blanc
2 fl oz-¼ pint milk
1 cup watercress leaves, and thin stalks
2 tbsps chopped fresh herbs
Juice and grated rind of ½ lemon
Salt and pepper

Combine the beans, water and salt in a casserole dish and cover loosely. Cook on HIGH for 4 minutes, stirring once or twice. Leave to stand while preparing the sauce. Heat the milk for 3 minutes on HIGH. If using low fat soft cheese, use the greater quantity of milk. Combine with the remaining ingredients, except the lemon rind, in a food processor and work until well blended. Drain the beans and pour over the sauce. Sprinkle on the lemon rind, and toss just before serving.

## Asparagus Tied with Fresh Herbs

**PREPARATION TIME:** 15 minutes

**MICROWAVE COOKING TIME:**
14 minutes

**SERVES:** 4 people

2lb asparagus spears
8 sprigs of fresh thyme or marjoram or
  8 chives
**SAUCE**
3 egg yolks

¾ cup butter
2 tbsps white wine
Squeeze of lemon juice
1 tsp chopped thyme, marjoram or chives
Salt and pepper

Trim the thick ends of the asparagus and place the spears in a shallow dish. Add ½ cup water and cover the dish loosely. Cook on HIGH for 10 minutes. Drain and keep warm. In a small, deep bowl, heat the wine and butter for 2 minutes on HIGH. Remove from the oven and gradually beat in the egg yolks. Cook on HIGH 10 seconds and then stir. Repeat the process until the sauce thickens, which takes about 2 minutes. Add the lemon juice, chopped herbs, salt and pepper. Tie up 4 bundles of asparagus with the chosen herbs. Serve the asparagus with the sauce.

## Broccoli with Toasted Sunflower Seeds

**PREPARATION TIME:** 10 minutes

**MICROWAVE COOKING TIME:** 4½-5½ minutes

**SERVES:** 4 people

*1lb broccoli*
*2 tbsps butter or margarine*
*1 cup toasted, salted sunflower seeds*
*Pepper*
*1 tsp lemon juice (if desired)*

Trim the ends of the broccoli stalks and separate into even-sized pieces. Place in a large casserole or shallow dish with ¼ cup water. Cover loosely and cook 4-5 minutes on HIGH. Melt the butter for 30 seconds on HIGH, stir in the sunflower seeds and add pepper and lemon juice. Drain the broccoli and sprinkle over the sunflower seeds to serve.

## Broccoli and Cauliflower Mold with Salsa

**PREPARATION TIME:** 25 minutes

**MICROWAVE COOKING TIME:** 7½ minutes

**SERVES:** 4-6 people

*1 small head cauliflower*
*8oz broccoli*

**DRESSING**
*3 tbsps oil*
*1 tbsp wine vinegar*
*1 tsp ground mustard*
*½ clove garlic, minced*
*Salt and pepper*

**SALSA**
*4-5 tomatoes, depending on size*
*1 green pepper, chopped*
*1 tbsp oil*
*1 green chili pepper, finely chopped*
*1 tsp cumin seed or ground cumin*
*4 green onions, finely chopped*
*Salt and pepper*

Divide the cauliflower into flowerets and trim down any long, thick stalks. Trim the broccoli stalks to within 2

**This page: Broccoli and Cauliflower Mold with Salsa. Facing page: Broccoli with Toasted Sunflower Seeds (top) and Brussels Sprouts and Hazelnuts (bottom).**

inches of the flowerets and combine with the cauliflower in a deep bowl. Add 2 tbsps water and a pinch of salt. Cover loosely and cook 3 minutes on HIGH. Mix the dressing ingredients together thoroughly. Drain the vegetables well and pour the dressing over the vegetables while still warm. Arrange the vegetables in a deep 2 cup bowl, alternating the 2 vegetables. Press lightly to push the vegetables together. Leave the vegetables to cool in the bowl and then refrigerate. Put

the tomatoes in a bowl of very hot water. Microwave 30 seconds on HIGH. Put the tomatoes into cold water and then peel and chop roughly. Heat the oil in a large bowl for 30 seconds on HIGH. Add the green pepper, chili pepper and cumin. Cook for 2 minutes on HIGH. Stir in the tomatoes, onions, salt and pepper and leave to cool. Turn out the vegetables carefully onto a serving plate and spoon the salsa around the base. Serve cold. Both the mold and the salsa may be prepared several hours in advance. If left overnight, the broccoli may discolor the cauliflower.

## Vegetable Stir Fry with Tofu

**PREPARATION TIME:** 20 minutes

**MICROWAVE COOKING TIME:**
7½ minutes

**SERVES:** 4 people

¼ cup oil
Blanched whole almonds
8oz tofu
4 spears broccoli
4oz pea pods
4oz bean sprouts
4oz baby corn-on-the-cob
1 red pepper, sliced
½ cup water chestnuts, sliced
1 clove garlic, minced
½ cup vegetable stock
2 tsps cornstarch
4 tbsps soy sauce
Dash sherry
Dash sesame oil
Salt and pepper
4 green onions, sliced

Heat a browning dish for 5 minutes on HIGH. Add the oil and fry the almonds for 5 minutes, stirring often to brown evenly. Remove the almonds from the dish and set them aside. Cut out the broccoli flowerets and reserve. Slice the stalks diagonally. If the corn cobs are large cut in half lengthwise. Cook the broccoli and the corn together for 1 minute on HIGH. Add the garlic,

red pepper, pea pods, water chestnuts and the broccoli flowerets. Mix the soy sauce, sesame oil, sherry, stock, and cornstarch together. Pour over the vegetables and cook 1 minute on HIGH. Add the bean sprouts, almonds, green onions and the tofu, cut in small cubes. Cook 30 seconds on HIGH. Serve immediately.

## Vegetables Mornay

**PREPARATION TIME:** 25 minutes

**MICROWAVE COOKING TIME:**
24-28 minutes

**SERVES:** 4-6 people

8oz new potatoes, scrubbed but not peeled
8oz button or pickling onions, peeled
1 tbsp butter
Pinch sugar
2-3 carrots, cut in strips
2 parsnips, cut in strips
4oz pea pods
4oz button mushrooms
2 tbsps butter
Salt

**SAUCE**
3 tbsps butter
3 tbsps flour
1 tsp dry mustard
Pinch cayenne pepper
2 cups milk
1 cup Cheddar cheese, shredded
Salt and pepper
Nutmeg

Cook the new potatoes in ¼ cup water with a pinch of salt for 8-10 minutes on HIGH in a deep, covered dish. Leave to stand 5 minutes. Cook the carrots and parsnips together in ¼ cup water in a covered dish for 6 minutes on HIGH. Combine the onions with the sugar and 1 tbsp butter in a deep bowl. Cook, covered, for 7 minutes on HIGH. Stir twice while cooking. Melt the remaining butter for the vegetables and add the pea pods and mushrooms. Cook for 2 minutes on HIGH. Leave all the vegetables covered while preparing the sauce.

Melt the butter for 1 minute on HIGH in a glass measure. Stir in the flour, mustard and cayenne pepper. Gradually whip in the milk and add the salt and pepper. Cook for 3-4 minutes on HIGH, whipping after 1 minute, until the sauce has thickened and is bubbling. Stir in the cheese to melt. Arrange the vegetables on a serving dish, keeping each different vegetable in a separate pile. Coat with some of the sauce and sprinkle on nutmeg. Serve remaining sauce separately.

## Brussels Sprouts and Hazelnuts

**PREPARATION TIME:** 20 minutes

**MICROWAVE COOKING TIME:**
20-21 minutes

**SERVES:** 4 people

½ cup hazelnuts
1lb Brussels sprouts
2 tbsps butter or margarine
Salt and pepper

Put the nuts into a small, deep bowl. Cover with hot water and heat 3 minutes on HIGH. Leave to soak for 10 minutes. Drain and rub off the skins. Leave the nuts to dry. Heat a browning dish 5 minutes on HIGH and drop in the butter. Add the nuts and cook 5 minutes on HIGH, stirring every 30 seconds to brown the nuts evenly. Cook the Brussels sprouts with 2 tbsps water and a pinch of salt in a lightly covered bowl or a cooking bag. Cook for 7-8 minutes on HIGH or until tender. Drain and combine with the nuts and butter.

**Facing page: Vegetable Stir Fry with Tofu.**

## Ginger Sesame Carrots

**PREPARATION TIME:** 10 minutes

**MICROWAVE COOKING TIME:**
7½-10½ minutes

**SERVES:** 4-6 people

*2lb carrots, sliced diagonally*
*2 tbsps butter or margarine*
*2 tbsps brown sugar*
*1½ tsps ground ginger or 1 small piece fresh*
*  ginger, grated*
*¼ cup sesame seeds*
*Dash soy sauce*
*Dash sesame oil*
*Salt and pepper*

Place the carrots in a casserole dish
with ¼ cup water. Add a pinch of salt,
cover and cook on HIGH for 7-10
minutes. Leave to stand while
melting the butter for 30 seconds on
HIGH. Stir in the brown sugar,
ginger, sesame seeds, sesame oil, soy
sauce, salt and pepper. Add 1-2 tbsps
of the cooking liquid from the carrots
to the sesame-ginger mixture. Stir in
the carrots to coat with the sauce.

## Pommes Noisettes

**PREPARATION TIME:** 15 minutes
plus overnight refrigeration

**MICROWAVE COOKING TIME:**
14-15 minutes

**SERVES:** 4-6 people

*1lb potatoes, scrubbed but not peeled*
*2 tbsps water*
*2 tbsps butter*
*Salt and pepper*
*½ cup grated Gruyère cheese*
*½ cup ground browned hazelnuts*
*Chopped parsley*

Prick the potato skins with a fork.
Put the potatoes and water into a
covered dish and cook 12 minutes on
HIGH until tender. Drain the
potatoes and cut in half. Scoop out
the pulp and mash with a fork or
potato masher. Beat in the butter,
salt, pepper and cheese. Allow to
cool and then refrigerate until cold.
Shape into 1 inch balls. Roll the
potatoes in the nuts. Place in a circle

on a baking sheet or serving dish and
heat 2-3 minutes on HIGH. Sprinkle
with chopped parsley before serving.

## Dilled White Cabbage

**PREPARATION TIME:** 10 minutes

**MICROWAVE COOKING TIME:**
8 minutes plus 5 minutes
standing time

**SERVES:** 4-6 people

**This page: Vegetable Mornay.
Facing page: Ginger Sesame Carrots
(top) and Pommes Noisettes
(bottom).**

*1 medium head white cabbage or Dutch*
*  cabbage, shredded*
*2 tbsps butter or margarine*
*Pinch sugar*
*2 tbsps dill seed*
*2 tbsps white wine vinegar*
*2 tbsps chopped fresh dill*
*Salt and pepper*

Place the cabbage in a large casserole or bowl with 2 tbsps water and the remaining ingredients except the chopped fresh dill. Cover loosely and cook 8 minutes on HIGH, stirring twice. Leave to stand, covered, 5 minutes. Before serving, sprinkle with the fresh dill.

## Beets with Sour Cream and Dill

**PREPARATION TIME:** 20 minutes

**MICROWAVE COOKING TIME:** 13-17 minutes plus 10 minutes standing time

**SERVES:** 4 people

*4-8 beets, depending on size*
*1 cup sour cream*
*½ tsp grated fresh horseradish*
*1 small bunch dill*
*Salt and pepper*

Place raw beets, unpeeled, in ½-1 cup water depending on the number of beets. Use a casserole or a bowl covered with pierced plastic wrap. Cook 12-16 minutes. Leave to stand 10 minutes before peeling. If using pre-cooked beets, just peel them and heat through 1 minute on HIGH. Slice into ¼ inch slices. Arrange in a serving dish. Mix the sour cream, horseradish, dill, salt and pepper together. Spoon over the beets and heat through 30 seconds to 1 minute on HIGH. Do not allow the sour cream to boil. Garnish with a few sprigs of fresh dill and serve immediately.

## Sweet and Sour Red Cabbage with Apple

**PREPARATION TIME:** 15 minutes

**MICROWAVE COOKING TIME:** 9-10 minutes plus 5 minutes standing time

**SERVES:** 4-6 people

*2 tbsps butter or margarine*
*1 medium head red cabbage, shredded*
*1 small onion, finely chopped*

*1 apple, cored and chopped*
*2 tbsps brown sugar*
*2 tbsps red wine vinegar*
*½ cup water*
*Pinch cinnamon*
*Salt and pepper*

**GARNISH**
*1 tbsp butter or margarine*
*1 apple, cored and chopped*
*Chopped parsley*

Melt the butter or margarine in a deep casserole dish for 30 seconds on HIGH. Add all the remaining ingredients except the garnish and cover with pierced plastic wrap. Cook on HIGH for 8 minutes. Leave to stand, covered, 5 minutes while preparing the garnish. Melt the butter or margarine 30 seconds on HIGH in a small bowl. Add the apple and cook 1 minute on HIGH, uncovered, to partially soften. Toss with the parsley and sprinkle on top of the cabbage.

**This page: Beets with Sour Cream and Dill. Facing page: Sweet and Sour Red Cabbage with Apple (top) and Dilled White Cabbage (bottom).**

## Creamed Green Onions

**PREPARATION TIME:** 10 minutes

**MICROWAVE COOKING TIME:** 5 minutes

**SERVES:** 4 people

*2 bunches green onions*
*1 tbsp butter or margarine*
*Salt and pepper*
*1 cup low fat soft cheese or fromage blanc*
*1 tsp chopped basil*
*1 tsp chopped parsley*
*½ cup milk*

the chopped watercress to the potatoes and beat in the hot milk. Add salt and pepper to taste and pipe or spoon the potatoes on top of the cheese sauce in the potato shells. Sprinkle on cheese and cook for 3 minutes on HIGH to heat through and melt the cheese. Alternatively, heat 5 minutes on a combination setting in a microwave convection oven. Garnish with the watercress and serve immediately.

## Mushroom Croquettes with Green Peppercorn Sauce

**PREPARATION TIME:** 25 minutes

**MICROWAVE COOKING TIME:** 16-17 minutes

**SERVES:** 4 people

1 cup finely chopped mushrooms
1¾ cups fresh breadcrumbs
2 tbsps butter or margarine
1 shallot, finely chopped
2 tbsps flour
½ cup milk
1 tsp chopped parsley
1 tsp chopped thyme
1 beaten egg
Salt and pepper

**COATING**
Remaining beaten egg
Dry breadcrumbs
2-4 tbsps oil for frying

**SAUCE**
1 tbsp butter or margarine
1 shallot, finely chopped
1 tbsp flour
2 tbsps vermouth or white wine
1 cup heavy cream
2 tbsps green peppercorns, drained and rinsed
1 small cap pimento, diced
Salt and pepper

them, one at a time into the water. Prick the yolks once with a sharp knife or skewer. Cook on MEDIUM for 3 minutes. Remove from the dish and place in enough cold water to cover them. Melt the 1 tbsp butter in a small bowl for 30 seconds on HIGH. Add the mushrooms and shallot. Cook for 1 minute on HIGH and set aside. Melt the butter for the sauce for 30 seconds on HIGH in a glass measure. Add the flour, mustard, and cayenne pepper. Stir in the milk gradually and cook 3 minutes on HIGH. Stir after

**This page: Pasta-Stuffed Cabbage Leaves (top) and Watercress-Stuffed Potatoes (bottom).**

1 minute. Add the cheese and stir to melt. Cut a slice off the top of each potato and scoop out the pulp, leaving a border inside the skin. Fill with the mushrooms and top with one of the drained eggs. Spoon over the cheese sauce. Mash the potato and heat the milk for 2 minutes on HIGH. Chop the watercress leaves and thin stalks in a food processor, reserving 4 sprigs for garnish. Add

Melt the butter for the croquettes for 1 minute on HIGH. Add the shallot and the mushrooms and cook 30 seconds on HIGH. Stir in the flour and add the milk gradually. Cook for

1 shallot, finely chopped
2 tbsps flour
½ cup milk
1 tsp chopped parsley
1 tsp chopped thyme
1 beaten egg
Salt and pepper

**COATING**
Beaten egg
Dry breadcrumbs
2-4 tbsps oil for frying

**SAUCE**
1 cup heavy cream
1 tbsp pear brandy
½ cup grated Parmesan cheese
Coarsely ground black pepper
Salt

**GARNISH**
4 small, ripe, unpeeled pears, halved and
    cored
Lemon juice
8 fresh sage leaves

Melt the butter for the escalopes for 1 minute on HIGH. Add the shallot and cook 30 seconds on HIGH. Stir in the flour and add the milk gradually. Cook for 2 minutes on HIGH until thickened. Add the remaining escalope ingredients and half the beaten egg. Spread the mixture into a square pan and chill until firm. Cut the mixture into 8 equal pieces and flatten into thin patties. Coat with the remaining egg and dry breadcrumbs, shaking off the excess. If the patties become difficult to handle, chill for 10 minutes in the refrigerator before coating with egg and crumbs. Heat a browning dish for 5 minutes on HIGH and pour in the oil. Heat for 30 seconds on HIGH, put in the escalopes and cover the dish. Cook for 2-3 minutes on HIGH, turning over halfway through the cooking time. Drain the escalopes on paper towels. Boil the cream and brandy for 6 minutes on HIGH in a glass measure. Stir in the cheese and pepper. Taste and add salt

**This page: Walnut Cutlets with Three Pepper Salpicon. Facing page: Mushroom Croquettes with Green Peppercorn Sauce (top) and Hazelnut Escalopes with Pear Brandy Cream Sauce (bottom).**

2 minutes on HIGH until thickened. Add the remaining croquette ingredients and half the beaten egg. Spread the mixture into a square pan and chill until firm. Cut the mixture into 16 equal pieces and shape into small ovals. Coat with the remaining egg and press on the dry crumbs, shaking off the excess. Heat a browning dish for 5 minutes on HIGH and pour in the oil. Heat for 30 seconds on HIGH and put in the croquettes. Cover and cook 3-4 minutes on HIGH, turning over after 2 minutes. Drain on paper towels. Heat the butter for the sauce for 30 seconds on HIGH in a small, deep bowl. Add the shallot, finely chopped and cook for 30 seconds on HIGH. Stir in the flour, vermouth or white wine and the cream. Season lightly with salt and pepper and cook for 3-4 minutes on HIGH, stirring

frequently. Add the green peppercorns and the pimento 1 minute before the end of cooking time. Arrange the croquettes in a serving dish and pour over the sauce to serve.

## Hazelnut Escalopes with Pear Brandy Cream Sauce

**PREPARATION TIME:** 25 minutes

**MICROWAVE COOKING TIME:** 17-18 minutes

**SERVES:** 4 people

1 cup ground hazelnuts
1⅓ cups fresh breadcrumbs
2 tbsps butter or margarine

if desired. Heat for 30 seconds on HIGH to melt the cheese. Place a spoonful of the sauce on each of 4 serving plates. Brush the cut sides of the pears with lemon juice and arrange on the plates with the sage leaves. Place on the cutlets and spoon over some of the sauce to serve. Hand the rest of the sauce separately.

## Walnut Cutlets with Three Pepper Salpicon

**PREPARATION TIME:** 25 minutes

**MICROWAVE COOKING TIME:** 17-18 minutes

**SERVES:** 4 people

**CUTLETS**
1 cup walnuts, ground
1⅓ cups fresh breadcrumbs
1 tsp chopped parsley
1 tsp chopped thyme
2 tbsps butter or margarine
1 shallot, finely chopped
2 tbsps flour
½ cup milk
1 beaten egg
Salt and pepper

**COATING**
Remaining beaten egg
Dry breadcrumbs
2-4 tbsps oil for frying

**SALPICON**
2 tbsps butter or margarine
1 small onion, thinly sliced
1 tbsp flour
Juice of 1 lemon
⅓ cup vegetable stock
1-2 green peppers, sliced
1-2 red peppers, sliced
1-2 yellow peppers, sliced
Pinch cayenne pepper
2 tsps capers
Salt and pepper

Melt the butter for the cutlets for 1 minute on HIGH. Add the shallot and cook 30 seconds on HIGH. Stir in the flour and add the milk gradually. Cook for 2 minutes on HIGH until thickened. Add the remaining cutlet ingredients and half the beaten egg. Spread the mixture

into a square pan and chill until firm. Cut the mixture into 8 equal portions and shape into cutlets or patties. Coat with the remaining egg and the dry breadcrumbs, shaking off the excess. Heat a browning dish for 5 minutes on HIGH. Pour in the oil and heat 30 seconds on HIGH. Put in the cutlets, cover the dish and cook 3-4 minutes on HIGH, turning over after 2 minutes. Drain on paper towels. Heat the butter for the salpicon 30 seconds on HIGH in a casserole. Add the onion and cook for 1 minute on HIGH. Stir in the flour and add the lemon juice and stock and cook for 1 minute on HIGH until very thick. Add the peppers and capers and cook a further 3 minutes on HIGH. Add the cayenne pepper, salt and pepper and serve with the cutlets.

## Pasta Primavera

**PREPARATION TIME:** 20 minutes

**MICROWAVE COOKING TIME:** 14 minutes plus 10 minutes standing time

**SERVES:** 4 people

6 cups pasta shapes, or noodles
8oz asparagus
4oz green beans
2oz mushrooms, sliced
2 carrots
3 tomatoes peeled, seeded and cut in strips
6 green onions
2 tbsps chopped parsley
2 tsps chopped tarragon
½ cup heavy cream
Salt and pepper

Cook the pasta 6 minutes on HIGH in 4 cups hot water with a pinch of salt and 1 tbsp oil. Cover and leave to stand 10 minutes before draining. Leave to drain completely. Slice the asparagus diagonally, leaving the tips whole. Cut the beans and carrots diagonally into thin slices. Cook the carrots and asparagus in 2 tbsps water for 4 minutes on HIGH, loosely covered. Add the beans and mushrooms and cook an additional 2 minutes on HIGH. Add to the drained pasta and stir in the cream, salt and pepper. Cook 1 minute on HIGH to heat the pasta. Add the tomatoes, onions, herbs and toss gently. Cook an additional 1 minute on HIGH. Serve immediately with grated cheese if desired.

## Eggplant Rolls

**PREPARATION TIME:** 25 minutes
**MICROWAVE COOKING TIME:** 20-23 minutes
**SERVES:** 4 people

2-3 eggplants, depending on size, sliced ½ inch thick
3 tbsps oil, or more as needed, for frying
1 cup grated mozzarella cheese

**SAUCE**
1lb can plum tomatoes
2 tbsps tomato paste
1 onion, finely chopped
Pinch sugar
Pinch oregano
1 bay leaf
2 parsley stalks
Salt and pepper

**FILLING**
8oz ricotta cheese
4oz pitted black olives, chopped
¼ cup grated Parmesan cheese
¼ cup pine nuts
1 tbsp white wine
1 clove garlic, finely minced
1 tsp each chopped parsley and basil
Pinch nutmeg
Salt and pepper

**Facing page: Pasta Primavera. This page: Eggplant Rolls.**

Lightly score the slices of eggplant on both sides and sprinkle with salt. Leave on paper towels to stand for 30 minutes to draw out any bitterness. Combine all the sauce ingredients in a small, deep bowl. Cook, uncovered, for 8 minutes on HIGH. Remove the bay leaf and parsley stalks and purée in a food processor. Strain to remove the seeds if desired. Rinse the eggplant and pat dry. Heat a browning dish for 5 minutes on HIGH. Pour in the oil and heat for 1 minute on HIGH. Add the eggplant slices and brown for 1 minute per side. Cook in 2 or 3 batches if necessary and add more oil if needed. Drain on paper towels. Mix the filling ingredients and fill half of each eggplant slice. Fill the bottom of a large, shallow baking dish with half the sauce. Fold the eggplant slices in half and place on top of the sauce. Spoon over the remaining sauce, cover the dish loosely with plastic wrap and cook 3 minutes on HIGH. Sprinkle on the cheese and cook, uncovered, a further 2-3 minutes on MEDIUM. Alternatively, coat with sauce and sprinkle on the cheese and cook for 8 minutes on a combination setting of a microwave convection oven.

## Vegetable Moussaka

**PREPARATION TIME:** 55 minutes

**MICROWAVE COOKING TIME:** 29 minutes

**SERVES:** 4 people

*2 potatoes, peeled and sliced*
*1 eggplant*
*4oz mushrooms sliced*
*2 zucchini*
*4 tomatoes, peeled and sliced*
*1 green pepper, sliced*

**TOMATO SAUCE**
*1 tbsp oil*
*1 onion, finely chopped*
*1 clove garlic, minced*
*1 14oz can tomatoes*
*1 tbsp tomato paste*
*¼ tsp ground cinnamon*
*¼ tsp ground cumin*
*Salt and pepper*
*Pinch of sugar*

**EGG SAUCE**
*2 tbsps butter or margarine*
*2 tbsps flour*
*1 cup milk*
*1 egg, beaten*
*½ cup feta cheese*
*Nutmeg*
*Salt and pepper*

Cut the eggplant in half and lightly score the cut surface. Sprinkle with salt and leave to stand for ½ hour. Put the potatoes into a roasting bag, seal and cook 10 minutes on HIGH. Heat the oil for the tomato sauce 30 seconds on HIGH. Add the onions and garlic and cook 1 minute on HIGH. Add the remaining ingredients and cook a further 6 minutes on HIGH. Wash the eggplant well and dry. Slice it thinly and cook in 2 tbsps oil for 2 minutes on HIGH in a covered dish. Remove the slices and drain. Add the

mushrooms to the dish and cook for 2 minutes on HIGH. Remove and set aside. Add the green pepper and the zucchini and cook for 1 minute on HIGH. Layer the vegetables, starting with the eggplant and ending with the potatoes. Spoon the tomato sauce over each layer except the potatoes. Cook the butter for the egg sauce for 30 seconds on HIGH. Stir in the flour, nutmeg, salt and pepper. Add the milk gradually and cook for 3 minutes on HIGH, stirring after 1 minute. Add the cheese and egg and stir well to blend. Pour over the potatoes and cook 4 minutes on HIGH or 5 minutes on a combination setting in a microwave convection oven, or until set.

**This page: Sweet and Sour Nuggets. Facing page: Vegetable Moussaka (top) and Mushrooms Florentine (bottom).**

## Sweet and Sour Nuggets

**PREPARATION TIME:** 25 minutes

**MICROWAVE COOKING TIME:** 15½-16½ minutes

**SERVES:** 4 people

*½ cup ground almonds*
*½ cup finely chopped water chestnuts*
*2 tbsps butter or margarine*
*1 shallot, finely chopped*
*2 tbsps flour*

1 tsp chopped parsley
1 tsp ground ginger
½ cup milk
1 beaten egg
Salt and pepper

**COATING**
Remaining beaten egg
Dry breadcrumbs
Sesame seeds
2-4 tbsps oil for frying

**SWEET AND SOUR SAUCE**
¼ cup brown sugar
¼ cup vinegar
2 tbsps tomato ketchup
2 tbsps soy sauce
8oz can pineapple pieces
2 tbsps cornstarch
1 green pepper
2 green onions, sliced
1 small can bamboo shoots

**ACCOMPANIMENT**
8oz bean sprouts

Melt the butter for the nuggets for 1 minute on HIGH. Add the shallot and cook 30 seconds on HIGH. Stir in the flour and add the milk gradually. Cook for 2 minutes on HIGH until thickened. Add the remaining nugget ingredients and half the beaten egg. Spread the mixture into a square pan and chill until firm. Shape the mixture into an even number of 1 inch balls. Coat with the remaining egg and the dry breadcrumbs and sesame seeds, shaking off the excess. Heat a browning dish for 5 minutes on HIGH and pour in the oil. Put in the nuggets and cover the dish. Cook for 3-4 minutes on HIGH, turning frequently. Drain on paper towels. Combine the sugar, vinegar, ketchup, soy sauce, pineapple juice and cornstarch in a small, deep bowl. Cook for 2-3 minutes on HIGH until thickened, stirring frequently. Add the peppers and onions and cook 1 minute on HIGH. Add the pineapple pieces and the bamboo shoots and cook a further 30 seconds on HIGH. Place the bean sprouts in a serving dish and heat 1 minute on HIGH. Put the nuggets in the middle. Coat over with the sweet and sour sauce to serve.

## Japanese Steamer

**PREPARATION TIME:** 20 minutes

**MICROWAVE COOKING TIME:** 13 minutes

**SERVES:** 4 people

3 packages tofu, drained
16 dried black mushrooms, soaked and stems removed
4oz small mushrooms
8 baby corn-on-the-cob
1 small daikon (mooli) radish, sliced
1 bunch fresh chives, left whole
4oz buckwheat noodles or other variety Japanese noodles
1 package dried sea spinach
1 lemon, sliced

**SAUCE**
1 small piece fresh ginger root, grated
½ cup soy sauce
4 tbsps vegetable stock
1 tbsp sherry or white wine
1 tsp cornstarch

Cover the noodles with 2 cups water and a pinch of salt. Cook on HIGH for 6 minutes and leave to stand, covered, for 10 minutes before using. Put the mushrooms and spinach into 2 separate bowls, fill both bowls with water and leave the spinach to soak. Put the mushrooms into the microwave oven and heat for 5 minutes on HIGH and set aside. Put the small mushrooms and the baby corn-on-the-cob into a small bowl with 1 tbsp water. Cover the bowl with pierced plastic wrap and cook for 2 minutes on HIGH and set aside. Combine all the ingredients for the sauce in a glass measure. Cook on HIGH for 3 minutes or until thickened. Stir after 1 minute. Slice the tofu into ½ inch slices. Drain the black mushrooms and remove the stalks. Drain the noodles and arrange in 4 separate serving dishes. Add the spinach, tofu, whole black mushrooms and small mushrooms, baby ears of corn, radish slices, and lemon slices. Pour some of the sauce over each serving and garnish with the fresh chives. Heat the dishes through for 1 minute on HIGH and serve the remaining sauce separately.

## Mushrooms Florentine

**PREPARATION TIME:** 20 minutes

**MICROWAVE COOKING TIME:** 17 minutes

**SERVES:** 4 people

¼ cup butter or margarine
1lb large mushrooms
2lb fresh spinach, stalks removed and leaves washed
2 shallots, finely chopped
4 tomatoes, peeled, seeded and diced
Salt and pepper
Nutmeg

**SAUCE**
3 tbsps butter or margarine
3 tbsps flour
2 cups milk
1½ cups grated Cheddar cheese
½ tsp dry mustard
Pinch cayenne pepper
Salt and pepper
¼ cup Parmesan cheese, grated
Paprika

Place the washed spinach in a large bowl or roasting bag with a pinch of salt. Cover or seal and cook 4 minutes in the water that clings to the leaves. Set aside. Melt the butter in a large casserole for 30 seconds on HIGH. Cook the mushrooms for 3 minutes on HIGH, turning often. Remove the mushrooms and set them aside. Add the shallots to the butter in the bowl, cover, and cook 2 minutes on HIGH. Chop the spinach roughly and add to the shallots with the tomato, salt, pepper and nutmeg. Place in the bottom of the casserole dish and arrange the mushrooms on top. Melt the butter for the sauce 1 minute on HIGH. Stir in the flour, mustard, salt, pepper and a pinch of cayenne pepper. Add the milk gradually, beating until smooth. Cook, uncovered, 4 minutes on HIGH, stirring twice after 1 minute's cooking. Add Cheddar cheese and stir to melt. Coat over the mushrooms and spinach and sprinkle the Parmesan and paprika on top. Cook 3 minutes until bubbling.

**Facing page: Japanese Steamer.**

## Escalopes d'Aubergines au Fromage

**PREPARATION TIME:** 25 minutes

**MICROWAVE COOKING TIME:**
14-15 minutes

**SERVES:** 4 people

*1 large or 2 small eggplants*
*Seasoned flour for coating*
*3 tbsps oil for frying*

**TOPPING**
*1 tbsp butter*
*2 shallots, finely chopped*
*2 tsps chopped tarragon*
*2 tsps chopped chervil*
*8oz cream cheese*
*1 cup grated Gruyère or Swiss cheese*
*¾ cup heavy cream*
*Dry breadcrumbs*

**VEGETABLES**
*12 small new potatoes*
*8 baby carrots*
*4 small turnips*
*4 small fresh beets*
*8 green onions*
*4 very small zucchini*
*4oz green beans, trimmed*
*4oz pea pods, trimmed*
*½ cup butter, melted*
*Chopped parsley*

Slice the eggplants into 8 1 inch thick slices. Score the slices lightly on both sides and sprinkle with salt. Leave to stand for 30 minutes to draw out any bitterness. Melt the butter for the topping for 30 seconds on HIGH. Add the shallot and cook for 2 minutes. Cool and mix with the other topping ingredients, except the dry breadcrumbs, and set aside. Cook the vegetables in ¼ cup salted water as follows:–
new potatoes for 10 minutes
baby carrots for 10 minutes
fresh beets for 8-9 minutes
turnips for 8 minutes
green onions for 2-3 minutes
green beans for 2-3 minutes
zucchini for 2-3 minutes
pea pods for 2-3 minutes.
Cook the vegetables in a loosely covered casserole and keep the beets separate. Melt the butter for 1 minute on HIGH and pour over the vegetables. Sprinkle the carrots and the new potatoes with chopped parsley. Leave the vegetables covered while preparing the eggplants. Rinse the eggplants well and pat dry. Mix the flour with salt and pepper and lightly coat the eggplant slices. Heat a browning dish for 5 minutes on HIGH. Pour in the oil and put in the eggplant slices. Cover the dish and cook for 2-3 minutes, turning halfway through the cooking time. Remove the eggplants from the browning dish and drain them on paper towels. Place them in a clean casserole or on a plate and top each slice with a spoonful of the cheese mixture. Sprinkle on the dry breadcrumbs and cook on MEDIUM for 2 minutes. Arrange on serving plates with the vegetables.

**This page: Escalopes d'Aubergines au Fromage. Facing page: Pasta Spirals with Walnuts and Gorgonzola (top) and Forester's Pasta (bottom).**

## Macaroni, Cheese and Tomato Squares

**PREPARATION TIME:** 15 minutes

**MICROWAVE COOKING TIME:**
14 minutes plus 10 minutes standing time

**SERVES:** 4 people

*3 cups macaroni*
*¼ cup butter or margarine*

*4 tbsps flour*
*Pinch dry mustard*
*Pinch cayenne pepper*
*3 cups milk*
*1 cup grated Cheddar cheese*
*Salt and pepper*
*2 tomatoes*

Put the macaroni into a large bowl with 4 cups salted water. Cook on HIGH for 6 minutes and leave to stand, covered, for 10 minutes before draining. Melt the butter for 1 minute on HIGH and stir in the flour, mustard, cayenne pepper, salt and pepper. Add the milk gradually and cook for 3-4 minutes on HIGH, stirring after 1 minute. Add the cheese to the sauce and stir to melt. Drain the macaroni well and mix it with half of the sauce. Press the macaroni mixture into a 8 inch square pan and chill until firm. Dilute the remaining sauce with 1 cup milk. When the macaroni mixture is firm, cut it into 8 squares and remove from the pan. Place on a serving dish and slice the tomatoes, putting 1 slice on top of each square. Reheat the sauce for 1 minute on HIGH and pour over the macaroni squares. Reheat the squares on a serving dish for 2 minutes on HIGH. Serve immediately.

## Forester's Pasta

**PREPARATION TIME:** 15 minutes

**MICROWAVE COOKING TIME:** 18 minutes plus 10 minutes standing time

**SERVES:** 4 people

*1lb spinach and plain tagliatelle/fettucine*
*2 carrots, shredded*
*3oz oyster or wild mushrooms*
*2 tbsps butter or margarine*
*1 clove garlic*
*2 tbsps chopped herbs such as thyme, parsley and sage*
*1 cup heavy cream*
*Salt and pepper*
*2oz fresh Parmesan cheese, ungrated*

Place the pasta in a large bowl with 4 cups hot water, a pinch of salt and 1 tbsp oil. Cook for 6 minutes on HIGH. Cover and leave to stand 10 minutes before draining. Rinse in hot water and leave to dry. Heat a browning dish 5 minutes on HIGH. Melt the butter 1 minute and add the garlic and carrots. Cook 1 minute on HIGH. The garlic should brown slightly. Add the mushrooms and cook 1 minute further on HIGH. Add the herbs, cream, salt and pepper and cook 2 minutes on HIGH. Toss with the pasta. Use a cheese slicer or a knife to shave off thin slices of Parmesan cheese to serve on top.

## Stuffed Vine Leaves

**PREPARATION TIME:** 25 minutes

**MICROWAVE COOKING TIME:** 26-34 minutes

**SERVES:** 4 people

*1 package vine leaves*

**FILLING**
*1½ cups rice*
*1 onion, finely chopped*
*2 tbsps butter or margarine*
*1 cup black olives, stoned and chopped*
*1 green pepper, chopped*
*1 cup pine nuts*
*1 cup feta cheese, crumbled*
*2 tbsps chopped parsley*
*1 tsp ground coriander*

**TOMATO SAUCE**
*1 14oz can tomatoes*
*1 tbsp tomato paste*
*1 onion, finely chopped*
*1 tbsp oil*
*1 clove garlic*
*¼ tsp cinnamon*
*¼ tsp ground cumin*
*Salt and pepper*

If the vine leaves are packed in brine, soak them in cold water for 30 minutes before using. Cook the rice 8-10 minutes in 2 cups water with a pinch of salt. Leave the rice to stand, covered, for 5 minutes. Melt the butter for 30 seconds on HIGH and add the onion, pepper and coriander. Cook for 2 minutes on HIGH. Stir in the drained rice, cheese, parsley, salt and pepper. Fill the leaves and roll them up, tucking in the ends. Arrange the leaves in a baking dish and set aside while preparing the sauce. Heat the oil for the sauce 30 seconds on HIGH and add the onion and garlic and cook for 1 minute on HIGH. Add the remaining ingredients and cook 6 minutes on HIGH. Leave to stand for 5 minutes before pouring over the vine leaves. Cook the vine leaves for 16 minutes on HIGH. Garnish with more chopped parsley if desired.

## Pasta Spirals with Walnuts and Gorgonzola

**PREPARATION TIME:** 15 minutes

**MICROWAVE COOKING TIME:** 12 minutes plus 10 minutes standing time

**SERVES:** 4 people

*1lb pasta spirals*
*1lb Gorgonzola cheese*
*1 cup walnut halves*
*1 cup heavy cream*
*Coarsely ground pepper*

**GARNISH**
*2 ripe figs*
*4 sprigs fresh thyme*

Place the pasta in a large bowl with 4 cups hot water, a pinch of salt and 1 tbsp oil. Cook for 6 minutes on HIGH. Cover and leave to stand for 10 minutes before draining. Rinse in hot water and leave to dry. Combine the cream and crumbled cheese in a deep bowl. Cook on MEDIUM for 4 minutes until the cheese melts. Do not stir too often. Add the walnut halves and the coarsely ground pepper. Taste, and add salt if desired. Pour over the pasta in a serving dish and toss to coat. Cut the figs in half and then in half again. Put one half fig on each plate with a sprig of thyme to garnish.

**Facing page: Stuffed Vine Leaves (top) and Macaroni, Cheese and Tomato Squares (bottom).**

# DESSERTS

## Avocado Creams

**PREPARATION TIME:** 25 minutes plus setting time

**MICROWAVE COOKING TIME:** 11½ minutes

**SERVES:** 4-6 people

*2 eggs, separated*
*4 tbsps sugar*
*1½ cups milk*
*½ tsp pistachio flavoring*
*1 tbsp gelatin or agar-agar*
*3 tbsps water and lemon juice mixed*
*1 large ripe avocado, well mashed*
*1 cup whipped cream*

**DECORATION**
*Pistachio nuts*
*Grated chocolate*
*Reserved whipped cream*

Sprinkle the gelatin or agar-agar onto the liquid and leave it to soak. Beat the egg yolks and sugar together until thick and lemon colored. Heat the milk for 5 minutes on HIGH until almost boiling. Gradually stir the milk into the eggs. Return to the microwave oven in a large glass measure. Heat for 6 minutes on LOW, whipping every 2 minutes until the mixture thickens. Have a bowl of iced water ready. Place the measure in the water to stop the cooking, and any time during cooking that the mixture seems about to curdle. Mash the avocado in a food processor until very smooth, combine with the custard and add the flavoring. Allow to cool. Melt the gelatin or agar-agar for 30 seconds on HIGH. Stir into the custard. Chill in the iced water until beginning to thicken, stirring constantly. Remove from the iced water while beating the egg whites until stiff but not dry. Fold into the custard with half of the whipped cream. Pour into the serving dish and chill until set. Decorate with the remaining cream piped into rosettes, pistachio nuts and grated chocolate.

## Pumpkin Pecan Pudding

**PREPARATION TIME:** 15 minutes

**MICROWAVE COOKING TIME:** 19-23 minutes

**SERVES:** 4-6 people

*½ cup chopped pecans*
*2 tbsps butter or margarine*
*2 cups canned pumpkin*
*1 tsp ground cinnamon*
*½ tsp ground ginger*
*Pinch ground cloves*
*Pinch nutmeg*
*⅓ cup cream cheese*
*⅓ cup evaporated milk*
*3 eggs*
*½ cup sugar*

**DECORATION**
*½ cup whipped cream*
*Preserved/crystallized ginger, sliced*
*Angelica, cut in thin strips*

Heat the butter for 30 seconds on HIGH. Stir in the pecans and cook a further 1 minute on HIGH. In a deep bowl, beat the remaining ingredients together until smooth. Add the buttered pecans. Cook on HIGH for 3 minutes, stirring halfway through. Reduce the setting to MEDIUM and cook 15-20 minutes or until thickened. Pour into a large serving dish or individual custard cups. Leave to stand at least 15 minutes before serving, or chill and decorate with piped cream and slices of ginger and angelica.

## Halva of Carrots and Cashews

**PREPARATION TIME:** 15 minutes

**MICROWAVE COOKING TIME:** 20 minutes

**SERVES:** 4-6 people

*2lbs carrots, peeled and shredded*
*1 cup heavy cream*
*¾ cup dark brown sugar*
*2 tbsps honey*
*¼ cup raisins*
*¼ cup butter or margarine*
*2 tsps ground coriander*
*1 tsp ground cinnamon*
*Pinch saffron*
*1 cup chopped, unsalted, roasted cashews*

**DECORATION**
*Candied violets*
*Silver leaf or silver balls*
*Desiccated coconut*

Cook the carrots, milk, sugar, honey and spices in a large bowl for 15 minutes on HIGH. Cook uncovered. Add the butter, raisins, nuts and cook for 5 minutes on HIGH, stirring frequently until thick. It may be necessary to add 2-3 more minutes cooking time to thicken. Allow the mixture to cool and pile onto serving dishes. Decorate with violets, silver leaf or balls and coconut. Serve warm or chilled with cream if desired.

**Facing page: Halva of Carrots and Cashews (top), Avocado Creams (center) and Pumpkin Pecan Pudding (bottom).**

# FROM CAVEMAN TO CULTIVAR

As civilization has developed, so has gardening. And though, biblical claims notwithstanding, man did not have his beginnings in a garden, our prehistoric forebears became cultivators and so, eventually, gardeners. For in early man's progress from a nomadic hunter-gatherer – in which he already made use of wild fruits and herbs for food and medicines – to form settled communities, he began to cultivate grasses, developing wild strains into cereals. He found that these could not only be stored against future hunger, but could be sown to propagate new, gradually improved crops.

This development from man the hunter to man the cultivator spanned many, many centuries, probably thousands of years. And it took place quite separately at different times, in different parts of the world – to give millet in Africa, maize in the Americas, rice in the Far East and rye in Europe and Asia Minor. He found that he could grow other plants as well; and through trade and the gradual movement of populations this 'produce' became cultivated in areas far distant from its wild origins. This process has continued and, in the absence of written records, has made it difficult for the modern botanist to establish where many of the plants we cultivate today – and which have been grown since prehistoric times – had their geographic origins. So unrecorded, save among artefacts which the modern archaeologist uncovers, man took his first tottering steps toward agriculture and thus horticulture, for over many centuries the two were to go hand in hand.

Gardens as we know them today are, in the historical sense, a very recent concept as far as Western civilization is concerned, though the Chinese were growing plants as an aesthetic expression – purely for the beauty of their colour and form – more than 2 000 years ago. In the West, early civilizations such as those of Egypt, Greece and Rome, cultivated vineyards, orchards and certain other plants – garlic, for instance, was grown as a vegetable and formed an important part of the ancient Egyptian's diet. in his *Georgics*, written in 36 BC, the Roman poet Virgil provides us with a long didactic epic devoted to husbandry of crops and orchards, and though he attributes much of the knowledge it contains to the earlier writings of Hesiod, and his verse form tends to obscure the practicality of his advice, the *Georgics* can lay arguable claim to being the first Western agricultural handbook. But – despite Virgil's digression into verse – such plants as he describes and our Western forebears tended were grown to a purpose, either as food, medicine or for ceremonial use.

It was for their medicinal use that plants were first studied and actively cultivated in gardens. Throughout medieval Europe, monasteries had herb gardens where they raised many of the plants which we still use to add savour to our meals. They tended others such as the paeony, which we cultivate only for its flowering charms, but which they grew in the belief that its roots provided a cure for madness.

In the fields, root-crops, a few of the *Brassicas*, and such 'pot herbs' as leeks were also grown but, even well into the 15th century, it was only the very wealthy who cultivated anything which was not of direct,

South African ericas proved extremely popular among the gardeners of 18th and 19th century Europe. This species, *Erica doliiformis* was dubbed ever-blooming French heather.

practical use. Those who did so were regarded as somewhat eccentric, and the term 'curious gardener' which the English were to apply to the botanists of the late 16th century did not always mean that the gentlemen concerned were regarded only as possessing a lively curiosity.

Probably the best-known of the plantsmen of the late 16th century was John Gerrard, today regarded less for his botanical knowledge – though it was substantial for his time – than for his *Herball, or generall historie of plantes*. Gerrard was renowned in both Britain and Europe for his physic garden and his *Herball*, published in 1597, stressed the medicinal uses of plants (and often their astrological significance) rather than how to cultivate them. Earlier, he had compiled what is the only extant reasonably full register of plants growing in the British Isles in his day. He listed some 1 000 species, but his work is largely forgotten today and it is his *Herball* which remains to delight the modern reader.

The quaint language and even quainter concepts are more than balanced by his acute observation and knowledge, a considerable body of which still remains valid. Typical of Gerrard's gems are his description of *Pyrethrum parthenium* as 'a small pale [fence] of white leaves set round about a yellow ball or button [which] joyeth to grow among rubbish', and of *Melissa officinalis* 'the juice of balme glueth together green woundes'. The latter observation has since been endorsed by modern medical science which recognizes that the balsamic oils make admirable surgical dressings.

The *Herball* was more a physician's than a gardener's handbook and had been preceded almost forty years earlier in a work written by another Englishman, William Turner, who had listed, with advice on their cultivation, all the plants in his garden near Richmond. But though both men were concerned with useful plants, they knew something of genera and species already being grown, ornamentally and for their rarity, in Britain and Europe. The ill-fated Cardinal Wolsey had incorporated a garden in the design for his palace at Hampton Court and reputedly planted the great vine which still grows there centuries after his death on his way to his execution in 1530.

## EXPANDING HORIZONS

The world's horizons were expanding, and as first the European seafaring nations and later Britain began to explore the scantily-mapped and unknown sectors of the globe, small wooden ships returned with strange plants from far-off lands; plants which fascinated the wealthy who vied with each other in collecting – and eventually cultivating – such exotica. The Spanish king established what was to become the Western world's first botanic garden and other royalty and nobles followed suit to become the first courtier-botanists. They developed magnificent gardens with these strange plants, often ignoring – rather as we do today – local flowers of considerable merit.

Botany, though still in its infancy, had by now become a science, and as more and more specimens became available to the scholars – be they in Leyden or Heidelberg, Padua or Oxford – they found it increasingly difficult to share their new knowledge with each other. It had been hard enough to cross linguistic boundaries when describing European plants which they all knew, but by common names that varied not only from country to country but from region to region within a particular country. Communication about the new wealth of flora which they faced was baffling.

They had overcome their earlier problems relating to common European species, albeit cumbersomely, by using Latin. Thus when in 1688 the naturalist Ray writing to a colleague on the Continent referred to '*Arbor exotica foliis fraxini instar pinatis et serratisi negundo perperam credita*' the recipient had no doubt that Ray was identifying what, in England at least, was known as the box elder.

## LINNAEUS AND THE NAMING OF PLANTS

It was into this quagmire of communication that the Swedish naturalist Carl von Linné stepped, to introduce to a delighted, if somewhat sceptical, scientific world the system of classification which we know as binomial nomenclature – the system which we have used in this book and allows each plant or living creature to be described by two words that indicate its genus and species, so making it instantly identifiable to modern botanists the world over.

Von Linné, who was so ardent a Latinist as well as naturalist that he altered his own name to Linnaeus, left his home in Uppsala in 1735 for Leyden and soon became a close friend of George Clifford whose zoological and botanic gardens at Haarlem were stocked mainly with plants from the Cape. These so fascinated the botanist that South African flora formed an important section of his book *Systema Naturae*, published in 1745, in which he systematically classified all known plants, animals and even minerals.

By the time the tenth edition of this work was published 13 years later he had given them each two names: one indicating the genus and the second the species. This system of 'binomial nomenclature' is still used today and though Linnaeus was not the first to formulate it (our friend the 'curious gardener' Gerrard had used a similar system in his *Herball*) it was through the efforts of Linnaeus that it was expanded and accepted by scientists.

In his *Species Plantarum* (1753) he applied the same two-name, or binomial, system to all the then known plants in the world. Linnaeus' system is only the tip of an overall system of classification of broader categories which scientists have applied to all living things. The plant kingdom, which is that of main concern to the gardener, is broken into smaller and smaller groups, all of which have a common identifying feature. The broadest of these groups is a phylum, and if one looks at the whole system of classification as a many-trunked tree, the phylum would be the root, the trunk would be the class, the branches would represent the orders while the twigs would be the families with the leaves representing genera and their veins the species. As the groups grow smaller so their shared features become fewer.

It is mainly with genera and species that the home gardener is concerned – though varieties and cultivars (see How to use this book, page 5) of many species have today outstripped their parents in terms of beauty and interest – and here our debt to Linnaeus' system is unlimited.

Nor was it introduced and accepted a decade too soon. As geographical knowledge expanded and settlement increased, the pioneers were followed not only by the missionaries (many of whom were scientists of a sort) but also by naturalists and botanists. The trickle of new seeds and specimens reaching botanical gardens and herbariums in Europe, soon became a stream and eventually a torrent.

Many of the genera and species which they discovered and described have been given their names, for it has remained a convention that the discoverers of 'new' plants, or species or varieties of plants are so remembered – though the names are latinized. Other specific names are more descriptive: *officinalis* indicates a belief in the plant's medicinal properties, *hirsutus* points to a plant's hairiness, *nudicaulis* refers to a bare stem and so on. Still others relate to a plant's site or geographical location so that *saxifraga* would indicate a preference for a rocky situation and *capensis* that it is indigenous to the Cape, though *australis* does not mean 'from Australia' but merely 'from the south'. For those who are interested, a list of the more common specific names, their origins and their meanings are appended to Botanical Terms and their Meanings (see page 378).

## HOW PLANTS GROW

But the botanists were not merely busy describing and naming the new plants. As the range of specimens available for study proliferated, and as attempts were made to propagate the new flora, the answers to many earlier speculative theories about how plants actually grew, reproduced themselves, and what their needs were, became apparent. It was established that most plants need light, moisture, warmth and fertile soil in which to grow and discovered, contrary to the earlier belief that the plant drew all its food from the soil, that it actually manufactures much of its own nutrient.

The way in which a plant lives is diagrammatically illustrated on page 32. Briefly, the plant's nourishment is derived by a process of absorption through the roots and the leaves. Minute root hairs near the growing tip of each root drink in the moisture containing salts and other nutrients by a process of osmosis. These root hairs, mono-cellular and about one millimetre long, are short-lived and replaced by others as the roots grow. Yet they are so numerous that they can provide the vital chemicals for a tree tens of metres tall.

While these root hairs are providing the salts, the leaves of the plant absorb carbon dioxide from the air. Then by a process of photosynthesis (literally 'manufacture from light') with the agency of chlorophyll, the leaves convert the carbon dioxide from the atmosphere into the starches and sugars which also feed the plant, at the same time releasing oxygen into the air. The excess moisture which results from this interaction is expelled through the leaves in a process known as transpiration, thus encouraging the sap containing the mineral-rich moisture from the roots to rise through the plant.

These botanists, too, discovered the principles of cross-pollination, and that by retaining the seeds or bulbs of a particularly strong specimen, its progeny were likely to reflect similar characteristics. Many attempts at cross-pollination were carried out and several theories advanced, but it was not until 1865 that the Abbot of Brno, Johann Mendel, succeeded in proving a theory of heredity and genes – based on a nine-year study of the pea – which we accept today as the Mendelian Theory.

Where the earlier explorer-botanists had opened up a new world of plants, Mendel opened the way to a vast range of improvements to many of these plants – to the hybrids and cultivars which are so important in today's garden. Thus the gladiolus, which today must rank as one of the world's most popular cut flowers, bears little resemblance to the shy flower which still is found in the wild, while the stone plants, or *Lithops* of Namaqualand seem totally remote from the multi-hued cultivars which Japanese experts have bred.

One of the earliest plants used by civilized man, other than for food or medicine, was *Cyperus papyrus* from which the ancient Egyptians made paper.

and many home-owners construct one near the vegetable garden which is usually screened from the rest of the garden and hidden from view.

A garden frame on the other hand is easily and cheaply built and takes up very little space. In frosty areas it can be used to over-winter tender plants, and is also useful for bringing on seedlings and cuttings. Because it is low and unobtrusive a frame can be situated within a garden without being an eyesore but it important to remember that, like the greenhouse, it must be sited so that it has as much light as possible and is protected from the prevailing wind.

**LAWNS. GENERAL POINTS.** Never split up a small lawn with several flower-beds. Leave the sweep of green undisturbed. Let the lawn be the garden carpet and, in small gardens, line the boundaries with flower-beds so that the eye will be drawn by their colour and the lawn be allowed to give the illusion of space.

Large lawns, on the other hand, can take one or two large flower or rose beds, or trees to give shade, or specimens which need space to be properly appreciated. Different trees can have a different effect on the grass growing beneath them. Grass will grow right up to the trunk of some deciduous trees but the heavy foliage of a pin-oak, plane or similar type trees will inhibit the growth. In this case you can create a pleasant effect by paving around the tree from near the base of the trunk out to the area where the grass is beginning to die. But never remove the lower branches of trees like the pin-oak (*Quercus palustris*), liquidamber, cedars and plane trees; their lower branches should be allowed to sweep the ground as befits their character and form if they are to be seen at their natural best. For further information see Chapter 4, 'Lawns and Grasses', paying particular attention to 'Preparing a Lawn' on page 46. This is a very important factor in your garden planning.

**LIGHTS.** Even in the smallest garden outdoor lighting can add an effective nocturnal charm, bringing to life a single striking specimen or piece of garden statuary which takes on a new beauty when seen from a patio or the windows of a house at night. A floodlit lawn and its adjacent beds, or a night-sparkling pool seem to attain a new dimension. More practically you may wish to light a path or, certainly, an outdoor flight of steps which is used at night. But avoid garishly-coloured light-bulbs; even at night Nature's own colours remain incomparable. When planning such an installation be guided by an expert electrician who should ensure that wires are adequately insulated and buried at sufficient depth to be safe from careless digging or cutting. And remember to place the control switch in, or conveniently close to, the house – you will avoid the stubbed toes and scratches which seem to accompany any night-time excursion into an unlit garden.

**PATHS.** Paths, steps and stepping-stones should be considered as a whole and similar materials should be used – not one in brick

and the other in crazy paving. It the path is grass-jointed, then let the steps also be grass-jointed.

Irrespective of whether it is curved or straight, a path which bisects a lawn on its route to the front door should not be bordered with flowers, especially if the lawn is on the

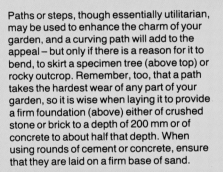

Paths or steps, though essentially utilitarian, may be used to enhance the charm of your garden, and a curving path will add to the appeal – but only if there is a reason for it to bend, to skirt a specimen tree (above top) or rocky outcrop. Remember, too, that a path takes the hardest wear of any part of your garden, so it is wise when laying it to provide a firm foundation (above) either of crushed stone or brick to a depth of 200 mm or of concrete to about half that depth. When using rounds of cement or concrete, ensure that they are laid on a firm base of sand.

small side. The presence of anything on either side of the path above its level (which should be flush with the lawn), only serves to magnify the division, destroying the illusion of space and making the lawn look half its real size. Rather flatter a lawn's dimensions by flower borders at its extreme boundaries.

Very large lawns can stand a bed on either side of a bisecting path, but such beds should then be at least the width of the path so that they are the feature and the path incidental to them. Never curve a path for the sake of curving it; nothing looks quite so silly as a path winding a tortuous way across a lawn when the obvious route is in a straight line. Paths should not be allowed to wander at random, they should always be the shortest way to a destination and if they change direction there should be a good reason. It adds variety and interest to the garden however if there are diversions which cause the path to curve naturally. It can follow a natural depression in a gentle downward slope and curve to bypass a tree or flower-bed, or you can contrive minor dips in the gradient of the garden by building up the soil at strategic points or constructing a rockery. Your own imagination will find the best scheme for your own garden.

Whatever the material chosen for your paths make certain the surface is smooth and easy to walk on and, if using stepping-stones to cross a lawn, set them on a base of sand and keep them flush with the lawn. Spaced stones look more attractive than ones laid in a straight line.

**PATIOS and BARBECUE AREAS.** Though Australians have not yet reached the stage celebrated in song by Flanders and Swann where 'the garden's filled with furniture and the house is full of plants', there are some homes which come uncommonly close to it. With our dedication to outdoor living and the barbecue, the patio provides an ideal connection between garden and house. Most newly-built houses incorporate a patio, many of them with an in-built barbecue and this is an area where pots of flowers, troughs and tubbed trees can come into their own. But — always avoid clutter and do not plant creepers or shrubs where their growth will eventually come within reach of the heat of the fire. Indoor plants can be brought out for effect when needed; tubs can be moved around as seasons change. The patio is an area to be used both for aesthetic and useful purposes. Throughout this book reference will be found to plants which can be used not only indoors but can be grown successfully in protected positions outdoors. See the relevant Chapter 18. The pleasure of 'outdoor living' is best realised when a patio is used to take advantage of all it can offer — and that is as wide as the imagination of the owner can range. The charm of a house often lies in the seemingly effortless way outdoor and indoor living blend. Both skill and art are needed to achieve this effect — simplicity is the keynote as it is in so many other garden endeavours. Time spent in planning this area is seldom wasted.

**PERGOLAS.** A pergola is seen and used to the best effect in the larger garden but, in a small garden, a car-port can be used as a base on which to train climbers such as wisterias and vines which need height to show off their drooping flower-panicles. In a garden large enough to contain a pergola or

Built-in flower troughs make ideal back rests for the seats of a shady patio.

Rambler roses and pot plants make this patio a comfortable transition from garden to home.

covered walk-way, it should be sited either in, or as the focal point of a vista, so that the climbing plants covering it can create a picture. A pergola should be sited to provide a view both into and out of the garden and should be provided with a seat or bench from which such a view can be enjoyed. The original purpose of a pergola was to provide a shady arbour but now it is mainly used to show off vines and creepers of particular beauty and can be a major feature in a garden. The range of lovely creepers and climbers is wide (see Chapter 10 'Climbers').

Pergolas may be constructed from a wide range of materials and to many designs. But whether the uprights are brick, stone, wood or concrete 'classical' columns you must give them firm foundations and make sure that the cross-pieces are strong and durable. Growing climbers exert considerable force and, in maturity, often attain substantial mass so, in selecting material and plants for your pergola

A pergola provides an ideal way to show climbers to their best advantage.

Statuary and rough stone combine with a lily pond to provide an air of tranquillity.

consider the creation of harmony in your garden – a rustic structure will look as incongruous in an orthodox, formal garden as a stream-lined modern style will look in a garden given to creating an atmosphere of old-world charm. A pergola can be covered by roses, but will then only show colour at one time of year; a clever choice of vines and creepers can make your pergola a source of beauty and colour throughout the seasons. Since few garden features create such an

effect it is worth planning very carefully to achieve maximum effect.

**YOUR GARDEN PLOT.** The fall of ground can vary from the flat to the precipitous, and here are advantages as well as drawbacks. If your plot is flat do not congratulate yourself too soon; it may make building the house easier but it will make the landscaping of the garden more difficult. Unless there is good reason to maintain a flat surface every effort should be

made to introduce slopes and contours which are both practical and pleasant. Flat land calls for a formal garden and does not permit the charming informal plantings which blend well with gentle slopes and flowing contours. In a new garden there may be builders' rubble etc. which can be used, banked and covered with earth, stone and rockery plants, to give a gentle rise and fall. You may have to bring in more soil to achieve the effect you like, but this can be done over a period of time as you shape your garden and create the atmosphere and amenities which give you and your family maximum pleasure.

Should your plot be gently undulating retain the natural contours as far as possible and let any other necessary slopes be in keeping with them. There should not be any sudden change in direction or gradient; such changes should be smooth, natural, almost imperceptible.

Where more extreme gradients are encountered, do everything possible to avoid terraces. They involve expensive retaining walls, steps, and create problems getting maintenance equipment from one level to another. Slopes, unless they are so steep that a mower cannot operate, are preferable to a terrace, or a series of terraces – and make for easier access, and reduce maintenance costs.

**PONDS and WATER GARDENS.** Even on the hottest of days the presence of a pond, no matter how small, lends an aura of coolness to any garden and is worth finding a space for in an overall plan. Whether planning a water garden for a new home or introducing it to an established landscape, there are several factors to be borne in mind. If small children are likely to have access to the garden, ensure that the pond is so sited that they will be protected from potential danger – a wickerwork fence supporting climbers, or a rough stone coping which blends with the rest of the garden should be adequate. Remember that most aquatic plants require some sun if they are to flourish; and, above all consider the proximity of any trees or shrubs; their thirsty roots, when the plant is fully-grown, will damage a pool's foundations. Bear in mind, too, that at some stage even the most natural pools will need to be emptied – to replace plants, separate overgrown rootstock and so on – so that some method of drainage should be incorporated in the design. Unless you intend to have fish in the pond, never site it near a bedroom window where mosquitoes can become a problem. (See also Chapter 15, 'Water Gardens', page 269.)

**POOLS.** Though you are unlikely to cultivate anything in your swimming pool, when siting it or deciding on the actual type of pool you intend to have installed, give some thought to its effect on the overall garden picture. Just as your house should blend with its environment, so should a pool. Most municipalities today insist that any pool should be safely fenced and closed off with a child-proof gate. Try to incorporate the fence into the garden whole, using creepers or climbers (see also Chapter 10, 'Climbers') and remember that

Natural stone and a cluster of aloes have been cleverly used to link the formal to the informal of this swimming pool.

pool-side pumps and gratings can be covered with several species of ground covers (see Chapter 5) whose tendrils may be moved and even rearranged without harming the plant.

**RARITIES.** As a keen gardener why not try to grow some species which are rare, unusually lovely or difficult to cultivate? If your garden is small just two or three types would do. Your friends will be fascinated and you will enjoy the challenge to your gardening ability. The plants in question will vary according to your geographical position, of course, as what is rare and difficult in one area can be commonplace in another. The lovely Waratah, the floral emblem of New South Wales, whose botanical and aboriginal names both mean 'seen from afar' is notoriously difficult to grow, not only away from its natural habitat but when transplanted within it, so think of the pride and the pleasure in being able to exhibit those great red glowing blossoms. There are other plants, not only difficult to grow but even to obtain.

**ROCKERIES.** The visual success of any rock garden, depends on its having a natural appearance. This is best achieved by placing the component stones and rocks so as to imitate the strata found in everyday formations. Even where bays and pockets for special massed effects are introduced, a little care will make possible this 'natural' look. (See also Chapter 16, 'Cacti and Succulents'.) If the rockery is to be given over to succulents and cacti, ensure that there is good drainage, as these plants resent the prolonged presence of moisture which tends to rot their roots.

'La Passionata', one of the ever-popular hybrid tea roses.
Tastefully chosen statuary can add charm and dignity even to a small garden.

**ROSES.** The width of an oblong rose-bed should be sufficient to take four or five rose bushes in a staggered line. The length of the bed should be little more than twice the width. The bed should be sited so that it can be seen, framed in the green of the lawn, from more than one angle. A circular bed should be about 4 m in diameter. If only one variety of rose is grown per bed uniform performance can be expected but few private gardens allow such luxury. But roses make good bedfellows and seldom clash with each other even though grown in mixed colours. A purist might object to such planting but Nature has a palette which allows a wide range of colours to blend, so do not be afraid, plant your roses together; the effect will always be lovely. One thing to remember – a standard is the only type rose which should be planted in a single hole in the lawn – a bush rose looks as out of place as an onion in a petunia patch. See pages 163-5 'Roses'.

**SCULPTURES.** The precast statuettes of the goose-girl, arms outstretched to bear a bird-bath, and the garden gnomes dangling a fishing rod into a pond that dotted so many suburban gardens in the 1930s have largely fallen from favour. Their plastic successors – no less mass-produced – are, to me, no less unappealing. Nevertheless, many gardeners find pleasure in them, and our gardens would be intolerably monotonous if we all shared identical likes and dislikes.

There is as wide a choice of garden statuary and sculpture as there are tastes – from finely executed copies of classical figures; to mass-produced, painted models of birds, animals, people and gnomes. But whatever the direction in which your taste runs, when siting a piece of garden sculpture bear in mind the need for balance and proportion. A full-size copy of the Venus de Milo will look as out of place in a suburban flower bed as would a painted garden gnome in the middle of a formal lawn at Versailles. One good sculpture is always preferable to several shoddy ones.

**SHEDS.** Few gardens today have space for a toolshed, let alone the luxury of a separate potting-shed. However, in planning a garden it is worthwhile trying to provide a covered space, no matter how small, in which tools, empty seedling trays and pots can be stored, and pesticides and other poisons locked away. If it is large enough to take a narrow work-top, so much the better – this will prove more comfortable when transplanting seedlings to pots, potting-on or even mixing sprays than doing the same task squatting on the garage floor. Try to site such a shed near a garden tap (and drain) for easy access when cleaning equipment. If you are unable to fit such a shed into your garden planning, a useful way to store tools and equipment is to hang them from trellis-work fixed to a garage wall (see Chapter 3, 'Equipment and Tools', page 37).

**SHRUBS.** Even the smallest garden can be enhanced by the judicious planting of one or more shrubs, grown for flowers or foliage. In planning where to site a shrub, bear in mind

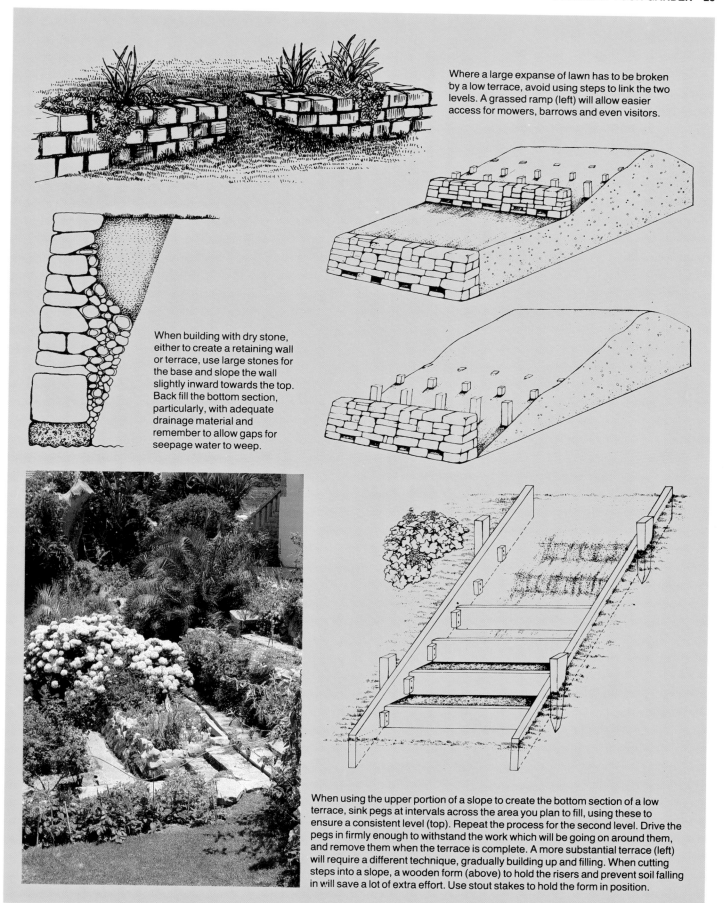

Where a large expanse of lawn has to be broken by a low terrace, avoid using steps to link the two levels. A grassed ramp (left) will allow easier access for mowers, barrows and even visitors.

When building with dry stone, either to create a retaining wall or terrace, use large stones for the base and slope the wall slightly inward towards the top. Back fill the bottom section, particularly, with adequate drainage material and remember to allow gaps for seepage water to weep.

When using the upper portion of a slope to create the bottom section of a low terrace, sink pegs at intervals across the area you plan to fill, using these to ensure a consistent level (top). Repeat the process for the second level. Drive the pegs in firmly enough to withstand the work which will be going on around them, and remove them when the terrace is complete. A more substantial terrace (left) will require a different technique, gradually building up and filling. When cutting steps into a slope, a wooden form (above) to hold the risers and prevent soil falling in will save a lot of extra effort. Use stout stakes to hold the form in position.

The almost severe lines of this modern home (above) have been softened by the use of natural stone which is echoed in the beds fringing the patio. The fronds of a potted palm blend happily with those of the cycads in the foreground to provide a pattern which harmoniously links Nature's very ancient with Man's most modern. Evergreen trees will add dimension to your garden; whether it is the towering arrowhead of a *Cupressus sempervirens* 'horizontalis' (left) or one of the small variegated cultivars of *Juniperus communis* (below), try to find a place for at least one specimen tree.

such factors as texture and leaf-colour as well as eventual size. If it is a deciduous species, take particular account of how it will appear in the barrenness of winter, after it has cast off its colourful autumn clothing. (For particulars see also Chapter 8, 'Shrubs and Roses'.)

**STEPS.** Unless a garden is as uniformly level as a bowling green it is likely to need steps somewhere within the boundaries. The lie of the land will often determine where they must be, though if the garden is terraced the planner has greater freedom of choice. The sort of material used for the steps is a matter of choice though, as with any other garden constructon, it should be harmonious with the general ambience of the garden scheme. There is a wide range of choice but one cardinal rule must be observed. Whether the steps are of stone, brick, concrete, turf or logs, the treads should always be wider and the risers shallower than those of an indoor flight. Outdoor steps become wet and slippery and wider treads reduce the risk of falls.

Always make sure that the treads are firmly based. In a loose bank of soil, this may mean excavating the entire area to be occupied by the steps and compacting the fill as the steps take shape. Where the slope is firm, only shaping of the steps may be necessary. In either case it is advisable to provide the bottom tread with a really firm foundation – concrete cast in a trench 100 mm deep, or crushed stone to twice that depth. This should extend to double the width of the tread, to bear the mass and stress of the first riser.

The edging will depend on the purpose of the steps and on individual taste; but at the planning stage it is worth bearing in mind that steps can be convenient seats, and that wide treads are useful stands for outdoor pot-plants and troughs.

**TAPS and WATERING.** When planning a new home from scratch it is easy to overlook such obvious requirements as garden taps and, as often as not, their siting is left to the builder or plumber. The tap outside the back door or against the garage wall is seldom a convenient source from which to water the entire garden. Ideally, stand-points should not be more than 50 m apart – most mains supplies are such that a normal 12 mm-diameter hose-pipe will deliver water over a distance of 25 metres to meet all ordinary garden requirements. Where a new tap or water source is to be installed, site it as unobtrusively as possible. Underground connections which make use of the bayonet principle (see page 40) have made unnecessary the vertical tap and its accompanying wooden support, which marred the lawns of a few decades ago. Several types of watering system are available today, and these are discussed in Chapter 3, 'Equipment and Tools', see page 40.

**TERRACES.** Should a terrace, or terraces, be inevitable, split the line of the terrace to create a grass ramp which will facilitate access between the levels. The lawn against a terrace wall should be framed by placing a flower border at its base, not on the upper wall level, where it will interfere with the view and shorten the vista. Should the view be unattractive, or there is some other reason for obscuring it, the upper level of the terrace wall presents a natural opportunity for introducing one of those highly ornamental garden fences in pre-cast concrete – or a pleasant simple picket fence. A permanent border may front the ornamental fence, using a mixture of perennials and annuals for seasonal colour. Alternatively, climbing roses may be grown, using the non-rambler type if you do not wish to obscure the form of the fence itself.

**TREES.** Providing your garden is large enough do see that you have one good specimen of a tree that is a tree; one which is stately enough to provide dimension, character and the suggestion of permanence such as a species of cedar, *Brachychiton acerifolium*, jacaranda, or *Grevillea robusta* – all of which are big, big trees if they can be allowed to grow, unfettered and unconstrained, to their fullest, majestic stature.

**VEGETABLE GARDENS.** Apart from the economic advantages, growing one's own vegetables ensures a freshness, whether for table or freezer, which bought produce cannot equal. A keen gardener will always find space for his own small allotment. When planning a vegetable patch bear in mind the need for adequate protection from wind and excessive

# THE GARDENER AND THE LAW

The tangled red tape of modern bureaucracy reaches even into today's garden – both in terms of actual planning, and in governing a range of everyday gardening activities. Not only does very necessary legislation cover the use and control of poisons such as pesticides and weed-killers, but certain laws and provincial ordinances specify certain plants that gardeners may not grow and others which they must actively eradicate. Water hyacinth and Kariba weed are disastrous to our rivers and dams, no matter how delightful these plants may appear. Legislation also strictly controls the importing of plants and seeds in a move to protect indigenous and other plants from disease.

As far as the gardener is concerned, common law provides him with protection and rights as well as facing him with certain obligations. Two spheres of garden planning seem most fraught with pitfalls for the home-owner – boundaries and building. Boundaries shared with neighbours are usually carefully surveyed and, in towns and cities at least, pegs fix the actual limits of each property. Strictly speaking, a fence or wall on the boundary line may only be erected with the agreement of both neighbours and, equally, may only be demolished or altered through their joint consent. A hedge or tree growing exactly on the line is viewed similarly in law. However, should the tree's branches extend into the garden, the owner of the garden may remove the branches or, in the case of a fruit tree, enjoy the fruits which grow on his side of the line. The law views similarly a tree which is actually on the neighbouring property. However in any such situation try to resolve it amicably; litigation is not only costly, but it never serves good neighbourliness.

Hedges or trees growing on a boundary which faces a road can cause a different set of problems for the gardener. Municipal or provincial authorities are empowered to order the home-owner to remove, at his own expense, any hedge or tree which may obscure a motorist's vision of, say, an intersection. Should a hedge be considered a fire hazard, the authorities may demand its removal, but in this case most authorities are obliged to make good the hedge with some type of fencing. If such situations arise, it is advisable to

check the local bye-laws for your area, as these are not the same in every State municipality.

Should the home-owner decide to excavate on or near his boundary, he must ensure that this is done in such a way as not to cause subsidence on the adjoining land. He, or his agents – if a swimming pool is being built, for instance – will be legally responsible for the costs of any repairs resulting from the excavation.

Most of the larger muncipalities have introduced bye-laws making the fencing of swimming pools compulsory. Your pool builder should be able to advise you on this, but it is a matter of common sense anyway. No-one wants a hazard to children in the garden.

Many parts of Australia are struck by drought at some time or other, and when this occurs, local authorities may well impose water restrictions, particularly on the suburban garden. These may take the form of limiting watering to certain hours or specific, staggered days and may even include a total ban on the use of hose-pipes. Annoying as these temporary decrees undoubtedly are, to deliberately disregard them is to court disaster. For in most cases water restrictions are enforced and transgressors fined. Though such restrictions will obviously affect your plants – particularly as such periods of drought are often accompanied by a heat-wave – there are certain steps which the gardener can take to reduce the effects. A heavy mulching will help keep the soil cool and reduce the loss of moisture through evaporation. Save bath and washing-up water and apply this from a watering-can, to keep particularly thirsty specimens happy, and to chirp up any plants which appear to be suffering thirst. If practicable, however, the best solution would be to tap an underground stream. For if you do have sweet, plentiful water fairly near to the surface in your garden, your problem would be solved and the cost of pumping equipment soon offset against savings in your water bill.

Building regulations also vary from local authority to local authority, and before putting up a garden shed, greenhouse or any other permanent or semi-permanent structure it is advisable to check that height, size and position come within local regulations.

sun. If the vegetable section is to be screened from the rest of your garden, avoid using greedy plants which will rob the soil of moisture and nutrients.

**WORK AREAS.** Though, strictly speaking, these are not the province of the gardener, unsightly washing-lines or outhouses often require screening. If this is to be achieved by

growing climbers on a trellis, remember that the supporting uprights will probably require as deeply-sunk foundations as would a fence. And if the work area is paved or walled, this is often a perfect place to grow plants, particularly herbs (see Chapter 14) – in pots or troughs. It can also be an ideal situation for the enthusiast to practise hydroponics or some other form of soilless cultivation.

and may be used for striking cuttings. Another plastic tray has 24 separate compartments, or divisions, and measures 220 × 320 × 60 mm. A more solid, white polyester tray – also with 24 divisions, but measuring approximately 130 × 330 × 60 mm encourages better growth. The young seedlings seem to thrive and are more easily removed from the container at planting-out time. Handled with care, these trays may be used again and again. Store plastic containers in a dry, cool and dark place. After use, wash each tray thoroughly in a moderate solution of disinfectant.

Should you plan to grow on rooted cuttings or young seedlings to a fairly advanced stage before setting them out, plastic bags are convenient, workable, and much cheaper than pots. They are readily available and a stock of two standard sizes (200 × 100 × 75 mm, and 230 × 125 × 100 mm) should meet the average gardener's needs. Use the small size first and, when the bag is full of roots and the plant about 200-300 mm high, ease it into the larger one, where it will be quite happy for another six to nine months. At this stage you must do one of four things: put it into an even larger bag; plant it out; give it to a friend; or donate it to charity.

If you wish to re-use the bags, and there is no reason why you should not, wash them and store them as you would seed trays.

**SHOVEL.** Similar in general appearance to the spade, but with a concave and rounded blade, the shovel is used to handle loose soil and sand. It will do this sort of work more efficiently than a spade. A good size is about 900 mm long with a blade 350 mm deep and 260 mm wide.

**SIEVES** are available in a variety of mesh sizes and overall dimensions. An outside diameter of 400-500 mm will allow a worthwhile amount of material to be shaken through at the one filling; the size of the mesh will depend largely on the material to be treated. For washed river sand, an 8 mm mesh is ideal. A 15 mm mesh is good for sieving soil and compost.

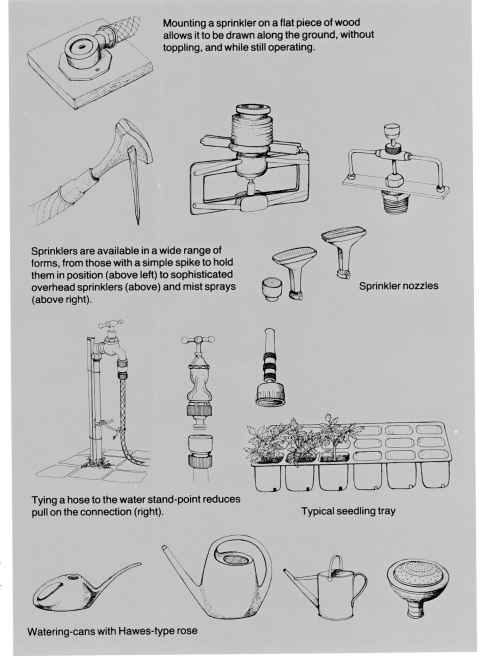

Mounting a sprinkler on a flat piece of wood allows it to be drawn along the ground, without toppling, and while still operating.

Sprinklers are available in a wide range of forms, from those with a simple spike to hold them in position (above left) to sophisticated overhead sprinklers (above) and mist sprays (above right).

Sprinkler nozzles

Tying a hose to the water stand-point reduces pull on the connection (right).

Typical seedling tray

Watering-cans with Hawes-type rose

A colourful display

**SPADES.** The standard spade has an overall length of 960 mm, with a blade which is 300 mm deep and 210 mm wide. The upper edge of the blade should have a flat metal rib about 20 mm wide which allows the foot to exercise maximum pressure. Spades smaller than standard are not very effective.

**SPRAYING EQUIPMENT.** Most of today's spraying apparatus is made from durable, strong plastic which will not corrode as a result of inter-reaction with spraying solutions. There are four main types of spraying units suited to home-gardening.
**a.** Knapsack spray. This has a capacity of 20 litres and is carried on the back. The pressure pump may be operated either left- or right-handed, leaving the other hand free to manipulate the delivery nozzle.
**b.** Pre-pump type. Less expensive than the knapsack type, this is pumped to pressure before use. When the pressure drops to an inefficient level, a few pumpings will quickly restore it. The unit usually has a capacity of 5 to 10 litres and may be carried slung over one shoulder.
**c.** Pump type hand spray. This looks like the old-fashioned fly spray. Mostly plastic, these units are sometimes available in stainless steel, and have a capacity of 500 ml to one litre.
**d.** Hand spray. Holding one litre of liquid, this is efficient and emits a fine, well-distributed spray.

Never leave unused liquid in a spray unit. Empty it in a safe area and wash it thoroughly in warm water to which a little liquid soap has been added, and pump some of the cleaning liquid through the nozzle before storing.

**WATERING-CANS.** A standard-sized can which holds about 10 litres of water is a basic requirement. Galvanized iron cans have largely been superseded by heavy plastic ones. If you still have a galvanized can you can prolong its life by giving it a coat of aluminium paint, inside and out. Detachable roses giving sprays of various drenching ability make it possible to use a can for different purposes.

Watering-cans come in different sizes, different spout-lengths and have roses which can deliver sprays to suit a purpose. Cans with long slender spouts and no rose are useful for watering plants in situations difficult to reach on the balcony or in the greenhouse, etc. The efficient gardener provides himself with a variety of cans so that all the watering he has to do, inside and out of doors, can be dealt with cleanly and effectively.

**WHEELBARROWS.** The standard garden wheelbarrow has a capacity of approximately four 10-litre buckets – useful to bear in mind when mixing soils for potting and so on. Barrows fitted with a rubber-tyred wheel are easier to push, run more smoothly and do least damage to the surfaces over which they are used.

The wheelbarrow is an expensive item of equipment and merits every possible care. When the outer coat of paint begins to wear off – particularly over the bottom of the tray – re-paint with a good quality paint (or aluminium) to prevent rusting. The tray is the first part of a wheelbarrow to wear and the erosion of metal is assisted by rust. After use, the inner tray or bowl of the barrow should be thoroughly washed out, dried, and then smeared lightly with an oily rag. Never allow the wheel to squeak for want of oil or grease. A wheelbarrow may last five years or a lifetime – it depends on how well it is looked after.

Backs can be strained by the incorrect use of wheelbarrows. Always ensure that the heaviest portion of the load rests above the wheel; lift the barrow, with knees bent and back upright – straighten the legs and you are ready to roll.

A well planted garden, planned for easy maintenance ▶

# LAWNS AND GRASSES

### CARPETING TO SET THE GARDEN SCENE

In any aspect of gardening, balance and harmony are the keynotes and this is never more so than in planning a lawn. In some of the world's outstanding gardens, superlative examples of horticultural art and craftsmanship, lawns impress by the major influence which their proportions exercise in attaining an almost incredible degree of harmony – a verdant carpet against which the splendours of other plants are set. And in these gardens – as well as in many closer to hand – the broad terraces, the quiet lawns and the sweeping, grassed vistas take up more than half, and sometimes as much as four-fifths of the area.

Yet this serves to emphasize the magnificence of the trees, the shrubs, and the colour borders and beds of the garden proper. The key to success was found in striking the right proportions – a lesson fundamental to the successful design of even the smallest suburban garden.

The lawn is not just something which should be planted to fill the space between shrubberies and flower beds – it is an integral part of the garden picture. And though our harsher conditions prevent the use of the softer greensward grasses which one associates with European lawns, there is a sufficiently wide range of species – some, like kikuyu and buffalo, tougher and more resistant than the fine grasses – to permit the establishment of a good lawn.

Instant lawns are becoming increasingly popular, and most major towns and cities boast commercial producers who supply turf in 'roll-on' sections. If you can afford it, this is the quickest, most effective and simplest way to establish a first-class lawn. Prepare the ground as you would for planting a lawn (see page 46) and lay the turfs or sods, as they are also called, directly onto this surface. Most commercial growers use fine grasses for their turfs, which are normally cut in sections about one metre long, 300 mm wide and about 30 mm thick.

If you are planning a new lawn from seed or cuttings, select a grass which has proved successful in your area. There is nothing more disappointing than to expend time and energy preparing the soil for a lawn, planting it and then finding that the grass springs up only in patches – if at all.

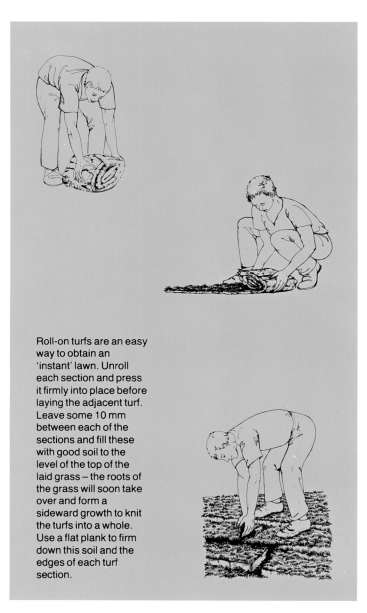

Roll-on turfs are an easy way to obtain an 'instant' lawn. Unroll each section and press it firmly into place before laying the adjacent turf. Leave some 10 mm between each of the sections and fill these with good soil to the level of the top of the laid grass – the roots of the grass will soon take over and form a sideward growth to knit the turfs into a whole. Use a flat plank to firm down this soil and the edges of each turf section.

The main species of grasses from which you can choose are:

**Bent** (*Agrostis tenuis*) see Brown top
**Bermuda** (*Cynodon dactylon*) see Couch grass

**Brown Top** (*Agrostis tenuis*) is one of the very fine-bladed grasses grown from seed and used extensively in New Zealand, whence it originates, Australia, the United States and Europe, for fine lawns and putting and bowling greens. It is effective when used with Chewing's fescue (*Festuca rubra* 'commutata'). Experiment with one part (by mass) brown top to three parts fescue. The soil surface must be finely levelled after having been brought to a very fine state of tilth; spread the seed evenly at a rate of 40 g/m² and rake over lightly before watering in with a fine, light sprinkler – the soil surface should not be allowed to dry out. Late spring is probably the best time for sowing. One month after germination give a light dressing of 3:2:1 and water well in. Do not allow the shoots to reach a height of more than 70 mm before making the first cut, using a cylinder-type mower. If at all possible, all seeded lawns should be maintained with a cylinder mower, either hand- or power-driven. For patching, sow a separate area and keep this well mown and in good condition, lifting sods for repairs when necessary.

**Pencross hybrid bent.** This creeping bent makes an evenly-covered lawn of good colour but is best used in cooler districts as it can be attacked by fungus in humid conditions. It should not be used for oversowing or mixing with other grasses and should be sown more sparingly than ordinary bent.

**Buffalo** (*Stenotaphrum secundatum*) is a first-class lawn grass for selected areas, succeeding probably better than kikuyu in coastal, frost-free areas, and where the soil may incline towards sand. Its winter dormancy in colder parts of the country has disadvantages, such as encouraging weed invasion, and in these areas one should rather think in terms of kikuyu. Buffalo is a vigorous, creeping perennial with extensive runners, those growing below ground being less aggressively invading than kikuyu. The matt of broadish leaves may appear coarse but is actually softer then kikuyu.

**Carpet grass** (*Axonopus affinis* or *Paspalum*) A low-growing tightly matted grass more brightly coloured than buffalo but useful in similar conditions.

**Chewing's fescue** (*Festuca rubra* 'commutata') is another fine-bladed grass grown from seed. This is a specially selected variety of the creeping-rhizomed New Zealand fescue. It is well worth trying in a mixture with brown top. In very hot areas, even where the rainfall is fairly good, a mixture of two parts Chewing's fescue to one part Kentucky blue grass, is most likely to succeed. Sow at a rate of 40 g/m².

**Couch grass** (*Cynodon dactylon*) You may know it as Twich or Bermuda grass. Good for lawns in a sunny position in warm to temperate climates it can withstand a baking in

1. *Agrostis tenuis* (brown top)

2. *Stenotaphrum secundatum* (buffalo)

3. *Festuca rubra* 'commutata' (Chewing's fescue)

# PREPARING A LAWN

Unlike annual and perennial borders, the rose garden and other parts of the garden which receive periodic overhauls and deep cultivation, the lawn is more permanent, so that its maintenance must remain largely a surface activity. Thus the initial preparation of the soil in which grass is to be planted must be particularly thorough.

Any soil in which weeds will grow will also support grass, but just how satisfactorily depends, largely, on the soil's physical condition and how much nutriment is added. Often one sees large quantities of screened material, or even the existing soil removed from the site of the intended lawn on the grounds that it is too stony, too shaly, too sandy or too 'something' equally inconsequential. Rather save the transport costs and put the money into extra compost, manure or fertilizers. The only stones that must be removed are those lying on the surface when the job is finished. Stones in the soil keep the ground cool and assist in conserving the soil moisture; those which lie on the surface will damage your equipment.

I also advocate deep digging, in spite of all the highly theoretical opinions advanced in recent years in support of the virtues of shallow cultivation. The only time it is ever necessary to sieve the soil is when kikuyu is present and one of the finer grasses has to be planted. Today, even this is quite unnecessary – a single spraying of weedicide at the correct strength will effect a 100% kill without leaving any harmful residue in the soil. (See 'Chemical Weedkillers', page 349.)

## Planting

The planting of large lawned areas by mechanical means is reasonably satisfactory and certainly so much cheaper that the method cannot be disregarded. Nevertheless, hand planting is considerably more effective so that, whenever possible, this should be done.

Fine grasses are usually planted staggered 100 mm apart in rows 150 mm apart. For coarse grasses such as kikuyu, make a continuous trench 60 mm deep, and lie the runners in rows the full length of the trench. Set the trenches 150 mm to 200 mm apart. Cover the runners with soil, raking it to leave a smooth, level overall finish, and water in thoroughly. Fine grasses such as bent (*Agrostis tenuis*) and Chewing's fescue (*Festuca rubra* 'commutata') should be dibbed in, again leaving the surface smooth and level and watering well. If there is adequate water, plant at any time. In our temperate to subtropical regions planting may take place throughout the year. Where the water supply is restricted, plant immediately after the first seasonal rains and thereafter throughout the rainy season.

Should you decide to lay an 'instant', roll-on lawn, remember to leave a gap of 10 mm between the turfs to allow the roots at the edges to knit into a cohesive whole. Fill these gaps with some of the topsoil which you have set aside for top dressing, tamping it down firmly to the level of the turfs' soil. Press the turfs into place, beating them firmly with the back of a spade, or by placing a plank along the edge, tramping once or twice along its length and then moving it forward, repeating the process until the whole turfed area has been covered. If you have children, so much the better – let them do the tramping, making a game of it. If they are young, supervision will be necessary.

It is wise to retain some of the original topsoil to use as a top dressing when the new grass is fully established. Screen the soil through a 10 mm sieve and add a little 2 3:2 fertilizer just before application.

# MAINTAINING A HEALTHY LAWN

The best time to top dress a lawn is in the spring, as soon as the grass begins to show signs of growth. At this stage, the extra stimulant is most effective and the top dressing is quickly absorbed. Of course, top dressing may be carried out at any time in the growing season.

Immediately before top dressing, the surface should be thoroughly and vigorously teased with a leaf rake. Most people do this teasing rather gently for fear of damaging the sward, but the roots of a fine grass are quite deep (much deeper than kikuyu) and the nearer the resemblance of your lawn to a battle-field, the more effective will the completed operation have been. Rake off the surplus, disrupted vegetation (which is invaluable for the compost heap) and then spread the prepared top dressing evenly over the surface to a depth of 5 mm to 7.5 mm, or about one cubic metre to every 150 m² of surface. The following specification for a top dressing is ideal, though the exact proportions need not be followed too rigidly: 50% compost; 25% good topsoil; 15% coarse river sand; and 10% peat.

Saturate the ground the day before top dressing, then do not water again until the grass is well through, or a crust may form. Should rain occur or watering become necessary, gently break away the resultant crust by tapping in with the back of a rake. All the ingredients of a top dressing should be well mixed and then passed through a 10 mm sieve before application. Water thoroughly immediately after active growth starts and keep moist until the first cutting.

To maintain the lush green that every gardener hopes of his lawn, a regular programme of fertilizer is essential – strong-growing grass eventually will draw out the nourishment from even the richest of soils. Several commercial fertilizers designed specifically for lawns are available and these should be fed together with top dressing at the start of the growing season and again eight weeks later. Water in well, and, whatever fertilizer you choose, ensure that it has a high nitrogen content.

To rejuvenate an old kikuyu lawn, rake off down to 1 mm below actual soil level; remove rakings together with the loose topsoil, and compost as described on page 35. Loosen and aerate the surface soil, using a tined fork at frequent intervals (say every 150 mm). Press the fork into the soil about 150 mm deep, and bend slightly so that not only aeration holes are made but the compacted soil itself is partially shattered. Top dress and water heavily, preferably with a fine sprinkler to give an even distribution; within a few days the lawn should appear as new.

Very old lawns of a finer grass benefit from a similar treatment but, instead of raking off the surface completely, first tease it thoroughly.

Large areas of kikuyu may be dealt with mechanically, using a hammer-knife type mower, whilst fine grass may be aerated by means of a power-drawn implement resembling the old-fashioned mole plough, or can be spiked with a garden fork perforating the soil at 5 cm intervals.

Before applying top dressing to an established lawn, tease the surface vigorously with a rake – the result should resemble a battlefield.

*Helichrysum* sp.

*Hypericum calycinum*  South Eastern
GUTTIFERAE  Europe/Asia Minor
🍂 300 mm ☾
Commonly known as the rose of Sharon, this evergreen has almost leathery leaves with glaucous undersides, and grows vigorously throughout the country. Reaching a height of about 300 mm, it is particularly useful as a ground cover in dense or semi-shade conditions, and bears masses of buttercup yellow flowers in summer. Propagate by division, planting 500 mm apart; its stolons will quickly fill the intervening spaces. Usually, pruning is not necessary.

**Ice Plant:** see *Lampranthus roseus*

*Juniperus horizontalis* 'Procumbens'
CUPRESSACEAE  North America
🍂 80 mm ☼
Literally hugging the ground, this hardy evergreen conifer has few equals as a ground cover, especially when planted amongst upright-growing conifers of contrasting foliage colours. Its branches take root as it splays across the ground, seldom more than 80 mm high.

The same may be said of *J. horizontalis* 'Douglasii', the foliage of which is normally silvery-blue, but assumes a plum colour in autumn. Plant both varieties about 1.5 m apart. They also look particularly well trailing over a low stone wall.

*Kennedia prostrata*  Australia
FABACEAE
🍂 ☼
Running postman is a very fast growing mat forming plant with attractive scarlet pea-

*Hypericum* sp.

*Hedera helix* 'Glacier' (English Ivy)

flowers from winter to early summer. Propagate from seed.

**Knotweed:** see *Polygonum capitatum*
**Lamb's Ear:** see *Stachys byzantina*

*Lampranthus roseus*  South Africa
🍂 50 mm ☼ to ☾
Ice plants form a genus of small, spreading, evergreen succulents which bear glistening, daisy-like spring flowers. They flourish even under unfavourable conditions which few other plants would tolerate. *L. roseus*, which bears rich pink flowers, is probably the most handsome species for the garden, but *L. aureus* (yellow-flowered), *L. amoenus* (mauve) and *L. coccineus* (carmine) may also be used to great effect. Propagate from rooted stem parts and set out approximately 600 mm apart.

**Lily Turf:** see *Liriope muscari* 'Variegata' and *Ophiopogon japonicus*

*Liriope muscari* 'Variegata'  Japan, China
LILIACEAE
🍂 200 mm ☼
An evergreen, lily turf grows to a height of about 200 mm and, having richly-variegated, grass-like leaves, should be treated rather as a group of tufted specimens, set some 400-500 mm apart, than as a complete ground cover. The young foliage is yellow-striped and in summer the plant bears muscari-like blue flowers. 'Variegata' is relatively hardy, but also succeeds well right through to the subtropics. Propagate by division.

*Lysimachia nummularia*  Europe
PRIMULACEAE
🍂 250 mm ☼ to ☾
This glabrous, creeping perennial, which thrives in most parts of the country and in all but the sandiest of soils, is useful in full sun or semi-shade, and its long runners make it

ideal as a screen for unsightly metal manhole or drain covers. In spring it bears attractive solitary, bell-shaped yellow flowers but it is in the profusion of almost orbicular leaves, about 20 mm long that its value lies. Propagate by division in autumn and plant out about 200 mm apart. The leaves of the species are a rich, glossy green, while those of 'Aurea' have a rich gold sheen.

*Ophiopogon japonicus*  Japan
LILIACEAE
🍂 300 mm ☼ to ☾
A hardy, close relative of *Liriope muscari*,

*Lampranthus aureus* (Ice plant)

*Lysimachia nummularia* 'Aurea'

*Polygonum capitatum* (Knotweed)

*Osteospermum jucundum* (Trailing Mauve Daisy)

*Polygonum capitatum*                    Himalayas
POLYGONACEAE
⬤ 300 mm ☼
This vigorous perennial can easily become a nuisance if its trailing stems, which root readily, are not kept under control. Knotweed, so named for the peculiar swellings at the joints of its stems, is ideal to cover large embankments or smaller slopes. Its variegated foliage is strikingly marked in shades of red, brick and carmine, and throughout spring and summer small, globular pink flowers are borne in profusion. Propagate from stem cuttings.

*P. setaceus* 'Nanus'                    South Africa
LILIACEAE
⬤ 500 mm ◉
There are several garden cultivars of the asparagus fern whose light green and grey-green fronds, often with viciously-curved thorns, are popular in floral decorations. 'Nanus' is horizontally-branching and enjoys a moist, shady situation. Liberal cutting for home flower arrangements will encourage a low lush habit. Asparagus ferns are semi-hardy. Plant out root divisions or seedlings 800 mm apart in spring.

*Protasparagus densiflorus*            South Aftrica
  'Compactus'
⬤ 400 mm ◉
Even if left uncut, this smaller-growing subject seldom reaches a height of more than 400 mm. Small white-pink scented racemes of summer flowers are followed by attractive bright red berries.

*Selaginella kraussiana*               South Africa
SELAGINELLACEAE
⬤ 250 mm ◐
This bright green tufted species, which is also an ideal subject for hanging baskets or the fringe of a marsh garden, succeeds well in all but the coldest parts of Australia. It is thirsty and spreads rapidly, its jointed creeping root system ideal for areas of moist shade, though it is quite happy in a situation where it receives moderate sun. Propagate by division of the roots or runners, setting out about 250 mm apart. Several attractive dwarf cultivars, which grow to about 100 mm, are available.

*Setcreasea purpurea*                      Mexico
COMMELINACEAE
⬤ 250 mm ☼
Sometimes known as purple heart, this fleshy-stemmed and leafed subject, with its rich purple foliage, is a genuine ground cover which can be used as a colour contrast with tremendous effect. Full sun brings out the best colour and a large patch of this, fronted by the emerald green of a lawn and backed by splashes of gold or silver foliaged subjects, has a mighty visual impact. Growing not more than 250 mm high, it should be planted out 300 mm apart. Trim lightly when necessary.

**Snow-in-Summer:** see *Cerastium tomentosum*

with which it shares the common name of lily turf, this is a valuable ground cover in both full sun and semi-shade. Also known as Mondo grass, its foliage tufts up to 300 mm and creates a quite unusual effect. Propagate by division in spring, planting 350 mm apart.

*Osteospermum jucundum*               South Africa
ASTERACEAE
⬤ 200 mm ☼ to ◐
The trailing mauve daisy is a perennial and is everything that its name implies. The evergreen foliage is a shiny dark green, and a profusion of mauve to wine red flowers are borne in spring, making it one of the finest ground covers available. Propagate from rooted stem parts or seed in summer and set out 1 m apart.

*Stachys byzantina*                                   Caucasus
LAMIACAE
🌑 200 mm ☼
A hardy evergreen ground cover, lamb's ear reaches a height of 200 mm. Its woolly, silvery-white foliage shows up well in any sunny situation. Propagate from seed or by division in spring, planting 400 mm apart.

*Tradescantia albiflora*                    Central America
COMMELINACEAE
🌑 25-125 mm ☾
This is the true wandering Jew, not to be confused with the closely-related, but botanically distinct, *Zebrina pendula*. The latter, depending on the degree of exposure to sunlight, has a mixed striping of green, purple and silver, with deep purplish undersides, while the wandering Jew has small dark-green leaves. There is also a more robust variegated form with light-green leaves in which yellow and white markings occur. All three have many garden uses, particularly indoors, but in temperate to subtropical zones they make splendid ground covers in partial shade. As a ground cover all three should be associated with shrubs of contrasting colour; but ensure that the shrubs arise from a single stem — those with a multiple rootstock are inclined to be invaded. Propagate from cuttings and plant any time, 500 mm apart.

*Setcreasea purpurea* (Purple Heart)

*Viola hederacea*                                     Australia
VIOLACEAE
🌑 150 m ☾ ☻
The native violet is a very pretty quick-growing mat plant for damp spots. The blue and white flowers are produced throughout most of the year. It spreads rapidly and can be easily divided.

**Wandering Jew:** see *Tradescantia albiflora*

*Dichondra repens* (Kidney Weed)

# ANNUALS

## PROVIDING A YEAR-ROUND BLAZE OF COLOUR

Australia is a vast country, with climatic zones ranging from tropical to cool temperate. In all zones there is a marked decrease in rainfall from the coast to the very dry inland.

In spite of this, there are very few regions where gardeners need be without a seasonal flower show of annual plants.

Annuals are those plants which grow from seed to plant to flower and again to seed — all within the space of one year.

These plants provide a wealth of colour and perfume in their short life span and are used extensively in large parks and public gardens to create all the shades of an artist's palette from season to season.

Although most park plantings keep up the traditional designs of severely formal garden beds of geometrical shapes, in the home garden a more natural look is preferred. Groups of plants are used in casual places in the border, where they will have a background of greenery from shrubs, trees, or perennials. A red brick house is not an aesthetically pleasing background for them, and regimented rows are not pleasing either.

Because annuals have such a short life, applications of fertilizer and other nutrients must be speeded up. Once seedlings are in active growth, fertilizer should be given (strictly in accordance with the recommended amount on the container), once every three weeks.

Small plants should have terminal leaf buds nipped out to encourage bushiness. This 'tip' pruning should

Alyssum, marigolds and cockscomb

be continued until the flower buds appear. After this, removal of dead flower heads will encourage an extended flowering season.

Home units, houses and flats now have decks or patios for entertaining and swimming pools have decorative surrounds. This has created a demand for container planting of flowering annuals, so that smaller and more compact forms of many well known plants have been developed. Tubs, troughs and window boxes are delightful fittings to work with and can be moved and altered to please any of the designs and colour schemes of the gardener.

Whether in containers or in the border itself, the following annuals will light up the garden.

## A NOTE ON GERMINATION

How long should a seed take to germinate? The seeds of different genera and even of different species in the same genus often vary considerably in the time they take in the first steps to becoming seedlings. Under ideal conditions, a seed may germinate in two days, but under adverse conditions, the very same seed might take anything up to six days. Thus I have been forced to compromise: where the text says 'from two days' then start looking — but it may take six. For instance, ideally petunias may germinate in four days, while under less favourable conditions anything up to 15 days may be required.

*Dorotheanthus bellidiformis* (Livingstone Daisy)

**African Daisy:** see *Arctotis X hybrid*
**African Marigold:** see *Tagetes erecta*

*Ageratum houstonianum*                    Mexico
ASTERACEAE
🌂 200 mm ☼ 🌐
The floss flower is summer-flowering in cold areas, and summer- and winter-flowering in the temperate to warmer parts of the country. The greatest joy is to be had from the F.1 Hybrid ranges, where the plants are often as much as 250 mm across and are free flowering over a long, long period. Traditionally powder blue, there is also a pure white cultivar. 'Blue Mink' is a lovely dwarf form. Plant out 400 mm apart. Germination is from five days.

*Amaranthus caudatus*                    Tropics
AMARANTHACEAE
🌂 1 m ☼ 🌐
Popularly known as love-lies-bleeding, this tall-growing subject droops panicles of rusty red, tassel-like tails throughout summer. Of the cultivars available, one bears green flower tassels and another has very dark red tassels. *A. caudatus* is useful to give height in

*Ageratum houstonianum* (Floss Flower)

*Amaranthus tricolor* (Joseph's Coat)

the mixed annual border or help fill out the herbaceous border. Plant out 300 mm apart. Germination is from eight days.

*A. tricolor*                    Tropics
Joseph's coat, which is grown in the East as a vegetable, is the parent of a number of excellent foliage forms, principal among which are the cultivars 'Flying Colours' and 'Flaming Fountain' with their brilliant scarlet and multi-coloured foliage.

*Anemone coronaria*                    Europe/Asia
RANUNCULACEAE
🌂 75-230 mm ☼ 🌐
Most of the popular garden anemones, such as 'De Caen' and 'St Brigid', derive from this species and are invaluable, brightly-coloured flowering subjects for winter-spring bedding purposes. Their colour range is good – scarlets, reds, pinks, purple, blue and white – and they provide a gay splash over a satisfyingly long period from early spring. Sow seeds in November for winter flowering and in February for spring blooms. Many prefer to buy corms and these should be set out in autumn, 100-120 mm apart and 50 mm deep. Seed germinates from 15 days.

**Annual Lupin:** see *Lupinus hartwegii*

*Antirrhinum majus*                    Europe
SCROPHULARIACEAE
🌂 200-750 mm ☼ 🌐
Snapdragons have declined in popularity in recent years because of the severe rust fungus. However, as more resistant strains have been bred and more effective anti-rust sprays developed, gardeners should be encouraged to try again with these wonderful flowers. Some reliable strains are 'Tetra Mixed', which grows to 600 mm, with big ruffled blooms in gold, mauve, orange, red and white — splendid for cutting; 'Semi-Dwarf Mixed' grows to 400 mm and comes in rose and pink shades; 'Bright Butterflies' strain has more open faced flowers and a wide colour range, and 'Tom Thumb', only about 200 mm high, provides a dazzling display of colour for rockeries, troughs, pots and window boxes. Seed can be sown in succession throughout most of the year in temperate areas, with spring and early summer sowings in cool districts. Germination is from 10 to 14 days.

*Arctotis* hybrid                    Africa
ASTERACEAE
🌂 600-750 mm ☼ 🌐
The African daisy, sometimes known as the Veldt daisy, is a first-class annual for the rock or wild garden. Its daisy-like flowers are silvery-white with a mauve-blue centre narrowly ringed in gold. The undersides of the petals are shaded lavender and can be seen when the flowers close in the evening. Breeding from *A. acaulis* and *A. breviscapa*, a fine range of hybrids has been evolved, their large blooms varying from pale yellow to orange and red. All *Arctotis* species and their cultivars enjoy full sun and the seed should be sown in February-March, either in situ, or in trays for planting out in April, about 250 mm apart. Germination is from six days.

*Anemone coronaria*

**Asters:** see *Callistephus chinensis*
**Australian Everlasting:** see *Helipterum manglesii*
**Baby Blue-eyes:** see *Nemophila maculata*
**Baby's Breath:** see *Gypsophila elegans*
**Balsam:** see *Impatiens balsamina*

*Begonia semperflorens*                    Brazil
BEGONIACEAE
🌂 500 mm ◑ 🌐
The bedding or fibrous rooted begonia is ideal for shaded gardens, but in humid areas, wide spacing of plants is desirable, as a greyish fungus mars the leaves if there is not ample air circulation. In sunny spots, the plants do quite well too, but more water will be needed. Few plants start flowering as quickly as these do, and even the leaves are colourful, being crisply succulent in reds, bronze and pretty shades of light and dark green. Colours in the glossy heads of flowers range from white and cream, through all the shades of pink to bright red. Seed is very fine and needs to be mixed with sand for effective

*Antirrhinum majus* (Snapdragon)

*Gomphrena globosa* (Globe Amaranth)

deep red flowers margined in yellow. Germination is from five days. Sow seed in late spring.

**Globe Amaranth:** see *Gomphrena globosa*

*Gomphrena globosa*                    India
AMARANTHACEAE
300 mm
The globe amaranth is a popular, long-flowering annual for the summer garden or for winter-spring blooms in temperate to sub-tropical areas. It grows compactly in poorish soils and bears flowers in globular heads, which are usually a harsh purple, but also appear in shades of white, carmine and deep rose. The foliage is an attractive blotched bronze, and the round flower heads may be dried for winter floral arrangements. Plant out in spring about 200-250 mm apart. Germination is from seven days.

**Grass Pink:** see *Dianthus plumarius*

*Gypsophila elegans*                    Asia Minor
CARYOPHYLLACEAE
450 mm
This is the annual representative of a delightful genus and is popular for its fine feathery foliage and the mist-like flowers – from which its common name baby's breath derives – much used for floral decorations. It is also very useful for dotting in the semi-herbaceous border or mixed summer border, to tone down harsh outlines or severe colour graduations between one group and another. White, soft pink and deep-rose flowers are borne in summer. Sow seed in early spring and plant out about 300 mm apart. Germination is from seven days.

*Helianthus annuus* (Sunflower)

*Helichrysum* sp. (Everlasting)

*Helianthus annuus*                    United States
ASTERACEAE
400 mm – 1,5 m
The common sunflower is of increasing garden interest in that a number of long-flowering, highly ornamental new strains have been introduced and these come in a wide range of colours, both single and double. One new hybrid growing to about 1.5 m bears large flower heads in creamy-white, bronzy-red, maroon, orange and intermediate shades. 'Sungold' grows 1 m tall with fluffy deep gold flowers. Sow seed in early spring. Germination is from six days. Plant out about 350 mm apart.

*Helichrysum* spp.                    Australia
ASTERACEAE
1,5 m
All the everlasting daisies are magnificent flowers for the border and for cutting. The group contains perennial as well as annual forms. Some have handsome greyish leaves in addition to the papery flowers in all shades of autumn colours and mauve. A number of worthwhile cultivars have been developed and are often raised from seed. Perennial or shrubby forms are normally raised from cuttings. Straw flowers need a warm sunny situation and sharp drainage. Seed is available in mixed colours. Germination is from five days.

Edmondia pinifolia (Syn. *Helichrysum humile*)

(250 mm) and its colours range from white through cream, pink, lilac and purple. Wonderful for the mixed winter-spring border, planted close together in large groups. The taller-flowered white, and hyacinth-flowered white are derived mainly from *I. amara* 'Coronaria' and are sweet-scented, bearing spikes up to 150 mm long. Sow seed in February-March. Germination is from four days.

**Iceland Poppy:** see *Papaver nudicaule*

*Impatiens balsamina*    India, Malaya, China
BALSAMINACEAE
200-400 mm
This truly annual balsam is distinct from the new F.1 Hybrid *Impatiens* and comes in two forms – one, camellia-flowered, reaches a height of 400 mm; the other, single- and double-flowered is dwarfish and about half this height. Among them are amazing ranges of colours – white, pink, salmon, scarlet, vermilion and all intermediate shades. They are summer flowering in the cooler parts and bear winter-spring blooms in the temperate to subtropical regions. A very lightly shaded position will prolong flowering and reduce bleaching of the colours. Sow seed in spring in the cooler areas and in autumn for winter-spring flowers.

*I. holstii:* see *I. walleriana*

Impatiens balsamina hybrid

*Helipterum manglesii*    Australia
ASTERACEAE
450 mm
The paper daisy is very popular in cultivation and produces white or pink flowers, which change colour as they fade giving a multi colour effect. They are long lasting as cut flowers and can be used in dried arrangements. They are spring flowering and seed can be sown in autumn. Germination is from seven days.

*Iberis umbellata*    Mediterranean
CRUCIFERAE
250 mm
The common candytuft is compact, dwarf

Iberis umbellata (Candytuft)

Impatiens walleriana hybrid

*I. walleriana*          East Africa
(🌢) 150-500 mm (◐) (⊕)

The Busy Lizzy is a bushy subject available in many forms ranging from 150 mm to 600 mm. These represent valuable additions to the garden scene, especially in the temperate to subtropical zones and, in addition to their groupings in shaded portions of the garden, may also be used with great advantage for specimen pot work and for indoor decoration, in containers. In their favourite areas, flowering is almost continuous throughout the plant's life-time. Once a collection has been established from seed, it can be maintained and increased by cuttings of semi-firm growing shoots, taken throughout the growing season. Germination is from about 12 days.

**Indian Pinks:** see *Dianthus* X *allwoodii*
**Japanese Pinks:** see *Dianthus chinensis* 'Heddewigii'
**Joseph's Coat:** see *Amaranthus tricolor*

*Kochia scoparia* 'Trichophylla' Garden origin
CHENOPODIACEAE
(🌢) 600 mm (☼) (⊕)

This particular variety retains the emerald green of the fresh cypress-like foliage – from which its common name summer cypress derives – throughout the summer and autumn. The variety 'Childsii', identical in its conical, softly formal habit, assumes reddish-bronzy shades in autumn. The main garden use for these two rather unusual forms is as dot plants in formal bedding schemes, here and there near a courtyard or a paved surface, or as specimens in containers among balcony plants. Sow seed in early September. Germination is from about six days.

**Larkspur:** see *Delphinium ajacis*

*Lathyrus odoratus*         Italy
LEGUMINOSAE
(🌢) 2 m (☼) (⊕)

The sweet pea must surely take pride of place among all annual climbers for sheer beauty of blossom, for its colour range, and for its value, not only in the garden, but also as a cut flower. Being climbers, sweet peas are a little difficult to place in the garden, but there are many options. Those who primarily want cut flowers could do worse than grow them on a dividing fence in the vegetable garden. For the winter-spring border, pea-sticks can be placed with the apex tied together to form a large pyramid. Clusters grown this way can be very effective. Or they may be grown on a trellis against an east-facing wall, or on a wall facing a mixed winter-spring border. The dwarf 'Bijou' strains are virtually self-supporting and may be grouped in the mixed border. The seed may be sown in situ in autumn, although I prefer to drop a single seed into a 70 mm pot and plant out when about 100 mm high. This way I know exactly how many plants there are in a group. Germination is about seven days.

*Lathyrus odoratus* (Sweet Pea)

*Limonium bonduellei*         Algeria
PLUMBAGINACEAE
(🌢) 450 mm (☼) (⊕)

The annual statice, or sea lavender, is a useful subject for the summer border. This particular species bears flowers with a yellow calyx and deeper yellow corolla.

*L. sinuatum*         Mediterranean
(🌢) 600 mm (☼) (⊕)

This strong-growing plant is taller than the previous species and comes in white, blue, purple and rose. Both are ideal for massing in the mixed summer border and are splendid as cut flowers. Sow seed in early spring. Germination is about ten days.

*Linaria maroccana*         Morocco
SCROPHULARIACEAE
(🌢) 250-400 mm (☼) (⊕)

One of the finest of all winter-spring flowering annuals for set border schemes, toad flax, blooms continuously throughout its season. The flowers resemble miniature snap-dragons, profusely produced on erect stems, compactly to a height of 400 mm in the taller strains and to 250 mm in the dwarf varieties. Colours range from white, cream through all shades of rose, pink and red to violet and purple. Sow in autumn and plant out about 100 mm apart. Germination is from five days.

*Lobelia erinus*         South Africa
LOBELIACEAE
(🌢) 200 mm (☼) (⊕)

There are two distinct cultivars of this valu-

*Lathyrus odoratus* (Sweet Pea)

able garden annual; the most used, 'Compacta', is available in a number of strains, foremost of which is 'Crystal Palace'. This has dark, bronzy-green foliage, is very compact, and bears dark blue flowers. Another compact form has pale blue flowers and light foliage, while still another comprises a blend of crimson-red, white and light and dark blues. All are ideal for edgings or for mixing in the formal summer bed with varieties of *Begonia semperflorens*, overplanted with

*Limonium sinuatum*

*Lobelia erinus*

standard fuchsias. When grouping together, plant out about 150 mm apart. Sow seeds of all forms in autumn for winter-spring flowering in the warmly temperate to subtropical areas or in September for summer flowering. Germination is from about eight days.

**Love-in-the-mist:** see *Nigella damascena*
**Love-lies-bleeding:** see *Amaranthus caudatus*

*Lupinus* spp.                           North America
LEGUMINOSAE
🌑 250-1000 mm ☼ 🌣
The annual lupins, particularly the 'Pixie' cultivars, are real gems for groups in the rock garden or for massed effect in the mixed winter-spring border. The taller strains are also ideal for the border. Sow seed in autumn either in situ, or individually in 70 mm pots. Colours of both forms range from shades of blue, yellow, rose and white. Germination is from about seven days.

*Malcolmia maritima*                    Mediterranean
CRUCIFERAE
🌑 150-200 mm ☼ 🌣
An old favourite for the early summer border, Virginian stock should be used in massed groups, sown in situ in spring. Quick growing, they flower in shades of pink, red, crimson, yellow and white. Germination is from six days.

*Matthiola incana*                      Mediterranean
CRUCIFERAE
🌑 300-700 mm ☼ 🌣
This is the species from which so many distinct strains of garden stocks have been derived. Outstanding amongst these are the giant column stocks (up to 700 mm) magnificent for cutting with their huge, single spikes. These are available in separate colours and are really good subjects for grouping in the mixed winter-spring border, or in a long,

narrow border backing onto a stone wall. The 'Giant Imperials' (up to 500 mm), as they are often called, are also available in separate colours and may be used similarly or for formal beds. In the shorter group (300 mm), the seven- and ten-week strains are ideal for bedding or for bays in the rock garden, and there is also a most colourful strain of single-flowered stocks. All are grown from seed sown in January, February and March for winter-spring flowering. Germination is from about eight days.

**Mignonette:** see *Reseda odorata*

*Mimulus luteus*                        North America
SCROPHULARIACEAE
🌑 350 mm ◐ 🌣
This species is a good subject for a somewhat damp, semi-shaded position where, in spring and summer, it will bear scented yellow flowers, blotched with rusty-crimson. The monkey flower has been crossed with *M. cardinalis* and its own cultivar 'Guttatus', amongst others, to produce a large-flowered race of hybrids. These hybrids are brightly coloured and blotched with contrasting shades. Both these and the following species are grown from seed in autumn. Germination is from about ten days. Plant out seedlings 250 mm apart.

*Myosotis alpestris*                    Europe
BORAGINACEAE
🌑 75-400 mm ◐ 🌣
This semi-perennial forget-me-not is self-

*Lupinus* sp

seeding under our conditions. The most popular and traditional blue forms are to be found in varieties of the species although others, derived from *M. scorpioides*, are also cultivated. These are useful subjects for ground work in formal spring bedding schemes, or for drifts in the winter-spring mixed border. Sow seed in February, March or April, and plant out 200 mm apart. Germ-

*Mimulus luteus*

ination is from about 12 days.

**Monkey Flower:** see *Mimulus luteus*

**Nasturtium:** see *Tropaeolum majus*

*Nemesia strumosa*                    South Africa
SCROPHULARIACEAE
🌢 200-300 mm ☼ 🐝
One cannot imagine a winter-spring border
without groups and drifts of this delightful
annual. The Cape Jewel is the parent of all the
modern and wonderful winter-spring flowering strains available today. 'Carnival Mixture'
is a compact cultivar, very free flowering in a
range including shades of blue, cream,
apricot, white, orange, flame and scarlet, all
blotched and mottled with other colours.
'Blue Gem' is clear sky blue and grows to only
200 mm. Sow seed in late autumn and plant
out 150-200 mm apart. Germination is about
six days.

*Nemophila maculata*                    United States
HYDROPHYLLACEAE
🌢 350 mm ☼ 🐝
This lovely little annual bears white summer
flowers blotched with purple, but despite this,
it is less widely grown than *N. menziesii*. This
has a similar habit, is also indigenous to the
United States and is commonly known as
baby blue-eyes, its sky-blue flowers having
white centres. The many cultivars include
white and blue edged with white, black-eyes
margined with white, and other combinations.
Sow both species in situ in spring. Germination is about seven days.

*Myosotis alpestris* (Forget-me-not)

*Matthiola incana*

*Nemesia strumosa* ('Cape Jewel') hybrids

# 74 ANNUALS

*Nigella damascena* — Spain, North Africa
RUNUNCULACEAE
500 mm

Love-in-the-mist had been all but forgotten in Australian gardens until recently. With fern-like foliage, the dainty and delicate flowers come in shades of blue, but white and pink shades are available. The strain 'Crown Jewels' is impressive and valued as a cut flower. The round seed pods are attractive for dried arrangements. Germination is from seven to ten days.

**Painted Tongue:** see *Salpiglossis sinuata*
**Pansy:** see *Viola tricolor*

*Papaver nudicaule* — Arctic Regions
PAPAVERACEAE
350 mm

Today there are many superb strains of the ever popular Iceland poppy which, in temperate to warm areas, flowers throughout winter and well into spring. It starts blooming in late winter and continues until the ground is wanted for other subjects in October – particularly if cut frequently for the house and no seed heads are allowed to form. 'Spring-song' is quite outstanding, free flowering, and bears flowers 100 mm and more across in a splendid range of colours. The 'Artists' Glory' and 'Sunglow' are also fabulous strains to grow and enjoy. Sow in January and February for winter-spring flowering. Germination is from seven days.

*P. rhoeas* — Europe

This is the species from which the corn, or shirley, poppies have been developed. Though they do not flower for as long as the Iceland poppy and are less popular, they are certainly worthy of a good place in every spring and early summer border. New strains offer a splendid range of pinks, reds and blushed white shades, both single and double. Plant out 250 mm apart or, better still, sow in situ in early spring.

*Petunia* X *hybrida* — Garden hybrid
SOLANACEAE
150 mm

What can one say of the petunia to describe adequately its unique role in our winter (temperate to subtropical) and summer garden schemes? There is no plant quite so easy to cultivate, more colourful, more consistent in its long flowering performance, and more adaptable to any garden pattern. It is equally indispensable for the window box or wall trough, and it is superb for pot and container work. In spite of the advent of the spectacular F.1 Hybrids, the old single bedding petunias still take a power of beating in the overall garden scene. In the F.1 Hybrid range there are the Multifloras, single and double, and the Grandifloras, also single and double, all in named colours or mixed selections and including the popular 'Elegant Cascade'. In the cooler areas, sow seed in a frame during autumn and spring and in the temperate to subtropical regions almost any time for year-round flowering. When sowing, do not cover the extremely fine seed. Germination is from four days.

*Phlox drummondii* — United States
POLEMONIACEAE
250-350 mm

Among the most colourful, long-flowering

*Primula malacoides*

*Papaver nudicaule* (Iceland Poppy)

*Papaver nudicaule*

*Papaver somniferum*

*Phlox drummondii* hybrids

annuals grown, this species should figure prominently in every garden. Both tall and dwarf strains of annual phlox are available in separate colours, a great advantage when planning set colour schemes. The taller forms (350 mm) are best in large groups in the mixed border, while the more compact (250 mm) come into their own in formal beds.

They are usually grown for the summer garden but in the temperate to subtropical areas also make a fine winter-spring showing. The cultivar 'Twinkle Star' is a welcome addition to this already glamorous family. Set the dwarfs out 150 mm apart and the taller strains 200 mm apart. Sow seeds according to your climatic area. Germination is usually from about seven days.

**Plumed Cockscomb:** see *Celosia argentea*
**Poor Man's Orchid:** see *Schizanthus pinnatus*

*Portulaca grandiflora*          Brazil
PORTULACACEAE
⚘ 350 mm ☼ ☻
As well as the traditional cultivars of rose moss, which are still very good in both singles and doubles, there are now new F.1 and F.2 Hybrids which are exceptionally uniform and free flowering in all brilliant colours except blue. Normally summer bloomers, they will also flower throughout winter and spring in the warmly temperate to subtropical areas. Seed may be sown in situ, but the new strains should be sown in trays and transplanted, as F.1 and F.2 Hybrid seed is too expensive to risk wasting and this subject transplants very easily. Plant out 100 mm apart. Germination is from five days.

*Primula malacoides*          China
PRIMULACEAE
⚘ 100-460 mm ❋ ☻
The most important garden primula flowers profusely throughout winter in favoured areas and in spring elsewhere in Australia. Any good cultivar of the original lavender species will still hold its own with the newer, more richly-coloured forms in purples, crimson, reds, white and shades of rose. A lightly-shaded position, particularly in the case of the new strains, will prolong the flowering period and prevent bleaching of the more

*Phlox drummondii* hybrid

*Petunia* X *hybrida* (F1 hybrid)

*Phlox drummondii* 'Twinkle Star'

*Portulaca grandiflora* (Rose Moss)
*Salpiglossis sinuata* (Painted Tongue, or Trumpet Flower)

sun-sensitive shades. Plant out 150 mm apart. Sow seed in trays in a shaded frame but do not cover. Germination is from about ten days.

*Ranunculus asiaticus*                    Asia Minor
RANUNCULACEAE
🌰 460 mm ☼ 🌐
Most people prefer to plant developed corms and, for the average gardener, this is probably the best option. For a massed effect plant out about 100 mm apart. Though late winter flowering in most parts of the country, in very cold areas they certainly brighten up the spring border. Ranunculas come in an amazing range of singles and doubles, self or variegated, in orange, yellow, cream, scarlet, red, white and all intermediate shades. Sow seed during early autumn in trays protected by a garden frame. Germination is variable, usually from 12 days.

*Reseda odorata*                          North Africa
RESEDACEAE
🌰 300 mm ☼ 🌐
An old favourite, the mignonette is much

salmon and white. Given constant warmth, moisture and humidity they are seldom out of flower and in such brief periods their heart-shaped leaves are a delight in themselves. In some cases this and the following species of *Anthurium* are grown solely for their ornamental foliage. See also Chapter 19, 'Bush House and Greenhouse Management', page 317.

*A. scherzerianum*                    Costa Rica
🌱 300 mm ⬤ 🌿
Smaller in habit than *A. andraeanum*, this species also bears scarlet, arum-like spathes. A native of Costa Rica, it is identical in requirements – and in the colour range of its varieties and cultivars – to *A. andraeanum*. However, its slender, lanceolate leaves are less attractive. This species will tolerate slightly lower temperatures than will the flamingo plant. The variety 'foliatum' has a sessile green leaf below the spathe.

Both species enjoy a soil medium-rich in leaf mould, and compost with plenty of fibrous material. Propagation is from seed sown in spring, or by division at any time the plant is not in flower.

*Aquilegia caerulea*            Northern Mexico
RANUNCULACEAE
🌱 200-750 mm ◐ 🌿
Columbines are a most unusual flower, in which much improved strains are now available. Although best suited to cooler climates, they grow well in temperate and coastal climates, where they will self-seed readily. A sunny position suits them but they will flourish in the filtered light of trees. The spurred flowers, held erect on stout stems, come in all shades of yellow, rose and blue, with many combinations of these as bi-colours. Seed can be sown in autumn, or in spring in cool regions. Germination is from about ten days.

**Arum Lily:** see *Zantedeschia aethiopica*

*Aster novi-belgii*          Eastern United States
ASTERACEAE
🌱 450 mm-1 m ◐ 🌿
This is one of the three species – all from North America – from which today's garden hybrid Michaelmas daisies are derived, the other two being the equally tall *A. novae-angliae* and the smaller (450 mm) *A. amellus*, some of whose varieties reach a mere 200 mm. Throughout winter, spring and early summer, the taller hybrids produce huge, branched heads of single or double blossom, in white and all shades of blue, violet, purple, rose and near red. The individual flowers are daisy-like – some as much as 50 mm across, in the large heads – others miniature. Michaelmas daisies are ideally suited to bold grouping in the border, either mixed or in separate colours, and the intermediate and dwarf varieties are equally impressive. In very warm areas, place them so that there is some shade from the afternoon sun. Propagate by division of the rootstock in late autumn, or immediately after flowering. Do not allow the clumps to grow for more than two flowering seasons before taking them up, dividing them and replanting in enriched soil.

*Amaryllis belladonna* (March, or Belladonna Lily)

*Anthurium andraeanum* (Flamingo Plant)
*Anthurium andraeanum* ▶
*Anthurium scherzerianum*

*Astilbe japonica*                    Japan
SAXIFRAGACEAE
🌱 500 mm ◐ 🌿
Though the very beautiful goat's beard is not generally suited to the Australian garden, our summers being rather too hot for it, it is well worth experimenting with if you have the right

conditions. These, unfortunately, are somewhat exacting: a permanent, cool, semi-shaded dell with cool, moist soil. Though this sounds simple, such places are few and far between. In late spring and early summer it sends up feathery, fluffy panicles of cream, soft rose and red flowers. Propagate by divi-

*Aster novi-belgii* (Michaelmas Daisy)

sion in autumn and plant out 450 mm apart.

*Aubrieta deltoidea*                    Italy, Persia
CRUCIFERAE
🌱 150 mm ☼ ❄

Another reluctant foreigner, purple rock cress succeeds reasonably well in the cooler areas, but seldom equals the brilliance of its spring display in Europe. It grows in a low, semi-trailing clump which in spring and early summer is almost hidden by the masses of small flowers in white, shades of purple, crimson, red and pink. Propagate from cuttings taken after flowering, or sow seed in autumn. Plant out 100 mm apart, in the rock garden or the front of the border. Cut back severely in late summer to prevent straggly growth, though you may find it more suitable to treat this species as an annual.

*Aurinia saxatilis*                         Europe
CRUCIFERAE
🌱 300 mm ☼ ❄

A very useful subject for the rock garden, golden tuft is a semi-woody perennial with a twisted, semi-prostrate habit. Golden-yellow flowers in the type and lemon and sulphur yellow, single and double, in the many cultivars, are borne in spring. Propagate from seed sown in February, or by division in autumn or spring, planting 300 mm apart.

*Babiana stricta*                      South Africa
IRIDACEAE
🌱 250 mm ☼ ❄

One likens the several species of Baboon flower to the crocuses of Europe and more charmingly beautiful flowers would be difficult to find, massed in a bay to themselves in the spring rock garden. *B. stricta* and its variety 'Villosa' are particularly pleasing, their scented flowers ranging in colour from purple, purplish-red and crimson to a sulphur yellow. Others well worth growing include *B. disticha*, *B. patersoniae* and *B. pulchra*.

**Bear's Breeches:** see *Acanthus mollis*
**Belladonna Lily:** see *Amaryllis belladonna*
**Bell Flower:** see *Campanula carpatica*
**Bird of Paradise Flower:** see *Strelitzia reginae*
**Blue Marguerite:** see *Felicia amelloides*
**Blue Squill:** see *Scilla natalensis*
**Bride's Bouquet:** see *Dimorphotheca cuneata*
**Brown Day Lily:** see *Hemerocallis fulva*
**Bush Lily:** see *Clivia miniata*

*Campanula carpatica*                   Carpathians
CAMPANULACEAE
🌱 450 mm ☼ ❄

A glabrous-leaved, spreading perennial, the bell flower provides an attractive clump for the border or rock garden. From spring, and continuing throughout summer, solitary bell-shaped flowers of an intense blue are borne on a profusion of long, erect stalks. There are many cultivars and hybrids of this species, ranging from shades of blue and violet to white.

*C. persicifolia*, found widespread throughout Europe and Asia, is also glabrous-leaved, but has a more spreading habit. In spring and summer, its creeping rootstock sends up taller flower stems (600 mm) on which the typical bell-shaped blooms are borne in shades of blue and white.

*C. poscharskyana*, a native of Dalmatia, is of similar habit and growth and a species well worthy of attention. Its shorter (300-400 mm) stems bear pale blue flowers.

*C. pyramidalis*, the vigorous, chimney bell flower from Europe, has stems up to a metre high, bearing striking, multi-flowered panicles of pale blue blooms with purplish bases.

All these species may be grown from seed sown in November or, as is more usual, propagated by division either in autumn or early spring. Plant out 300-600 mm apart, depending on the habit of the species.

*Babiana disticha* (Baboon Flower)

*Canna* hybrids                        Garden origin
CANNACEAE
🌱 2 m ☼ ❄

Few realize that at one time the canna was grown almost entirely for its foliage effect, the flowers, borne at the apex of stems up to 2 m high, being more or less insignificant. *C. warscewiezii*, *C. edulis* and their progeny were mainly responsible for the introduction of the bronzy and purplish foliage of many modern cultivars. Where this attraction is prominent – particularly in the rich scarlet and bronzy-orange colours – these make good subjects for the tropical bed and for foliage colour contrast in the canna border.

Few perennial subjects are more valued than cannas – always providing that they are properly cared for. But because they are so easily grown and are so accommodating, cannas are often neglected. The moment the plants become overcrowded, the soil cannot support them and deterioration sets in, with both flower and stem growing progressively smaller. To maintain a vigorous plant, capable of continuously producing strong stems bearing large blooms, there are two essentials. First, once a stem has finished flowering it must be removed at ground level; second, the clump must be lifted after every second year's flowering, the rhizomes broken up and replanted after the bed has been thoroughly dug over and heavily manured and fertilized. Plant the divided rhizomes 400 mm apart and, after the first year's flowering, cut back all stems to ground level and give the soil a heavy top-dressing of well-prepared compost. As soon as growth resumes give a dressing of balanced fertilizer. In warmly temperate to subtropical areas, cannas will flower throughout the year – all the more reason why the plants should be rejuvenated biennially.

Cannas may be grouped in separate colours in the border or along the border of a driveway. Dwarf cultivars grow to some 600 mm, taller ones to some 1.5 m. Flowers may be fringed, mottled, striped or self, in pale cream, lemon, white, gold, apricot, pinks, reds and scarlet. A superb new cultivar with golden, striped foliage is outstanding for contrast colour effect in the border or in bedding schemes.

*Canna* hybrid

*Canna* hybrid

*Canna* hybrid

*Campanula glomerata*

*Campanula persicifolia*

# DAHLIAS: PRIDE OF MANY SHOWS

So wide is the range of cultivars and forms of today's garden dahlia that many gardeners find it hard to believe that these members of the ASTERACEAE family stem from two Mexican species introduced to Europe via Madrid's Botanic Gardens in 1789. Most of the singles, pompons and show types derive from *Dahlia rosea*, while the cactus forms have their origins in *D. juarezii*.

The descendants of these two species make up the 11 main divisions of dahlia for gardens and showing designated by the National Dahlia Society of Great Britain and the Royal Horticultural Society. In addition, *D. imperialis*, the tree dahlia, is widely grown in larger gardens. This grows as tall as 3.5 m and is magnificent in a semi-woodland setting, particularly in areas where early frost does not catch the late autumn flowers. The blooms, which vary in colour but are usually rose-lilac, are borne abundantly from mid-summer through to late autumn or early winter. Like most others of the genus, the tree dahlia can be grown from seed but is best propagated from divisions of the tubers.

The 11 categories (and their subdivisions) into which our garden dahlias have been placed are:
**Single-flowered** which comprise:
Show Singles, whose flower heads must not be more than 80 mm across, have only eight rays (or petals) with slightly recurved tips, and which are broad, smooth and overlap to form a perfect round;
Singles, whose rays do not overlap as much and have separated tips; and
Mignon Dahlias, whose flower heads are similar to those of the Singles but are dwarf of habit (not more than 450 mm tall).

**Anemone-flowered,** which have one or more series of flat ray-florets surrounding a dense group of tubular florets that are longer than the disc florets of the Singles and usually differing in colour from their rays.

**Collarette Dahlias** have one or more series of flat rays similar to those of the Singles, but above each series is a ring of florets (the collarette) only half the length of the rays and usually of a different colour. There are three groups:
Collarette Singles, with a single series of rays and a collarette with a yellow disc;
Collarette Paeony-flowered, which have heads with two or three series of rays and collars, also with a yellow disc; and
Collarette Decorative, a fully double version of the Paeony-flowered type.

**Paeony-flowered** have heads of two or three series of ray-florets and a central disc, and are divided by size into four types: Large, with flowers more than 180 mm wide; Medium, with flower heads 130-180 mm in diameter; Small, with heads less than 130 mm across, and Dwarf, which comprise plants not more than 750 mm high.

**Formal-decorative** are divided into four sub-classes similar to those of the Paeony-flowered, except that the flower heads are fully double and show no disc. All the florets are regularly arranged with their edges curving slightly inwards but flattening towards the rounded or broadly-pointed tips.

**Informal-decorative** differ from the former only in that the florets are not regularly arranged, and more or less flat or slightly twisted, and have acutely pointed tips. This class is also divided, according to size, into four sub-classes similar to those of the Paeony-flowered and Formal-decorative dahlias.

**Show** bear almost globular, fully-double flower heads which are more than 80 mm wide. The central and outer florets are alike, but the smaller florets are tubular or cup-shaped with incurved margins giving them a short, blunt mouth. A sub-class, Fancy Dahlias, have white-tipped or striped florets.

**Pompons** are similar to Show dahlias, but have smaller flower heads which, for show purposes, must not be more than 50 mm across.

**Cactus** have fully-double flower heads; the margins must twist for at least three-quarters of their length and the central floret forms a filbert-shaped group. These, too, are sub-classed according to size: Large-flowered, with heads more than 110 mm; Small-flowered, with heads less than this; and Dwarf, whose plants are not more than 750 mm high.

**Semi-cactus** have the same divisions according to size, and are similar to the Cactus dahlias save that their florets are broader at the base and the margins twist slightly for only about half their length.

**Star** have small, cup-shaped flower heads formed by two or three series of pointed rays which hardly overlap, surrounding a central disc.

Among gardeners, the most popular are certainly all classes of Singles, the Cactus and Semi-cactus, the Pompon, the Paeony-flowered, the Collarettes and the

Decoratives.

The Singles are particularly valuable massed in the mixed summer border, whilst the Mignons are excellent for formal beds. Purple-leafed, scarlet-flowered cultivars make useful dot plants in the tropical bed. Ordinary Singles and the 'Coltness Gem' strain may be produced from seed, with especially good forms being reproduced from these plants in following years. The taller-growing Singles provide fine cut flowers and are more widely grown and generally more adaptable than any other class. The Dwarfs can be set out 300 mm apart and the taller strains at about 500 mm intervals.

Those metre-high Cactus and Semi-cactus varieties noted for their long stems and firmly upheld heads, are also excellent for cutting. And though some of the most colourful forms do not make good cut flowers, they merit a place in every summer or semi-herbaceous border. They should be planted out 450-500 mm apart, depending on their vigour and habit – our concern here is for massed effect, not plants whose blooms are to be exhibited.

Dwarf Pompons reach a height of 450 mm and the taller strains grow from 600 mm to a metre high, all being eminently suited for border planting and providing good cut flowers.

Both Paeony-flowered and Collarettes are popular. But, beyond the ordinary cultivars, among the Decorative classes and the 'specials', the emphasis is on exhibition and specialisation rather than garden use. However, the Decoratives do have a place in the large semi-herbaceous border and can contribute a striking splash of colour. But the border must be big enough for them not to dominate it – otherwise their presence is as incongruous as a set of traffic lights in the middle of a paddock. They should be planted at least a metre apart and like all tall-growing dahlias, whose stems are brittle, should be carefully staked throughout their growth.

All dahlias are gross feeders and require deep, well-prepared soil, enriched with compost, as well as ample water throughout their growth. Instead of incorporating the richest manure in the soil at the time of planting, as this may induce rank early growth, give the plants a heavy mulching of well-rotted but rich manure just as the buds form. Well-watered, this will provide all the necessary nutriment.

**Storage and Propagation**
There is nothing really complicated about the winter treatment of dahlia tubers and their subsequent propagation. Tubers should be lifted as soon as the foliage dies down or is cut back by early frost – where this occurs. Cut off the old stems a few centimetres from the tuber and store in perfectly dry sandy soil, covering the tuber entirely and leaving only the stems show-

**DAHLIA TYPES:** Clockwise page 88,
Semi-cactus
Paeony-flowered
Collarette
This page clockwise,
Cactus
Cactus
Star

ing. (For reference when replanting, tie identification labels to these stems.) In dry, frost-free areas the tubers may be stored outdoors, but in winter-rainfall regions they must be kept under cover, and nowhere should they be allowed to become moist or be touched by frost. Examine them occasionally and remove any showing signs of disease.

Probably the finest plants are produced from cuttings, and here some propagation facilities are needed.

When the shoot has developed two joints it should be removed as a cutting, planted in a small pot (filled with a sandy medium and with extra sand at the base of the cutting) and placed in a closed frame. As soon as the plants show signs of rooting, these pots should be transferred to an open case. Label each pot so that even if they become mixed, you will make

no mistake as to the cultivar or type when planting out.

Much the same results – though they will take longer – can be achieved using a garden frame. Treat the tubers as described above, ensuring that they are shaded from strong sunlight. The cuttings you obtain will be of firmer wood and may be inserted in lines in pure sand overlying a mixture of equal parts of loam, peat and sand. Depending on the weather, both cuttings and tubers should be syringed from once to three times daily, though not on dull, overcast days. As soon as the cuttings are rooted, plant them out into separate pots.

Propagation from cuttings is, of course, the best way to increase stock, as each crown will produce an extraordinary number of shoots. If you wish only to set out tubers, ensure that a piece of old stem bearing a bud is taken with each tuber. Plant the tuber some 150 mm deep.

*Catharanthus roseus* and *C. roseus* 'Albus'

*Chrysanthemum* X *morifolium*

**Cape Gooseberry:** see *Physalis peruviana*
**Carnation:** see Special Spread, page 115
**Cardinal Flower:** see *Lobelia cardinalis*
**Carpet Geranium:** see *Geranium incanum*

*Catharanthus roseus*          Madagascar, India
APOCYNACEAE
🐚 310-620 mm ☼ or ◑ 🐦
There is nothing to surpass the periwinkle for planting in an odd shady corner where, with its dark, glossy-green leaves and sprawling habit, it is most at home. The summer and autumn flowers of the species are a rosy-purple. Recently-developed dwarf cultivars are available from seedsmen. It is also ideal as a ground cover under trees. Propagate from seed or cuttings in spring and plant out 250 mm apart.

**Cat Mint:** see *Nepeta* X *faassenii*
**Chimney Bell Flower:** see *Campanula pyramidalis*
**Chincherinchee:** see *Ornithogalum thyrsoides*

*Chrysanthemum coccineum*          Persia
ASTERACEAE
🐚 350 mm ☼ 🐦
This species is one of the best true perennials. Providing excellent cut flowers, it should be planted in bold groups where its profusion of long-stemmed, daisy-like summer blooms, 80 mm across, which spring from clumps of foliage 200 mm high, are seen to best effect. Several named cultivars are available, with petal colours ranging from white to deep scarlet, all centred on a yellow disc. Propagate by division in autumn, or early spring in the colder regions, planting out about 300 mm apart. It may also be grown from seed sown in spring.

*C. maximum*          Pyrenees
🐚 400-500 mm ☼ 🐦
The shasta, or moon daisy, is another excellent source of cut flowers as well as being an asset to the border. Forming dense clumps from a low-growing rootstock, it bears white, daisy-like summer flowers on long stems. The large flowers (70-100 mm across) may be double or single, ruffled or frilled. Named varieties do not come true from seed and should be propagated by division in early spring and planted out 700 mm apart.

*Chrysanthemum* X *morifolium*

*C. parthenium* 'Aureum'          Europe
🐚 930 mm ☼ 🐦
The golden feather has insignificant flowers but is frequently used for edging, as a carpet bed, or as a splendid dot plant among plantings of dwarf red salvia. Unless kept trimmed throughout summer, this native of Europe may lose its clear, golden-yellow foliage, which will revert to green. Pluck the flower heads as soon as they form. Sow seed from November to February for use the following spring-summer, and plant out 200 mm apart.

**Cinquefoil:** see *Potentilla nepalensis*

*Clivia miniata*          South Africa
AMARYLLIDACEAE
🐚 400 mm ☼ 🐦
Well-known and strictly protected in South Africa the bush lily or fire lily enjoys semi-shade, adequate moisture when growing, and a cool root-run with lots of leaf mould, all in a well-drained situation. The trumpet-shaped flowers, borne in late spring and early summer, are orange-red in the type. Twelve to 20 flowers form an umbel on a stem some 400 mm high. There are two other species of *Clivia* and, somewhere along the line, horti-culturists have produced hybrids in a variety of colours, from pale lemon through deep yellows and reddish-orange to salmon and flame. All are very beautiful, either in the shaded garden or in pots for balcony decoration. Propagate by careful division of the bulbous stock at the end of winter, or from ripe seed, that is, while the seeds are still red and fleshy.

**Coral Bells:** see *Heuchera sanguinea*
**Crane Flower:** see *Strelitzia reginae*

*Cyrtanthus contractus*          South Africa
AMARYLLIDACEAE
🐚 400 mm ☼ 🐦
The fire lily, so named because it frequently appears in the veld after bush fires, is one of several species of the *Cyrtanthus* genus which must surely become popular garden plants. All bear loose umbels of pendulous, tubular flowers. Those of *C. contractus* are 500 mm long, brilliant scarlet, and borne in spring. Propagate by division of the bulbous clumps in autumn – but only when these become overcrowded – or from seed sown in spring. Bear in mind that plants grown from seed will not flower until three to five years after planting.

*C. macowanii*          South Africa
🐚 250 mm ☼ 🐦
The ifafa lily has a shorter flower stem than

the previous species and bears spring umbels ranging from white through cream to yellow, apricot and on to deep red. Propagate as for *C. contractus*.

*Cyrtanthus* species are ideally suited to planting in rock garden bays where they can be grown undisturbed until overcrowding makes division necessary.

**Daffodil:** see *Narcissus* spp.
**Dahlia:** see Special Spread, pages 88 and 89

*Delphinium* X *belladonna*                    Europe
RANUNCULACEAE
🌑 450 mm ☼ ⊕
Most of these hybrids are lower growing than the original wild species – up to 900 mm. Apart from the dazzling display of pure colours on stout stems, these hybrids have a prolonged flowering as they make new side stems throughout the growing season. Reds, bright blue and shades of these are available. Germination of seed is from 14-21 days.

*D. elatum*                                      Europe, Asia
🌑 2 m ☼ ⊕
The 'Pacific' strain is the dominant form available these days. These are very tall – up to 1.8 m and in most cases need some sort of support. The strong stems are covered in flowers of a satiny texture, in every shade except yellow – some with a paler or darker central marking in each flower. The plants are long lasting, tolerating frost after the first season. Germination of seed may take up to 28 days.

*Dianthus* X *allwoodii*                         China, Japan
CARYOPHYLLACEAE
🌑 150-500 mm ☼ ⊕
There is now a bewildering array of delightful hybrids from the original small flowering pinks, all adaptable to a wide variety of soils

and preferring very well drained conditions. Masses of erect stemmed flowers in mauves, pink, reds and white are borne above the fine foliage. Most make ideal subjects for the rock pocket or the pebble garden, growing to 200 mm high. 'Baby Doll' and 'Mini Glow', very compact with prettily marked flowers are only two of the dozens available. An established clump can be increased by short cuttings. Germination of seed may take up to 14 days.

*D. caryophyllus:* see Special Spread, page 115

*Dierama pendulum*                             South Africa
IRIDACEAE
🌑 600 mm ☼ ⊕
This lovely species forms a mass of grass-like, erect foliage 600 mm high. From this clump, long, arching flower stems arise in early summer, bearing panicles of pale pink or mauve-rose flowers which hang like pendant bells. *D. pulcherrimum* is similar but stronger in every way, and the flowers are much larger and purplish-red. Propagate by division in autumn and plant out 400 mm apart.

*Dimorphotheca cuneata*                        South Africa
ASTERACEAE
🌑 300-450 mm ☼ ⊕
A semi-woody perennial, bride's bouquet is a useful subject for the rock garden. Spring-blooming, it bears daisy-like white flowers with gold in the reverse. Sow seed in February or March and plant out 250 mm apart.

*D. ecklonis:* see *Osteospermum ecklonis*
*Diplacus glutinosus:* see *Mimulus glutinosus*

*Echium candicans*                             Canary Islands
BORAGINACEAE
🌑 1,8 m ◖ ⊕
A somewhat woody perennial of shrub-like

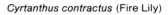

*Clivia miniata* (Bush, or Fire Lily)

*Cyrtanthus contractus* (Fire Lily)

appearance, pride of Madeira has attractive, long and pointed silvery foliage. Panicles of deep blue, bell-shaped flowers are borne in spring. Though it will tolerate very light frost, *E. candicans* is more at home in a truly temperate climate. It looks good grouped in the foreground of a shrubbery, but can also be dramatic in a well-placed container on a patio, or as an isolated specimen at a high point in the rock garden. Sow seed when ripe and plant out 600 mm apart.

*Eucomis comosa*                               South Africa
LILIACEAE
🌑 600-750 mm ☼ to ◖ ⊕ ⊛
The dense, yellow-green raceme of the early summer blooms of the pineapple flower is borne above long, strap-like leaves, and is tipped with a rosette of feathery green leaves to give the whole plant the appearance of the fruit from which its common name derives. Plant this and other species of *Eucomis* in autumn, setting out the bulbs about 300 mm apart and about 100 mm deep in well-drained sandy soil. Lift the clumps of bulbs in winter or early spring every two or three years, and propagate from offsets. Seed sown in spring will take up to five years to mature.

**False Dragon Head:** see *Physostegia virginiana*

*Felicia amelloides*                           South Africa
ASTERACEAE
🌑 300 mm ☼ ⊕
A low, bushy perennial, the blue marguerite

*Dimorphotheca sinuata* is similar in habit to *D. cuneata*

*Felicia amelloides* (Blue Marguerite)

bears sky blue flowers in spring — or, in the warmest parts of the country, for much of the year. Though it will tolerate light shade, it prefers full sun. The blue of these felicias is so unique that one of these days there must surely be another official colour category — 'Felicia blue'. Propagate from seed sown when ripe, and plant out 300 mm apart.

**Fire Lily:** see *Clivia miniata* and *Cyrtanthus contractus*
**Flag Iris:** see *Iris* spp.
**Flamingo Plant:** see *Anthurium andraeanum*
**Four O'Clock:** see *Mirabilis jalapa*

*Freesia* X *hybrida*　　　　South Africa
IRIDACEAE
🌺 200-400 mm ☼ ☙
The spikes of this spring-flowering hybrid, excellent for cutting, vary in colour from greenish-yellow to bright yellow. All are heavily scented. The popular coloured hybrid forms in pink, rose, orange and intermediate shadings, veined and spotted, are usually classified as *F.* X *hybrida* and arise largely from crossings of *F. refracta* and *F. armstrongii*. The latter species bears white tubular flowers, yellow-throated and purple-fringed. All may be raised from seed sown in January, and the corms lifted in November after flowering in August-September. Store the corms in the usual way, or give them cold storage treatment as described on page 110.

*Furikia subcordata:* see *Hosta plantaginea*
**Garland Flower:** see *Hedychium coccineum*
**Gay Feather:** see *Liatris pycnostachya*

*Gazania* hybrids　　　　South Africa
ASTERACEAE
🌺 200 mm ☼ ☙
The treasure flower has been improved so much now that it has left the old black-eyed Susan far behind. Types are both lax bran-

*Eucomis autumnalis* (Pineapple Lily)

ched and clump forming and are an essential part of the sea coast garden, withstanding salt droplets, dryness and poor soil. Yearly dressing with complete fertilizer will improve their growth. In addition to the old yellows with the dark contrasting zones, there is a wide range of shades of apricot, pink and red, some with very individual markings and stripes on the petals. One of the species now possesses a double form difficult to recognise as a gazania. Plants can be increased by breaking up the clumps and discarding the older stems. Most types average about 250 mm high.

**Geranium:** see *Pelargonium zonale*

*Geranium incanum*　　　　South Africa
GERANIACEAE
🌺 150 mm ☼ ☙
Almost all plants previously known as geraniums are now classified under *Pelargonium* and the carpet geranium, a South African gem for the rock garden, is about the only species left in the genus. It forms a low clump of soft foliage up to 150 mm high, and from this dense mat arise masses of light heliotrope blooms, borne on short stems. Flowering is in spring in temperate areas, and in late spring and summer in the colder parts. Propagate by division in autumn or sow seed when ripe, planting out about 250 mm apart.

*Gerbera jamesonii*　　　　South Africa
ASTERACEAE
🌺 450 mm ☼ and ☼ ☙
The Transvaal daisy is known and loved by all for its long-stemmed, spring and summer daisy-like flowers, scarlet in the type and with singles and doubles, in orange, pink, flame, lemon, white, salmon and scarlet in the hybrid range. As cut flowers they last up to ten days and, apart from being so useful florally, they make a brilliant splash of colour in the garden. They can be accommodated with advantage in the semi-herbaceous border, grouped in the rock garden, and used with reckless abandon in the wild garden. The new strains of singles are quite lovely, named cultivars of doubles are outstanding and, perhaps best of all, the new strains of Dutch hybrids, which are super singles in an astonishing array of pastel shades.
Propagate all Transvaal daisies, except the doubles, from seed, the best time for sowing (in trays) being immediately the seed is harvested. Divide the plants in January, between the first and second flush of flowering, and plant out about 350 mm apart. They appreciate a well-drained soil in which there is

*Freesia* X *hybrida*

*Gazania* hybrid

*Gerbera jamesonii* (Transvaal Daisy) hybrid

plenty of well-prepared compost, and prefer full sun in the morning and semi-shade in the afternoon. Double cultivars are propagated by division in very early spring or late autumn.

**Gladiolus Hybrids:** see Special Spread, page 95

*Gladiolus alatus*                    South Africa
IRIDACEAE
🌐 150-200 mm ☼ ☽
This flowers in early summer and is a little gem found wild throughout the western Cape, bearing pink, sometimes old rose, heavily-veined, spikes of blooms. It prefers sandy and gravelly soils. Plant the corms of this and all the following species about 150 mm apart, setting out the spring-flowering species in autumn, and the autumn-flowering species in spring.

*Freesia refracta*

*Gladiolus alatus*

*G. natalensis*       Natal
🌰 750 mm ☼ ✺
Bright red flowers with a greenish-yellow throat are borne on one side of the spike in late autumn. The Natal lily is one of the parents of the modern gladiolus hybrids.

*G. primulinus*       Tanzania
🌰 620 mm-1,24 m ☼ ✺
The hybridization of this species has led to an entirely new range of gladiolus hybrids with hooded flowers. The spikes of flowers, borne in late summer, are often branched. A wide range of soft shades is exhibited by the hybrids, though the species itself is yellow-bloomed. The influence of this species will probably lead to an entirely new race of cut flowers, daintier and more attractive than the present hybrids.

*Gloriosa rothschildiana*       Tropical Africa
LILIACEAE
🌰 2,45 m ☼ ✺
The flame lily is a climber, supporting itself by means of tendrils produced at the tips of the leaves. It is a beautiful and showy subject, bearing yellow and crimson flowers in late summer.

*G. superba*       South Africa, Tropical Africa,
🌰 1,5 m ◐ ✺       Tropical Asia
A bulbous climber, but requiring support, this is another 'flame lily' and one of the real gems of the floral world. Deep, rich orange and red flowers are borne in mid-summer. It requires semi-shade, and is best supported by a trel-

lis, though some gardeners prefer to grow it in a border on a support of stakes. The plant dislikes disturbance, and the bulbs are poisonous. *G. superba* is usually propagated from seed sown in spring.

**Goat's Beard:** see *Astilbe japonica*
**Golden Feather:** see *Chrysanthemum parthenium* 'Aureum'
**Golden Marguerite:** see *Anthemis tinctoria*
**Golden-rayed Lily of Japan:** see *Lilium auratum*
**Golden Rod:** see *Solidago canadensis*
**Golden Tuft:** see *Aurinia saxatilis*
**Guernsey Lily:** see *Nerine sarniensis*
*Haemanthus katherinae:* see *Scadoxus multiflorus* 'Katherinae'
*H. magnificus:* see *Scadoxus puniceus*

*Hedychium coccineum*       India, Burma
ZINGIBERACEAE
🌰 1,5 m ☼ ✺
Popularly known as ornamental ginger or garland flower, this species has canna-like foliage and is excellent for decorative purposes, especially near water. Sweet-scented flowers are borne in spring, those of *H. coccineum* being red, of *H. coronarium*, pure white and scented, and of *H. flavum*, orange-yellow. All may also be used for tropical bedding effect, in containers for patio decoration, and as specimens in the indoor garden. Propagate by division of the rhizomes. Some are more sensitive to cold than others but, generally, they are best suited to the warmer temperate regions. If planted as a group, set out 500 mm apart.

*Helianthus angustifolius*       United States
ASTERACEAE
🌰 1,5 m ☼ ✺
Although the perennial swamp sunflower will tolerate dry conditions, it is most at home and does best in a permanently moist, well-drained position. It produces a generous mass of golden-yellow, daisy-like flowers from summer through to late autumn. Wood-

land conditions, especially near water, suit it perfectly, but it may also be grouped in the background of a large semi-herbaceous border. Plant out 500 mm apart.

*Helinium autumnale*       North America
ASTERACEAE
🌰 1 m ☼ ✺
Sneezewood is a stalwart of the summer border, and several varieties and cultivars are available. Long stems bear daisy-like flowers in yellow, gold, bronze and splashed crimson. Flowering is more or less continuous throughout summer. Propagate by simple division in autumn and set the plants out 450 mm apart.

*Heliopsis helianthoides*       United States
ASTERACEAE
🌰 1,5-2 m ☼ ✺
Gardeners often confuse members of the *Heliopsis* genus with species of *Helianthus*. Though they look alike, the rays of the former have pistils while sunflowers do not. The metre-high 'Orange King' is tolerant of most conditions, and its compact habit makes it an excellent subject for the semi-herbaceous

*Gloriosa superba* (Flame Lily)

# GLADIOLUS HYBRIDS

*Gladiolus* hybrid

*Gladiolus* hybrid

*Gladiolus* hybrid

Today's gladiolus hybrids bear only a slight resemblance to their ancestors. With their stiff, sword-shaped leaves – the name derives from the Latin word *gladius*, meaning a sword – and spikes of trumpet-shaped blooms, they are among the most popular of all our cut flowers, and florist shops are seldom without them.

This 'cut flower' image is unfortunate, for gladioli can be had in flower in succession from November through until April and would undoubtedly enhance our herbaceous borders. Certainly, it is only in successive groups in the border that the gladiolus's true garden beauty can be fully appreciated.

But for all the hybrids' beauty and vast range of colours, several indigenous species of this genus in the family IRIDACEAE make splendid garden subjects. Three in particular spring to mind:
*G. cardinalis*, the waterfall gladiolus, is the parent of many of the hybrids. Growing some 70 mm high, it blooms in mid-summer, bearing flattish spikes of crimson flowers whose lower petals are tinged with deeper red.
*G. psittacinus*, the parrot gladiolus, found throughout most of south east Africa, on each spike bears as many as 20 hooded, orange flowers, tinged with yellow. Arching to a height of almost one metre, this

species makes an impressive autumn show.

For all species and hybrids, plant the corms 120 mm deep, in succession from mid-August onwards. They take about three months – give or take a week – to come into flower, depending on the species or particular cultivar.

Gladioli are particularly susceptible to virus and mosaic infection, spread mainly by thrips, so the foliage should be sprayed twice weekly from the time the first blades appear until the flower spikes show colour. (See page 339 for suitable pesticides and spraying frequency.)

Theoretically, it should be possible to get two flowerings of gladiolus in one year, but in practice this does not work. For instance, corms planted in mid-August will flower about mid-November and can be lifted in mid-December. If these are lifted, cleaned and replanted only about 20% will flower again. In other words, the corms must be rested and this is why they should be lifted, cleaned and stored as soon as the foliage dies back or becomes yellowish to the soil level.

## STORAGE OF CORMS

When the corms have been lifted and cleaned they should be dipped in a fungicide with a copper sulphate base, as a

protection against such storage diseases as dry rot. Then place them on racks in a cool, airy room.

Unless the room is particularly cool, it will be impossible to retard activity in the corm after late August or early September so that later successions are only possible through refrigerated storage at a temperature of about –4°C but not higher than 0°C. Place locally-saved corms in such cold storage at the end of July, keeping them up to the end of November for a final planting.

To store corms under refrigerated conditions, place them in dry shallow trays, about two-and-a-half corms deep, leaving a space of 70 mm between each tray to allow air to circulate freely.

*Hedychium coccineum* (Ornamental Ginger)

*Hemerocallis lilioasphodelus* (Day Lily)

border. Throughout summer it bears a profusion of deep yellow flowers, which are good for cutting. Propagate by division in autumn or early spring, planting out 400 mm apart. To maintain maximum floral performance the plants should be divided and replanted every two years, the beds being re-enriched whenever this is done.

### *H. fulva*                                            Eastern Asia
🌑 1,8 m ☼ ☀

Taller growing than the day lily, in the type the brown day lily has orange flowers borne throughout summer, though it actually starts blooming in winter in the warmer areas. It is this species which has provided such a galaxy of colours in its various cultivars, coppery-red, red-blotched, white-striped, and recently a double form. Flower-spikes are as much as 450 mm long. Propagate as you would *H. lilioasphodelus.*

### *Hemerocallis lilioasphodelus*          East Asia
LILIACEAE
🌑 350 mm ☼ and ☀ ☀

One of the most useful plants for the semi-herbaceous border, the day lily does remarkably well here. It has grass-like foliage, fleshy, tuberous roots and lily-like, lemon-coloured flowers which last only a day, but are borne continuously throughout summer. Six to nine flowers form each corymb, and many of these are produced simultaneously. In very cold areas the foliage is frosted back but, in temperate to subtropical zones, it remains green

and flowers continue to appear spasmodically throughout the winter. Divide the clumps in very early spring and plant out 400 mm apart.

### *Heuchera sanguinea*                     New Mexico
SAXIFRAGACEAE
🌑 450 mm ☼ ☀

A neat-growing perennial, coral bells is better suited to the rock garden than the herbaceous border. It produces a low-growing leafy clump, or rootstock, with attractive foliage from which numerous flowering scapes, 450 mm long, and bearing terminal panicles of white, pink and red flowers, appear in summer. All are very dainty, though I am inclined to favour the deep, brick red colour. Propagate by division in early spring, or from seed sown in early autumn; plant out 500 mm apart.

### *Hibiscus moscheutos*                   United States
MALVACEAE
🌑 1,25 m ☼ ☀

Bearing enormous, single, summer flowers, often as much as 200 mm in diameter, this species is available in a wonderful array of colours – crimson, reds, rose, pink and white with a red 'eye' are just a few. It is difficult to believe that a *Hibiscus* species can produce such giant flowers – but seeing is believing. Propagate from seed sown in autumn, planting out 750 mm apart, for flowering the following summer.

### *Hippeastrum hybrid*                    South America
AMARYLLIDACEAE
🌑 620 mm ☼ and ☀ ☀

Fully dealt with in Chapter 19, 'Bush House and Greenhouse Management', the huge, trumpet-like flowers of the amaryllis, or

Barbados lily, in whites, reds, scarlets and burnt orange, mottled and striped in a variety of colours including a greenish-yellow, are a splendid addition to the winter border in warmer areas.

Flower scapes are 300-450 mm long and usually bear two or four blooms, each 100-150 mm across, if grown outdoors, plant out 350 mm apart.

### *Hosta plantaginea*                              Japan
LILIACEAE
🌑 450 mm ☀ ☀

Sometimes known as the plantain lilies, these perennials with their broad, plantain-like leaves, have long been known to gardeners as Funkia. This species and its variety 'Grandiflora' have large, broad leaves, making a handsome clump some 450 mm high, from which rise summer spikes bearing large, white bell-mounted flowers with an orange-like fragrance. *H. sieboldiana*, another species indigenous to Japan, has narrower leaves, tinged metallic blue and striated with green. Its flowers are slender tubes of blushed lilac. *H. fortunei* has smaller leaves and the racemes grow well clear of the foliage clump. The flowers are pale lilac and there are a number of varieties. *H. lancifolia* 'Marginata' is a form with creamy-white marginal leaves; and *H. undulata* has ovate and waved, green leaves, splashed white, and 150-200 mm long. Pale lilac flowers are borne on a 600 mm scape.

All require a deep soil, well enriched with compost, a cool root run and the shade of trees, making them ideal for woodland conditions. Propagate by division of the clumps in early spring. They are best planted singly; but if grouped, set out 750 mm apart.

**Ifafa Lily:** see *Cyrtanthus macowanii*

*Hippeastrum* hybrid

*Iresine herbstii* 'Aureo-reticulata'

*Iresine lindenii*

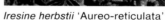

*Incarvillea delavayi*    China
BIGNONIACEAE
🌿 600 mm ☼ ⊛
This is one of those special perennials which merits a place in all gardens where winters are not too severe. Under favourable conditions it makes a clump of handsome, pinnate foliage up to 300 mm tall, from which 450-600 mm summer flower-scapes rise, bearing at their apex a number of trumpet-shaped, gloxinia-like flowers in a soft rosy-magenta, and some 50-70 mm long. A good subject for the rock garden or semi-herbaceous border, it thrives in ordinary soil.

*I. mairei* var. *grandiflora*    China
🌿 450 mm ☼ ⊛
Another summer-flowering species, this has shorter leaves, and bears rosy-red blooms on scapes 450 mm high. Both *Incarvillea* species may be grown from seed, but are usually propagated by division of the tuberous rootstock in early spring. Set the plants out 450 mm apart.

*Iresine lindenii*    Ecuador
AMARANTHACEAE
🌿 450 mm ☼ ⊛
This erect herb is noted for its brilliant foliage, rich, deep, blood red, in the type and gold, veined with crimson and streaked with green. *I. lindenii* is much used as a dot plant in tropical and formal beds (trimmed) and for edgings or grouping in the shrubbery or the semi-herbaceous border. It will tolerate any amount of trimming and may be kept to any height up to 450 mm. If grouped, or planted in a row set out 350 mm apart.
    *I. herbstii*, another South American species, has cordate leaves which are deep bronzy-maroon above, crimson beneath, and are borne on deep red stems and branches.

'Aureo-reticulata' has green leaves, mottled gold, and red stems. Both species and cultivar may be treated as for *I. lindenii* and all may be raised from cuttings during the active growing season. Trim whenever necessary.

*Iris* spp.    Garden hybrids
IRIDACEAE
There are two major divisions in the genus *Iris*: those which, like the English, Spanish and Dutch, have a bulbous root; and those, like the tall bearded iris and *I. kaempferi*, the Japanese iris, which have a rhizomatous rooting system. The tall bearded iris represents the most important group in Australian gardens, particularly in the cooler areas. Their origin is somewhat involved, but initially the two European species *I. pallida* and *I. variegata* were crossed, their progeny being joined later by the Asian species *I. cypriana* and *I. trojana*. Later still, *I. mesopotamica* and *I. gatesii* were bred into the strain to produce the gorgeous hybrids we know today. Hybridizing continues, both here and overseas, and new cultivars are constantly added to an already dazzling range of colours. While shades of blue are prominent, white with other markings, cream, lemons and varying shades of pink are all popular.
    These irises demand a well-drained site, but are otherwise most accommodating, in that they do not require rich, well-manured soil; indeed the presence of fresh manure often induces the incidence of fungoid disease. Give them a biennial dusting of agricultural lime and dressings of super phosphate and bone meal in late winter of alternate years. Permanent shade induces lank growth and diminished flowering, but they do appreciate a little shade from the full heat of the sun. The most limiting factor is

wind, and they must be protected from this. In general garden practice they should be lifted and divided every third year, though certain particularly vigorous forms may need lifting every second year. After lifting, dig over the bed thoroughly, adding leaf mould if possible. Divide, selecting the outer rhizomes for replanting, each 50-100 mm long with a fan growth of foliage attached. Plant these 350 mm apart with the rhizomes just below soil surface and tramp the roots down firmly so that, when watered in, the upper surface of the rhizome is just above ground level but firmly anchored underneath. At this time cut back the leaves to about half their length to avoid undue loss by transpiration. All this may be carried out when the main flush of flowering is over, usually in December or January. The flag iris enthusiast usually grows them in a special place solely for their cultivation. If used in the semi-herbaceous border, plant fairly large groups, preferably each of one colour.

### I. kaempferi — Japan
🌑 400 mm ☼ 💧

The Japanese iris is widely grown but it won't grow just anywhere; where it does succeed, however, it is very, very good. It is probably happier in the cooler areas, possibly in a not-too-shady woodland setting, and where the soil is deep, cool and fairly moist. In the type, the flower, borne in spring and summer, is a dark red and purple, but many cultivars are available, with 70 mm flowers ranging from a creamy white to violet, lavender and pink. Plant out 300 mm apart any time after flowering.

### I. laevigata — Japan
🌑 1 m ☼ 💧

A true swamp iris, this early summer-flowering species enjoys permanent moisture. In the type, the flower is a clear uniform blue, but there is also a white form and new cultivars cover various exciting shades of contrasting blue. Propagate by division in early spring; plant out 450 mm apart.

### I. sibirica — Central Europe, Russia
🌑 1 m ☼ 💧

Closely related to the Japanese I. sanguinea, which has purplish-red blooms, this species bears purplish-blue flowers in spring, and many colour variations are available in hybrids of the two. Both species and their hybrids look well near water. They require normal soil conditions, full sunlight and plenty of moisture during the active period of growth and flowering. There is no need to disturb them for a number of years; division, when necessary, should take place in autumn. Plant out 450 mm apart.

### I. unguicularis — Eastern Mediterranean
🌑 350 mm ☼ 💧

This really lovely, winter-flowering species, is quite low growing and bears beautiful, lavender-blue blooms. It likes a loose, friable soil which is not too rich and contains some lime. Plant out divisions of the rhizomes in early spring, 300 mm apart.

### I. xiphium — Southern France, Portugal
🌑 1 m ☼ 💧

The bulbous Spanish iris, which bears deep blue and yellow-gold summer flowers excellent for cutting, has been largely superseded – particularly as a cut flower – by the Dutch iris. The latter has developed from I. xiphium through generations of hybridization.

Bulbs of all the preceding species should be lifted at least every two years, though some growers prefer to lift them annually. This is done just as the foliage assumes a wilted, dried appearance. Divide the bulbs and allow them to dry out thoroughly in the open air, under a tree and protected from direct sun. Store in a cool, dry shed and replant (80 mm deep and 200 mm apart) during February or March, mulching with dried grass or similar litter.

There is a host of other Iris species, varieties and cultivars which, although delightful subjects, are largely for the specialist or collector. Among these are such gems as the miniature I. reticulata and I. histrioides, which have a character and beauty all their own. I do not want to be labelled 'anti-progressive', but I hope that the more delicate and completely charming characteristics of true species will not be sacrificed in the breeding of bigger, better and more spectacular hybrids which often have everything – but about as much character as a well-formed turnip.

Bearded Iris hybrid

Bearded Iris hybrid

Bearded Iris hybrid

Bearded Iris hybrid

*Iris kaempferi*

*Ixia viridiflora*     South Africa
IRIDACEAE
500 mm
This cormous species is one of the very few green-flowered plants of real worth anywhere in the world, and is one of the most widely grown. The duck-egg green flowers are borne on long, wiry stems in summer. Ixias are easy to cultivate and all may be grown from seed in March, taking two to three years to flower. Once a stock has been established, increase by division of the corms, which should be lifted when the foliage wilts after flowering. Store in a cool, dry shed and plant out again in March, setting the corms about 60 mm apart. The popular, multi-coloured hybrids have been derived largely from the species *I. monadelpha* and *I. maculata*.

**Jacobean Lily:** see *Sprekelia formosissima*
**Japanese Anemone:** see *Anemone japonica*
**Japanese Iris:** see *Iris kaempferi*
**Jockey Caps:** see *Tigridia pavonia*

*Kalanchoe blossfeldiana*     Madagascar
CRASSULACEAE
300 mm
Winter flowering succulents of great appeal, with rounded satiny leaves and brilliant masses of tiny flowers in heads about 50 mm across. Scarlet is the original colour, but further strains have produced clear yellows, apricots and orange. All need as much sun as possible, and a rich, well drained soil. Ideal for mass effects and for container planting. Most can be propagated by dropping the leaves on damp soil and many produce adventitious roots on side pieces. These can be cut off and used for increasing the stock.

*Kniphofia praecox*     South Africa
LILIACEAE
1,5 m
Generally regarded as the most widely distributed species in nature, its common name – red-hot poker – is applied even to yellow-and-white flowering species as well as to many hybrids and varieties. There is still some confusion as to their exact botanical classification and this is likely to become even more involved with the bringing together of many newly-cultivated species and their consequent hybridization. Be that as it may,

Louisiana Iris hybrid

*Ixia viridiflora*

as far as the home gardener is concerned an ever-increasing range of *Kniphofia* is available – both winter/spring- and summer-flowering, either as new species, cultivars of these, or as hybrids. Many species such as *K. macowanii*, are quite dainty (growing to no more than 300-450 mm) while the giant *K. multiflora* reaches an overall height of three metres. Flowers may be whitish in some forms, or yellow with reddish tips in others. The general, popular run of red-hot pokers grow to about one metre, are summer or winter-spring flowering, and are invaluable for the large semi-herbaceous border. Plant them in bold clumps grouped with agapanthus. They are also ideal to edge driveways and for the wild garden. The smaller-growing species are excellent in rock garden pockets, while the magnificent *K. multiflora* is very much at home and looks grand beside an informal water or marsh garden, where its roots can reach permanent moisture.

Kniphofias are easily grown from seed sown when ripe, and usually flower in the third season. However, they are normally propagated by division of clumps soon after flowering. Ensure that the divisions do not dry out

either before or after planting. They enjoy a deep, well-drained situation with plenty of moisture, especially during their growing season.

*Lachenalia aloides*     South Africa
LILIACEAE
100-200 mm
In Australia, New Zealand, Europe and the United States Soldier lilies are widely grown, indoors and out, and are highly prized. Hybridists have also been very busy with them, and their range of hybrid lachenalias is quite remarkable. *L. aloides* is green, red and yellow, while the cultivar 'Aurea' is bright orange-yellow, 'Lutea' is all yellow, and 'Nelsonii' is bright yellow. Other worthwhile species include:
*L. bulbiferum*, which can reach a height of 250 mm, and has pendulous, tubular flowers in deep purple, red and yellow.
*L. pendula:* see *L. bulbiferum*
*L. purpureo-caerulea*  bears purplish-blue bell-shaped flowers.
*L. rosea* is ruby-red, while *L. rubida* is similar, but richer in colour.
*L. tricolor:* see *L. aloides*

favour among gardeners because of its coarse habit and vigorous spread, invading and ousting its immediate neighbours. The new, lower-growing hybrids (up to 1 m) are superior garden subjects and should soon gain popularity. A group of these, with their striking sprays of golden or lemon yellow flowers, liven up the summer-autumn border as do few other plants. Propagate every two years by simple division after flowering, and plant out 450 mm apart.

**Spanish Iris:** see *Iris xiphium*

*Sparaxis grandiflora*              South Africa
IRIDACEAE
🌱 200 mm ☼ ✿

A corymbose perennial species closely akin to the ixias, and most suitable for a pocket in the rock garden, the wild freesia bears purple, but variable flowers in spring. *S. tricolor*, also indigenous to South Africa and spring blooming, bears orange, yellow-throated and black spotted flowers. Both species are easily grown from seed, though normal propagation is by separation of the corms. Once established, leave undisturbed for three or four years. Plant about 100 mm apart, in groups.

*Sprekelia formosissima*              Mexico
AMARYLLIDACEAE
🌱 300-400 mm ☼ ✿

A close relative of the *Amaryllis*, in which genus it was once classified, the Maltese cross, or Jacobean lily, flaunts beautiful, showy, orchid-shaped flowers in October and November. Borne on 300-400 mm scapes, which appear before the leaves, the large flowers are usually crimson, though sometimes white, and make a grand show when filling an entire bay of the rock garden. Leave the bulbs undisturbed unless they become overcrowded, when they should be separated and replanted. Otherwise propagate from seed sown in spring. Plant the bulbs 150 mm apart.

**Stokes' Aster:** see *Stokesia laevis*
*Stokesia cyanea:* see *S. laevis*

*Stokesia laevis*              United States
ASTERACEAE
🌱 600 mm ☼ ✿

Stokes' aster, which resembles the Michaelmas daisy, is a strong-growing perennial with daisy-like, double, lilac-blue flowers 80 mm across. The cultivar 'Alba' has white flowers. 'Blue Danube' has darker richer blue blooms, up to 130 mm across and is a beauty. They bloom right through summer into autumn and are ideal for cutting. Stokes' asters dislike heavy, clay soil and enjoy comparatively dry conditions. Propagate by division in early spring; seedlings produce variable results but some may prove quite colourful, ranging from white through rose and mauve to purplish-blue.

*Strelitzia reginae*              South Africa
STRELITZIACEAE
🌱 1,5 m ☼ ✿

The striking perennial bird of paradise, or crane flower, has leathery banana-like leaf

*Sparaxis* hybrids

*Sprekelia formosissima* (Maltese Cross, or Jacobean Lily) ▶

blades some 500 mm long, with thick, extremely tough stalks projecting from the rhizomatous roots. Erect and densely produced, this upright mass of stalk and foliage gives the plant an almost shrubby appearance and from it the flower stalks arise, bearing their unique bird-like flowers of orange and purple-blue. Though slow to mature, after the first two years these are freely borne at all favourable times. The strelitzia prefers full sun, though it will also tolerate some light shade, and does best in a deep, moist, nutrient-rich soil. It does not like to be disturbed; if this must be done, do it in early spring and, if the plant is to be divided, don't be greedy and try to make too many divisions from a single specimen. It just won't stand for it. Strangely, the crane flower, which is the floral emblem of Natal, is also that of the city of Los Angeles in the United States.

The larger-growing, shrubby, evergreen species *S. alba* and *S. nicolai* – both also indigenous to South Africa – are included here for easy reference.

*Strelitzia reginae*
(Bird of Paradise, or Crane Flower)

*S. augusta* has a very short stem with leaf stalks up to 2 m long and banana-like leaf blades of about one metre. The spathe is purple and the unequal outer and inner flower segments are white.

*S. nicolai*, the wild banana of the Natal coast, has a stem up to 5 m and large, banana-like leaves. The outer flower segments are white, the inner blue, and the spathe is brownish-red.

Unlike *S. reginae*, these two species are grown not so much for their flowers, as for their special impact on the landscape. *S. nicolai*, particularly, can impart an immediate tropical effect, and as an isolated specimen in just the right position, its influence can be quite dramatic.

**Swamp Rose-mallow:** see *Hibiscus moscheutos*
**Swamp Sunflower:** see *Helianthus angustifolius*
**Tall Bearded Iris:** see *Iris* spp.

*Thalictrum dipterocarpum*          China
RANUNCULACEAE
🌼 1 m ◐ ✤
A really choice summer-flowering perennial for the colder and cool temperate parts, meadow rue is highly prized both for its border display and for floral arrangements. It likes semi-shade and well-drained soil, with a permanently cool, moist root run. It produces panicles of dainty violet flowers with golden anthers from a network of fern-like foliage. Grow it in groups of about half a dozen, planting out about 400 mm apart at the back of an east-facing border. Once planted it does not like disturbance. Sow seed in February for flowering the following summer.

**Tiger Lily:** see *Lilium tigrinum*
**Tree Dahlia:** see *Dahlia imperialis*, pages 88 and 89

*Strelitzia reginae*

*Tigridia pavonia*          Mexico, Guatemala
IRIDACEAE
🌣 500 mm ☼ ⊕

In the species the jockey caps bears large, glowing red blooms, spotted wit yellow and purple in their cup-like centres. These appear in summer on tall, nodding stems surrounded by stiff, strap-like leaves. Cultivars have been developed in many colour combinations and include pure, pearly-white flowers, yellow and red blooms, salmon red flowers with darker spots of the same colour, and various shades of red, blotched and streaked with yellow and orange. Plant the tigridias in spring, 50 mm below the surface of a well-drained, loam-rich soil, setting the bulbs out 150 mm apart. In the colder parts of the country they should be lifted for dry storage before the first frosts. Propagate by offsets taken in spring. Seeds sown in spring will bloom the following year.

*Tritonia crocata*              South Africa
IRIDACEAE
🌣 600 mm ☼ ⊕

Of the many species of these cormous plants, many hybrids are now available. All are spring flowering and *T. crocata* is at its best in October, when it bears saffron flowers. Varieties and forms are also available in orange-red, purple, scarlet and blood red. As with babianas, *Ixia* and *Sparaxis*, give them a pocket in the rock garden, and give yourself real pleasure in something that is beautiful. Sow seed in autumn, or propagate by division of the corms when they become too crowded. Plant out about 150 mm apart.

*Tulbaghia fragrans*            South Africa
LILIACEAE
🌣 350 mm ☼ ⊕

A rhizomatous perennial 350 mm or so in height, wild garlic bears terminal umbels of rose-lavender flowers. Now quite widely grown, this sweetly-scented subject, which has quite a long-flowering spring season, is excellent for floral arrangements. *T. violacea* has purple flowers, freely produced, and is a good subject for massing in the wild garden. Unlike *T. fragrans*, it emits an odour of garlic – 'odour' if you do not like garlic – otherwise 'scent'. Propagate from seed, or by division of overcrowded rhizomes. Plant out both species about 250 mm apart.

*Verbascum phoeniceum*          South Eastern
SCROPHULARIACEAE     Europe, Asia Minor
🌣 750 mm-1 m ☼ ⊕

Most verbascums grown in this country are hybrid perennials, propagated from seed sown in November-December for flowering late in the following spring or in early summer, according to local climate. They have a semi-procumbent rosette of woolly-grey foliage from which flower-spikes rise, varying in colour from pink to violet-red, lilac, deep rose and purple. *V. phoeniceum* is probably the principal parent of these hybrids which are excellent grouped 350 mm apart in the semi-herbaceous border. The species is smaller and has red, purple or mauve flowers. All prefer a semi-woodland condition, or at least semi-shade in the afternoon, as long as it is well-drained. *V. nigrum* is taller, having a

*Tigridia pavonia* (Jockey Caps)

*Tritonia* hybrid

1.2 m branched, woolly spike of masses of yellow flowers, each a little less than 100 mm across and with filaments of purple hairs. They may also be grown from root cuttings (pieces of root severed from the old crown).

Before planting out, place the cuttings in sand until the foliage appears and rooting is evident.

*Vinca rosea*: see *Catharanthus roseus*

*Tulbaghia violacea*

*Watsonia* X *hybrida*          South Africa
IRIDACEAE          and Garden hybrids
🌣 500 mm ☼ ⊕

The bugle lily was despised for many years in Australia as a poor relation of the gladiolus, but the modern hybrids are not only attractive flowers for the garden and for cutting, but are as easily grown as the old-fashioned species, which in many areas of Australia can be seen naturalized. The sword-like bright green leaves are a pleasant contrast to other plants and the cream pink, apricot and reddish flowers are carried on stalks up to one metre long. Full sun or part shade suits them and the soil does not need to be over rich. The corms can be left in the ground for a number of years before separation, and this is the method of increase. In the wild garden, you should not expect any seedlings which appear to be the same as the parent plant.

**Wild Banana:** see *Strelitzia nicolai*
**Wild Freesia:** see *Sparaxis grandiflora*
**Wild Garlic:** see *Tulbaghia fragrans*
**Yellow Tiger Lily:** see *Lilium henryi*

*Zantedeschia aethiopica*          South Africa
ARACEAE
🌣 600 mm ☼ ⊕

This is the common arum lily which, together with *Z. oculata*, is described in Chapter 15, 'Water Gardens', page 275.

*Z. elliottiana*          South Africa
🌣 600 mm ☼ ⊕

Growing upwards of 600 mm and called the calla lily, this species has attractive green foliage with transparent silvery markings and spring-summer flowers of bright buttercup yellow. Propagate by division of rhizomes in autumn and plant out 300 mm apart.

*Z. rehmannii*          South Africa
🌣 150-240 mm ☼ ⊕

A dwarf gem, this species bears flowers

*Watsonia angustifolia*

*Watsonia humilis*

ranging from white and blush-pink, through red to a deep purplish-red. Invaluable for grouping in the rock garden, it does not object to full sun and a fairly dry position if, during the growing and flowering season, it receives plenty of water. In nature this species is usually found among rocky outcrops, on the edges of forests and even in marshy ground. It will probably keep its colour best in a semi-shaded position but, when massed, this is not particularly relevant. Propagate all species by division of the rhizomes after flowering, or from seed sown between November and February. Seedlings should stay in the same seed bed for at least a year. During spring, 18 months later, plant them out about 200 mm apart.

*Dianthus caryophyllus* hybrids (Carnation)

*Zantedeschia rehmannii*

*Zantedeschia aethiopica* (Arum Lily)

# CARNATIONS: BUTTONHOLES TO THE WORLD

Few cut flowers enjoy greater popularity than the carnation (*Dianthus caryophyllus*) in its multiplicity of hybrid forms. The carnation reached peak popularity in the 18th and 19th centuries – French aristocrats wore the carnation while attending executions: Napoleon selected carnation-red for the rosette of the Legion of Honour; and Boulanger's followers wore it as the symbol of socialism, which it remained for more than a century. Though the vogue for this flowering perennial is no longer so great, it is a popular florists' flower. Many tend to choose the annual sub-species in its varying forms – in double and single pinks. However, the true perennial carnation merits serious consideration by any gardener.

Though *D. caryophyllus*, the best-known member of the family CARYO-PHYLLACEAE, has its geographical origins in central and southern Europe, it was first actively cultivated by the Muslims in north Africa, who used it for flavouring. From them it spread back to Europe as a cultivated and already hybridized plant. But it was in the United States that the perpetual-flowering carnation – the popular cut flower of today – was first bred, earning for its creator a reputed sum of $3000. Hybridists and other plantsmen have been working at it ever since and every year new named forms become available.

The problem is that the perpetual-flowering carnation is neither a bedding nor (strictly speaking) a border plant. Probably the ideal place to site perpetual carnations is in a narrow border fronting a wall, in full sunlight. Here the wiring and staking needed to produce first-class blooms will not clash with the other plants of the general border, and will also allow for the extra dressing of lime on which they thrive – carnations will not tolerate soil acidity. The true carnation enthusiast will probably find a suitable spot somewhere in his flower beds, and disregard appearances.

Carnations demand excellent drainage; a loose, gritty soil consisting of good loam with lime rubble incorporated is ideal. The lower reaches of the bed should contain a generous application of well-rotted stable or cow manure. The carnation's life span is seldom more than three years, but it is easily propagated by taking cuttings from the strong young shoots which arise at the base. If these are taken in late autumn or early spring each year (depending on local climate) a constant supply of fresh flowering material will be available. When taking cuttings of the growing nodal shoots, shorten back the foliage by removing some of the lower leaves, to reduce the rate of transpiration. Root the cuttings in pots of sand and syringe frequently. They should be firmly established within a month and ready to plant out within two months. Set out 400 mm apart, and pinch out the tops of the young growing plants to encourage stocky basal growth.

*Dianthus caryophyllus* hybrids (Carnation)

# SHRUBS 8 AND ROSES

## PREPARING A PALETTE OF EVER-CHANGING TINTS

Shrubs provide a wealth of uses in the garden – they afford shade and shelter, bring together house and garden, adorn perimeters, conceal an unsightly view or fence and provide privacy. Carefully selected, they are a permanent asset and with the modern trend towards outdoor entertaining in Australia's warm and congenial climate, they provide interest, colour and beauty throughout the year.

There is a great increase in the number of exotic species available to the gardener as well as an outstanding range of indigenous plants from which to choose. Exotic and native plants may be planted harmoniously together or you may wish to create an entirely 'Australian' section in the garden. Native shrubs also provide nesting sites and food for native birds – and birds will keep insect pests under control.

Many plantsmen believe that no garden, however small, is complete without a rose bush or two.

Except in the formal rose-garden, shrubs should be planted in such a way as to avoid any suggestion of sameness. For large shrub borders, follow the same principle with regard to heights as for herbaceous borders; avoid any uniform slope from back to front. Rather plant three or five of each species in groups, with some almost forming a promontory which nearly reaches the front of the border. Plants such as agapanthus, salvias and strelitzia, as well as some of the annuals, associate happily with shrubs. Used boldly, they add to the seasonal colour and provide continuity of texture and interest.

Striking effects can be attained with shrubs of distinctive foliage – variegated with silver, gold, red, purple and even many self shades. The soft greyish colours and weeping foliage of many natives also provide a harmonious contrast and can be grouped to form delightful associations. Consider the habits and growth of the various shrubs when it comes to their grouping.

Many shrubs are noted for their beautiful fragrant flowers and there are glorious scents to be gained from the leaves of some aromatic plants. Arrange your scented plantings along walkways or near windows and doors so that the perfume may drift into the house. Fragrance may also be more noticeable in a protected position where the wind does not disperse the scent.

Because the shrub border, once established, is more or less permanent and little changed, its soil preparation should be particularly thorough. Trenching to a depth of 600 mm is essential and though the natural fertility of the soil will dictate how much rotted manure or compost to add, incorporate at least a barrow load to the top 400 mm of every 2 m². This should be supplemented, at least annually, with a surface dressing of compost, lightly forked in. It is usually unnecessary to use chemical fertilizers and these should always be used sparingly for native shrubs.

When planting, it is important to allow each plant sufficient space for its complete development. The patch of bare ground may be carpeted with ground covers or filled with herbaceous perennials that can be moved when occasion requires. Evergreen and most native shrubs should be planted during autumn, or immediately before growth starts in spring. Deciduous shrubs may be planted at any time during dormancy. Do not disturb the roots and water well in dry periods.

Unless they have grown undisturbed for three years or more, shrubs are not difficult to transplant. But those which have been established longer, especially evergreens, may prove troublesome. In such instances, and where circumstances permit, dig around the plants severing all the roots, during the early spring preceding removal. The cut should be about 400 mm away from the stem, or even further in the case of larger specimens more than 2 m tall. The plant should be watered well immediately after root pruning. Evergreens are usually transplanted the following autumn and deciduous species the following winter. Prepare the hole to receive the transplant some days beforehand and soak it thoroughly at least two days before planting.

The following is a fairly extensive list of worthwhile shrubs. Unless otherwise indicated, all are hardy.

Dew beads the flowers of *Caesalpinia pulcherrima*.

Abelia X grandiflora

**Abelia floribunda**     Mexico
CAPRIFOLIACEAE
1,5-2 m
A summer-flowering species, this evergreen has rosy-red pendulous flowers borne closely on the wood of the previous season. The five sepals are at first green and later turn a brick red, and the purple-bronze foliage is particularly striking during winter.

**A. X grandiflora**     Garden origin
1,5-2 m
This hybrid is the most widely seen in Australia. It flowers almost continuously throughout summer, bearing white-tinged pink blooms with two to five purplish sepals. Its long (500 mm) dark, glossy green foliage makes it a good year-round subject. Light pruning is needed after flowering to keep good shape. Propagate from semi-soft cuttings during summer or autumn.

**A. longituba:** see A. schumannii

**A. schumannii**     China
to 1,5-2 m
Deciduous in cold areas and semi-deciduous in temperate areas, this species bears solitary, richly rosy-pink, bell-shaped flowers in the axils of short shoots on previous years' growth and the arching new shoots are tinged with purple. Prune immediately after flowering.

**Abutilon hybridum**     Garden origin
MALVACEAE
1 m
Many of these numerous summer-flowering cultivars show characteristics which might suggest A. pictum parentage. In temperate zones their summer flowering extends well into winter. The pendulous flowers range in colours from white and yellow to orange, pink and red. Propagate all species by cuttings, either hardwood in winter or semi-soft in summer. Shape lightly after flowering.

**A. megapotamicum**     Brazil
1 m
The extremely pretty Chinese lantern flower bears small, lantern-like red and yellow flowers with prominently protruding brown anthers. Though it blooms mainly in summer, its flowering period varies according to climate. In 'variegatum', the leaves are prettily mottled with bright yellow. This is much smaller growing than the species and is useful for the rock garden or against a wall. Both are free flowering.

**A. pictum**     Guatemala
2 m
Though there is some confusion about the nomenclature of this variety, I refer to the most attractive, bushy plant which used to be described as Abutilon thompsonii. Grown for its leaves, which are heavily variegated and mottled with gold. Prune back large plants heavily in spring as the young, fresh growths give rise to far richer leaf colourings.

**A. thompsonii:** see A. pictum

**Acacia:** for taller varieties see 'Trees' page 198

**Acacia acinacea**     Australia
MIMOSACEAE
1-2 m
Suitable for small gardens, this dense shrub produces masses of bright yellow ball flowers in late winter and spring. As with all acacias prune lightly after flowering to improve bloom production and shape.

**A. buxifolia**     Australia
2-3 m
The box-leaf wattle is a slender, blue-green shrub with masses of bright yellow loose balls from August to October. Widely grown it is moderately frost and drought tolerant.

**A. cardiophylla**     Australia
2-3 m
A garden favourite with soft ferny drooping foliage and bright yellow flowers from July to September. This very hardy attractive shrub tolerates a wide range of conditions.

**A. drummondii**     Australia
1-2 m
This ferny-leaved shrub with slender arching branches bears spectacular long yellow rods of flowers in late winter and early spring. It grows well in a wide range of soils, but requires good drainage.

**A. myrtifolia**     Australia
1-2.5 m
Myrtle wattle is a long-lived hardy shrub suited to a wide range of soils and conditions. Cream coloured ball flowers appear in spring. The stems, young growth and immature pods are often brilliant red.

**A. vestita**     Australia
3-4 m
This tall beautiful weeping shrub has soft blue-green foliage and masses of bright yellow flower balls in spring. An outstanding specimen shrub, it is also suitable as a hedge or windbreak plant. It will tolerate drought and frost.

**Acalypha hispida**     India
EUPHORBIACEAE
1,5 m
All the acalyphas succeed well outdoors in warmly temperate to subtropical regions, but in colder areas must be grown in glass houses. Propagate from hardwood or soft tip cuttings in spring. The red-hot cat's tail, sometimes known as the chenille plant, takes its name from the rusty red, tassel-like pendant flower-spikes, up to 350 mm long, borne in summer. It has large, attractive, deep green leaves with paler undersides.

**A. wilkesiana**     Fiji
1,5-2 m
The copper leaf or Fijian fire bush with large variegated red and pink leaves makes a striking accent among green foliaged plants. It has many good varieties and cultivars, the best known 'Marginata' has large, olive-bronze leaves with a distinct rosy-carmine margin. All varieties require good growing conditions, adequate moisture and protection from winds which damage the large leaves.

**Adam's Needle:** see Yucca filamentosa
**Adenium obesum:** see 'Cacti and Succulents', page 280

**Agave americana**     Mexico
AGAVACEAE
1,5 m
Thick, fleshy leaves – their edges toothed and their tips sharply pointed – radiate from the central rosette of the century plant. The golden cultivar 'Marginata', with white or gold

*Abutilon megapotamicum*

*Abutilon* sp.

*Acalypha hispida*
(Red-hot Cat's Tail, or
Chenille Plant)

*Acalypha wilkesiana*
(Fijian Fire Bush)

*Correa alba*          Australia
RUTACEAE
⬇1 m ☼ ⊕
A low hardy compact shrub with oval foliage covered with soft down. The white or sometimes pink flowers in small clusters are produced in winter. Does well in coastal gardens and is useful as a sand-binder.

*Correa reflexa*        Australia
⬇1,5 m ◐ ⊕
There are many lovely forms of this attractive bird attracting species. The ovate leaves are downy and the fuchsia-like tubular flowers are displayed over a long period in autumn,

*Correa reflexa*

winter and spring. Although the flowers can be cream, green or pink, the usual colour is coral-red with yellow anthers. Propagate from cuttings taken in autumn.

*Cotinus coggygria*     Southern Europe, Asia
(Syn. *Rhus cotinus*)
⬇1,5 m ☼ ⊕
A bushy spreading shrub with smooth green leaves which take on lovely ornamental orange and red colourings before falling. Summer flowers, in smoky feathery heads, add further to its attraction. 'Foliis Purpureis', one of the best of all purple-foliaged shrubs, maintains the rich purple-red colour of its

leaves well into autumn. Prune back in winter to produce an abundance of spring foliage.

*Cotoneaster* spp.
ROSACEAE

These spineless shrubs from the northern hemisphere are quite at home in our more temperate regions. All are hardy and easily grown, many species being strikingly attractive with their display of orange-red, crimson or black berries. Most are evergreen, and all are grown from seed, or late summer cuttings. Natural hybridizing occurs and there is some confusion among growers as to the true identity of some species.

*C. X cornubius*       Garden origin
⬇3 m ☼ ⊕ or ⊕
In its true form, this fast-growing, large-leafed hybrid is one of the very best cotoneasters. Heavy, pendulous masses of brilliant red berries are produced all along the arching branches in autumn.

*C. franchetii*         China
⊕ or ⬇3-4 m ☼ ⊕ or ⊕
Semi-evergreen in some areas, this is another fast-growing species with spreading, graceful branches and very downy shoots. Pink summer flowers are followed by bright orange-red, medium-sized berries.

*C. frigidus*         Himalayas
⬇7 m ☼ ⊕ or ⊕
This tall-growing, deciduous species has long oval dull green leaves which have downy undersides when young. White flowers, borne in summer, are followed by an abundance of small, bright red fruits, which persist throughout winter.

*C. horizontalis*        China
⬇500 mm ☼ ⊕ or ⊕
A low-growing evergreen, this species has herring-bone, horizontal branches which spread along the ground when the plant is young and gradually increase in height with age. Pale pink flowers, borne in summer, are followed by bright red berries. *C. horizontalis* makes an excellent specimen for the rock garden.

*C. lacteus*         China
⬇3 m ☼ ⊕ or ⊕
Though tall-growing, this evergreen can also be pruned to make a superb, trimmed hedge. The white summer flowers with their red anthers are followed by masses of small bunches of long-lasting dazzling red berries.

*C. pannosus*         China
⊕ or ⬇4 m ☼ ⊕ or ⊕
A graceful semi-evergreen, its arching branches are covered with small ovate to elliptic leaves. Mid-summer white flowers are followed by large clusters of dull red berries.

*C. salicifolius*        China
⬇3 m ☼ ⊕ or ⊕
Its long, slender, arching branches make this evergreen a graceful shrub for the large garden. Insignifiant summer flowers are followed by masses of bright red autumn berries.

*Pyracantha angustifolia,* a close relative of the cotoneasters

*Crotalaria* sp.

*Crotalaria laburnifolia*                    Australia

🌺 3 m ☼ 🔆

The bird flower grows vigorously, but is at its best in frost-free areas. In temperate to subtropical regions, cut back this evergreen fairly hard after summer flowering. This encourages a second show of the large, greenish-yellow flowers, each shaped like the beak of a bird. It needs a sheltered position, and its branches break easily in the wind. Propagate from root cuttings in spring.

**Croton:** see *Codiaeum variegatum,* 'Indoor and Balcony Plants', page 299

*Crowea exalata*                    Australia
RUTACEAE

🌺 700 mm ☼ to 🔆

This woody plant has star-shaped, white to pink flowers, 2 cm in diameter, in summer and autumn. It is native to the eastern states of Australia, and prefers well-drained soils and full sun to half shade.

**Crown of Thorns:** see *Euphorbia milli*

*Cuphea ignea*                    Mexico
LYTHRACEAE

🌺 500 mm ☼ 🔆

Small and compact, the evergreen cigar bush flowers almost continuously throughout the year, its bright red blooms tipped with purple and white. It is very much at home in the rock garden where it is best mass-planted. It is happiest in frost-free areas. Propagate from cuttings of small side shoots.

*C. micropetala*                    Mexico

🌺 800 mm ☼ 🔆

A much-branched evergreen with oblong leaves and masses of small, tubular flowers. These are scarlet, but yellow at the apex and throat and are borne from late summer through autumn and even into winter in frost-

free areas. A white-flowered variety is also attractive. Propagate from cuttings taken in spring.

*Cussonia paniculata*                    South Africa
ARALIACEAE

🌺 4 m ☼ 🔆

Although this is an evergreen tree, it is included in this section because – in spite of its height – it takes up so little space. A fairly hardy, quick-growing plant, it lends a palm-like quality to whatever position it occupies, be it garden, patio or courtyard. It bears large heads of coarsely-pinnate, lobed but variable leaves. Small, insignificant spikes of yellow flowers are borne in summer. Propagate from cuttings taken in summer and struck in sandy soil.

*Cydonia japonica:* see *Chaenomeles japonica*

*Cytisus albus*                    Spain
FABACEAE

🌺 1,5 m ☼ 🔆

White Spanish broom each year puts up a magnificent spring show of sweetly-scented white flowers. A bush evergreen, it is quick growing. Hybrid 'Lilac Time', bears pretty lilac-pink flowers.

*C. X racemosus*                    Garden origin

🌺 1,5-2 m ☼ 🔆

This evergreen hybrid is an old-time favourite. Scented, bright-yellow flowers are freely produced in spring and summer. Ideally this is a subject for the large garden. Propagate from cuttings of firm side shoots.

*Cuphea micropetala* (Large Cigar Flower)

*Daphne odora*                                    China
THYMELAEACEAE
🌐 1,5 m ◑ ☀
Most popular of the daphnes, this lovely
winter flowering shrub bears waxy reddish
buds opening to pinkish white beautifully
fragrant flowers. 'Rubra' is especially lovely
with tight clusters of fragrant flowers of a
reddish-purplish shade. As a cut-flower these
will last a long time indoors. Var. 'alba' has
pure white flowers, often larger, but equally
fragrant. All daphnes are lime-haters and
require a well drained rich soil, preferably a
little elevated to prevent collar rot. Do not
overwater, especially in winter. Propagate
from cuttings.

*Darwinia citriodora*                         Australia
MYRTACEAE
🌐 1 m ☀ ☀
This very attractive native plant has a greyish-
green foliage which emits a lemony scent
when crushed. The pretty reddish flowers
appear over a long period in spring and are
useful in attracting birds to the garden. Easily
propagated from cuttings taken in early
spring or autumn.

*Deutzia* spp.
HYDRANGEACEAE
Of the several species, varieties and cultivars
of bridal wreath which are cultivated, all are
deciduous and free flowering forming bushes
ranging from 1 m to 3 m high. Pruning is not
necessary unless to shape. Will tolerate
extreme cold. Propagate from hardwood cuttings taken in either autumn or winter.

*D. X lemoinei*                                  France
🌐 2 m ☀ ☀
Stemming from the crossing of *D. gracilis* with
*D. parviflora*, this hybrid is especially valued
for its pyramidal panicles of pure white
flowers borne in spring. It is very free flowering and grows taller than most bridal wreaths.

*D. longifolia*                                   China
🌐 3 m ☀ ☀
This striking species is the tallest growing of
the cultivated bridal wreaths. An outstanding
variety is 'veitchii', which in summer bears
large, rich rosy-purple flowers.

*D. X rosea*                                      France
🌐 1 m ☀ ☀
Compact and with arching branches, this
hybrid is the result of crossing *D. gracilis* and
*D. purpurascens*. Bell-shaped, soft rose
flowers are borne in spring and summer.

*D. scabra*                                       Japan
🌐 3 m ☀ ☀
A deciduous shrub, that bears large single
pure white flowers. It is adaptable to most
soils and positions and is drought and frost
resistant.

*Daphne odora*

*Dichorisandra thyrsiflora* and right, close-up of flower

*Dodonaea viscosa* (Hop Bush)

**Dichorisandra thyrsiflora**            Brazil
COMMELINACEAE
⊕ 1,5 m ◐ ⊛
Reed-like, with dark green, sheathed leaves, this evergreen bears 170 mm-long, terminal branches of glistening, waxy dark blue flowers in summer and autumn. A lovely subject for a shady position in the temperate and subtropical areas. It will not tolerate frost. Propagate by division or from stem-cuttings.

*Diosma ericoides: see Coleonema pulchrum*
*Diplacus glutinusus: see Mimulus*
*aurantiacus*

**Dodonaea viscosa**    Australia, New Zealand
SAPINDACEAE
⊕ 3 m ☼ ⊛
Grown for its foliage, the hop bush is extremely accommodating, succeeding almost anywhere outside the tropics. 'Purpurea' makes a fairly upright bush and has attractive green-purple foliage which, depending on the season, is sometimes intensely purple. Though their flowers are insignificant, both species and cultivar add interest and colour to the garden. Propagate from semi-hardwood cuttings in spring.

**Dombeya tiliacea**            Africa
(Syn. *D. dregeana*)
STERCULIACEAE
⊕ or ⊛ 3 m ☼ ⊛
Soft-wooded and openly rounded, this semi-evergreen frequently adopts a deciduous habit and is suited to frost-free areas only. Its rosy flowers are borne in large umbels in late winter and early spring. Similar in habit and equally attractive is *D. natalensis* with downy, poplar-like foliage and fragrant white flowers. Propagate from hardwood cuttings taken in spring or early summer.

**Dryandra formosa**            Australia
PROTEACEAE
⊕ 3 m ☼ ⊛
This beautiful shrub is noted for its attractive narrow divided foliage as well as the showy fragrant flowers it produces in winter and spring. The flowers are a rich yellowish-orange and are lovely as cut flowers in water or in dried arrangements. All dryandras require excellent drainage in sandy soil with a little lime. They do not like root disturbance and newly planted specimens may require staking to prevent wind damage. Propagate from cuttings in sandy moist soil or by heat treated seeds.

**D. praemorsa**            Australia
⊕ 2 m ◐ ⊛
The cut-leaf dryandra with broad prickly leaves and large yellow flowers is considered the easiest dryandra to grow in the eastern states. It is an excellent bushy specimen shrub and will attract nectar-seeking birds to the garden.

**D. speciosa**            Australia
⊕ 1 m ☼ to ◐ ⊛
This is a particularly attractive shrub for the small garden or rockery. It bears pendant, browny-pink silky flowers in autumn and winter which make an outstanding cut flower.

**Duranta erecta**        Mexico, West Indies
(Syn. *D. repens*)
VERBENACEAE
⊕ 3 m ☼ ⊛
Semi-hardy and relatively fast growing, this species is suited only to the large garden. Numerous lilac-blue flowers borne over a long period in summer, are followed by golden-yellow berries. 'Alba' has white

flowers and golden fruits, while the leaves of 'Variegata' have silvery-cream margins, and its blue flowers are followed by golden berries. Propagate from hardwood cuttings in late winter or early autumn.

**Elaeagnus pungens**            Japan
ELAEAGNACEAE
⊕ 1,5 m ☼ ⊛
The cultivars developed from this spreading evergreen species have long, intertwining branches which are clothed with leathery oval or oblong leaves. In 'Aurea' their margins are edged with gold, while the leaves of 'Aureo-variegata' have a bold central blotch and those of 'Argenteum-marginata' have a sil-

*Duranta erecta*

very margin. All are worthy of a place in the garden, particularly where a colour association is sought. All are very hardy and best suited to the colder parts though they also succeed in temperate regions. Propagate from semi-hardwood cuttings in spring.

**English Holly:** see *Ilex aquifolium*
**English Lavender:** see *Lavandula angustifolia*
**Ericas:** see Special Spread, pages 140-142
*Erythrina* spp.: see 'Trees', page 210

*Escallonia* spp.           South America
ESCALLONIACEAE
✿ 2 m ☼ ✿

It is as hybrids and cultivars that this group of evergreens are better known to Australian gardeners. The species *E.* X *langleyensis* is the parent of many fine cultivars, 'Apple Blossom', a dwarf, with large trusses of soft pink flowers; 'C. F. Ball', with carmine-red flowers; 'Donard Seedling', white; 'Donard Brilliance', dark crimson; 'Slieve Donard' with apple-blossom pink blooms. All make rounded bushy shrubs which require only pruning to shape after flowering. They are readily propagated from hard or semi-soft cuttings taken in late autumn or winter.

*Eucalyptus kruseana*         Australia
MYRTACEAE
✿ 3 m ☼ ✿

This very beautiful ornamental shrub has attractive stem-clasping, blue-grey rounded foliage and clusters of creamy yellow flowers in autumn to winter. It is drought resistant and will tolerate a little frost. Prune only lightly to maintain shape.

*E. rhodantha*               Australia
✿ 3 m ☼ ✿

This lovely shrub has silvery, broadly-oval foliage, which alone is enough to ensure it a place in every garden. But its flowers, freely-produced throughout summer, are strikingly attractive. These are large (about 70 mm across) balls of rich rosy-red wi h predominant golden anthers. A similar species is *E. macrocarpa*, the most ornamental of all eucalypts, both in foliage and flowers. The flowers of this species are huge (up to 120 mm across) and pinkish-red, arising from a highly ornamental bud. These species like a deep, sandy, well-drained soil. They are drought resistant and thrive in drier climates.

*Euonymus japonica*            Japan
CELASTRACEAE
✿ 2 m ☼ ✿

This species is an extremely useful evergreen with shiny, thick leaves. It may be grown as an upright single specimen or trimmed to a hedge (as low as a metre), a role in which it has proved particularly popular at the coast. Ornamentally, it is better known in its varie-

gated forms, of which the following are among the most satisfying: 'Albo-marginatus' has leaves with a thin white margin; in 'Aureus' the leaf centre is gold surrounded by a thin green margin, but as this feature is liable to revert to type, prune out all plain green growths; while 'Ovatus-aureus' is my favourite, having an oval leaf with a broad margin of rich yellow.

All these cultivars are smaller growing than the type and bear insignificant flowers. Propagate from hardwood or semi-hardwood cuttings taken in spring.

*Euphorbia* spp.
EUPHORBIACEAE
The genus *Euphorbia* is huge, containing more than 1000 species, widely distributed over the world. All produce a milky latex, which can be poisonous in some of the species. The flower-like arrangements are not flowers, but a series of highly-coloured bracts surrounding a group of inconspicuous flowers. Some species are succulents and are often mistaken for cacti.

*E. fulgens*                Mexico
✿ 1 m ☼ ✿

This desirable little evergreen will not tolerate any frost and is suited to warmer areas only. In winter and spring its long, arching branches are clothed with clusters of small flowers, whose bracts are a brilliant scarlet. It grows to a graceful bush about a metre tall, and eventually reaches a similar spread. Propagate from hardwood cuttings in summer.

*E. jacquiniiflora:* see *E. fulgens*

*E. milii*               Madagascar
✿ 600 mm ☼ ✿

Widely known and cultivated, the low-growing crown of thorns is useful in the rock garden or cavity wall, and is often used as a low hedge in coastal areas. Its arching to horizontal stems are heavily thorned and bear more or less terminal, emerald green leaves. Though the flowers, borne in winter, are small, they are surrounded by very colourful, orange-scarlet bracts. Propagate from stem cuttings in spring.

*E. pulcherrima*             Mexico
✿ 2 m ☼ ✿

Poinsettias are worth growing in frost-free areas. Though light frost will not kill them, it will damage the coloured bracts which appear throughout winter on the large bare stems of this deciduous species. The colours of the bracts vary from singles in white, yellow and through salmon and pink to red, and those of the doubles are mostly red and vary considerably in quality and size, according to the variety or cultivar. Before the leaves appear in spring and immediately after the bracts have fallen or faded, prune poinsettias hard back to encourage strong shoots which will bear the following year's terminal flowers. Poinsettias are often grown in pots for indoor winter decoration. The 'Paul Mikkelsen' strain will 'flower' freely in pots, holding its bracts for five or six weeks.

*Euonymus* sp.

*Euphorbia pulcherrima* (Poinsettia)

◀ *Dryandra formosa*

*Fabiana imbricata*                                Chile
SOLANACEAE
🌓 2,5 m ☼ 🕸

This hardy, heath-like evergreen bears white, bell-shaped flowers in great profusion during summer, and is a worthwhile subject for the temperate, to cooler and very cold, areas. Propagate this and the following species from hardwood cuttings in spring.

*F. violacea*                                      Japan
🌓 1,5-2 m ☼ 🕸

This species is very similar to *F. imbricata*, but is more spreading, and bears flowers varying from pale mauve to a bluish-lilac.

*Fatsia japonica*                                  Japan
ARALIACEAE
🌓 3-4 m 🕸 🕸

Usually cultivated as a spreading bush, the evergreen rice paper plant or figleaf palm may be trained into a single-stemmed tree whose thick stem shows the prominent scars

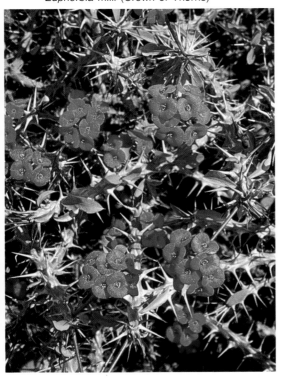

*Mussaenda erythrophylla*

*Euphorbia milii* (Crown of Thorns)

of fallen leaf stems. It has glossy green, creamy white inconspicuous flowers and fruit of small black berries. This handsome plant is well worth growing for the bold effect of its foliage. It thrives in cool to warm temperate areas, and is propagated from seed or stem cuttings taken in autumn.

**Featherhead:** see *Phylica pubescens*

*Feijoa sellowiana*                         South America
MYRTACEAE
🌓 2,5-3 m ☼ 🕸

A strong, upright evergreen, the fruit salad plant, or pineapple guava, has attractive leathery foliage which is dark green above and felted white beneath. It is quite hardy and also succeeds in temperate regions. The dark crimson, summer flowers, not unlike those of some eucalypts, have crowded, long stamens. The flowers are followed by large, berry-like fruits, which many consider a delicacy. As with the flowers, these fruits are mainly hidden by the foliage. Propagate from seed or hardwood cuttings, in spring.

**Figleaf Palm:** see *Fatsia japonica*
**Fijian Fire Bush:** see *Acalypha wilkesiana*
**Fire Thorn:** see *Pyracantha coccinea*
**Flowering Quince:** see *Chaenomeles japonica*

*Forsythia* X *intermedia* 'Spectabilis'    Garden
OLEACEAE                                          origin
🌓 2 m ☼ 🕸

This deciduous hybrid is excellent, especially for the very cold parts of the country. In spring, immediately before the leaves appear, deep, golden-yellow flowers are borne all along the arching branches. These are particularly profuse when a warm spring follows a very cold winter. Prune back hard after flowering, and propagate from hardwood cuttings in summer.

*F. suspensa*                                      China
🌓 2 m ☼ 🕸

This deciduous parent of 'Spectabilis' enjoys similar conditions to its offspring, but is rambling and needs some form of support. Golden-yellow, tubular, bell-shaped flowers are produced during spring and again intermittently, throughout summer and autumn. Because the golden bell occupies considerable space, it is suitable only for the large garden – there are other selected forms preferred to the type including 'Atrocaulis' with slender branches that can be trained over an archway and the flowers a pale-lemon colour.

**French Tamarisk:** see *Tamarix gallica*
**Fruit Salad Plant:** see *Feijoa sellowiana*

*Fuchsia magellanica*                              Chile
ONAGRACEAE
🌓 1,5 m 🕸 🕸

This hardy species is a large free-flowering shrub. The long, arching branches bear an abundance of dainty pendulous flowers in the leaf axils. The bright red calyx encloses purplish petals with prominent stamens. The

many varieties available include *F. magellanica* 'Alba', which has a white calyx with pale pink petals. Though most fuchsia species are indigenous to Central and South America, it is in New Zealand that the two extremes of the genus are found – the deciduous *F. excorticata*, a tree reaching 10 m or more and with papery peeling bark, and *F. procumbens* a wiry, evergreen trailer.

*F.* X *hybrida*                              Garden origin
🌓 1 m 🕸 🕸

Members of this group of more than 2000 evergreen hybrids have their parentage in the South American species *F. magellanica* and the Mexican *F. fulgens*. With so many internationally-registered cultivars to choose from, it would be pointless to describe any in detail; suffice it to say that these hybrids come in doubles and singles and in an incredible range of colours. Some are strong, upright-growing and may be cultivated as standards; some are miniature or procumbent; and others have a lax habit which suits them ideally to hanging baskets.

Fuchsias may be grown in most climatic conditions, but will not tolerate severe frost and will rarely survive a hot, subtropical coastal situation. In colder areas give them winter protection, but in very hot parts it is wisest to regard them as annuals, renewing them each year and allowing them to flower to exhaustion. Generally, they enjoy semi-shade, are ideal plants and are very successful in the cool greenhouse.

Fuchsias are rather greedy and like plenty of extra food during active growth and while flowering. A friable, free-draining soil is ideal. Pinch out the growing tips of young plants frequently, to encourage a very bushy growth – the more branched and bushier the plant, the more abundant will be its flowers. Soft tips, 60-100 mm long and with two or three nodes, root readily in early spring. Plant them in washed river sand, under bell jars, or assisted by a mist spray.

*Gardenia globosa:* see *Rothmannia globosa*

*Gardenia augusta*                          China, Japan
(Syn. *G. jasminoides*)
RUBIACEAE
🌓 1,5 m ☼ or 🕸 🕸

This bushy evergreen is suited to frost-free areas. It is the most common species found in cultivation and is the popular fragrant gardenia of the floral world. The white, thick-petalled flowers appear near the ends of the shoots and the variety 'Florida' produces double flowers. Gardenias require constant warmth, shelter, plenty of water and feeding at least once a month. Propagate from cuttings taken in late winter.

*G. thunbergia*                              South Africa
🌓 2 m ☼ 🕸

The tree gardenia is a desirable and exceptionally beautiful shrub which succeeds best in temperate to subtropical areas. Solitary, large, white terminal flowers which are sweetly-scented appear usually in autumn.

Garland Spiraea: see *Spiraea* X *arguta*

*Fuchsia corymbiflora* 'Marinka'

*Rhododendron* hybrid

*Fuchsia* hybrid 'Winston Churchill'

*Gardenia thunbergia*

*Fuchsia* hybrid 'Mrs Rundle'

**Garrya elliptica**  United States
GARRYACEAE
🌑 1,5 m ☼ ⊕
This hardy evergreen's male plants produce the highly ornamental, pendant catkins of silky grey to sulphur yellow. These appear for several weeks in winter. The female catkins are shorter and less showy and for this reason the male form only is propagated. This is an outstanding decorative winter-flowering shrub. Propagate from hardwood cuttings in late summer.

**Genista monosperma**  Spain, North Africa
FABACEAE
🌑 2 m ☼
This species is under revision and may be classified as *Retama monosperma*. It is most spectacular when in full bloom. Deciduous and broadly bushy in spring it becomes a mass of white, sweetly scented pea-shaped flowers, borne on long arching branches. Propagate from semi-hardwood cuttings in autumn.

**Geraldton Wax-Flower:** see *Chamelaucium uncinatum*
**Giant Protea:** see *Protea cynaroides*, page 150

**Glory Tree:** see *Clerodendrum philippinum*
**Golden Bell:** see *Forsythia suspensa*
**Golden Elder:** see *Sambucus nigra* 'Aurea'
**Golden Privet:** see *Ligustrum ovalifolium* 'Aureo-variegatum'

**Grevillea alpina**  Australia
PROTEACEAE
🌑 1 m ☼ ⊕
This small variable shrub is one of the oldest grevilleas in cultivation. It varies in habit, leaf shape and flower colour, but most of its forms are well worth cultivating. It will tolerate very cold conditions and during the growing period is nearly always in bloom. The spidery flowers range from red and yellow, to white pink or yellow.
    This species is a member of a large genus of decorative Australian shrubs. Many species are in cultivation and have proved themselves reliable and attractive ornamental shrubs, mostly with bright flowers and attractive foliage. A number of species are low-growing, suited to the small garden or rockery, while others are tall growing specimen plants. Many species produce excellent cut flowers and most attract native birds to the garden. Generally grevilleas are winter and spring flowering, and prefer a well-drained soil in full sun, with little root disturbance. Propagation is from cuttings taken in mid to late summer.

**G. banksii**  Australia
🌑 3 m ☼ ⊕
This upright shrub from Queensland is a handsome specimen plant for frost-free areas. It bears large heads of bright red flowers for most of the year. Foliage is dark green and deeply lobed. There is also a creamy-white flowered form.

**G. baueri**  Australia
🌑 1 m ☼ ⊕
This bright winter flowering species is usually a dense rounded shrub with several forms. The flower colour is pink to deep red and the new growth is often bronze. Lightly prune in early summer.

**G. caleyi**  Australia
🌑 2 m ☼ ⊕
This beautiful spreading shrub bears red tooth-brush type flowers from late winter to summer. Its handsome, bold, deeply-cut foliage further enhances its appeal. Prune regularly to encourage compact shape.

**G. juniperina**  Australia
🌑 2 m ☼ ⊕
This very hardy plant has finely pointed

leaves and apricot or red flowers produced in early winter and spring. Prostrate forms suited to rockeries and tubs are available from nurseries.

*G. 'Robyn Gordon'*　　　　Australia
🌑 1 m ☼ 🐦
This popular hybrid is widely cultivated for its continuous display of large red flowers for most of the year. It is a hardy, beautiful, compact specimen shrub and attracts native birds to the garden. Pruning will encourage dense growth.

*G. rosmarinifolia*　　　　Australia
🌑 2 m ☼ 🐦
This dense growing, spreading shrub has narrow dark green foliage and spidery, rosy-red flowers for most of the year. An easily grown shrub, it will tolerate most soils and conditions. Prune to maintain shape. 'Canberra Gem' is a hybrid between forms of *G. rosmarinifolia* and *G. juniperina*. It has a compact habit, needle-like leaves and bears its rich red, spider-like flowers in pendant clusters.

*G. sericea*　　　　Australia
🌑 1.5 m ☼ 🐦
This upright plant bears its deep pink spider flowers in terminal clusters for most of the year.

*G. speciosa*
🌑 2 m ☼ 🐦
Fast growing and bird attracting, this outstanding species produces bright red spider flowers in spring and summer.

*G. victoriae*　　　　Australia
🌑 3 m ☼ 🐦
The royal grevillea is a rounded shrub, with grey-green leaves. The marvellous rusty-red flowers in pendulous clusters appear in winter and spring. This hardy plant will grow in moist conditions and tolerates frost and snow.

*Hakea corymbosa*　　　　Australia
PROTEACEAE
🌑 1 m ☼ 🐦
This compact bushy shrub has rigid pointed leaves and terminal clusters of pale yellow

*Grevillea juniperina*

*Grevillea* 'Robyn Gordon'

▼ *Grevillea juniperina*

flowers. There are many forms of hakeas in this large genus of some 140 Australian natives. They vary from small to medium woody shrubs to small trees, with attractive foliage and flowers. All have woody seed cases and these often form an attractive part of the plant. These are great in dried arrangements. Hakeas are generally hardy and prefer open, sunny well-drained positions. They are propagated from seed.

*H. nodosa*                                    Australia
🌳 3 m ☼ 🌀
A very hardy plant which is quick growing and will tolerate dry or moist situations. This plant bears clusters of yellow flowers along the branches in autumn and winter, followed by attractive woody fruits.

*H. purpurea*                                  Australia
🌳 1.5 m ☼ 🌀
A showy species that has proved hardy in most soils and full sun. The sharp needle-like leaves are often forked and in spring the bush is covered with clusters of deep crimson flowers.

*H. sericea*                                   Australia
🌳 2 m ☼ 🌀
This erect bushy shrub has sharply pointed, needle-like leaves and white or pink flowers in winter and spring. The attractive woody fruits are large and prominent.

*Hebe speciosa*                         New Zealand
SCROPHULARIACEAE
🌳 1 m ☼ 🌀
The genus *Hebe*, of 100 or more species, was formerly included in the genus *Veronica*. Mainly from New Zealand, this useful group of shrubs are attractive in landscape work or as low hedges. Winter pruning is essential to maintain a good shapely bush. Propagation is easily carried out from cuttings at the end of the flowering season. *H. speciosa*, a desirable species, with deep green foliage and purple brushes of flowers has given rise to a number of brightly coloured cultivars such as 'Andersonii Variegata' with spikes of lavender-blue flowers and variegated foliage; 'Autumn Glory', with deep blue blooms; and many others whose flowers range from purple and deep red to pale lilac, pink and white.

*Helianthemum nummularium*              Europe
CISTACEAE
🌳 500 mm ☼ 🌀
Delightful little hardy evergreens, rock roses are particularly suited to the rock garden, where they enjoy a well-drained soil with plenty of lime, and full sunlight. Small, rose-like flowers are borne throughout summer. Garden forms are available in a wide range of flower colours – white, sulphur yellow, buttercup yellow, bright red, coppery red, pale rose and crimson, as well as many intermediate shades – in both single and double form. Though hardy they will also succeed in the cooler temperate regions. All are derived largely from seedling variations of *H. nummularium*, or from hybrids of this and closely allied species. Propagate from semi-soft-

wood cuttings, assisted by gentle bottom heat, in autumn.

*Heliotropium arborescens*                   Peru
BORAGINACEAE
🌳 600 mm ☼ 🌀
An attractive, tender little evergreen, cherry pie will grow taller than its usual 600 mm in warmly temperate areas, where it can be cultivated as a standard. A number of dark-leafed varieties and cultivars are available, and flowers range from white to pale mauve and deep violet-purple. Propagate from semi-soft cuttings taken in summer, after flowering. Seedsmen now offer heliotrope seeds which flower in mixed colours and are grown and treated as perennials; the species *H. arborescens* figures prominently in their parentage.

*H. peruvianum:* see *H. arborescens*

*Hibiscus mutabilis*                           China
MALVACEAE
🌳 3 m ☼ to ◑ 🌀
The quick- and strong-growing, semi-deciduous tree hollyhock needs the space of a large garden. Though it will grow in favoured inland areas, it is frost tender and is best suited to temperate and subtropical parts. The pink buds of the autumn flowers are 70-100 mm across and open to reveal white blooms, initially flushing to pink, and deepening to dark red by evening. Sow seeds or propagate from semi-hardwood cuttings in spring.

*H. rosa-sinensis*                            China
🌳 2 m ☼ 🌀
Though there are many other beautiful species, *H. rosa-sinensis* and its many splendid varieties and cultivars are closest to the Australian gardener's heart. Its numerous, named garden forms are all showy evergreens, some even flamboyant in their dazzling abundance of blooms. At times throughout summer and autumn these almost cloak the shrubs, and in warmly temperate to subtropical parts flower well into the winter. Liberal amounts of water and fertilisers should be applied during flowering. Bushes are best if pruned back to near half height each winter to maintain a good shape and encourage good blooms the following summer. Though a few varieties are propagated by grafting, most are propagated from hardwood cuttings taken in winter.
    Among the outstanding cultivars are 'Agnes Gault', with single, bright satin-pink flowers; 'Camdenii', one of the most hardy reds, bright scarlet, single flowers; 'Conqueror', with buff-yellow flowers with crimson base; 'Mrs George Davis', an extra-large double with cerise-red flowers; 'Norman Scoble', rich apricot double; 'Wilder's White', large white single with crimson pistils.

*H. schizopetalus*              Tropical East Africa
🌳 3 m ☼ 🌀
This tall, glabrous evergreen has slender, arching branches bearing brilliant orange-red flowers in summer. Each bloom has recurved, finely-cut petals and protruding stamens. It is suited only to larger gardens in temperate to subtropical areas.

*Hebe speciosa* 'Purple Queen'

*H. syriacus*                                   Asia
🌳 2 m ☼ 🌀
The hardiest species, the shrubby althea or Syrian Rose makes an upright, deciduous shrub, and although not as flamboyant as some varieties of *H. rosa-sinensis*, is still colourful and free flowering and is able to withstand cold climates. Available in white, shades of pink, soft red, mauve and violet-blue, its mid-summer flowers – single, semi-double or double – are borne over a reasonably long period. Propagate from hardwood cuttings in winter.

*Hibiscus rosa-sinensis*

Hibiscus schizopetalus

Hibiscus rosa-sinensis 'White Wings'

Hibiscus rosa-sinensis 'Princess Marina'

# ERICA SPECIES

Of more than 640 species of the genus *Erica* some 600 belong to South Africa, and towards the end of the 18th century, when Masson and Thunberg were busily identifying new species, the 'Cape Heaths' as they were popularly known, were much in vogue in Europe. Records show that by 1811, no fewer than 186 species of *Erica* were being grown at Kew. However, the difficulties of growing these 'exotica' in the cold northern climate – often requiring greenhouse protection – led to a gradual decline in their popularity.

And while the South African ericas do not take kindly to the colder climate, their northern relatives – the European heaths and heathers – can be grown without difficulty in the coldest parts of Australia.

South African species like warm conditions and full sun. When cultivated in summer-rainfall areas they should be watered generously during winter. They are more showy than the species from Europe and, although comparatively shorter-lived, cover a gratifying range of colour and variety. All ericas may be propagated from seed sown in spring or from semi-softwood cuttings taken after flowering.

Ericas are related to rhododendrons and most species will not tolerate lime or animal manure. Nor do they like root disturbance. They are peat-loving plants and enjoy a humus enriched soil. Often they are grown in a separate raised garden bed where these special requirements can be easily maintained.

There are many favourites from the ERICACEAE family. Following is a selection of the best known.

Erica bowieana and below close-up of flower

*Erica* X *autumnalis*       Garden origin

Autumn heath is a hybrid, with tiny narrow foliage, to 1 m. Its early flowers are masses of tiny, deep rose bells.

*E. bauera:* see *E. bowieana*

*E. bowieana*       South Africa

There are white, mauve and rosy-mauve forms of this strong growing species. Though it bears masses of flowers throughout most of the year, this erica is at its best in early summer. It is inclined to be straggly and reaches a height of 1.5 m or more, but is useful for cut-flower decoration.

*E. canaliculata*       South Africa
  (Syn. *E. melanthera*)

One of the loveliest of the ericas and probably one of the most popular and hardiest of the South African species. It forms a neat bush to 2 m and bears

*Protea caffra* (Highveld Protea)

*Protea scolymocephala*

*Protea grandiceps* (Peach Protea)

*Protea cynaroides* (Giant, or King Protea)

*Protea aurea*, another fine cultivated species

*Protea scolymocephala*

Nerium oleander 'rubra' (Oleander)

Nerium oleander        Mediterranean
APOCYNACEAE
🌼 2 m ☼ ⊛

A handsome, drought-resistant evergreen, the oleander is noted not only for its summer flowers but for its flexible branches bearing long, leathery and tapering leaves. Its masses of single and double flowers range from white, through cream to a vivid apricot and from shades of pink to deep red. A word of caution here – the oleander's sap and leaves are poisonous and can prove fatal to children; there are also recorded instances of people being poisoned by meat cooked on the embers of its branches. A variety with fine

Olearia pimeleoides

cream-variegated foliage is available, but is not outstanding. Propagate from semi-firm tips or semi-hardwood cuttings.

**New Zealand Flax:** see *Phormium tenax*
**New Zealand Manuka:** see *Leptospermum scoparium*
**Ngaio:** see *Myoporum laetum*
**Oak-leaved Hydrangea:** see *Hydrangea quercifolia*

Ochna atropurpurea      South Africa
OCHNACEAE
🌼 1,5 m ☼ ⊛

The carnival bush, a hardy evergreen, grows best in a hot, sunny position. The primrose yellow flowers are borne in spring and are followed by scarlet calyces in which shining black fruits nestle. Both fruits and calyces last well into summer. This is an unusual and thoroughly worthwhile shrub. Propagate from fresh seed, sown immediately, or from half-ripe cuttings assisted by bottom heat.

**Oleander:** see *Nerium oleander*

Olearia lirata           Australia
ASTERACEAE
🌼 5 m ● ⊛

The snow daisybush is a graceful tall shrub best suited to a shaded position where ample water is provided. In summer the bush is covered in large heads of white daisy flowers. It will grow in most soils and is frost hardy. Propagate either by cuttings or seeds.

O. microphylla          Australia
🌼 1 m ☼ ⊛

This small hardy shrub has very small leaves and bears masses of small white daisy flowers in spring. Prune regularly to encourage compact growth.

Osmanthus fragrans    Himalayas, China,
OLEACEAE                 Japan
🌼 1,5 m ☼ ⊛

This relatively hardy, compact, evergreen bears clusters of fragrant, small white flowers in spring. The finely-toothed leaves are oblong-lanceolate and have slender points. Propagate this and *O. heterophyllus* from cuttings of semi-firm wood in later summer.

O. heterophyllus       Japan, Taiwan
🌼 3 m ☼ ⊛

This very hardy and quick-growing evergreen has holly-like foliage with leaves in opposite not alternate, pairs. Shepherd's holly bears clusters of white, fragrant flowers in autumn. The leaves of 'Aureo-marginatus' are margined with yellow, while those of 'purpurea' are purple, especially when young.

O. ilicifolius: see O. heterophyllus

Pachystachys lutea          Peru
ACANTHACEAE
🌼 1 m ☼ ⊛

The beautiful, evergreen golden candles has attractive and broadly-lanceolate, dark green leaves which contrast well with the erect, terminal inflorescences whose rich golden-yellow bracts burst with a profusion of yellow-

Ochna pulchra is similar to O. atropurpurea

Pachystachys lutea (Golden Candles)

powdered, white flowers borne almost continuously throughout the year. In warmly temperate and subtropical areas it may be grown outdoors in a sheltered, shady position, and makes a fine subject for pots and tubs. Prune back hard after flowering. Propagate from cuttings of firm, terminal shoots in spring.

**Parasol Flower:** see *Holmskioldia sanguinea*
**Peach Protea:** see *Protea grandiceps*, page 150

Pentas lanceolata      Tropical Africa
RUBIACEAE
🌼 1,5 m ☼ ⊛

For favoured inland parts and temperate to subtropical areas, this *Pentas* species, in all its various colours, is one of the most rewarding evergreens and, if lightly pruned after each flush of flowering, the bushes will bloom most of the year – particularly in very warm situations. Small flowers are produced in coryms, as much as 80 mm across, and range in colour from white, cerise, pale and deep pink to shades of red, lilac, magenta and purple. These are excellent for floral arrangements. Propagate from cuttings of slightly firm shoots.

**Petrea volubilis**      Mexico
VERBENACEAE
🌳 1 m ☼ ⊕
The beautiful evergreen purple wreath which twines and builds itself to form a shrub, may also be trained as a climber, when it will reach a height of 5 m or more. The rich violet-blue flowers, usually with lilac sepals, are borne on the ends of long, arching shoots. In the warmer, favoured areas, both inland and coastal, it flowers profusely several times a year. Elsewhere its blooms are confined to summer. It has tough, leathery leaves. A pure white variety, although not as spectacular as the blue, is nevertheless worth growing. Propagate from cuttings of firm shoots.

**Phaenocoma prolifera**      South Africa
ASTERACEAE
🌳 500 mm ☼ ⊕
A small-growing, hard-wooded evergreen with glabrous, scale-like leaves, this is a fine 'everlasting' whose daisy-like flowers range from white to deep pink. It blooms more or less continuously from late spring until early autumn and is at its flowering peak in summer. Under cultivation it requires a well-drained situation in full sun and is at home in a rock garden with its roots rammed against a rock. Propagate from seed or cuttings of firm, young side shoots.

**Philadelphus coronarius**      Asia Minor
HYDRANGEACEAE    South Eastern Europe
🌳 2,5 m ☼ ⊕
Very widely grown, particularly in the colder parts, mock orange will also succeed in temperate areas of the country. It is prized for its masses of creamy-white, orange-like blossoms. These heavily-perfumed flowers are produced in early summer. There are a number of cultivars and hybrids of this deciduous species. Prune heavily immediately after flowering – this helps to keep a good shape and ensures flowering wood for the following season. Propagate from hardwood cuttings.

**Phlomis fruticosa**      Eastern Europe
LAMIACEAE
🌳 1 m ☼ ⊕
An old-fashioned favourite and member of the salvia family, Jerusalem sage has evergreen, silvery foliage and produces circular tiers of yellow flowers in summer. It is an absolute 'must' for foliage contrast grouping and it will stand almost any climatic conditions, even salt-laden wind. Propagate from semi-firm cuttings.

*Pentas lanceolata*

*Petrea volubilis* (Purple Wreath)

◀ *Philadelphus coronarius* (Mock Orange)

*Phaenocoma prolifera*

*Phormium tenax*                    New Zealand
AGAVACEAE
🌷 1,5 m ☼ ✇
Although it is more at home in perpetually moist soil (see also Chapter 15, 'Water Gardens', page 274), New Zealand flax will grow under ordinary garden conditions. Its flexible, sword-like leaves are 2-3 m long, and its panicles of dull red flowers, borne in summer, are more interesting than showy. 'Atropurpureum' has rich, plum-purple foliage; 'Rubrum' is more dwarf, with coppery to

*Phlomis fruticosa* (Jerusalem Sage)

purplish-violet foliage; and 'Variegatum' has leaves striped creamy-yellow and green. Propagate by simple division.

*Photinia glabra* 'Rubens'                Asia
ROSACEAE
🌷 or 🌑 4 m ☼ ✇
This species has found its way into Australian gardens, being most highly valued for its attractive foliage. *P. glabra* 'Rubens' is a neat bushy shrub. Its new growth in spring is a rich coppery red, later turning to dark green. This is an outstanding species in its colour performance. *P. X fraseri* 'Robusta' is fast-growing to 3 m, its large leaves when young are a brilliant bronze-red.

*Phygelius capensis*                South Africa
SCROPHULARIACEAE
🌷 1 m ☼ ✇
Thick, angular stems and finely-toothed ovate-lanceolate leaves distinguish the Cape figwort or Cape fuchsia, an evergreen which, even cut back by severe frosts, will recover quickly in spring. In summer it bears scarlet, tubular flowers, slightly enlarged at the mouth. 'Coccineus' has brighter scarlet flowers and, like the species, is worthy of a place in every garden. Propagate mostly from firm stem cuttings in summer.

*Phylica pubescens*                South Africa
RHAMNACEAE
🌷 1,3 m ☼ ✇
This attractive small bush is densely covered with slender, hairy, yellowish-green leaves,

while the growing tips of each stem and branch are capped with rosettes of feathery, golden-yellow 'floral' leaves. These are produced during midwinter. Known as the featherhead or flannel bush, this species prefers a compost-rich soil and frequent water from autumn to spring. Prune back after flowering to preserve good shape and prolong life. Propagate from stem cuttings in autumn.

*Phyllanthus nivosus:* see *Breynia disticha*

*Phylica pubescens* (Featherhead)

*Pimelea rosea*

*Pimelea ferruginea*                Australia
THYMELAEACEAE
🌷 1 m ☼ ✇
Often seen in cultivation, this showy native has oval glossy leaves and bears its plentiful heads of pink flowers at the ends of the branches in spring and summer. It is a neat compact bush and should be pruned after flowering to maintain shape. Propagate from cuttings.

*P. rosea*                        Australia
🌷 1 m ☼ ✇
In spring, this handsome little bush bears

abundant heads of pink, sometimes white, flowers at the tips of the branches. Needs a sunny or partly shaded position.

**Pincushion:** see *Leucospermum bolusii*
**Pineapple Guava:** see *Feijoa sellowiana*

*Pittosporum crassifolium*          New Zealand
PITTOSPORACEAE
🌷 2,5 m ☼ ✇
Frequently grown as an evergreen windbreak or hedge, karo is as much at home in parts where frosts are not too severe as it is facing salt-laden winds at the coast. Brown terminal panicles of fragrant flowers are borne in spring, but karo is grown mainly for its glossy green, obovate foliage, which is covered in fine white felt when the leaves are young. The leaves of 'variegatum' have bright silver markings and make it a fine foliage subject. All *Pittosporum* species may be grown from seed, or raised from cuttings.

*P. eugenioides*                  New Zealand
🌷 2,5 m ☼ ✇
The evergreen lemonwood bears clusters of yellow, honey-scented flowers in summer. Though less frost-resistant than karo, it is also frequently used as a hedge and sometimes is grown as an isolated specimen. Its oblong to ovate leathery leaves provide a pleasant splash of new green in the mixed-foliage shrub border. The variety 'variegatum', whose leaf has a creamy-white margin, is one of the better variegated subjects.

*P. nigricans:* see *P. tenuifolium*

*P. tenuifolium*                  New Zealand
🌷 4 m ☼ ✇
Good evergreens are not so plentiful and this species, with its small, dark green leaves, is one of the best. It is quick-growing, fairly hardy and compact. The flowers, insignificant but fragrant, are borne in the leaf axils. 'Silver Queen', with silvery-grey foliage, is superb.

*Plumbago auriculata*              South Africa
PLUMBAGINACEAE
🌷 3 m ☼ ✇
This rambling, semi-hardy evergreen, said to have been Cecil Rhodes' favourite shrub, succeeds best in temperate and subtropical areas. Leadwort bears spikes of sky blue flowers throughout summer, and in bloom makes an extremely colourful garden subject which may also be trained into a metre-high ornamental hedge. *P. auriculata* also grows well in a tub – one way of controlling its vigorous suckering. Propagate from suckers, root cuttings, or semi-hardwood cuttings in spring.

*P. capensis:* see *P. auriculata*

*Podalyria calyptrata*            South Africa
FABACEAE
🌷 1,5 m ☼ ✇
The downy hairs covering the grey-green leaves of the sweetpea bush give an almost grey appearance to this compact evergreen. Though fairly hardy, it will not withstand severe frost. In spring a profusion of pea-

shaped flowers, either white or in varying shades of magenta-pink, stand out in brilliant splashes of colour against the grey of the foliage.

*P. sericea*                    South Africa
🌐 1 m ☼ 🏵
So profuse are the felt-like hairs of the foliage of this small species that the leaves take on an almost silver sheen and give *P. sericea* its common name of satin bush. It bears scented, mauve flowers from late autumn until mid-spring and these are followed by silver seed pods, which last well into summer, giving the bush a glistening silver appear-

*Plumbago auriculata* (Leadwort)

ance. Propagate both species from seed in spring or from cuttings of young semi-hard wood after flowering.

**Poinsettia:** see *Euphorbia pulcherrima*

*Polygala myrtifolia*          South Africa
POLYGALACEAE
🌐 2,5 m ☼ 🏵
The young leaves of this evergreen are tinged with purple, the shade echoed by the pink pea-shaped flowers. These blooms are borne in early spring on somewhat straggly twigs and branches. Neither this species nor the related purple broom can withstand frost, and

*Polygala myrtifolia* and its flower

are suited best to the temperate parts of the country. However, they will grow, but less satisfactorily, in subtropical areas.

*P. virgata*                    South Africa
🌐 2 m ☼ 🏵
Long, fleshy stems grow to 2 m or so before developing into the much-branched head which characterizes purple broom. Though this species is slightly hardier than *P myrtifolia* it abhors frost. Throughout winter it bears graceful racemes, up to 200 mm long, of purple to flesh-coloured flowers.

**Pomegranate:** see *Punica granatum*

*Potentilla fruticosa*     Northern hemisphere
ROSACEAE
🌐 1 m ☼ 🏵
This evergreen sub-shrub has graceful, pinnate, fern-like foliage, and in summer freely produces buttercup yellow flowers, 30 mm across. It is ideal for the rock garden, grown in pockets in stone walls and in similar situations. Propagate from seed sown in spring, or from cuttings of firm shoots.

**Pride of Barbados:** see *Caesalpinia pulcherrima*
**Primrose Jasmine:** see *Jasminum mesnyi*

*Prostanthera nivea*               Australia
LAMIACEAE
🌐 1,5 m ☼ 🏵
Most *Prostanthera* species are compact evergreens with highly aromatic foliage which has earned their common name of mint bush. This species bears white flowers, occasionally blue, in spring. Prune back after flowering to

*Prostanthera cuneata*

pruning. It depends largely on what role you wish the rose to fill in your garden. You will not achieve the effect of the traditional formal bed if you depart from traditional practice. If, on the other hand, you want to include roses in your shrubbery, or make a shrubbery of them, then long pruning seems the answer. We are not concerned with pruning to produce show blooms, but even here the answer is not to be found in extremes, but rather in pruning correctly according to experience of a particular variety, under given soil and climatic conditions. In other words, let us have a little less dogma and a little more reason.

Firstly, and irrespective of the type of pruning you intend, cut out completely all dead or diseased wood and weak and straggly growth. On the good remaining wood make all pruning cuts slantwise and immediately above a dormant eye – not above an eye which has prematurely broken into growth. The sloping cut directs the flow of sap towards the eye where it is required; it also throws moisture off quickly and heals more rapidly.

## NEW ROSES
In July, cut back newly-planted bushes to within four eyes of the base unless they are standards, which should be cut to six eyes. Do not prune climbing hybrid teas at all in their first year as many varieties are then inclined to revert to bush form. Ordinary climbers and ramblers may be cut back to half their length at the time of planting in warm areas, or in the last week of July in cold areas. Any rose reared in containers should be lightly trimmed or not at all – depending on its condition, shape and cleanliness – at the time of planting.

## ESTABLISHED ROSES
### Bushes, Standards and Hybrid Teas
*Traditional.* As a general rule, bushes growing on light sandy soils should not be pruned as heavily as those on heavier soils, nor should one be too severe on the less vigorous growing varieties. Remove all weak, diseased, exhausted or dead wood, either back to firm wood or, if necessary, to the base; cut out all twiggy central growths and crossing branches. Now you will be left with a strong open framework of well-developed shoots of the previous season's growth. Cut these back to half their length, to outer buds on strong growers and inner buds on varieties which tend to sprawl. Treat standards in the same way, paying more attention to keeping the head symmetrical.
*Long Pruning.* Here the plant is built up into a bushy shrub and the only wood removed (apart from dead and diseased) is that which failed to produce good shoots during the previous season. Branched stems are reduced to single strong shoots but are not materially shortened.

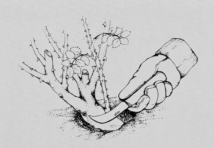

Water-shoots or suckers should be removed as close to the stock as possible, making an upward-sloping cut.

There is no need to be hesitant about pruning a strong-growing rose bush. The illustration above shows the extent to which removal of old growth may be taken to encourage a strong, floriferous plant.

### Hybrid Dwarf Polyanthas
Remove all dead or diseased wood in autumn and, in spring, cut out all the older flowering stems and any which did not flower the previous year. Shorten back the rest of the roots.

### Hybrid Polyanthas
In July, after removing all unwanted or diseased wood, cut back the previous season's strong growths to about two eyes below the original flowering head and prune back two-year-old wood to within two eyes of the base. In these, as distinct from the dwarf polyanthas, keep the centre open and remove all crossing branches.

### Ramblers and Climbers
The Wichuraiana ramblers such as 'Dorothy Perkins', and 'American Pillar' bloom on the new growth of the previous year's wood. Cut away all the older growths and tie the previous year's growths in place. The large-flowered Wichuraianas, such as 'Paul's Scarlet', require less drastic pruning; remove only the older stems from time to time so that there is always a reasonable balance between new, vigorous growths and older wood. Prune sublaterals of the newer stems back to four eyes in July.

### Climbing Hybrid Teas
Treat these as you would 'Paul's Scarlet'.

Grow species such as *Rosa hugonis*, and *R. moyesii* as shrubs and prune them to shape after flowering or, where the fruit is ornamental, in autumn, merely removing dead or unwanted wood and maintaining an attractive shape.

Water-shoots or suckers should be removed as close to the stock as possible, making an upward-sloping cut.

There is no need to be hesitant about pruning a strong-growing rose bush. The illustration above shows the extent to which removal of old growth may be taken to encourage a strong, floriferous plant.

A well-tended rose garden flaunts its charms.

# HEDGES AND WINDBREAKS

## GROWING PROTECTION FOR HOMES AND PLANTS

Whether it is ornamental or used to divide garden features, a protection against wind or used merely to provide privacy, the garden hedge or windbreak is an important feature and merits as much planning and consideration as any other planting. Remember that a hedge is, essentially, a collection of plants – usually of the same genus or species – and the only difference from others is that these are grown close together in a row and trimmed to keep them thick, orderly and tidy. Just as any other cultivated plant needs attention if it is to succeed, so hedge specimens require good cultivation, good soil treatment and adequate water.

The two most common mistakes made in planting a hedge are a lack of adequate preparation of the soil and insufficient pruning when the plants are still small. The latter omission is understandable; the average gardener wants his hedge to reach its intended height as quickly as possible – and in his haste forgets that a plant can never be well-furnished and thick at the base, unless it has been severely cut back while young, and its young growing tips pinched out frequently during all periods of active growth. This is particularly important to the formal hedge fronting your property or forming the boundary between you and your neighbours, and to the hedge planted as a garden feature or screen. Both must be of uniform appearance.

Once a hedge has become leggy, it is virtually impossible to get it properly furnished again – and not all species will tolerate the necessary remedies. So, if you want a good hedge, cultivate it correctly from the start; later is too late to rectify mistakes.

Good hedges make good neighbours – a psychological fact that may have something to do with the old adage about 'familiarity breeding contempt'.

## PREPARATION

Hedge plants do better in prepared trenches than in individual holes. Dig your trench at least 600 mm wide and to the same depth, and if the bottom half of the soil is very poor and lacking nutrient, remove this and turn the top 300 mm into its place. Over this (and before replacing either imported top soil or the original, if your soil is good enough) spread one barrow-load of manure or compost to every 2 m of trench. Place about half of your remaining top soil over the manure, lightly forking the two together and then replace the balance, treading the soil firmly into position. This deeper incorporation of manure will encourage the roots to go down in search of it, thus moving quickly away from the surface where they are most susceptible to drought. Preferably, prepare the trench at least six weeks before planting and as soon as this is done flood it with water. Repeat this flooding three days or so before planting. When planting, give each seedling a little initial encouragement by sprinkling a handful of compost at the base of the planting hole.

Planting distances and notes on pruning are discussed under each individual entry. I have deliberately omitted the privet group. These plants are such soil robbers, and there are so many alternatives, that recourse to the privet is quite unnecessary. Symbols at the top of each entry indicate whether the plant is evergreen or deciduous and the height it can be expected to reach if left unpruned. However, details of families, botanical origins, and methods of propagation are omitted as these are detailed under the entries for the plant concerned, in Chapters 8, 'Shrubs and Roses,' and 11, 'Trees'.

A hibiscus hedge in all its summer glory

◀ This well-furnished hedge is a tribute to the topiarist's art

*Abelia* X *grandiflora*, like *A. floribunda*, is an ideal hedge plant.

*Acalypha hispida* (Chenille Plant) makes a bushy hedge for warmer parts.

*Abelia floribunda*
🌼 1,75 m ☼ 🌐

This attractive evergreen is well suited as an ornamental hedge plant in cooler areas, and has the advantage of both colourful foliage and abundant flowers. It is hardy, but may also be grown successfully in temperate, frost-free areas. Plants 350 mm high are ideal and should be planted 600 mm apart. When the young plants have grown a further 150 mm, cut back to 300 mm from the ground and, in the following late spring, again cut back to a height of about 550 mm. Thereafter, prune lightly from time to time, to encourage a trim, compact growth to the desired height and width. The maximum manageable height of *A. floribunda* as a hedge is 1.75 m.

*Acalypha wilkesiana*
🌼 1,5 m ☼ 🌐 🅕

The copper leaf, or Fijian fire-bush and its many cultivars make excellent, thick ornamental hedges, especially in the warmer temperate to subtropical parts, though they should not be exposed to direct sea winds. Plant about one metre apart and prune back twice during the growing season for the first three years. From then on, when the plants are about 1.5 m tall prune only when shaping is required. This is best carried out in early spring and, once the hedge is growing soundly, serves to bring out the best of foliage colour. Keep hedges comprising *A. wilkesiana* cultivars to one colour.

*Berberis* X *stenophylla*
🌼 2 m ☼ 🌐

This hybrid should be used much more widely for boundary hedges in cooler areas, for it has many attributes which commend it to this role. It is evergreen; has long arching branches which, in spring, bear masses of tiny orange flowers; and, above all, it provides an impenetrable boundary protection. Set out the plants one metre apart and cut them back hard in the late spring of their first year's growth. Cut back to about 600 mm in the following year and to 1.25 m in the third; thereafter prune immediately after flowering each year. Its maximum manageable height is about 2 m.

*B. thunbergii* 'Atropurpurea'
🌼 2 m ☼ 🌐

Neither this cultivar of the Japanese species nor its various sub-forms should be overlooked when considering an internal hedge, particularly in the cooler regions of Australia. They require minimal pruning and their colourful foliage is a delight throughout the growing season. Plant them out 600 mm apart and prune back only when their dimensions exceed your requirements.

*Bougainvillea* spp.
🌼 variable ☼ 🌐 🅕

Time and patience are required to develop a good bougainvillea hedge, but the result can be most rewarding and provides total protection as well as seasonal colour and good foliage effect. There is no reason why the colours should not be mixed, if the growth-rate of the species or cultivars planted is

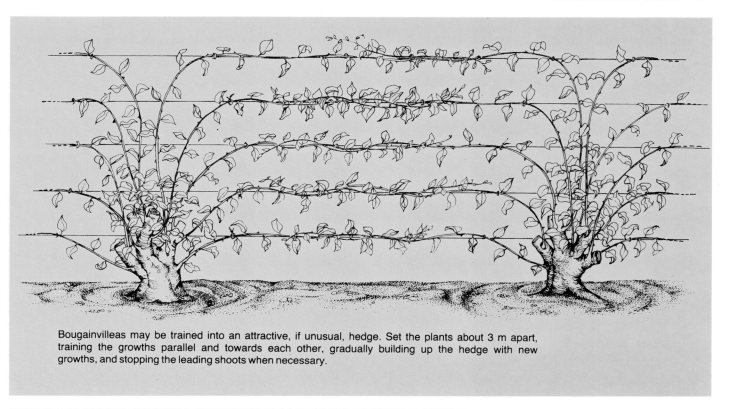

Bougainvilleas may be trained into an attractive, if unusual, hedge. Set the plants about 3 m apart, training the growths parallel and towards each other, gradually building up the hedge with new growths, and stopping the leading shoots when necessary.

*Bougainvillea* bracts and flowers

more or less the same. For instance, 'Donyo' being strong-growing, should be grown alone, but cultivars such as 'Brilliance', 'Golden Glow', 'Lady Mary Baring', 'Killie Campbell', 'Orange King' and 'Poulton's Special' may be mixed. Plant about 3 m apart and pin the growths parallel to the ground in the direction of the next plant in the line of the proposed hedge. Continue this, gradually raising the height of the parallels and stopping the leading shoots when necessary. Tie with ordinary string as this will rot before it

can cut into the expanding stems. When you have established the framework of the hedge, trim to shape after flowering.

### Breynia disticha
🌳 1 m ☼ ☺ 🄵

Particularly in its cultivar 'Roseo-picta', the snow bush will make an excellent small hedge a little more than one metre high, grown as a feature in the garden rather than as a boundary hedge. Plant in a trench at 750 mm intervals, and shorten back regularly

each year, until a thick base develops. Thereafter trim to shape.

*B. nivosa:* see *B. disticha*
*Carissa grandiflora:* see *C. spectabilis*

(Syn. *Acokanthera oblongifolia*)
### Carissa spectabilis
🌳 3 m ☼ ☺

*C. spectabilis* forms a fine hedge. The foliage is most attractive throughout the year and it will fruit and flower even as a tightly trimmed hedge. Plant 1.25 m apart and keep nipping out the growing tips to encourage a thick, bushy base.

### Casuarina equisetifolia
🌳 up to 5 m ☼ ☺

At the coast this Australian native is invaluable and will succeed under the most trying conditions. For a protective windbreak, plant in a triple, staggered row 2 m apart. Cut back hard twice during each of the first two growing seasons. Once established, it may be stopped at any desired height.

### Cedrus deodara
🌳 6 m ☼ ☺

It is not generally realized that this evergreen can be formed into a densely compact specimen. This is achieved by constantly removing the side growing tips, but leaving the main leading shoot untouched. Used in this way deodars can make a highly ornamental windbreak, particularly in cold and exposed areas – but only for the large garden. Plant 4 m apart or, if quick protection is required, at half this distance, subsequently removing every alternate plant. Prepare individual holes 600 mm

*Mandevilla splendens*
*Lonicera hildebrandiana*

*M. splendens*                                          Brazil
🌱 2,5 m ☼ 🌢 🅖

There is no more sought-after climber than this evergreen with its freely-produced, shell pink flowers which are as much as 80 mm across and borne from early summer well into autumn. Essentially a trellis rather than a wall subject, it likes air and freedom all around. Though frost tender, it will still do well in favoured inland spots, and is, of course, completely at home in temperate to subtropical areas. If you find *M. splendens* is not doing so well in one particular situation, move it to another in full sun; it has tubular roots and will move quite readily, given decent treatment. Propagate from cuttings of growing stems.

*Mandevilla suaveolens: see M. laxa*

*Manettia inflata*                                          Brazil
RUBIACEAE
🌱 4 m ☼ 🌢 🅕

An unusual and graceful evergreen climber, the cigarette creeper is suited only to temperate and subtropical areas and thrives particularly well along the coast. Small, tubular flowers are freely produced over a long period in spring. Their lower tubes are bright scarlet, while the upper parts are yellow. Propagate from cuttings of medium soft shoots, using bottom heat.

**Mexican Trumpet:** see *Phaedranthus buccinatorius*
*Mina lobata: see Quamoclit lobata*

*Monstera deliciosa*                                          Mexico
ARACEAE
🌱 2,5 m and upwards ☼ 🌢 to 🌢 🅕

Popularly grown as an indoor or warm greenhouse evergreen, the fruit salad plant is a vigorous outdoor climber for the warmly temperate to subtropical areas, where it is usually grown against the support of a large tree. It is not a showy plant, but its large shining green leaves, perforated and with deeply incised edges, lends a curious tropical atmosphere to any garden. Its arum-like flowers, borne in summer, are followed by cone-like fruits with a delicious pineapple flavour. As the plant climbs, it puts out long aerial roots, many of which do not reach the ground. Propagate from stem cuttings any time during the active growing period. (See also Chapter 18, 'Indoor and Balcony Plants', page 305.)

*Muehlenbeckia complexa*                     New Zealand
POLYGONACEAE
🌱 3 m ☼ 🌢

The New Zealand wire vine has small. glossy green rounded foliage on wiry, rapidly twining stems. The flowers are tiny, but fragrant. The plant can be trained on wire netting to make an attractive soft fence. Propagate by seed or by division of roots in spring.

Pandorea pandorana

shade, though its colouring is better in the latter situation. The young leaves open a lovely waxy red and its autumn tints are frequently spectacular.

**P. tricuspidata** China, Japan
4 m ☼ ⊕
'Lowii', the cultivar of the deciduous Boston ivy has much smaller leaves than the species, to which, in many respects, it is preferable. Its leaf pattern against a wall is more artistic and its autumn colours are simply glorious.

**Passiflora antioquiensis** Colombia
PASSIFLORACEAE
☀ 3 m ☼ ⊕ 🅕
A slender-stemmed evergreen climber which in summer bears rich, rose-red, passion fruit-like flowers, 100-120 mm across. Best suited to temperate and subtropical areas. In summer, *P. X allardii*, a fine evergreen hybrid, bears white flowers, flushed pink, with a white and deep purple corolla. All *Passiflora* species and cultivars are fine cover for a wire fence; and may be propagated from semi-firm cuttings of growing shoots, though true species are often best propagated from seed.

**Nepal Trumpet Climber:** see *Beaumontia grandiflora*

**Pandorea jasminoides** Australia
BIGNONIACEAE
☀ 3-4 m ☼ to ◑ ⊕ 🅕
Flowering from the first year of planting and thereafter more or less continuously – particularly in our warmer regions – this is one of the better evergreen climbers. And it is better behaved than most; it does not elbow its way into its neighbours' living space as so many other climbers do. Numerous ice-cream pink flowers with deep carmine throats are borne in compact panicles some 50 mm across. The deep green, pinnate foliage is leathery, though not coarsely so, and considerably enhances the climber's appearance. This species is easily propagated from cuttings of semi-firm growing stems at any time.

**Parthenocissus henryana** China
VITACEAE
☀ 6 m ◑ ⊕ 🅕
A strong-growing, self-clinging, deciduous climber, this species somewhat resembles the Virgina creeper, but has silver and pink leaf veinings. The young leaves open a shiny red and colour well again in autumn. It is slightly frost tender and prefers semi-shade. Propagate this and all *Parthenocissus* species from summer cuttings of growing stems.

**P. quinquefolia** United States
☀ 7 m ☼ to ◑ ⊕
The hardy, self-clinging, deciduous Virginia creeper is too well-known to require further description. It will thrive in full sun or semi-

Parthenocissus tricuspidata (Japanese Ivy)

*P. caerulea*          Brazil

❀ 5 m ☼ to ◐ ⊛

The hardiest of its genus, the blue passion flower is a widely-grown, vigorous, evergreen creeper noted for its greenish-white flowers and blue-white and purple corolla. The faintly-scented flowers are borne in late spring and throughout summer.

*P. manicata*       Colombia, Peru

❀ 3,5-5 m ☼ ⊛

A moderately strong-growing, evergreen climber suited to hot, dry and frost-free, or warmly temperate to subtropical parts, the red passion flower is probably the most showy of all its family. Vivid scarlet flowers, up to 120 mm across and fringed pale blue, are borne in summer.

*P. mollissima*           Andes

❀ 5 m ☼ ⊛ **F**

Rapid-growing and a vigorous evergreen climber, the banana passion fruit requires lots of space and is best suited to the warmly temperate to subtropical areas. Its flowers, borne in summer, are a delightful rose-pink, 80 mm across, and are followed by edible, yellow fruits resembling bananas. These are delicious, raw on their own or in fruit salads – but may require protection against fruit fly – and well worth cultivating for the home table. (See also Chapter 12, 'Fruit Trees and Vines', page 248.)

*P. quadrangularis*    Tropical America

❀ 6-10 m ☼ ⊛ **F**

The strong-growing, evergreen giant grana-dilla does particularly well in the tropics, where it is worth growing for its large, elongated fruits. These have a purplish, slightly acid juice and follow the attractive flowers, which are pinkish-white inside, have a white corolla with blue and purple-red bands, and are borne in summer. Territorially this is probably the most demanding of all the members of the genus *Passiflora*.

*Pelargonium peltatum*    South Africa
GERANIACEAE

❀ 1 m ☼ ⊛

A well-known sub-shrub or semi-woody sprawler, the ivy-leafed geranium is most at home climbing over a low stone wall or tree stump. It is tolerant of most conditions and, according to its habitat, blooms over an extended period in winter, spring and summer. It makes a brilliant show, its flowers ranging from shades of crimson, through to lavender and salmon and even red-purple. A double rosy-purple variety is very popular and is frequently used on low fences. Propagate from stem cuttings at almost any time.

**Pelican Flower:** see *Aristolochia grandiflora*

*Pereskia aculeata* 'godseffiana'     South
CACTACEAE               America

❀ 5 m ☼ ⊛ **F**

While the gorgeous variety of this species, 'godseffiana', will grow in temperate areas, it is only at its best in the subtropics. Planted

Passiflora quadrangularis (Giant Granadilla)

Passiflora antioquiensis

against a wall on the sunny side of the house, the evergreen lemon vine will climb as much as 5 m or so. Its beauty lies in its attractive, broadly-elliptic, fleshy leaves which assume the most incredible colours, basically yellow-green, but tinted in coppery shades of salmon red. At its best it must be seen to be believed. Propagate from semi-firm stem cuttings, under a bell jar with bottom heat, during the growing season.

*Petrea volubilis:* see Chapter 8, page 153

*Phaedranthus buccinatorius*      Mexico
(Syn. *Distictis buccinatoria*)
BIGNONIACEAE

❀ 3-4 m ☼ ⊛

This rather tender, evergreen, summer-flowering climber is widely grown and best known under its old name of *Bignonia cherere*. Its blood red or scarlet, curved trumpet flowers – yellow at the base and the reason for its common name, Mexican trumpet – are borne in terminal racemes. It is strong growing and very showy when happy. Propagate from semi-hardwood cuttings during the growing season.

*Philodendron selloum*    Brazil, Paraguay
ARACEAE

❀ 3,5 m ◐ ⊛ **F**

Grown elsewhere as an indoor plant (see page 306), this evergreen is also extensively used as an outdoor climber in the warmly temperate to subtropical zones. Planted against a tree or some other suitable support in the shade of trees, this species, along with

Mandevilla laxa (Chilean Jasmine)

Pelargonium peltatum (Ivy-Leaf Geranium)

Phaedranthus buccinatorius

*Sollya heterophylla*

*Monstera deliciosa*, lends a distinctly exotic effect to any garden. Propagate from nodal cuttings of the stem during the growing season.

*Podranea ricasoliana*                    South Africa
BIGNONIACEAE
🌳10 m ☼ 🌱
The pink tecoma is a beautiful climber which bears trusses of large pink bell-shaped flowers during summer on arching canes. This showy plant is useful for covering low fences or tree stumps in tropical or subtropical regions. Propagate from hardwood cuttings.

*Polygonum aubertii*          Western Szechwan
POLYGONACEAE
🌱6 m ☼ 🌱
In many current classifications this species is now placed in the distinct genus *Fallopia*, as *F. aubertii*. An extremely vigorous deciduous climber, the silver lace vine bears sprays of silvery-white flowers, much prized for floral bouquets, throughout most of the summer. It has large, heart-shaped leaves, and grows so rampantly that it should be given ample space to itself. Propagate from hardwood cut-

tings taken during autumn in the colder parts and in winter in warmer areas, or from semi-hardwood cuttings at any time during the growing season.

*P. baldschuanicum*          South Turkestan
🌱10 m ☼ 🌱
Often classified as *Fallopia baldschuanicum*, this hardy, deciduous and rampant grower is splendid as a rapid cover for an unsightly building. The Bokhara vine's feathery sprays of white flowers are borne in summer, but it is a strictly utilitarian climber and should not be mixed with other choice climbers. Propagate from hardwood cuttings in spring, or from ripe seed.

**Potato Creeper:** see *Solanum wendlandii*

*Pothos longipes*                            Australia
ARACEAE
🌱10 m ☼ 🌱 🌱
This vigorous root climber will cover rocks or tree trunks. It has bright green leaves, small flowers and bright red fruit. It is cultivated from seed and grows slowly, preferring a shady position. In its natural state, this

species is found growing in rainforests.

**Purple Coral Pea:** see *Hardenbergia violacea*
**Purple Wreath:** see *Petrea volubilis*

*Pyrostegia venusta*                            Brazil
BIGNONIACEAE
🌳10 m ☼ 🌱 🌱
This beautiful evergreen climber flowers over a long period in summer, and in warmer climates, spasmodically throughout autumn and winter. As its common name implies, in full flower the whole aspect of the plant resembles a golden shower, especially when cascading over a tree, massed clear gold flowers being borne in drooping panicles. Propagate from cuttings of firm growing stems after flowering.

*Quisqualis indica*                    Tropical Asia
COMBRETACEAE
🌳10 m ☼ 🌱 🌱
Suited only to frost-free parts of the country, the evergreen Rangoon creeper requires plenty of space and a rich, loamy soil in which to grow. It requires some support, and the drooping spikes of flowers, borne in summer and autumn, are seen to best advantage when this woody species is trained on a pergola or overhead trellis. The fragrant, broadly trumpet-shaped flowers are each some 75 mm long, comprising a green tube from which the white petals emerge; these darken to pink or red with age. Propagate in autumn from softwood cuttings, preferably with bottom heat.

**Rangoon Creeper:** see *Quisqualis indica*
*Rhoicissus capensis:* see *R. tomentosa*

*Rhoicissus tomentosa*                  South Africa
VITACEAE
🌳10 m ◑ 🌱 🅵
The wild grape is found wild in many South African forests and is an ideal, quick-growing cover for unsightly walls or wire fences. The shiny, dark green leaves resemble those of a grape vine and the new foliage is particularly showy. Insignificant summer flowers are followed by clusters of berry-like fruits, which make fine jam or jelly. It prefers good, compost-rich soil and requires regular watering. Propagate from semi-firm cuttings in spring.

*Rhynchospermum jasminoides:* see
    *Trachelospermum jasminoides*
*Rosa banksiae:* see Chapter 3, 'Shrubs and
    Roses', page 158
**Scarlet Honeysuckle:** see *Lonicera*
    *sempervirens*
*Sellowiana selloum:* see *Philodendron*
    *selloum*
**Silver Lace Vine:** see *Polygonum aubertii*

*Solandra grandiflora*                        Jamaica
SOLANACEAE
🌱2,5-6 m ☼ 🌱
A vigorous evergreen with large leaves, the trumpet flower is a rather coarse climber requiring a lot of space. In winter and spring it bears huge, trumpet-shaped flowers which are cream at first, turning rich yellow with age.

*Pyrostegia venusta* (Golden Shower)

*Quisqualis indica* (Rangoon Creeper)

Both this and the flowering species are frost tender and suited only to larger gardens. Propagate from semi-hardwood cuttings taken in autumn.

*S. maxima* — Mexico

3-6 m

Often mistaken for *S. guttata*, this evergreen climber is another with a coarse habit and requiring considerable space. However, the masses of large, deep yellow flowers which cup-of-gold bears throughout spring and summer tend to compensate for these shortcomings.

*Solanum jasminoides* — Brazil

SOLANACEAE

or 3 m

This quick-growing climber is evergreen in all but the cooler parts, where it is semi-evergreen. It is semi-hardy and in summer bears clusters of bluish-white flowers, lightly fringed with blue. Propagate both this species and *S. seaforthianum* from cuttings of firm growing stems.

*S. seaforthianum* — South America

3 m

This semi-woody, deciduous climber is somewhat tender and in autumn bears masses of flowers in drooping axillary panicles. Though variable in colour, these blooms are mostly lavender-purple with prominent yellow stamens and are followed by charming, long-lasting, red berries.

*Solandra maxima* (Cup-of-Gold)

*S. wendlandii* — Costa Rica

2-5 m

The potato creeper is a striking, evergreen climber for the warmer parts and in summer bears huge trusses of light sky-blue to lilac flowers. Where it is happy, it grows vigorously and needs plenty of space. It is seen at its best covering a pergola or on a trellis against a white wall. Propagate from semi-hardwood cuttings after flowering.

*Senecio tamoides* (Canary Creeper) with bougainvillea

*Sollya heterophylla* — Australia

PITTOSPORACEAE

2 m

The bluebell creeper is a delicate light-growing climber with aromatic leaves and nodding clusters of blue, pink or white flowers in late spring. It can be trained up trellises or walls or as a cover for fences. Propagate from cuttings in warmer months.

**Star Jasmine:** see *Trachelospermum jasminoides*

Solanum seaforthianum

Solanum wendlandii (Potato Creeper)

Stephanotis floribunda

*Stephanotis floribunda*                    Madagascar
ASCLEPIADACEAE
🌳 2,5 m ☽ 🔆

Frequently grown as a greenhouse plant in cooler parts, this evergreen is a 'must' outdoors in the warmly temperate to subtropical areas. Madagascar jasmine has attractive, dark green foliage and is a tidy climber, which in spring bears clusters of small, waxy, very fragrant, creamy-white, star-like flowers. It does best on a trellis in semi-shade. Propagate after flowering from cuttings of firm, growing wood, assisted by bottom heat.

*Stigmaphyllon ciliatum* (Golden Vine)
Amazon Climber)

*Stigmaphyllon ciliatum*                    Brazil
MALPIGHIACEAE
🌳 5-10 m ☼ to ☽ 🔆 🟢

An evergreen climber, the golden vine or Amazon climber succeeds best in warmly temperate to subtropical areas and prefers full sun or semi-shade. In autumn it bears umbels of three to six delicately-fringed, clear yellow flowers. Propagate from cuttings of semi-firm, growing stems in summer, with bottom heat if available.

*Tacsonia antioquiensis:* see *Passiflora antioquiensis*

*T. manicata:* see *Passiflora mollissima*
*T. grandiflora:* see *Campsis grandiflora*

(Syn. *T. Thunbergia gibsonii gregorii*)    Africa
ACANTHACEAE
🌳 2 m ☼ 🔆

The glory vine is a light-growing twiner covered with lovely, bright orange trumpet flowers for most of the year. It enjoys a warm protected position. Propagate this and the following *Thunbergia* species from seed or semi-mature cuttings in summer.

*T. grandiflora*                            India
🌳 3,5-5 m ☼ 🔆 🟥

This very strong, but somewhat tender, evergreen climber is useful for quick cover over an unsightly building or similar structure. It requires a lot of space. In summer and autumn rich, deep blue flowers are freely produced over long periods.

*T. mysorensis*                             India
🌳 4 m ☼ 🔆

The evergreen lady's slipper must also be grown over a pergola so that its 300 mm-long racemes may hang down, clear of the foliage. Its slipper-like flowers are old gold with the base sheathed in chocolate brown bracts, and are borne over a long period in summer. A really delightful and unusual climber, it may flower several times a year in the warmly temperate to subtropical zones.

**Tickey Creeper:** see *Ficus pumila* 'Minima'

*Trachelospermum jasminoides*              China
APOCYNACEAE
🌳 5 m ◉ 🔆 🟢

A fairly hardy, strong-growing evergreen climber, star jasmine bears masses of fragrant, starry white flowers in summer. It may also be used as a ground cover and will tolerate full shade. 'Variegatum' has attractive silver-white leaf markings. Propagate from semi-hardwood cuttings in autumn.

**Trumpet Flower:** see *Solandra grandiflora*
**Virginia Creeper:** see *Parthenocissus quinquefolia*

*Vitis coignetiae*                          Japan
VITACEAE
🌳 5-7 m ☼ 🔆

An extremely vigorous, deciduous climber, the crimson glory vine has the largest leaves of all the hardy vines. It is noted particularly for its autumn foliage, richly coloured in shades of yellow, crimson and scarlet. Propagate from cuttings of semi-firm wood in winter.

*V. henryana:* see *Parthenocissus henryana*
**Wild Grape:** see *Rhoicissus tomentosa*
**Winter Honeysuckle:** see *Lonicera fragrantissima*

*Wisteria sinensis*                         China
FABACEAE
🌳 10 m ☼ 🔆

This well-known and vigorous deciduous

*Thunbergia grandiflora*

climber may also be trained into a standard. A hardy subject, it requires a cold winter to bring out the best of its spring-flowering potential. Seedlings vary greatly in flower colour – from lilac to shades of mauve. Insist on a grafted plant of a good colour, for many of the seedlings are not worth growing. Though similar, *W. venusta* with its slightly-scented, pure white flowers will never oust *W. sinensis*, in its best blue varieties, as the favourite. Propagate from cuttings or by layering in summer.

**Wood Rose:** see *Ipomoea tuberosa*

*Wisteria sinensis*

*Thunbergia gregorii* is a quick-growing annual climber

# BOUGAINVILLEAS: LOVED AND VERSATILE CLIMBERS

The bougainvillea, in all its many permutations of species and cultivars, is certainly the best-known, most widely cultivated and probably the most versatile of any climber grown in Australia. Its showy bracts, borne throughout much of the year, adorn buildings and fences in most of the warmer parts of the country. And, once established, this member of the botanic family NYCTAGINACEAE is one of the few cultivated plants which seems almost to thrive on neglect. At the other end of the scale, probably more bougainvilleas die in the garden as a result of excessive care, particularly in their early stages of growth when they are highly sensitive to too much watering and overfeeding. When young, bougainvilleas cannot absorb all the water and food, and once they have settled down they do not need it.

Bougainvilleas may be trained as arches or hedges, grown as standards, used as ground covers on steep slopes where little else will grow, and trained against a wall or trellis as climbers. They are singularly resistant to most insect pests and to fungus attack, as well as being highly drought resistant. They enjoy an enriched light sandy soil, long sun hours and regular watering in hot, dry weather. Most species and their hybrids are rather frost-tender and can be easily cultivated in warm climates only.

Obliging though they are when established, newly-planted bougainvilleas are often slow to get started. Whatever purpose they are to serve, dig the planting hole 700 mm square and 50 mm deep. Place well-prepared compost mixed with a complete plant food into the hole. Water this well three days before planting and again after planting. Then leave well alone, watering only when absolutely necessary.

If the bougainvillea is to be trained as a colourful standard it should be 'cartwheeled'. That is to say, as soon as every shoot rising from the base is some 300 mm long, it should be tied around the outside of the plant to form a cartwheel shape (see illustration) which eventually will create a low, flat-topped barrel effect.

The complete establishment of the plant is indicated by the appearance of strong, fast-growing water shoots. Select the best of these for your purpose, then gradually shorten back, and finally remove, all the other shoots, including the original cartwheel base.

Flowering period is early spring and can extend well into summer. Pruning is after the flowering is over and vigorous plants can be heavily pruned without harm. If you are developing a standard, trim back to about 200 mm any side shoots which appear on the main stem. Remove these only when the stem is thick enough to support the weight of the head. This process may need to be carried out for several years. Propagation is by tip cuttings in spring or hardwood cuttings, setting these in river sand, preferably in late winter.

Botanical classification of this South American genus remains somewhat enigmatic. There has been an enormous increase in the new varieties of bougainvillea in the past few years and the origin of some of these is difficult to trace. Quite often some of these may be sold under different names.

### B. X buttiana
This hybrid is probably the result of crossing the Brazilian *B. glabra* with *B. peruviana* found extensively in nature from Colombia to Peru. Its main cultivars are listed below:

'**Apple Blossom**', also known as 'Jamaica White' and 'Snow White', has unusual bracts of sea-foam white which become tinged with pink in cooler weather.
'**Barbara Karst**' is a shrubby grower with masses of fiery red flowers.
'**Brilliance**' makes an excellent standard and its multi-coloured bracts show in a range of changes of varying shades of red.
'**Golden Glow**', formerly 'Millar's Seedling', is fairly strong growing and flowers heavily; its bracts opening golden-yellow and slowly turning to cerise flushed with pink.
'**Killie Campbell**' is another very popular form, its garnet-brown and vibrant, fiery rose bracts suffused with terracotta.
'**Mary Palmer**' is an outstanding, multi-toned bougainvillea. It bears attractive, large white bracts, some of which are suffused with pink, light carmine and pale magenta.

'**Mrs. Butt**' is a very free-flowering and popular cultivar, its rich crimson bracts accounting for its former common name 'Crimson Lake'.

### B. glabra
As well as being a parent of the hybrid cultivars, this strong-climbing Brazilian species is represented by several splendid forms. These varieties will stand moderate cold in winter.

'**Alba**' is a vigorous pure white single.
'**Beryl Lemmer**' has small, pale green leaves and large white bracts.
'**Formosa**', also known as 'Pride of Singapore', is a rampant, free-flowering cultivar which may be used in topiary or allowed to scramble. Strong lilac bracts cover the entire length of the branches.
'**Harrisii**' is a natural dwarf with violet bracts and variegated foliage.
'**Magnifica**' is extremely vigorous and slightly frost-tolerant. Its wide bracts are brilliant purple.

### B. spectabilis
This Brazilian species and its cultivars are characterized by their particularly dense growth, hairy foliage and a greater number of spines than other bougainvilleas.

'**African Sunset**' is of moderate growth. Its bracts are a mixture of pink, salmon, orange and red.
'**Lateritia**' of wide spreading growth has bright brick-red bracts fading to bronzy-orange.
'**Scarlet O'Hara**' is a beautiful variety with young reddish bracts which mature to a brilliant orange-scarlet and then burning crimson.

Three steps in 'cartwheeling' a bougainvillea: All the young shoots are wound round upon each other; strong leaders are allowed to develop upwards; finally, the bottom growths are removed.

'**Turley's Special**' is a popular cultivar, easy to grow and bearing very large, deep rose-pink bracts.

## DOUBLE BOUGAINVILLEAS

One of the most exciting horticultural developments in recent years has been the advent of double bougainvilleas. These seem to have been cultigens – they were not bred but developed as natural cultivars. All are vigorous growers, free flowering and a distinct contribution to our gardens. All produce huge heads (as much as 220 mm across) or closely-packed, double bracts.

'**Bridal Bouquet**' is a lovely bi-colour; its rich cerise-pink bracts are blotched with white on the outer edges and the throat of each is off-white.
'**Carmencita**' has lovely apricot and crimson bracts.
'**Golden Dubloon**' provides a charming mixture of colours. Its bracts are suffused with yellow, orange and pale pink which darken with age.
'**Klong Fire**' has brilliant crimson bracts.
'**Pagoda Pink**' has beautiful pink bracts tinged with lavender.
'**Pink Champagne**' is a semi-dwarf with pale rose pink bracts which deepen with age.
'**Raspberry Ice**' has cerise bracts and variegated foliage.
'**Temple Fire**' is a semi-dwarf suited to container growing. It has attractive bronze-pink bracts which deepen with age.

Bougainvilleas

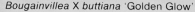

Bougainvillea X *buttiana* 'Golden Glow'

Bougainvillea grown as a standard

# TREES

## AN ENDURING FRAME TO THE GARDEN PICTURE

If a lawn is the canvas on which a gardener paints the colours of the flower beds and shrubbery, it is trees which provide the frame. But, unlike the frame of a painting, which can be changed if it is unsuitable – or even at the owner's whim – a tree, which has possibilities of longevity beyond that of any animal, should be planted to endure. Some of the world's largest trees, notably the sequoias of the redwood forests of California, are estimated to be more than 3000 years old. This estimate is based on a count of the trees' annual rings, these being the continuous rows of cells formed each year around the trunk, just below the bark.

Thus, of all your garden's plants, how much more careful you must be in choosing and planting a tree. Its ultimate beauty is in its maturity and there is no consolation in accepting, when it is too late, that you have planted unwisely or without sufficient thought. Only one horticultural crime is greater than cutting a tree down – that is to plant it in the wrong place, for, inevitably, the result will be the same.

So, think before you choose; and think again before you plant. Study the requirements of the type of tree you wish to plant and determine its height, spread and rooting characteristics. If it is going to be too tall or too spreading, or its roots may cause structural damage, or it may have to be severely lopped – rather than pruned – to keep it to its allotted space, plant something else. Never write a tree's death warrant on the day you prepare the site.

Having decided on the species you wish to grow and chosen the most suitable site, prepare the hole in which the tree is to be planted several weeks beforehand.

In uncultivated ground, the size of the hole should never be less than 600 mm square by 600 mm deep. In shaly or rocky ground the hole must be square, not round, for the sound practical reason that in hard ground the tree's roots will take the line of least resistance and go round and round the perimeter of a circular hole, whereas, if it is square, they will penetrate into the fissures at the corners, so forcing their way out into new ground. If the soil is good it can be excavated and replaced, returning the subsoil to bottom and replacing the topsoil where it came from.

When back-filling, press the soil firmly in place and incorporate about half a barrow-load of well-rotted manure or prepared compost about 300 mm down in each hole. If the soil is poor, after excavating replace only the top spit – this time at the bottom of the hole. Make up with good imported soil to which the half barrow-load of manure has been incorporated. Water a few days before planting to ensure that the surrounding soil is moist. Though most trees can be propagated by seed, most home gardeners prefer to buy seedlings from a nursery.

When buying trees – or any other plants – the average gardener is very much in the hands of the nurseryman. The buyer assumes that the plant is true to name; that, if budded or grafted, it is on the correct stock; and that the nurseryman has given its roots the correct nursery treatment. Though he must depend largely on the nurseryman's reputation, there are a few precautions he can take.

Examine the roots. When deciduous trees and conifers are raised in the open ground, it is correct nursery practice either to dig round the young tree once a year, severing the long roots, or to transplant it. The former practice, which is called wrenching, encourages the growth of numerous fibrous roots which are important to successful transplanting. If the tree has only a few bare roots, varying in thickness between the size of your finger and wrist, it certainly has never been wrenched or transplanted, and its chances of survival are remote. If, however, there are numerous smaller roots and additional fibrous roots, you can be satisfied that the nurseryman has done everything he can be expected to have done to ensure success.

Next, examine the stem. In the production of such standards as pine, oak, ash, elm and flowering peach, it is practice to tie the leading shoot so that it grows straight, and to leave the side shoots (feathers) on the leading stem until the head has reached a certain height and the stem's circumference has thickened accordingly. These feathers, whose function is to ensure the development and thickening of the stem so that it can support the weight of the head, are gradually shortened back as the young tree grows. If this is not done, the stem will remain thin and spindly, will

◀ The ever-popular golden cypress (*Chamaecyparis lawsoniana* 'Lutea')

*Acer palmatum* 'Osakazuki' (Japanese Maple)
*Bauhinia purpurea* 'alba' (Camel's Foot, Orchid Tree)

*Acer japonicum* 'Aureum', another popular cultivar
*Brachychiton acerifolius* (Illawarra Flame Tree)

need staking for an unduly long period, and may never develop into a strong clean specimen. Use you own judgement in this matter, rejecting the specimen with a smooth, spindly stem and a heavy head.

If the roots and the stem are satisfactory, only two things can be wrong with the head. If the tree is one which should have a leader (e.g. pin oak, silky oak, plane or liquidamber) be sure this is intact and undamaged.

This is less important in trees such as species of *Tipuana* or *Gleditsia*, which are not necessarily uniform in growth and do not depend on such uniformity for their ultimate grace and beauty. The other point to check is that the branches are free from pernicious scale or other insect pests.

When moving conifers they must be tightly balled (see illustration page 376) and thoroughly soaked beforehand. Should they dry out there is little hope of recovery. A conifer which has been regularly wrenched in a nursery develops a tight ball of fibrous roots and will transplant quite safely. The roots of deciduous trees must never be allowed to dry out and this is best prevented by covering them with damp hay or moss and then wrapping – not too tightly – with wet sacking or hessian. If the roots are a little dry on arrival, stand them in a bucket of water for 24 hours before planting.

If you examine the new plant carefully, you will notice a distinct line (the soil line) indicating the exact depth at which the plant grew in the nursery; the bark of the stem is usually harder above this line and darkly shiny below. This should coincide with the soil level when you have finished planting. Decide on the depth of your superficial excavation with this soil line in mind; spread the roots out level (or slightly down and out from the centre of the stem); throw in two to three spadefuls of soil; and then shake the stem so that the disturbed soil filters in snugly around the roots. Tamp firmly, keeping the stem upright, and keep on filling and tamping until planting is complete. Mound round the surface of the tree so that water is contained when good soakings – about 50 litres at a time – are given; once a week while the tree is dormant, and twice a week when growth starts, and particularly during hot, sunny weather.

To support the young tree, drive a 2.5 m stake about 0.75 m into the ground beside the stem and tie firmly, first wrapping the stem with canvas or rubber where the cord embraces the tree. Examine the tie periodically and adjust it when necessary so that the tree is neither strangled nor chafed by being too loose. Labels fastened to the plant with thin wire or string must be removed or suitably re-tied. Planting from open ground should take place while the tree is dormant, or, with evergreens, when growth is least. Planting from pots or tins may be carried out almost throughout the year, although I do not favour planting during the coldest months. Unless otherwise indicated, all trees may be propagated from seed, sown when ripe.

In the individual entries which follow, I have tried to be as practical as possible about the behaviour of each species and have restricted my list to those trees which I consider best suited to the average gardener's needs.

*Acer buergerianum*　　　　　　China, Japan
ACERACEAE
⊕ 6 m ☼ ☺
The small Chinese maple, extensively used for street planting because of its size, is also eminently suited for use as a lawn specimen, either in its normal habit or as a standard. It is also excellent as background for a large shrubbery. Deciduous, it loses its distinctly three-lobed leaves rather early, but often in a blaze of colour. The 50-70 mm-long leaves are a lovely, shining green in spring.

*A. negundo*　　　　　　North America
⊕ 20 m ☼ ☺
A deciduous species, the box elder succeeds well in all but the very dry parts of the country, and makes a good, rounded tree. Of particular interest to gardeners are its smaller variety 'variegatum', whose leaves have silvery-white variations, and the cultivar 'Aureovariegatum', with clear golden variations. These are amongst the most effective of all variegated small trees and are really striking, either as isolated lawn specimens or as a background to shrubbery. The leaves appear in very early spring, and are inclined to drop just as soon as there is a feeling of autumn in the air. When impoverished or neglected, the two forms mentioned are susceptible to attack by red spider.

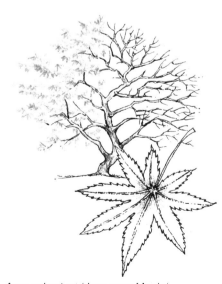

*Acer palmatum* (Japanese Maple)

*A. palmatum*　　　　　　Japan
⊕ 8 m ◑ ☺
With bright green, typical three-lobed leaves which turn to brilliant golds and reds in autumn, the small Japanese maple is ever a visual delight. Like most other maples, it will take all the cold in the world. It will also succeed in the more temperate regions, but because of our intense summer heat, *A. palmatum* requires a woodland situation where the sunlight is broken and filtered. However cold the winter, it is unlikely to survive the summer months in the full blaze of the sun. If the species succeeds in your garden, try also the two especially good cultivars 'Purpureum', which has purple foliage, and 'Dissectum Atro-purpureum', also purple-leafed but with finely dissected leaves. Both are much smaller than the species, the former growing to about 4 m and the latter only to about 1.5 m.

*A. trifidum*: see *A. buergeranum*

*Agonis flexuosa*　　　　　　Australia
MYRTACEAE
⊕ 14 m ☼ ☺
Also called peppermint tree, the willow myrtle

takes about fifteen years to reach maturity. It is a broad-leaved evergreen which blossoms in November when its long branches are sprayed with small white flowers in early summer. It succeeds best in temperate climates but, once well-established, will tolerate a fair degree of frost and drought.

*Ailanthus altissima*                    China
SIMAROUBACEAE
⚥ 25 m ☼ ☻

Though a fine specimen, the height of the tree of heaven makes it suitable only for the very large garden – and even here your neighbours will not thank you for planting the tree near their boundary as, whenever its spreading roots are cut, suckers arise profusely. If you can accommodate this tree, plant it well away (20 m) from any cultivated area. Its bold, pinnately compound leaves, its panicles of terminal summer flowers whose seed is a striking rusty red, and its superb autumn tints make it well worth planting. The tree of heaven gives good shade and though deciduous, it loses its leaves for only a short period in winter. In some areas of New South Wales this species is a proclaimed noxious weed.

*A. glandulosa:* see *A. altissima*

*Alectryon subdentatus*               Australia
SAPINDACEAE
⚥ 11 m ☼ ☻
The foliage of this tree is very attractive. It has shiny pinnate leaves and small red flowers. The red fruit are also very attractive. Cultivated from seed, this tree tolerates dry and exposed areas.

*Araucaria araucana*                      Chile
ARAUCARIACEAE
⚥ 35 m ☼ ☻
Either you like the monkey puzzle or you hate its grotesque appearance and its twisted and contorted branches, bearing whorled leaves which cannot decide if they should really be needles. Even in a garden large enough to accommodate it, this remarkable evergreen requires careful placing; it does not harmonize with other trees and probably looks best as an isolated feature. All *Araucaria* are propagated from seed. Best suited to colder areas.

*A. bidwillii*                          Australia
⚥ 40 m ☼ ☻
Despite a towering height, which gives it tremendous landscape impact, the bunya-bunya takes up relatively little space so that even a moderate-sized garden can accommodate it comfortably. Its thick, resinous bark peels to give the trunk a mottled effect, while the branches – growing in almost-horizontal whorls – produce long, pendant branchlets. The long, leathery, dark green leaves narrow to a stiff point.

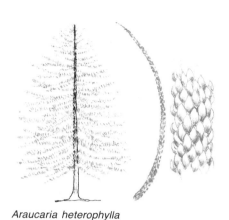
*Araucaria heterophylla*

*A. cunninghamii*                       Australia
⚥ 45 m ☼ ☻
This species is similar in height and general appearance to the bunya-bunya, except that the branchlets on the horizontal branches of the hoop pine are densely tufted at their apex. Another difference is that the bark peels in horizontal bands.

*A. excelsa:* see *A. heterophylla*

*A. heterophylla*                   Norfolk Island
⚥ 60 m ☼ ☻
This is a magnificent evergreen. The beauty of the Norfolk Island pine lies in the perfect symmetry of its branches, held rigidly horizontal to the vertical trunk. It reaches heights of 50-60 m in Australasia, but is smaller in other parts of the world. Ideal in the coastal to warmer inland areas, elsewhere it is tender to frost. Tubbed and its growth contained, it is a perfect indoor subject if given plenty of sunlight.

*A. imbricata:* see *A. araucana*
**Arbor-Vitae:** see *Thuja occidentalis*
**Arizona Cypress:** see *Cupressus arizonica*
**Atlantic Cedar:** see *Cedrus atlantica*
**Australian Bush Cherry:** see *Syzygium paniculatum*
**Australian Flame Tree:** *Brachychiton acerifolius*
**Australian Frangipani:** see *Hymenosporum flavum*

*Backhousia citriodora*                Australia
MYRTACEAE
⚥ 10-15 m ☼ ☻
The lemon ironwood flourishes either as a shrub or small tree in the warm temperate areas of Queensland. Its white flowers with their green calyces grow in large clusters, and are set off by the shiny pointed leaves, velvety underneath, which are lemon scented. A valuable commercial oil is extracted from its foliage.

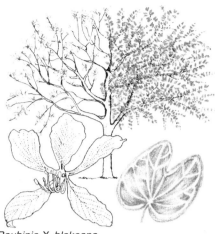
*Bauhinia X blakeana*

**Bailey's Wattle:** see *Acacia baileyana*
*Bauhinia alba:* see *B. variegata* 'Candida'

*Bauhinia X blakeana*                     China
LEGUMINOSAE
⚥ 5 m ☼ ☻
This relatively low-growing, small deciduous tree is widespread and quite unlike any other cultivated bauhinia. It bears large, red-burgundy-purple flowers resembling huge orchids over a long period during winter. It does not set seed and consequently there is no aftermath of pods. Grow it as an isolated specimen, for its flowers contrast harshly with anything other than white. Semi-tender, it is easily propagated from hardwood cuttings.

*B. purpurea*                  India, Burma, China
⚥ 4 m ☼ ☻
For coastal areas and the warmer inland parts, the deciduous camel's foot, or orchid tree, is wonderful in flower and excellent for shade. A well-grown specimen in full bloom is a sight not quickly forgotten. The flowers, profusely borne in spring just before the foliage appears, vary from near-white to a rich shade of purple, the basic colours being blotched or shaded with intermediate tones. Propagate this and all other bauhinias; except *B. X blakeyana*, from seed.

*B. variegata*                        Tropical Asia
⚥ 10 m ☼ ☻
This species is very similar to the foregoing in habit, but the rose-coloured petals of pink camel's foot are veined and variegated with red and yellow. The cultivar, 'Candida', has the characteristic shape, but is smaller growing and bears pure white flowers. Try and place these bauhinias against a darkly-foliaged background; as an isolated specimen on high ground, the galaxy of colour is often lost against the sky.

*Betula alba:* see *B. pendula*

# ACACIAS: TREES OF ORNAMENTAL CHARM

Of the more than 1000 species of *Acacia* found throughout the world, most are native to Australia, though they are represented on other continents as well, notably Asia, the Americas and Africa. The genus name, derived from a Greek word *akakia*, meaning 'sharp', was first used to describe an Egyptian plant, *Acacia arabica*.

Acacias belong to the same family as peas (Leguminosae), and they have long pods like the more typical peas. Indeed, these pods, known as 'phyllodes', replace the leaves. The phyllodes are mostly flattened stalks which usually have a leaf-like shape.

The genus includes a great variety of species which can be grouped according to function. One group contains species of economic importance. These provide fodder for cattle, oil for perfume, and even glue. Most importantly, perhaps, their timber is beautiful and very valuable. The species of a second group affect the environment: some are capable of binding the soil; others are salt-tolerant and so are suitable for seafront planting. A third group is classed as ornamental, and a fourth group contains the nuisances: species whose foliage is poisonous to cattle, and others whose vicious spikes lacerate the flesh.

My list of species is by no means exhaustive but it serves to show the wide range of acacias available and suited to the average garden. All species listed are propagated from the extremely hard seed which, under natural conditions, takes a long time to germinate. An early, even germination can be assured however, if the seed is soaked in hot water before planting. I drop the seed into water which has come to the boil, leaving it until the water cools and then drying it off and sowing it immediately in individual 50 mm containers.

*Acacia baileyana*  Australia
LEGUMINOSAE
🌳 10 m ☼ 🐦
A small evergreen with a moderate spread and roundish habit, the Cootamundra or Bailey's wattle is reasonably frost resistant and fairly tolerant of drought. In spring, clusters of rich yellow, fluffy, ball-shaped flowers contrast strikingly with its silver-grey, pendulous foliage. Pruning back after flowering encourages its capacity for blooming. Under favourable circumstances, *A. baileyana* is inclined to seed itself, but never becomes a nuisance. A recently developed cultivar bears distinctly purplish-blue foliage.

*A. cambagei*  Australia
🌳 15 m ☼ 🐦
This is gidgee, also known as 'stinking wattle', an appellation deriving from the unpleasant odour given forth by the leaves when they are wet. Gidgee is native to the dry inland, where stands often spring up in depressions. The lance-shaped phyllodes are covered with fine greyish flakes, which give the foliage an ashen hue. The bark is rough and brown, the flowers are few, and the seed pods smooth. The timber, which is hard and resistant to termites, is useful for fence posts and for firewood.

*A. cultriformis*  Australia
🌳 3 m ☼ 🐦
The knife-leaf wattle is widely grown and deservedly popular because of its erect panicles of small yellow flowers which are held well clear of the foliage and are borne in early spring. The silvery-grey leaves are oblique or triangular. Clipped to a height of 1.5 m this evergreen species would make an attractive hedge.

*A. decurrens*  Australia
🌳 15 m ☼ 🐦
The black wattle is a prominent natural feature of the landscape in the high rainfall areas of coastal New South Wales, though it is naturalised in other Australian states. It is a beautiful tree, tall and straight with dark green, feathery foliage, and densely massed cream to yellow flowers which appear in the spring. The seed pods are flat and slightly curved. The tree grows quickly but is a target for borers and may, therefore, be shortlived.

*A. elata*  Australia
🌳 30 m ☼ 🐦
The cedar wattle is a broad-leaved, long-living evergreen which is often used to screen unsightly views. In the Canberra Botanic Gardens it is used as a screen plant in a simulated rainforest environment. It need hardly be mentioned that the views there are not unsightly. It is inclined to wilt in heavy frost areas, and to break under heavy winds. Plantings intended for shelter should therefore form double rows. Although essentially utilitarian, in spring it bears attractive panicles of yellow flower heads.

*A. estrophiolata*  Australia
🌳 10 m ☼ 🐦
The ironwood is a hardy species native to Australia's dry inland. In its life cycle it undergoes radical changes in form. From a dense shrub, it becomes a dense tree, and finally a weeping willow with the dejected air typical of this group. As its common name would indicate, its timber is enduring. The tree itself also endures for a long time.

*A. floribunda*  Australia
🌳 5 m ☼ 🐦
A charming, small evergreen, this species

*Acacia melanoxylon* (Blackwood)

is widely grown throughout the world for the abundance of its yellow flowers in spring and summer. Its branches are slightly weeping, and it succeeds best in areas of generous rainfall.

*A. melanoxylon*  Australia
🌳 30 m ☼ 🐦
The blackwood is a tree for the large garden and in nature reaches 40 m. Tough, hardy and drought resistant, it makes a splendid, isolated lawn specimen, for the grass will grow right up to the base. It casts a pleasing shade, and dark green foliage lends to the tree an air of dignity and unusual character. The wood is used extensively in the furniture industry and related crafts.

*A. podalyriifolia*  Australia
🌳 8 m ☼ 🐦
Perhaps the best of all ornamental acacias in the small garden, the Mount Morgan, or Queensland silver wattle has silvery-white foliage and bears masses of large, deep yellow, fluffy balls in winter. Evergreen, it is quick growing, and is semi-hardy.

*A. pycnantha*  Australia
🌳 5-10 m ☼ 🐦
The golden wattle is Australia's floral emblem. It is only a small tree, with a short slender trunk from which branches begin to extend not far above ground level.

It occurs throughout southern Australia, where its beauty bursts forth in the spring in the form of fluffy golden and highly perfumed flowers. These are set off by the plant's shiny green foliage.

The plant grows freely in gardens and along the edges of country roads. It is a quintessential part of the Australian bush.

*A. salicina*  Australia
🌳 14 m ☼ 🐦
Known as native willow or cooba, this tree is, in an unconventional way, as beautiful

as the true willow, and it does not have the latter's troublesome root system.

It is neither its foliage nor its flowers which make it beautiful. The phyllodes are long, narrow and fleshy, and the cream flowers quite inconspicuous. Its beauty lies in its form, in the rounded crown and the sadly drooping branches which move even in the stillness of the inland.

The native willow ranges through the dry interior from Victoria's western border to the coast of Western Australia, springing up in depressions which once held water. Shoots emerge freely from the roots and serve to bind the loose soil. It is a long-lived species, despite the rigours of its environment.

*Acacia baileyana* (Cootamundra Wattle)

*Acacia pycnantha*

*Acacia podalyriifolia*

*Acacia decurrens*

# CARING FOR OLD TREES

Sometimes drastic treatment, even surgery, is required for the treatment of disease or deterioration in old trees. Before undertaking this it would be prudent to acquaint yourself with the regulations of your local municipial council. If the treatment indicated involves infringement of council regulations and the tree dies, despite your best efforts, you could have placed yourself in legal jeopardy.

The most common cause of deterioration in mature trees is decay in the hollows formed where branches join the trunk, particularly where three or four main leaders arise from a common point. Should this occur, remove all the spongy matter and decayed wood down to firm timber. Wash the cleaned surface with a carbolic acid solution (one part commercial liquid carbolic acid to 20 parts of methylated spirits). When dry, paint the area heavily with coal tar. If the area of decay is too deep-seated to cure in this manner, probe the hollow with a piece of No. 8 wire to establish its lowest location. This must be 'tapped'; use an auger to drill an upward-sloping hole towards the base of the inner depression. Once this aperture has been successfully sited, leave until the hollow has dried out thoroughly. The drilled hole can then be force-filled with cement or plugged with an oak stick. Fill the main hollow with coarse aggregate cement and finish this off smoothly with cement plaster so that water will run off the treated area.

Heavy or dangerously weak branches are best supported by bracing them with an iron bar, threaded at both ends, either from the branch in question to the trunk, or through parallel branches. A 20 mm hole is bored through the centre of the weak limb and a corresponding hole through another support – either a limb or the trunk. The bar is then passed through the holes and plates are fitted at either end and moulded against the shape of the particular part of the limb or trunk they are to support. The nuts should be very tightly turned so that the brace actively relieves pressure; the nuts can be loosened as growth demands.

Moving large trees is another art, though easily acquired once the fundamental principles are understood. Here I refer to trees which have been moved at least once before, such as a nursery-produced tree which at one time or another has had its tap root severed. A

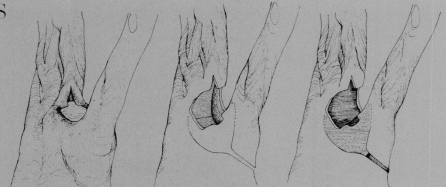

When decay forms in the hollows of old trees – usually where a large branch joins the trunk – this should be treated immediately. Remove the spongy wood down to fresh, good growth and probe the hollow to establish its lowest point. Drilling upwards, tap the hole at this point and allow any moisture in the hollow to drain, and the surrounding wood to dry out thoroughly before force-filling with cement.

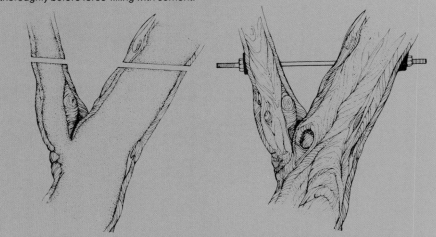

A dangerously weak branch may be supported by threading an iron bar through a hole bored in the trunk of the tree and a corresponding one through the weak branch. Plates, fitted to the outside contours of both branch and trunk, allow nuts to hold the bar in place. These nuts may be tightened or loosened according to the tree's growth needs.

tree from seed which has grown in situ for several years cannot be removed successfully as it will not produce the necessary network of fibrous roots to support it during the transition period. These fibrous roots are the key to the problem, for only the fine root-hairs are capable of absorbing moisture.

Any large, previously transplanted tree, even if it is 8 m high, can be successfully transplanted if, in good time beforehand, it is induced to produce a good network of fibrous roots. This is achieved by cutting all round the tree – say one metre from the stem – so that all its roots are severed. Preferably this should be done in mid-spring. The ball thus exposed is tightly wrapped, sewn in stout sacking, and the hole refilled with light sandy soil. The tree is moved to its new position in early spring the following year, immediately before budding. Immediately before moving, spray the covered root-ball with the new latex material developed for this purpose to protect the roots and retain moisture. Make certain that, in its new position, the stem cannot move, so that the young roots are not broken, dislodged or disturbed.

---

*Betula pendula*                     Europe
BETULACEAE
(‡) 18 m ☼ to ◑ ⊛
One of the most graceful of all small deciduous trees, the silver birch with its delightfully decorative form merits the attention of every keen gardener, however small his garden. Graceful, and usually with a paper-white peeling stem, it has pendulous branchlets which

bear small, shiny green, ovate leaves. It is best suited for cooler climates. It is immune to the heaviest frost, and its main requirement is a cool, well-drained but permanently moist soil. Propagate from seed.

**Bhutan Cypress:** see *Cupressus torulosa*
**Blackwood:** see *Acacia melanoxylon*.

**Blue Gum:** see *Eucalyptus* spp.

*Brachychiton acerifolius*            Australia
STERCULIACEAE
(‡) 7-10 m ☼ ⊛ **G**
The Illawarra, or Australian, flame tree has the unusual characteristic of dropping its foliage in spring when the flowers appear. These are bell-shaped, a brilliant red and long-lasting. A

*Betula pendula* (Silver Birch)

*Brachychiton acerifolius* (Illawarra Flame Tree)

*Brachychiton discolor* (Queensland Lace Bark)

full-grown Illawarra flame tree in full blossom is a striking sight. The tree has a fine pyramidal habit, and can hold its own as a specimen even when not in flower. It is frost tender and suited only to temperate to sub-tropical areas. As with the other species of this genus, propagation from seed is easy.

*B. discolor*　　　　　　　　　　Australia
🌢 30 m ☼ 🌢 **F**
The Queensland lace bark, also called white kurrajong and a relation of the Illawarra flame tree, thrives only in temperate to subtropical areas and cannot withstand frost. When it is happy, the species bears an abundance of

*Brachychiton rupestris*

large, bell-shaped summer flowers which are pink with rusty felt undersides.

*B. populneus*　　　　　　　　　Australia
🌢 20 m ☼ 🌢
The kurrajong derives its name from an Aboriginal word meaning 'fibrous plants'. In the past, Aboriginals used to make nets from its bark fibres. Today, its beauty, utility and hardiness make it a familiar tree not only in the country, where it provides fodder for cattle, but also in suburban streets and parks. This is particularly so in the eastern part of the continent.

The rounded crown and thick, shade-giving summer foliage make it a very attractive tree. When young the kurrajong's heart-shaped leaves are a pale green which becomes dark as the tree matures. The cream-coloured flowers with their reddish brown hearts, which appear in early summer, are not particularly noticeable. Kurrajong is tough too, being resistant to both drought and pests. Its only enemies are the weevils which sometimes destroy its bark.

*B. rupestris*　　　　　　　　　Australia
🌢 15 m ☼ 🌢
The common name of this tree, bottle tree, derives from the shape of the trunk. Its appearance suggests age but, under warm to temperate conditions, the bottle takes less than ten years to form. With its narrow, lance-shaped leaves and small pale flowers, the bottle tree is unspectacular but it is a curiosity to have within a garden. These unusual trees are most common in Queensland.

**Bunya-Bunya:** see *Araucaria bidwillii*

*Bursaria spinosa*　　　　　　　Australia
PITTOSPORACEAE
🌢 7-10 m ☼ 🌢
Early settlers, homesick for northern hemisphere species, were reminded by this tree of the English box tree: hence its common name native box. An alternative common name is blackthorn. According to its habitat, it may be a thorny shrub or a tree which is as tall as 10 m. In midsummer its small, highly perfumed flowers appear, attracting bees in swarms to the garden. The name of the genus derives from the purse-like shape of the seeds (Latin: *bursa*, a purse). It may be propagated from seed.

*Callistemon salignus*　　　　　Australia
MYRTACEAE
🌢 9 m ☼ 🌢
Bottle brushes, which may be large shrubs or small trees, form a large group of which the willow bottle brush of south-east Australia is typical. It is a small tree, yet within the bottle brush group it is relatively tall, a triton among the arboreal minnows. It often produces two flowerings within the same year, the pale yellow flowers appearing in spring and autumn. Though common, like other bottle brushes, it is sought after because of the fine display of its masses of stalkless blooms.

*Callitris columellaris*　　　　　Australia
CUPRESSACEAE
🌢 18 m ☼ 🌢
This tree is a member of a group with a long history. The ancient Egyptians are believed to have used the durable wood of one of its species to make the coffins in which they encased their mummies. Subsequently, 'sad cypresses' became emblems of mourning for the dead. Today, the wood is sought by the building trade because of its resistance to termite attack. *C. columellaris* is one of the conifers (cone-bearing trees) which are found in every Australian State, but more particularly in New South Wales and Queensland. In South Australia it is a feature of the spectacular scenery of the Flinders Ranges. In a garden or park native cypress pines create a formal effect. They are column-like in form, with foliage reaching almost to the ground. Their rough bark is grey and the greyish-blue leaves are small and scale-like, growing in whorls along the branches. The cones contain winged seeds which germinate freely.

*Cassia fistula*　　　　　　　India, Ceylon
LEGUMINOSAE
🌢 9 m ☼ 🌢
One of the most beautiful of all small, flowering trees, the semi-deciduous golden shower or pudding-pipe tree is often likened to the English laburnum for its long, pendant racemes of fragrant, golden flowers, borne in summer. It has a well-shaped head and makes a perfect shade specimen when isolated on a lawn. It is suited only to the warmly temperate and subtropical areas, and may be propagated from seed or root cuttings, the latter taken in early summer.

*C. grandis*　　　　　　Tropical America
🌢 15 m ☼ 🌢
The pink shower, also an excellent shade

*Cassia spectabilis*

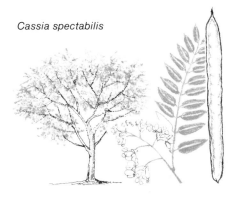

*Chamaecyparis lawsoniana* 'Lutea'

*Acacia fimbriata*

*Macrozamia communis*

◀ *Cycas revoluta*

cies, *L. hopei* (syn. *Macrozamia hopei*) and *L. peroffskyana* (syn. *Macrozamia peroffskyana*). They inhabit the moist coastal forests of eastern Australia, the former in northern Queensland and the latter in the south of that State and in northern New South Wales. These are the tallest Australian cycads, having slender trunks from the top of which emerge long pinnate leaves. The cones are about 65 cm long, those of the male plants being slender and those of the female resembling enormous pineapples. They are elegant plants and would make fine indoor or garden specimens.

*Macrozamia* spp.                    Australia
ZAMIACEAE
⊕ 1-7 m
The genus *Macrozamia* comprises 14 spe-

cies, one of which is found solely around a couple of isolated central Australian waterholes. Another species occurs only in the south-west of the continent; the remainder inhabit coastal forests from central Queensland to the Victorian border. Some species have tall, graceful trunks; for example, *M. moorei* from southern Queensland and northern New South Wales, which may reach a height of 7 m. Other species are trunkless like the members of the genus *Bowenia*: instead of a trunk they have fleshy underground stems, sometimes with many 'branches'. *M. communis*, the trunk of which is usually less than 1 m high, is present in reasonably large numbers in New South Wales forests. Its graceful, dark green, shiny leaves may be 1.5 m long and the spiny cones of the male are as long as 45 cm.

*Citharexylum quadrangulare* (Fiddlewood)

'Minima-aurea' is a very dwarf variety with
gold foliage;
'Minima-glauca' is also very dwarf but has
glaucous leaves;
'Pygmaea-argentea' is low-growing and has
semi-globose foliage, the young leaves
having dark blue tips;
'Stewartii' is compact, but taller-growing than
most, its foliage yellow rather than gold;
and
'Triomphe de Boskoop' is a striking small tree
with open, glaucous foliage.

**Cherry Laurel:** see *Prunus laurocerasus*
**Chinese Elm:** see *Ulmus parvifolia*
**Chinese Juniper:** see *Juniperus chinensis*
**Chinese Maple:** see *Acer buergeranum*
**Chinese Persimmon:** see *Diospyros kaki*

*Chorisia speciosa*                    Brazil
BOMBACACEAE
🌲 10-12 m ☼ ☺ 🄵
The flowering, deciduous kapok tree has a
spreading, rounded head which is smothered
in blooms in summer. It is only semi-hardy
and is very tender when young. Not unlike
huge orchids, the individual flowers are 100
mm or more across, satin pink in the best
forms, with brown markings at the throat.
Large conical, bluntly thorn-like protuberances stud the growing trunk of young trees.
With maturity, these, protuberances fall off
and the theory is that this is Nature's way of
protecting the young bark from grazing
animals. Propagate from seed.

*Cinnamomum camphora*          China, Japan
LAURACEAE
🌲 30 m ☼ ☺
Strictly a specimen evergreen for the very
large 'estate', its habit and growth allow the
camphor tree no place in the small garden.
Nor is it a shade tree, for it is widely based
and almost pyramidal. However, when trimmed, it is a good plant for tub work as it will
take any amount of clipping. A suitable subject for the topiarist, the camphor tree is
easily propagated from seed.

*Citharexylum quadrangulare*       West Indies
VERBENACEAE
🌲 12 m ☼ ☺ 🄵
Although the fiddlewood is frost tender, it is
otherwise very accommodating, particularly
as regards soil. Few other deciduous trees
anywhere in the world put up such a magnifi-

cent show of autumn colour which persists
well into the winter and frequently even longer. The predominant autumn leaf colour is a
reddish-bronze, blended with shades of
yellow and orange. The leathery leaves are
entire and elliptic-oblong. Propagate from
hardwood cuttings in late winter.

**Cockscomb Coral Tree:** see *Erythrina
crista-galli*
**Cockspur Thorn:** see *Crataegus crus-galli*
**Common Beech:** see *Fagus sylvatica*
**Common English Hawthorn:** see *Crataegus
laevigata*
**Cootamundra Wattle:** see *Acacia baileyana*
**Cork Oak:** see *Quercus suber*

*Crataegus* X *carrierei:* see *C.* X *lavallei*

*Crataegus crus-galli*          North America
ROSACEAE
🌲 3-4 m ☼ ☺
Wide-spreading and sometimes flat-topped,
the cockspur thorn has narrowly obovate
leaves. The white summer flowers are borne
in clusters and are followed by bunches of
round red berries, each about 12 mm across.
The handsome species succeeds well in the
colder areas. Propagate both this and the
following species from seed.

*C. laevigata*                      Europe
🌳 8 m ☼ ☺
Where the common English hawthorn succeeds, it grows and flowers well, but not with
that spontaneous flush and super-abundance
of summer blossom that characterizes it in
colder climates. The summer flowers are
followed by glossy, dark berries. Some of the
better hybrids and cultivars are now obtain-
able and most will succeed in climates ranging from cold to temperate.

*C.* X *lavallei*                    France
🌳 6 m ☼ ☺
This deciduous hybrid developed in France is
one of the best hawthorns. It has 50-70 mm-
long, coarsely-toothed obovate or oval
leaves with downy undersides and its summer flowers, white with red anthers, are borne
in clusters. These are followed by persistent,
roundish, orange fruits about 30 mm across.
All hawthorns appreciate a cold winter. Propagate this species by budding.

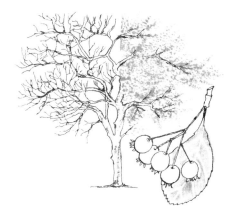

*Crataegus crus-galli* (Cockspur Thorn)

*Cupressus arizonica* (Arizona Cypress)

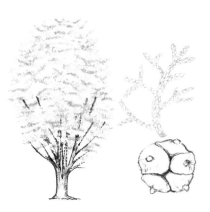

*Cupressus macrocarpa* (Monterey Cypress)

*C. oxyacantha:* see *C. laevigata*

*C.* X *prunifolia*              Garden origin
🌲 3-4 m ☼ ☺
This deciduous hawthorn is superb, with lush
foliage, profuse flowers and fruit, and rich
autumn colouring. It has brilliant dark green
leaves, about 60 mm long and mostly
roundish-ovate. White summer flowers borne
in clusters are followed by bunches of bright
red berries, each about 15 mm across. This
species is best propagated by budding.

**Creeping Juniper:** see *Juniperus horizontalis*

*Cryptomeria japonica* 'Elegans'      Japan
TAXODIACEAE
🌲 40 m ☼ ☺
A really lovely conifer, the soft, emerald green
spring foliage of the Japanese cedar is lightly
tinged bronze, but turns a striking purple-
bronze in autumn and winter. Light trimming
throughout the early growing seasons encourages a compact habit which greatly adds
to its effectiveness as a specimen. Like most
conifers, it must not be allowed to dry out in
periods of drought. It is best suited to temperate and cool regions. Propagate from seed
sown when ripe.

*Cupressus arizonica*           North America
CUPRESSACEAE
🌲 12 m ☼ ☺
A tall, pyramidal conifer with pale glaucous-
blue foliage, the Arizona cypress is extremely

*Citharexylum quadrangulare* (Fiddlewood)

*Cercis siliquastrum* (Judas Tree)

*Chamaecyparis lawsoniana* (Lawson's Cypress)

*Ceratonia siliqua* (Locust Bean)

hardy and unusually tolerant of dry, rigorous conditions. It makes a fine, attractive specimen and is also frequently used for windbreaks. In Australia, 'Swanes Golden' variety is very successful. Propagate this species and all other cypresses from seed.

*C. lawsoniana:* see *Chamaecyparis lawsoniana*

*C. macrocarpa*                                    North America
ⓣ 12 m ☼ ⊕
The Monterey cypress is only of garden interest as an isolated specimen in a very large garden, or park. However, this tall evergreen is invaluable as an untrimmed windbreak in coastal or favoured inland areas.

*C. sempervirens* 'Stricta'          Southern Europe
ⓣ 5-9 m ☼ ⊕
In its true form, the Italian cypress is strictly fastigiate, very compact and upright. Overseas this evergreen is mainly reproduced from cuttings true to form, so that only the best forms are distributed. It is useful for the formal garden, but don't overdo the numbers as you may create a funereal aspect.

*C. torulosa* 'Compacta'          Western Himalayas
ⓣ 4-7 m ☼ ⊕
Another slender, tapering evergreen, this compact cultivar of the Bhutan cypress is a lighter green than the previous species. Whereas the Italian cypress may, with age, open up its branches to spoil its pencil-like effect, this cultivar will never do so, thus making it a much more reliable subject for formal gardens.

*Cyathea dealbata*
(Syn. *Alsophila tricolor*)          New Zealand
CYATHEACEAE
ⓣ 2-4 m ◐ ⊕
This New Zealand evergreen ranks in the forefront of all tree ferns. Like most ferns, the silver tree fern appreciates the filtered sunlight of semi-woodland conditions and a permanently moist position. The dark green leaves are firm and bi-tripinnate, with almost pure white undersides. Propagation is from spores.

*Davidia involucrata*                      Western China
DAVIDIACEAE
ⓣ 15 m ☼ ⊕
There is only one species of the dove tree, and it was not discovered until the twentieth century. Alternative names are ghost tree and handkerchief tree. The North American dogwoods are distant relations. The egg-shaped leaves are long, broad and pointed, and downy on the underside. The flowers are small and nondescript, and surrounded by two abnormally large white leaves. The fruit is a pear-shaped drupe. This tree will grow only in cool mountainous country, and in such country it can be propagated from seed.

*Diospyros kaki*                              China, Japan
EBENACEAE
ⓣ 12 m ☼ ⊕
This highly ornamental deciduous tree may

grow to 12 m or more in the species, less in the true fruiting varieties and only to 1.5 m in its dwarf forms. Known as the Chinese or Japanese persimmon, it has shining green leaves and bears colourful fruits in late summer and early autumn. The apple-sized fruits follow small, insignificant flowers and are deep glowing red when ripe. In autumn the foliage is often spectacular. The species is reasonably tolerant of frost.

*Elaeocarpus reticulatus*                      Australia
ELAEOCARPACEAE
ⓣ 30 m ☼ ⊕
The blueberry ash belongs to a large genus of southern hemisphere species. The name of the genus is derived from the Greek, *elaia*, an olive, and *carpos*, fruit, which describes the olive-like form of most species. The fruit is an edible, lobeless drupe or capsule with a fleshy outer covering and, as the common name would indicate, it is blue in colour. The flowers are pink or white and are delicately fringed. It is found in its natural state on the east coast of Australia.

**English Oak:** see *Quercus robur*

*Eriobotrya japonica*                              China
ROSACEAE
ⓦ 4-6 m ☼ ⊕
This round-headed evergreen with its crinkled, dark glossy green foliage, woolly underneath, is probably known to everyone from childhood – who hasn't climbed a loquat tree to collect its attractive yellow autumn fruits? Fragrant, yellowish-white flowers are borne on stiff, woolly, terminal panicles in summer. Propagate from seed or softwood cuttings in spring. The loquat requires little, if any, pruning; trim to shape after harvesting.

*Erythrina crista-galli*                              Brazil
LEGUMINOSAE
ⓣ 6 m ☼ ⊕ ⊖
A brilliant deciduous species, the cockscomb coral tree bears handsome spikes of large, bright crimson, pea-shaped flowers in spring. It should be pruned hard immediately after flowering, to produce flowering stems for the following season. It is hardy in all but severe frost areas.

*E. vespertilio*                                    Australia
ⓣ 15 m ☼ ⊕
Known as the tiger claw, coral bean and batwing coral, this Australian species is mainly confined to north-eastern Australia. Other members of the genus are distributed through the tropical parts of the world. This coral tree is an interesting rather than a beautiful tree, with a stark, forbidding aura. The branches are sparse and covered with sharp thorns, and the leaflets, which are arranged feather-like on both sides of a stalk, suggest a bat's wing, as one of the tree's common names indicates. The flowers are large and pea-shaped, and they range in colour from pink to red. It is an adequate shade tree but is deciduous and looks rather naked in winter.

*Fagus sylvatica*                                    Europe
FAGACEAE
ⓣ 30 m ◐ ⊕
In Europe as well as in many other parts of the world, the common beech, together with its varieties and cultivars, is much prized as a large deciduous tree. This is the species most often grown in Australia. It has smooth grey bark and shining green leaves which are downy when young. These leaves turn a reddish brown in autumn, the season when the tree is seen in all its glory. The beech is hardy and will thrive unless exposed to high winds or salt spray. It does best in areas which resemble its natural environment, that is, in cooler regions and at relatively high altitudes.

**Fan Palm:** see *Chamaerops humilis*

*Ficus macrophylla*                              Australia
MORACEAE
ⓔ 60 m ☼ ⊕
Trees of this genus are widespread in the tropics. They are generally too massive for any but the most extensive garden, and even in parks they dominate the landscape. The Moreton Bay fig, also known as the Australian banyan tree, is no exception. It is common in the coastal areas of New South Wales and Queensland. In the rainforests it attains a great height; its trunk is thick, the bark grey and rough; and the tough leaves are a dark glossy green above and brownish below. The fruits are purple globules. The early settlers planted many of these trees, but few are planted now because of their spreading root system which endangers property. Often the seeds lodge in the branches of other trees. When the seeds germinate they send down aerial roots which can strangle the host tree.

**Flowering Almond:** see *Prunusa amygdalus*
**Frangipani:** see *Plumeria rubra*

*Ginkgo biloba*                              Western China
GINKGOACEAE
ⓔ 40 m ☼ ⊕
Slow-growing when young, the maidenhair tree – of which the male and female plants are separate – moves quite well after the first four years. It does well in temperate to warm conditions and thrives best in areas with good rainfall. Although not an outstandingly beautiful tree, its peculiar habit of growth and its almost complete difference from most other trees, combine to give it a strangely elusive charm. Remarkably resistant to air pollution, it is widely used as a street tree in industrial areas of the United States.

*Gleditsia triacanthos*                      North America
LEGUMINOSAE
ⓔ 8-10 m ☼ ⊕
Rarely more than 10 m high and nearly as much across, the honey locust is a splendid shade tree and is particularly valuable in areas of little rainfall, with hot summers and cold winters. A deciduous species, it has attractive fern-like foliage, and in autumn its masses of long brown pods rattle eerily in the slightest breeze.

*Eucalyptus*                                    Australia
MYRTACEAE

Eucalypts are as Australian as the koala. Indeed, the two go together, with the leaves of five species of eucalyptus providing the staple diet of these little animals.

There are at least 600 eucalypt species recorded in Australia, and others in New Guinea, Indonesia and the Philippines. Species identification is complicated by the fact that there is often variation between the foliage of juvenile and adult forms of the same tree.

People often refer to eucalypts as 'gums' or 'gum trees'. The English explorer William Dampier, who landed on the coast of Australia almost one hundred years before Captain Cook, so described the sticky substance oozing from the bark. The substance is, in fact, 'kino' which is used in medicine, as a tanning agent and for dyeing cloth.

*Eucalyptus ficifolia* (Red Flowering Gum)

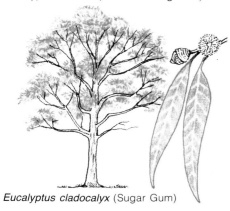

*Eucalyptus cladocalyx* (Sugar Gum)

Eucalypts are certainly the dominant genus among Australian trees. They are found throughout the continent in habitats ranging from the freezing conditions of the snow country to the heat and aridity of the interior. It is due to the wide range of species that make them a popular gardening choice for almost any situations where a tree is desired.

Habitat also determines the form of the tree. The snow gum of the Alpine region is a stunted tree with crooked branches. At the other extreme, in the low rainfall areas of the interior, eucalypts are also stunted. Aboriginals called

these dwarf eucalypts mallee. Under the favourable conditions of the temperate plains the trees have straight trunks and rounded heads.

Eucalypts are valued for their timber, for their beauty and for the role which they play in stabilising the environment. These versatile evergreens provide excellent shade and their large root systems protect the soil from erosion by holding the soil together. Eucalypts propagate easily from seed and are among the fastest growing of all hardwood trees. Within only a few years of planting they can make very effective windbreaks.

Most eucalypts are suitable for cultivation but it depends entirely on the type of species as to where it can be cultivated. For example, many of the mallees exist quite will in drier, arid conditions where their large root systems enable them to extract sufficient water from the soil in times of drought. At the other end of the scale many eucalypt species, for example, the snow gum, can survive very well in much colder climates, although no eucalypt can survive in frozen soil.

Often you will find only one eucalyptus tree in your average garden because they grow very tall and may dominate the garden. However, there are smaller species, such as the mallee, which grow to approximately 1 metre in height and some hybrids, which grow up to two or three metres, that can be planted to make a beautiful addition to your garden.

Eucalypts are very popular because of their wide range of flowers and fruits which display a large variety of colours. Their beautiful foliage and majestic trunks, which range in colour from deep brown, orange to silvery grey, are also an attraction.

The eucalyptus trees have two very distinct types of foliage. Juvenile leaves, which are blue in colour, are stalkless, heart-shaped and grow in pairs on either side of the stem, while the adult leaves are green and sickle-shaped. The adult leaves have short stalks and hang vertically, reducing water loss. The aromatic, volatile oil, which is contained in the oil glands of these leaves, is exclusive to the eucalyptus trees and form that distinct scent so familiar to the Australian bushland.

These native trees have been known to live past 200 years old and form a practical and delightful addition to your garden.

Listed are a few examples of the many species grown in Australian gardens.

*E. caesia*                                    Australia
MYRTACEAE
🌳 8 m ☼ 🌀

This stunning tree has brown bark that cracks and peels at the base of the trunk with silver branches. It bears large pink flowers with blue-green buds and fruit, and requires a well-drained position and protection from the wind. It prefers a sunny position and is drought and frost resistant.

*E. cladocalyx*                                Australia
🌳 10 m ☼ 🌀

The sugar gum is a spreading tree that is very fast growing. It has pale bark and is very hardy being suitable for most soils and conditions. It

is a low maintenance tree and is frost and drought resistant.

*E. cornuta*                                    Australia
🌳 20 m ☼ 🌀

This is an evergreen tree with an erect and branching stem. It has a dark fibrous bark, with bluish-green narrow leaves. The flower buds are orange occurring in clusters, the flowers, which appear in summer, are bright yellow. The fruit are deep brown and capsule-like. This tree prefers a sunny position and is resistant to drought and frost.

*E. curtisii*                                   Australia
🌳 7 m ☼ 🌀

This relatively small eucalypt is suitable for large or small gardens. It is an outstanding feature in any garden with its display of creamy flower clusters. It is best suited to areas where the soil is sandy and well drained. It tolerates frost and also thrives in tropical areas.

*E. ficifolia*                                  Australia
🌳 9 m ☼ 🌀

This spectacular species, which adds splashes of colour to our roadsides as well as many of our gardens, the red flowering gum has deep glossy green leaves and, at best, bears masses of flowers from late summer though until early spring. The colour of the flowers range from white-to-pink and red-to-orange. Its fruit is large and urn-shaped. This tree survives very well in heavy soils but does not thrive in sandy conditions.

*E. globulus*                                   Australia
🌳 30 m ☼ 🌀

The Tasmanian blue gum has blue-to-grey foliage as a juvenile and dark green as an adult. It is best suited to larger gardens, however, there are various hybrids suitable for smaller gardens. It is popular with florists for its decorative foliage and is valued as a shade tree for colder climates. The buds and fruit are a mealy white.

*E. mannifera*                                  Australia
🌳 15 m ☼ 🌀

This eucalypt is an evergreen and is drought and frost resistant. It prefers a sunny position with shady and well-drained soils. Its trunk is smooth and white and changes to an orange colour in mid-summer. The creamy flowers appear in summer and the fruit are dark brown and capsule-like.

*E. pulverulenta*                               Australia
🌳 8 m ☼ 🌀

This is another species ideal for bedding schemes. It has highly decorative silvery-white leaves. It is a twisted looking tree and due to its contrasts in foliage is often used in floral arrangements. This frost-hardy and attractive tree may be used as a feature in any garden.

*E. socialis*
🌳 12 m ☼ 🌀

The grey mallee prefers heavy soils in a sunny position. It is drought and frost resistant and is suitable for large or medium size gardens. It has light grey bark with pale green leaves. The flowers are white and appear from winter to spring.

*Eucalyptus ficifolia* (Red Flowering Gum)

▼*Eucalyptus cornuta*

*Fagus sylvatica* 'Cuprea' (Common Beech)

*Cassia artemisioides*

*Acacia dealbata* (Silver Wattle)

*Liquidambar styraciflua*          North America
HAMAMELIDACEAE
(\$) 30 m ☼ ☻
Beautifully shaped, upright and almost pyramidal, the liquidambar or sweet gum succeeds in most parts of the country, but does
best in areas of good rainfall. It is deciduous,
and prefers a deep, loamy situation, though it
will tolerate less favourable soils. Because of
its pyramidal habit, it is not a shade tree in the
true sense, but there are few other trees
which have as much appeal, especially when
grown as an isolated lawn specimen. Its
triangular leaves are emerald green in spring,
fiery in autumn and its winter aspect is that of
a well-ordered grey ghost.

*Liriodendron tulipifera*          North America
MAGNOLIACEAE
(\$) 10 m ☼ ☻
Though in its natural habitat the deciduous
tulip tree reaches heights of 30 m, it is rarely

*Lagerstroemia indica* (Pride of India)

*Lagunaria patersonia* (Pyramid Tree)

more than one-third as tall when cultivated. It
has lovely, three-lobed leaves which are a
soft green, changing to delicate shades of
yellow in autumn. Tulip-shaped flowers are
borne in summer, and these are a pastel
green, rimmed with yellow and orange. The
flowers are not conspicuous, being hidden in
the foliage. At its best it is a good shade tree.

**Locust Bean:** see *Ceratonia siliqua*
**Lombardy Poplar:** see *Populus nigra* 'Italica'
**London Plane:** see *Platanus* X *acerifolia*
**Loquat:** see *Eriobotrya japonica*
*Magnolia conspicua:* see *M. heptapeta*
*M. denudata:* see *M. heptapeta*

*M. discolor:* see *M. quinquepeta*

*Magnolia grandiflora*  Southern United States
MAGNOLIACEAE
(\$) 25 m ◐ ☻
The glossy green leaves and abundant, large,
creamy-white, lemon-scented flowers of the
southern magnolia, or bull bay, combine to
make it one of the most desirable evergreen
trees available. In full bloom, its summer
show of flowers makes it an unforgettable
sight. It is tolerant of a certain amount of frost.
Fine cultivars are available, among them
'Nigra', with large purple flowers; 'Alba', with

*Ligustrum lucidum* (Large-leafed Privet)

pure white flowers; and 'Rustica Rubra', with
purplish red flowers. Magnolias enjoy a
slightly acid soil and a semi-woodland condition. This species is best propagated from
seed or hardwood cuttings of terminal
growths.

*M. denudata*          China
(\$) 15 m ☼ ☻
There is some controversy about the name of
this species and it is sometimes classified as
*M. heptapeta*. Of the deciduous magnolias
this is my favourite, with its creamy-white
spring flowers which are long, bell-shaped
and faintly perfumed. The flowers of the Yulan
magnolia, which are abundantly produced,
appear just before the leaves. Though this
species can be propagated from hardwood
cuttings, these give poor results and – as with
all the following species and varieties except
*M. grandiflora* – it is wisest to reproduce by
layering.

*M. kobus*          Japan
(\$) 10 m ☼ ☻
Another favourite deciduous species, this
also bears creamy-white spring flowers, but
these are 100 mm across and have a faint
purple line at their base.

*M. purpurea:* see *M. quinquepeta*
*M. quinquepeta:* see *M. liliiflora*

*M. liliiflora*          China
(\$) 3-4 m ☼ ☻
The spring flowers of this deciduous species
are bell-shaped, 70-100 mm long and are
purple outside with white flushed purple
inside. It is quite widely grown, usually under

the name of *M. purpurea*. The variety 'nigra' is
well known, with long petals which are a very
dark purple outside and paler within.

*M.* X *soulangiana*          Garden origin
(\$) 7 m ☼ ☻
In seedling forms, the flower colours of this
deciduous hybrid are extremely variable,
ranging from white inside petals to shades of
stained purple outside. The following named
seedling cultivars of this spring-flowering
hybrid are best propagated by means of
layering. 'Alba superba' has almost clear
white flowers; those of 'Alexandrina' are
white, stained purple at the base; 'Lennei' has
rosy-purple outside and white within; while
'Rustica Rubra' has large cup-shaped petals,
rosy-red outside and paler within. Perhaps the
best of these cultivars is 'Spectabilis', with
large, almost pure white flowers.

*M. stellata*          Japan
(\$) 3 m ◐ ☻
The deciduous starry magnolia is an absolute
gem, with masses of white star-like flowers
borne in spring. These are about 80 mm
across and comprise some 16 or so petals
and sepals which are flat at first and then
reflexed. The cultivar 'Rosea', even more rare,
opens a deep, flushed pink.

**Maidenhair Tree:** see *Ginkgo biloba*

*Malus* spp.          Mainly garden hybrids
ROSACEAE

This is the genus of *Malus pumila*, the wild
apple from which all of today's varieties are
derived. This is true both of eating apples, *M.
domestica*, of which there are more than a
thousand varieties, and of the tangy crabapples. All belong to the rose family, their fruit
corresponding to the fruit of the rose, the rose
hips. Growing apples in the back garden is an
uneconomic proposition. Apples are susceptible to attack by insects and disease, and the
cost of combatting these evils is often pro-
hibitive. This leaves the gardener with the
crabapples, which offer two gifts. The first is
the pectin-rich fruit from which jams and,
more particularly, jellies are made, the pectin
providing a setting agent. The second is the
visual delight which the blossoms offer, a
delight so intense as to inspire songwriters to
produce memorable lyrics. This deciduous
flowering apple is native to the temperate
areas of the northern hemisphere but
nurserymen have produced very good cultivars which will grow in warm, dry areas as
well. The following – all of which are propagated by budding or grafting – represent a
selection of some of the best. All are garden
hybrids unless otherwise indicated.

*M.* X *aldenhamensis*
(\$) 3 m ☼ ☻
This is a good garden hybrid with purplish
leaves and purplish-red flowers followed by
yellow fruits.

*M. X arnoldiana*
✤ 4 m ☼ ⊛

With a graceful growth to a probable maximum of 4 m, this form has similar, but larger, flowers and fruit to *A. X aldenhamensis*.

*M. X astrosanguinea*
✤ 3 m ☼ ⊛

Often also catalogued as *M. floribunda* 'Purpurea', this is another excellent hybrid with flowers of a very rich rose.

*M. floribunda* 'Purpurea': see *M. X astrosanguinea*

*M. X lemoinei*
✤ 4,5 m ☼ ⊛

Tall-growing where it is happy, this hybrid has bronzy foliage and bears vivid purply-crimson flowers in profusion.

*M. X micromalus*
✤ 6 m ☼ ⊛

Derived from *M. spectabilis*, this excellent

*(continued on page 222)*

*Malus* X *lemoinei* (Purple Crab-apple)

*Malus spectabilis* (Chinese Crab-apple)

# PALMS: PROVIDING THE EXOTIC TOUCH

Be they tall, towering specimens grown outdoors where the wind makes gentle sussurations in their fronds, or smaller indoor specimens cultivated in a strategically-placed tub or stand, palms lend an air of the exotic to any home. There is an immediate suggestion of tropical islands or desert oases in most members of the PALMAE or ARECACEAE family; an air, almost, of romance.

And though most palms are indigenous to the tropics or subtropics, there are few which will not thrive outdoors in all but the coldest parts of this country. Some are tall and graceful, others – their trunks subterranean and almost root-like – are squat, their fronds creating a spiked, bushy effect; but all have an undeniable charm. Generally, they fall into two groups – those with feathery, or plumose, leaves.

All the palms listed are best propagated from seed sown, preferably in situ, as soon as it is ripe. I have found from bitter experience that unless one obtains fresh, ripe seed, germination may take as long as 18 months. Seed of *Phoenix reclinata* and *Arecastrum romanzoffianum*, on the other hand, sown immediately it falls, will germinate in only a few weeks. Most species do well in any well-drained soil, enriched with a moderate application of compost. In terms of pruning, the only attention palms need is the removal of dead fronds. This is, of course, impractical when a specimen has reached a height of 10 m or more, but though the dropping dead fronds may be briefly unsightly, the wind or time will usually do the task where the pruning saw cannot reach.

Some of the most popular palm genera and species for Australian conditions are:

*Arecastrum romanzoffianum*　　　Brazil
✤ 15 m ☼ ⊛

Recently classified as a synonym of *Syagrus romanzoffiana*. Widely grown throughout the temperate and coastal regions of this country, the handsome queen palm bears plumose, green fronds, some 3 m long, on stout stems, which are greyish and smooth. The old leaves drop away without leaving discernible scars. Deep yellow, edible fruits are borne in drooping panicles.

*Chamaedorea elegans*　　　Mexico
✤ 2 m ☼ ⊛

Graceful and relatively fast growing, though it seldom reaches more than 2 m, the good-luck palm is ideal for indoor use. Its plumose, pinnate leaves are broadly-lanceolate and dark green. It is better suited for indoor work than *Ptychosperma elegans* which it closely resembles when young. It is sometimes sold as *Neathe elegans* – a name with no botanical standing.

*Chamaerops humilis*　　　Mediterranean
✤ 1 m ☼ ⊛

Although in nature the slow-growing attractive fan palm may grow to 3 m, under indoor, greenhouse or home garden cultivation it is seldom more than 1 m high. Its fan-shaped leaves, up to 450 mm long, are grey-green and borne on long, spined stems. The variety 'elegans' is a more refined, slender subject much used for greenhouse and indoor decoration.

*Cocos nucifera*
✤ 40 m ☼ ⊛

In coastal areas the coconut palm reaches to 15 m. Its slender stem, much thickened at the base, bears pinnate fronds, anything from 2-5 m long, whose leaflets are more or less pendant. The coconut palm is difficult to grow outside the tropics.

*C. plumosa*: see *Arecastrum romanzoffianum*

**Date Palm:** see under *Phoenix canariensis*

*Dictyosperma album* 'rubrum'　　　Mauritius
✤ 10 m ☼ ⊛

In nature the princess palm – one of only

Two fine ornamental palms: *Phoenix canariensis* and *P. reclinata*

two species in its genus – is almost extinct, although a number of varieties are widely cultivated, of which 'rubrum' is probably the best known in this country. It is an attractive palm, reaching some 10 m at maturity, with numerous vertical cracks in its dark grey, otherwise smooth, slender trunk. The leaves are at least 2.5 m long, comprising drooping leaflets up to 500 mm in length and 30-40 mm wide. The prominent red veining of the fronds gives an overall reddish appearance to the foliage. On the whole, the princess palm prefers warmer climatic conditions than most.

**Fan Palm:** see *Chamaerops humilis*
**Good-luck Palm:** see *Chamaedorea elegans*

*Howea forsteriana*          Lord Howe Island
🌰 3 m ☼ 🌰

There are only two species of *Howea* and for indoor and general cultivation, the sentry palm is generally thought to be superior to *H. belmoreana*. These are spineless palms, with ringed stems and long (up to 2 m) plumose leaves. Usually known by nurserymen as *Kentia*, these are foremost among all ornamental palms for indoor decoration where there is ample space.

*Livistona australis*          Australia
🌰 6-26 m ☼ 🌰

Known as cabbage tree palm and Gippsland palm in Victoria, this Australian native is found along the east coast from Fraser Island to Victoria. It is the only species occurring naturally in Victoria. It has a long history here: the cabbage-like heart of its leaves was used for food by Aboriginals and later by white explorers. Early settlers wove broad-brimmed hats and baskets from its leaves. The cabbage tree palm is single-trunked with fan-shaped fronds and long drooping leaves. The flowers, which grow in clusters among the fibrous leaf bases, are small and yellow; the fruits are spherical and purplish black. A species planted more than a hundred years ago in the Sydney Botanical Gardens is now only about 9 m tall, so fast growth cannot be expected. Environmental pollution has taken its toll on this palm which was once familiar in coastal cities and suburbs. In Sydney only a few stands remain, in the northern coastal suburbs. When the palm is small it makes an attractive indoor plant which can later be transplanted outdoors. Propagation is from seed.

*Lytocaryum*          Brazil
   (Syn. *Microcoelum weddellianum*)
🌰 1,5 m ☼ to ◑ 🌰

One of the most elegant of all small palms for indoors, this species is equally at home in shady gardens in temperate to sub-tropical areas. Its slender stem bears graceful, arched fronds 300-900 mm long. These are deep green with glabrous undersides.

*Arecastrum romanzoffianum* (Queen Palm)

*Cocos nucifera* (Coconut Palm)

A palm garden lends a touch of the exotic

*Cocos nucifera, Livistona australis, Roystonea regia, Howea forsterana* and *Phoenix dactylifera* (Date Palm)

*Tipuana tipu* (Tipu Tree)

*Tibouchina granulosa*

# LEAF SHAPES

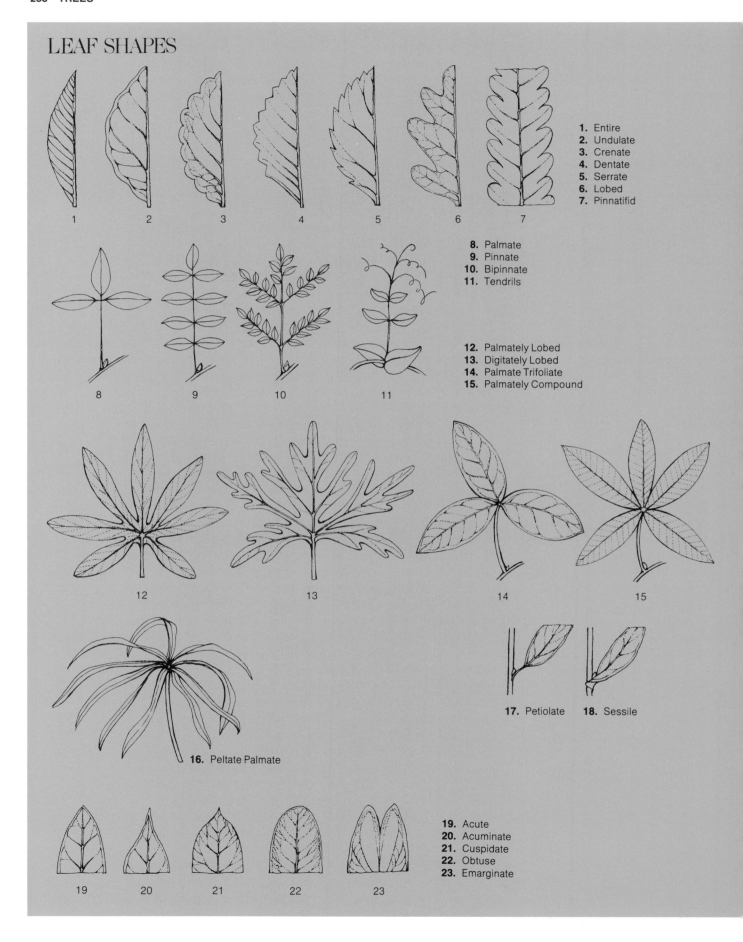

1. Entire
2. Undulate
3. Crenate
4. Dentate
5. Serrate
6. Lobed
7. Pinnatifid

8. Palmate
9. Pinnate
10. Bipinnate
11. Tendrils

12. Palmately Lobed
13. Digitately Lobed
14. Palmate Trifoliate
15. Palmately Compound

16. Peltate Palmate

17. Petiolate
18. Sessile

19. Acute
20. Acuminate
21. Cuspidate
22. Obtuse
23. Emarginate

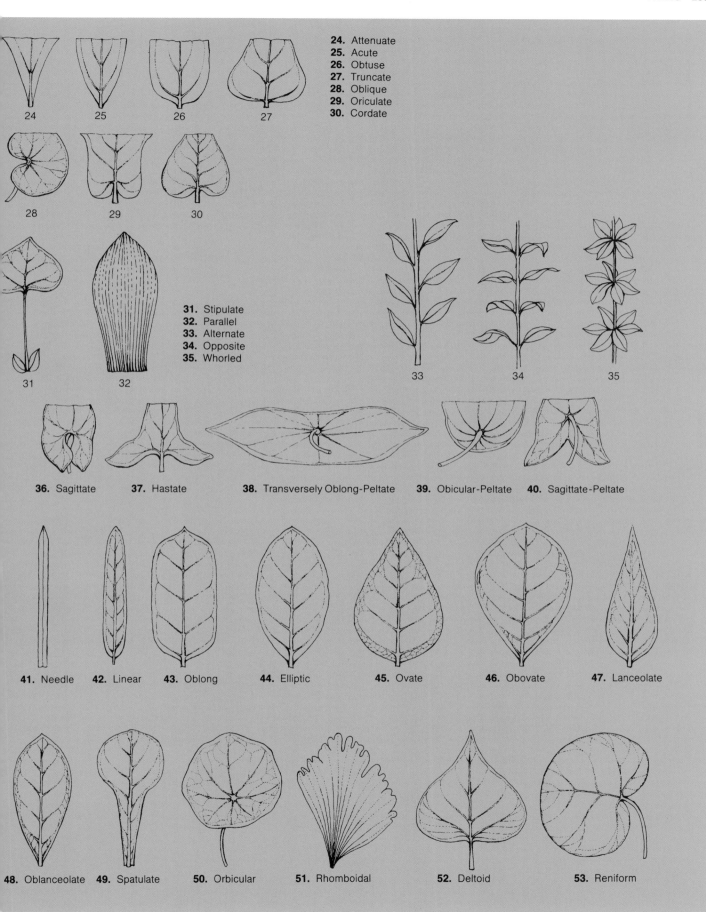

24. Attenuate
25. Acute
26. Obtuse
27. Truncate
28. Oblique
29. Oriculate
30. Cordate

31. Stipulate
32. Parallel
33. Alternate
34. Opposite
35. Whorled

36. Sagittate    37. Hastate    38. Transversely Oblong-Peltate    39. Obicular-Peltate    40. Sagittate-Peltate

41. Needle    42. Linear    43. Oblong    44. Elliptic    45. Ovate    46. Obovate    47. Lanceolate

48. Oblanceolate    49. Spatulate    50. Orbicular    51. Rhomboidal    52. Deltoid    53. Reniform

# FRUIT TREES 12 AND VINES

## FRESHNESS AND FLAVOUR FOR THE PLUCKING

Gone, probably for ever, are the days when abundant fresh fruit and vegetables were available at prices which today seem risibly cheap and the word 'glut' was commonly used in relation to agriculture's bounty. Improved cold storage techniques, airfreight and a lively export industry have seen to that, leaving the housewife to scramble for the remnants. Unless there is a farmer in the family we must do as much as we can for ourselves.

Space is often a problem, but the inclusion of fruit trees or other food-bearing plants is not incompatible with aesthetics and it is remarkable how careful planning can allow much to be produced from a relatively small area. When designing a new garden the planner should take into account, as far as possible, household needs in terms of fruit and vegetables – and even existing gardens may be restructured with this in mind.

I deal with vegetable-growing in the following chapter, but mention vegetables here because many of them grow well in combination with fruit trees. For instance, in subtropical and warmly temperate areas, properly spaced lines of papaws provide the ideal shade for lettuce, peas, beans, carrots or beetroot. Citrus fruits such as lemons, oranges, mandarins, grapefruit and tangelos are not incongruous grown among shrubs in the border, while an orange tree, prominently placed near the house, can prove highly ornamental.

Three factors will largely determine the nature of a fruit garden – space, climate, and the lengths to which the gardener is prepared to go to protect his plants from pests and diseases.

Where space is limited, the grower may be wise to concentrate on loganberries, blackberries, strawberries, Chinese guavas, papaws, grapes, tree tomatoes, and passion fruit – by no means a dull list. Plum, nectarine, peach, apple and some citrus trees require liberal space to mature satisfactorily and provide optimum fruit, but there is no reason why a pecan nut or a mulberry should not be used as a specimen shade tree in a small garden. Both are highly productive; pecan nuts store well for use throughout the year while mulberries are ideal for stewing, for pies and especially for jam-making.

As far as climate is concerned, deciduous trees – the stone fruits and apples, pears and quinces – do best in cold to cool temperate regions. However, many suppliers offer varieties of apple, peach and plum trees which are suited to the warmer, temperate regions. Orange, fig, persimmon trees and grape vines prefer warmer conditions. Tropical fruits, such as bananas, papaws, pineapples, mangos and litchis, may succeed in subtropical zones as well as in favoured, frost-free spots in warmly temperate areas.

Protection against insect pests and fungus diseases can be a major bugbear. While passion fruit, loganberries and mulberries need very little protection, other fruits require a regular spray programme and should not be planted unless you are prepared to attend to all their particular requirements. Quite apart from anything else, such neglect would be totally unfair to your neighbours, whose plants might also be attacked.

### PURCHASE OF PLANTS

Fruit trees of any description – already established in plastic containers – are available from most nurserymen all the year round. But while this is very convenient, the wise gardener will plan his planting to take advantage of the much lower price of all important deciduous fruit trees offered during the dormant months. Evergreens such as avocado, litchis, mangos and citrus are usually available in containers and may be planted out any time. All these, as well as the macadamia nut and the deciduous pecan nut, may be bought as seedlings, but it is wise to pay a little more for named cultivars as these usually fruit earlier and perform consistently. Your nurseryman will be able to advise which is the best type for your particular soil and climate.

Soil preparation for fruit-bearing plants is no different from that for other trees and shrubs so that I need add little more. Remember, however, that citrus trees are shallow-rooting so that the holes should be wide rather than deep; do not cultivate around these trees – rather maintain a fairly deep mulch which will discourage other growth. When planting loganberries, youngberries, passion fruit and grape vines, a well-prepared trench is preferable to individual holes.

◀ The spiny skin of a pineapple belies the succulent sweetness which it hides.

# HOME-GROWN VEGETABLES

## CRISP GREENS ON YOUR DOORSTEP

In the horticultural sense, a vegetable is any edible herbaceous plant, or part of such plant, which is commonly used for human consumption. And though there is a technical term – olericulture – for vegetable gardening, it is one of many such words which has never achieved popular usage.

In some countries melons and tomatoes are regarded as fruits; the Americans on the other hand regard both as vegetables, while in Australia we tend to regard melons as fruit and tomatoes as vegetables. In fact it is almost impossible to find a simple definition which will embrace all vegetables, omitting none. But the term 'vegetable' is so well known – 'Eat up your vegetables' remains an early childhood admonition – that we have little difficulty in applying it, and making ourselves understood in everyday speech. Actually it remains much easier to talk or write about vegetables than to grow them.

I have deliberately omitted such vegetables as asparagus, the onion, garlic and celery. Crops which occupy space for as much as nine months and more – and then may or may not prove successful – have no place in the home garden. Equally, Brussels sprouts require space and do not always succeed. These vegetables are best left to the farmer or market gardener who, as well as having more space, has the enormous advantage of being able to choose the best site in terms of soil and drainage, for whatever crop he wishes to plant. The home grower must take what there is and do the best he can with it. But, if it is fully open to the sun, almost any piece of ground can be worked and treated so that it becomes fertile and capable of providing a wide range of good vegetables.

Deep digging over the whole area is vital. Together with the initial heavy application of farmyard manure or good compost, this is the only way of improving the physical texture of the soil so that it will be loose, mellow and fertile, capable of holding moisture and producing crops quickly. Deep digging means trenching to a depth of at least 600 mm and then thoroughly breaking up the bottom 200 mm, thus loosening the soil to an overall depth of 800 mm. Into the top 300 mm thoroughly incorporate the equivalent of a 200 mm layer of manure or compost. Not all vege-tables, particularly carrots and similar root crops, appreciate fresh manure in the near surface soil, and the quickest way of bringing all the soil into an acceptable home for vegetables is to plant an initial crop of potatoes, peas or beans.

Here, too, crop rotation can play a valuable rôle; for though its application is essentially agricultural, it is important in creating good tilth as well as making optimum use of the soil, no matter how large or small your vegetable plot. Briefly, shallow- and deep-rooting vegetable crops are rotated on a particular piece of ground to exploit the different soil levels most effec-tively. Rotation also reduces the risk of plant diseases building up in the soil, a danger heightened by grow-ing the same crop in the same place for several consecutive harvests. At the same time, because some vegetables demand larger quantities of a par-ticular food element than others, crop rotation reduces the creation of deficiencies which might stem from these demands.

Although planting for a succession of vegetables is not strictly a matter of crop rotation, it forms part of the pattern. Not long ago, the gardener wanting his own steady supply of different vegetables had to plan carefully the staggered sowing and planting out of each crop. But the advent of the deep-freeze has changed all that, and today's wise gardener plans his production in relation to his capacity for storage. Though no home gardener can produce directly from his garden to the plate all the family vegetable require-ments every day of the year, with the aid of the deep-freeze he can come very close to it. In these days of spiralling prices and often falling quality, a good vegetable garden can make a worthwhile contri-bution not only to the household budget but to the savour of one's food.

Peas and beans exemplify how the system of grow-ing for the deep-freeze works. By and large, beans are a summer and peas a winter crop. At the beginning and again towards the end of each season, make a major sowing of each. Each crop can be picked at its peak and deep-frozen without waste, even if this entails (as it will do) picking and packing away every third day or so throughout the period of the crop. I

Pumpkins nestle among the green of their leaves.

have followed this pattern with most vegetables for years and there is scarcely a day of the year when we cannot put our hands on peas, beans, carrots, cauliflower, broccoli, beetroot and pumpkin.

In the selective list for the home grower which follows, I have included notes on deep-freezing. Over the past years my wife and I have established that blanching is best achieved by steaming, rather than immersion in boiling water, and that rapid cooling in iced water is quite unnecessary – equally good results and a superior flavour are achieved by natural cooling. Place the blanched vegetables on a grid until cold enough to pack away. We find a large double boiler is the best steaming apparatus, substituting a perforated inner pot for the inner part of the boiler; otherwise, use any large pot and a metal or enamelled colander with fairly well-fitting lid. The times I have given for blanching rate from the moment the water starts to boil furiously. We pack away the 'prepared' vegetables in ordinary standard size 220 × 300 mm plastic bags with just enough in each for a family meal for two, three or four. Unless otherwise indicated in the text, pack the blanched vegetables firmly, roll the pack to exclude as much air as possible and stack away.

**Aubergine:** see **Egg Plant**

**Bean** (*Phaseolus vulgaris*) Tropical America
LEGUMINOSAE
The dwarf bean is generally more convenient for the home gardener to grow than the runner bean and provides a crop which matures in eight to ten weeks, thus providing regular pickings for about three weeks. It is particularly successful in ground which has been heavily manured for a previous crop and should be supplemented by light dressings of complete plant food every ten days after sowing. Give soils deficient in phosphates a dressing of superphosphate five days before you sow.

Depending on local climate, it is probably best to sow the first main crop in September and the second main crop in mid-December. If, for some reason beyond your control, either crop should fail, there is still time to sow again before the season ends. Space rows of dwarf beans 500-600 mm apart and sow seeds every 70-100 mm along each row. Pick the beans when they are in perfect condition, young and succulent; to deep-freeze, your only pre-blanching activity will be 'topping and tailing' and cutting in half. Extra large, young beans may also be halved, lengthwise.

Blanch or steam them for two minutes, or until they just turn bright green.

**Beetroot** (*Beta vulgaris*) Europe, Asia Minor
CHENOPODIACEAE
A relatively quick crop, beetroot matures eight to ten weeks after sowing. Beetroot is not particular about soils, but it is good practice to give a dressing of complete plant food several days before sowing, and after that a light side dressing every 15 days or so until just before harvesting. Sow thinly in rows about 300 mm apart, thinning the seedlings out to about 120 mm apart when about 70 mm high, using transplants to fill any gaps. To deep-freeze beetroot, prepare and cook them in the usual way; when cool, slice or dice, place in small containers, seal with lid and pack away. Do not add onion or vinegar until required for the table.

**Broccoli**
(*Brassica oleracea* 'botrytis') Western Europe
CRUCIFERAE
Sow broccoli between December and March in most areas of Australia.

To make the most of space in the home garden, sow broccoli, cauliflower and cabbage, particularly, in trays and pot on into 120 mm-diameter containers where they should grow or until they are about 200 mm high and are ready for planting out. This saves considerable space and you also know the plant will succeed. Stagger the plants 500 mm apart with about 500 mm between rows. Before planting, a light dressing of lime will prove beneficial and thereafter, until harvesting, dress lightly with complete plant food every ten days, giving enough water to keep the plants growing well and fast. Allow about 12 weeks for maturing and, for the home garden, keep the plant growing strongly after the main head has been cut to ensure continuous cropping. Lesser heads will continue to grow from the lower stem, and though these are smaller, together with their tender stems and succulent small leaves, these deep-freeze beautifully. Before freezing, blanch the picked broccoli for three minutes.

**Cabbage**
(*Brassica oleracea* 'capitata') Western Europe
CRUCIFERAE
Australia's warmly temperate climate allows cabbage to grow well throughout the year and deep-freezing is not necessary. Heat-resistant varieties, modern hybrids, and the use of summer shade cloth, permit round-the-year cropping except in tropical regions where they may be difficult to grow in the wet season. As with cauliflower and broccoli, it is wise to grow plants in individual pots. However, because cabbage is not a one season crop it should be grown in succession. I find that putting out a dozen plants every month is not only enough for home needs, but provides a few cabbages to give away.

The soil must be rich, properly prepared with compost, and pre-limed; to keep the crop growing fast give adequate water whenever required. Every ten days give a side dressing of complete plant food. Plant out smaller types 600 mm apart, and the larger at 800 mm centres.

For deep-freezing, prepare the cabbage as you would for the pot, then steam-blanch for two minutes, cool, and put in plastic bags the quantity required for one meal.

**Capsicum**
(*Capsicum annuum*) Tropical America
SOLANACEAE
This group includes the sweet green, the sweet yellow and red peppers as well as the hot chili pepper – which may be large or

Beans (*Phaseolus vulgaris*)

small, green or red. In cooler areas sow seed under protection and grow on in pots, so that well-developed plants are ready for setting out as soon as the danger of frost is past. Whether in warm or cold areas, the ideal is to have the longest possible fruiting season; once peppers start to fruit this continues until the cold stops them.

A marvellous, 'one-stop' flavouring for fish dishes, stews, soups, meat pies and so on, may be made as follows: Wash and clean a little more than 500 g of medium-sized red peppers – not the very little ones popularly known as 'Red Devils' – skin the cloves of one large garlic bulb and mince together. Place in a pot with 750 ml of sunflower oil and simmer gently for 30 minutes. Strain, cool and pour the oil back into the same bottle. The liquid will last indefinitely, and should be used sparingly, drop by drop, until the flavour is just to your taste. There were red faces and hot tongues until I realized its potency. Do not throw away the strainings; pack them into a jar, place in the refrigerator, and use to flavour stews. Surprisingly, the strainings are less potent than the oil.

Plant out at 450 mm intervals in staggered rows set 600 mm apart. Peppers enjoy a well-drained loamy soil to which a generous quantity of organic material or compost has been added. Every fortnight give a side

Peppers (*Capsicum annuum*)

dressing of a complete plant food. The yellow and green sweet peppers deep-freeze well and are handy for stews, soups and similar dishes. Blanching time for these peppers is 40 seconds.

**Carrot** (*Daucus carota*)  Garden origin
APIACEAE
The carrot does best in deep, loamy to sandy soil which has been well-manured for a previous crop. Fresh manure, or even too much fertilizer in the upper soil, will cause the roots to fork. Plant carrots from August to March in most areas.

Bring the seed bed to a very fine state of cultivation, firming down before sowing. Some gardeners prefer to broadcast the seed, but rows are often more convenient, in which case sow very thinly in rows 300 mm apart. When the plants are about 60 mm high thin out to 70 mm apart. Carrots need constant and ample watering and the seed bed or seed rows should be kept moist until germination. Always use fresh seed from a reliable source. The old variety 'King Chantenay' is still very popular.

The carrot deep freezes beautifully, but use only the best, the youngest, the most succulent. Carrots may be prepared for the deep freeze in many ways, such as ringing and dicing, but we find the quickest method is to slice them lengthwise, cutting the smaller roots in half, quartering the larger, and shortening where necessary. Blanch for two minutes.

**Cauliflower**  Western Europe
(*Brassica oleracea* 'botrytis cauliflora')
BRASSICACEAE
Generally, cultivation is the same as for cabbage and broccoli, and although the 'winter' season of the cauliflower has been extended by the introduction of new cultivars – and perhaps a better understanding of its cultural requirements – you will probably find two crops convenient. The cauliflower is sensitive and must be grown without check from the seedling stage through to maturity. When they start, they mature quickly so that two staggered crops give a better chance to cope with deep freezing. The head is at its best for only a few days.

Prepare for deep-freezing in much the same way as you would for the pot – cut off the small heads and dice the thicker, secondary stems. Do not discard the tender leaves at the base of each head; divide them among the packs for deep freezing. Blanch for two minutes or until the bright green is evident in the tender leaves.

**Cucumber** (*Cucumis sativus*)  Southern Asia
CUCURBITACEAE
This worthwhile vegetable takes up little space when grown on wires or, ideally, on a trellis which can then be used in winter for climbing peas. Along the base of the support dig a trench 400 mm deep and 250 mm wide and enrich this with good compost and a light dressing of complete plant food. From September through to December sow two or three seeds in groups 300 mm apart along the trench. Give supplementary feeds every

Carrot (*Daucus carota*)

Cabbage (*Brassica oleracea* 'capitata')

ten days or so after planting out to keep them growing fast. Water copiously when necessary.

**Egg Plant**  Africa, Asia
(*Solanum melongena* 'esculentum')
SOLANACEAE
The egg plant, or aubergine, takes some time to establish itself and begin to bear. Sow the seed in October or November, three or four seeds per pot, peat pots are excellent for this. By the time all danger of cold snaps and frost is past, you will have sturdily developed plants. Pinch out the growing points as the plants develop. Any well-drained soil with liberal quantities of compost, well worked in, is suitable. Give a side dressing of complete plant food every ten days, and water plentifully during dry periods.

A dozen plants, put out at 600 mm centres, will provide ample egg plant for the average family, with sufficient left for deep-freezing.

For deep-freezing, slice the fruit and blanch for one minute before packing into firm containers.

Egg Plant, or Aubergine (*Solanum melongena* 'esculentum')

Lettuce (*Lactuca sativa* 'capitata')

**Gem Squash:** see **Pumpkin**
**Hubbard Squash:** see **Pumpkin**

**Kohlrabi** *(Brassica oleracea)* Western Europe
CRUCIFERAE
This relative of the cabbage will thrive in all but the hottest climates. The thick stem is eaten rather than the sparse and bitter-tasting leaves. Kohlrabi has similar soil and water requirements to cabbage and is also cultivated in the same way. Sow seed in situ, from February through to late autumn, in rows about 300 mm apart, thinning out the young seedlings so that individual plants are about 180 mm apart. The seeds take about six weeks to reach maturity and weekly plantings will ensure a regular crop until early winter. Harvest kohlrabi when the stems are about 50 mm in diameter; they are inclined to bolt and if allowed to grow any larger than this, tend to become woody. Cook as you would turnips.

**Lettuce** *(Lactuca sativa)* Garden origin
ASTERACEAE
This is one of the very few vegetables which cannot be stored for long, so that crops must be grown in succession. Fortunately, there are few parts in the country where this cannot be done throughout the year. Lettuce is an easy crop but it must be grown fast with plenty of food and abundant water during hot, dry spells. Any deep, well-drained, medium to light loamy soil, well worked with liberal quantities of compost or farmyard manure, suits all varieties of lettuce. Depending on type, the crop matures in six to nine weeks, and putting out 15-20 plants each month will more than satisfy the needs of the average family. Raise plants for the home garden in a compartmented polyester tray, filling each section with equal parts of river sand and fibrous loam. Drop two seeds into each compartment, cover the seed very lightly and after germination thin to one. When the plantlets are well rooted and about 50 mm high, plant

out 300 mm apart in staggered rows. Alternatively sow directly into clumps or stations 200 mm to 300 mm apart. Seedlings emerge in six to seven days. Thin each station to the strongest seedling. Nine to twelve plants in successive sowings each three to four weeks should supply the average family. 'Great Lakes' is good and will tolerate heat better than most.

**Marrow** North America
(*Cucurbita pepo* 'Ovifera')
CUCURBITACEAE
Though it cannot be preserved or stored as one would, say, a pumpkin, the vegetable marrow is a most useful summer vegetable. The low, bushy plant takes up very little room

and produces its green-striped or yellow fruit close to the parent. Some growers delight in producing huge marrows – as much as 500 mm long and 150 mm in diameter – but this exhausts the plant and reduces the crop to two or three. Cut either as baby marrows (zucchinis) or allow the fruits to grow to only about 250 mm, and the plants will produce three times as many and over a much longer period. Marrows enjoy a well-drained loamy soil, to which a moderate quantity of good compost has been added. Excessive use of animal manure or chemical fertilizers may lead to rank growth and little productivity.

**Pepper:** see **Capsicum**

Sweet Green Pepper (*Capsicum annuum*)

Potatoes (*Solanum tuberosum*)

## Peas (*Pisum sativum*)     Eurasia
### LEGUMINOSAE

Frozen peas are always available, but one's own cost so much less that home growing and deep-freezing is really worthwhile. As peas are a winter vegetable, April is a good month to sow the first, main crop, following it with a second crop in June. Dwarf and semi-dwarf varieties are best suited to the home garden, but even these need some form of twiggy support. Soil previously heavily manured for another crop, is ideal and should be given a dressing of 2:3:2 about five days before sowing.

Sow the seed 40 mm deep in double rows – two lines of seed staggered 100 mm apart in each row – leaving 500 mm between the double rows. This is heavy coverage, but if the soil is in good shape and side feedings of a balanced fertilizer are given every 10-12 days until flowering, an optimum crop should be expected. To obtain the best return, pick when the first pods are full and continue this chore every third day until the whole crop is reaped.

Picking and packing away in the deep-freeze every few days may prove a bother, but you will be surprised at the quality and quantity of the total crop. Repeatedly cultivate the surface of the soil to a depth of 50 mm, eliminating weeds and conserving soil moisture, and water well during flowering and harvest periods.

For storage, blanch peas for about two minutes or until they become bright green, then freeze in meal-sized packs.

## Potatoes     South America
(*Solanum tuberosum*)
### SOLANACEAE

Though the potato is suitable only for the larger vegetable garden, I include it because, irrespective of size, the new home garden is usually best brought into condition for future vegetable growing by planting it, heavily manured, with potatoes. The potato loves a well-drained soil, rich in organic matter, and other plant foods should be supplied every 15 days or so throughout the active period of growth. The initial application of farmyard manure, or well-prepared compost, should be as heavy as the grower can manage. However, because the 'seed' should not come into direct contact with fresh manure or concentrations of fertilizer, try to prepare the soil some six weeks in advance.

To obtain even growth it is good practice to sprout seed potatoes before planting out. To do this spread the tubers out in a brightly lit position and turn them over after a few days to encourage even greening. Small potatoes can be planted out whole once sprouts have erupted, larger potatoes can be halved or quartered so that each piece has two or three shoots sprouting from it.

Dig trenches 650 mm apart, approximately 120 mm deep, and the width of a spade. Plant the sprouts upright, 400 mm apart, and back fill the trench, covering the tubers well. When the sprouts are about 120 mm high, draw up the soil on either side, so that only a few centimetres of their tips remain showing. Continue this ridging process until you have a broadly-based ridge some 350 mm high. This not only protects the tubers, but provides a ready means of applying water – furrow irrigation is much healthier for the potato than overhead spraying. Water whenever required and remember that occasional soakings give more benefit than frequent light applications; never allow to dry out. Feed lightly with a complete plant food six weeks after planting. Reduce watering and stop fertilizing as soon as a slight yellowing of the foliage indicates a decline in growth. This will allow the tubers to mature.

During dry weather the mature potatoes can safely be left in the ground for quite some time; lift them as you need them. But if it rains or the earth is wet, lift the tubers as soon as they are ready or they may turn glassy or begin to grow again. When lifting potatoes, remove everything of the old crop from the ground – stems, rotten tubers, old seed and so on – as a precaution against pests and fungus diseases.

## Pumpkin     South America
(*Cucurbita maxima*)
### CUCURBITACEAE

Pumpkins grow on large rambling vines and require a large area of the garden. It's best to provide substantial support for them – a fence or a garden shed can be very suitable. Popular varieties include Queensland Blue a very large fruiting variety and Butternut and Baby Blue which are both smaller and more suited to the home vegetable garden.

To get pumpkins or squash into the ground as early as possible, grow them singly in 120 mm pots, under protection. Early in spring make mounds of soil, heavily enriched with farmyard manure and compost. Each mound should be 1.5 m in diameter and stand about 400 mm high. Set the mounds about 2.5 m apart; plant three to five plants on each mound. After planting out, give a good dressing of complete plant food and repeat this three weeks later. Water copiously during the very active growing season, tailing off as the vegetables mature. Pumpkin may be deep-frozen as soon as it has reached full size, leaving the ground available for other plantings.

> To prepare effectively for the deep-freeze: cut into slices – making it easier to remove the hard skin and pulpy seed – then cut into conveniently-sized small blocks and blanch these for two or three minutes.

## Radish (*Raphanus sativus*)     Europe/Asia
### BRASSICACEAE

This crop matures in about six weeks, so that monthly sowings should provide a succession of young radishes – far less 'burpy' than large ones – practically all year round. The radish is relatively pest-free, but do not plant them in the same piece of ground again and again as this will inevitably encourage the development of fungus disease in one form or another. The plants are not fussy, but the soil should be finely worked and sufficiently well enriched to sustain rapid growth. Tardy growth results in an unpalatably strong flavour. If the soil is well enriched two or three weeks before sowing, using a well-decomposed manure or compost, one light dressing of a complete plant food ten days after germination should bring the crop through nicely. Sow the seed thinly in rows 200 mm apart and when the plants are 30 mm high, thin them out to 50 mm apart.

## Silver-beet (*Beta vulgaris*)     South West Asia
(*Spinacia oleracea*)
### CHENOPODIACEAE

The Swiss chard type of spinach gives the best and easiest crop in the home vegetable garden. 'Fordhook Giant' with a broad white stem and large, crinkly green leaves is the most popular variety. Don't discard the fleshy white stems – cooked with the rich green leaves they are quite delicious.

The life of each crop depends largely on the frequency of cutting; regular harvesting can lead to plants lasting a year or more. Sow the seed thinly in rows 500 mm apart, or sow in a tray, later setting the young plants out 400 mm apart in the rows. Silver-beet does not

Pumpkins (*Cucurbita maxima*)

have difficult soil requirements, but very light soils should be heavily worked with farmyard manure or good fibrous compost. A side dressing of balanced fertilizer every 20 days or so should keep the crop in fine shape. Frequent watering is essential as growth is more or less continuous. Because of the plants' long productive lives, deep freezing is not recommended.

*Squash:* see **Pumpkin**

**Sweet Corn** (*Zea mays*)       Tropical America
GRAMINEAE
Sweet corn requires a sunny position and well drained soil rich in organic material such as fibrous compost or well dug in farmyard manure. Sow the seed directly into position 20-30 mm deep in rows about 500 mm apart in spring and summer. During preparation of the bed, and again when the plants are about 500 mm tall, apply a complete plant food, and when they have doubled this height give them a top dressing of nitrogenous feed. The plants take about 12 weeks to reach maturity and the cobs are best harvested at the 'milk' stage, when the kernels are still young and tender. Some varieties now mature in eight to nine weeks.

**Tomatoes** (*Lycopersicon esculentum*)Andes
SOLANACEAE
Highly sensitive to cold and very prone to fungus diseases during periods of high humidity or prolonged wet weather, the tomato is not the easiest vegetable to cultivate really successfully. Nevertheless, it is certainly one of the most gratifying – pleasing both the eye and the palate.

In temperate parts of the country, tomatoes can be grown throughout the year. Even where there is some frost, plants in a sheltered north-west aspect – especially if grown in pots – will survive and often fruit very well. Tomatoes require a well-drained soil, enriched with organic material, and are best grown on ridges which allow furrow watering. Never use overhead irrigation for tomatoes.

Sow seeds individually in a compartmented polyester tray and when the seedlings are about 50-70 mm high, transfer them to 120 mm pots to grow on to a height of 200 mm before planting out. This way the roots are virtually undisturbed and there is no check to the plants' growth – a vital factor in successful home garden cultivation.

Prior to planting out prepare the bed with plenty of fibrous compost or well rotted farmyard manure. Set out the plants at 400 mm intervals in rows one metre apart. Pinch out any side shoots in the axils of the leaf stems on the main leader; and when five or so trusses have formed, stop the main leader. Like most other 'salad' plants, the tomato should be grown fast. Water copiously whenever necessary and feed with a complete water soluble plant food every 10 days or so.

Dust regularly with tomato dust to prevent fungus diseases and caterpillar attack. Check the makers' instructions carefully with regard to safety intervals between dusting and harvesting.

Silver-beet (*Beta vulgaris*)

## SOWING TIMES

| | Temperate Climates | Cool Climates | Tropical Climates | Maturity |
|---|---|---|---|---|
| Beans, dwarf | Late Sep-late Feb | Oct-Jan | All seasons | 8-10 weeks |
| Beans, climbing | Late Sep-Feb | Oct-Jan | All seasons | 10-12 weeks |
| Beetroot | Aug-Apr | Sep-Mar | All seasons | 10-14 weeks |
| Broccoli | Jan-Mar | Jan-Mar | Jan-Feb | 20-26 |
| Brussels sprouts | Dec-Mar | Dec-Feb | Unsuitable | 25-30 weeks |
| Cabbages (small) | Aug-May | Aug-Apr | Mar-Jul | 15-18 |
| Capsicums | Oct-Nov | Oct | Sep-Feb | 18-20 weeks |
| Carrots | Aug-Apr | Sep-Mar | Mar-Sep | 10-12 weeks |
| Cauliflowers | Dec-Mar | Nov-Mar | Feb-Mar | 18-30 weeks |
| Cucumbers | Sep-Dec | Oct-Dec | Jul-Mar | 8-10 weeks |
| Egg-plants | Oct-Nov | Oct | Sep-Feb | 18-20 weeks |
| Khol-rabi | Apr-Aug | Mar-Aug | Apr-Jun | 10-12 weeks |
| Lettuce | All seasons | All seasons | All seasons | 9-10 weeks |
| Marrows | Oct-Jan | Oct-Dec | Aug-Mar | 8-10 weeks |
| Peas | Feb-Sep | Jul-Oct | Mar-Jul | 12-15 weeks |
| Potatoes | Aug-Sep & Feb | Aug-Sep | Feb-Apr | 16-20 weeks |
| Pumpkin | Sep-Jan | Oct-Nov | Aug-Feb | 16 weeks |
| Radishes | All seasons | Sep-Mar | All seasons | 4-6 weeks |
| Silver-beet | Aug-Apr | Aug-Mar | Mar-Aug | 10-12 weeks |
| Sweet Corn | Sep-Feb | Oct-Dec | Aug-Feb | 12 weeks |
| Tomatoes | Aug-Dec | Sep-Oct | All seasons | 16-18 weeks |
| Turnips | Feb-May | Feb/Mar & Jul/Sep | Mar-Jul | 12 weeks |

Surplus ripe tomatoes can be cleaned and put through the blender. Bring the pulp obtained to the boil, skim off any foam and immediately pour the juice into sterilized screw-top bottles, capping tightly. Place the bottles in a cool dark cupboard. This tomato pulp is an invaluable addition to stews, curries and similar dishes.

### Turnip (*Brassica rapa*)   Europe
BRASSICACEAE
Easy to grow and taking up very little space, the humble garden turnip is a useful quick crop for a sunny piece of vacant ground. After four to five weeks feed regularly with a complete plant food. Work the soil well and dress it five days before sowing. Sow thinly in rows and prick out the weaker plants to leave the remaining seedlings 100 mm apart when they are about 40 mm high. Turnips thrive in the cooler months.

Neatly tended rows in a well-kept vegetable garden

*Limnanthemum thunbergianum:* see
   *Nymphoides indica*

*Mimulus guttatus*       North America
SCROPHULARIACEAE
⚘ 150-500 mm ☼ ☙
Ranging in height from 150-500 mm, this
evergreen perennial, which flowers in late
spring and early summer, is a natural choice
for the marsh garden. Racemes of yellow
flowers with purple-brown spotted throats
bring splashes of vivid colour to the clumps
of the monkey musk's leaves. Found in nature
in climatic extremes as varied as those of
Alaska and Mexico, this species has no difficulty in adapting itself to Australian conditions. Both this and the following species may
be propagated from seed, but as this is an
involved process, the average gardener will
find it much easier to increase the plants from
cuttings or by division in autumn.

*M. luteus*       Chile
⚘ 900 mm ☼ ☙
Similar in habit and appearance to the
monkey flower (see page 102), with which it is
often confused, this species also bears
yellow flowers but these are distinctively
marked with two red or purple spots on the
throat.

**Monkey Musk:** see *Mimulus guttatus*

*Myriophyllum aquaticum*       Brazil
HALORAGADACEAE
The stems of the vigorous, aquatic parrot's
feather carry dense whorls of feathery foliage
which grows 150-220 mm out of the water
before drooping or arching over. The tips
finally recurve upwards turning shades of
crimson in late spring and early summer. To
propagate, put cuttings in loam and sub-
merge them in water.

*Nelumbo nucifera*       Asia
NYMPHAEACEAE
Perhaps because its flowers are sacred to
Buddhists, the East Indian lotus is often confused with the sacred lotus of Egypt; but this
species can be distinguished immediately by
its characteristic, raised foliage which stands
as much as 750 mm above water level. These
leaves are glaucous, entire, and 450-600 mm
across. The strongly-scented flowers are
white, flushed pink or rose towards the tips.
There are many cultivars of this species,
some larger than the type, some double and
varying from white to cream and from flushed
pink to a very deep red. Plant so that the
crown is ultimately covered by water to a
depth of about 300 mm. Propagate by division of the crowns in autumn.

**New Zealand Flax:** see *Phormium tenax*

*Nymphaea caerulea*    North, Central Africa
NYMPHAEACEAE
Though this species, often depicted in
ancient Egyptian paintings, has a delicate
appearance, it, like most water lilies, is surprisingly hardy and vigorous. Its faintly-
scented, typical water-lily flowers are light
blue and seem to nestle on the surface

*Nelumbo nucifera* (East Indian Lotus)

among the deep green leaves, which have
purple-blotched undersides and are 300-400
mm across. All water lilies may be propagated from ripe seeds, but as these often take
as long as four years to mature, *Nymphaea*
are best propagated by division of the
tuberous rootstock.

*N. capensis*       South Africa
This has been extensively bred and hybridized, particularly in Japan, but the true form
can still hold its own as one of the finest. Sky
blue, fragrant flowers, 150-200 mm across,
are held proudly above the water on slender
stems, and a large pool or pond, its surface
covered with the soft green of the leaves and
a carpet of blooms nodding, provides an
unforgettable sight. The variety 'zanzibarien-
sis', bears deeper blue flowers of almost
startling intensity, and these are larger –
sometimes double the size of the true
species. The variety 'rosea' has deep carmine
to pink blooms.

*N. lotus*       Tropics, Old World
There has always been disagreement
between the proponents of *N. lotus* and *N.
caerulea* on the one hand, and of *Nelumbo
nucifera* on the other, as to which is the true
sacred lotus of the ancient Egyptians. Since
*Nelumbo nucifera*, known throughout the
ages in the East as the lotus lily, is not found
in the Nile, I am convinced that *N. lotus* is the
true white sacred lotus and *N. caerulea*, the
true blue sacred lily. *N. lotus* has large, floating, peltate leaves, with hairy undersides. The
large (up to 300 mm across), unscented,
white or flushed pink flowers open only in the
morning, closing again in the afternoon. Plant
so that when the pool is full, 450-500 mm of
water stands above the crown.

*N. stellata*       South and East Asia
This species, which bears pale blue flowers

about 150 mm across, is, with *N. caerulea*, the
parent of many popular hybrid cultivars. Its
leaves differ from those of *N. caerulea* in
having violet, or sometimes pinkish, undersides. Flowers of a form found only in India
are frequently white or pink.

*Nymphoides indica*       Tropics
MENYANTHACEAE
This floating species, which bears a myriad of
bright yellow flowers throughout summer, is a
delightful addition to the pool, tub garden or
aquatic window box. Until fairly recently this
useful and charming species was known as
*Limnanthemum thunbergianum*. Propagate
by division in spring or autumn.

**Parrot's Feather:** see *Myriophyllum
aquaticum*

*Nymphaea capensis*

A frog he would a-wooing go . . . *Nymphaea caerulea*

A fine spread of *Nymphaea capensis*

*Pontederia cordata*

*Phormium tenax*                    New Zealand
AGAVACEAE
As well as producing fibre which is of considerable economic importance, New Zealand flax, with its many varieties and cultivars,
is most attractive planted in the raised zone of
the marsh garden. All will grow under
ordinary garden conditions (see page 154)
but are particularly at home in such a permanently moist situation where they will reach
heights of 2 m or so.

*Pontederia cordata*                    North America
PONTEDERIACEAE
🌢 600 mm ☼ 🌢
One of the most handsome of all aquatics,
this species should be grown in water not
deeper than 300 mm, or in mud near the edge
of the pool with as little as 120 mm of water
above the rootstock. Growing to 450-600
mm, it has a tidy habit and pleasing, smooth,
olive green leaves, about 300 mm long and
some 180 mm wide. Many consider it to be
the finest blue-flowering aquatic in cultivation. Long spikes of densely packed, sky
blue flowers are borne in summer. Propagate
by division of the rootstock during autumn.

**Red-Hot Poker:** see *Kniphofia* spp.

*Salix apoda*                    Europe
SALICACEAE
This charming dwarf willow with its delicate
tracery of branches is an excellent subject
for, and is particularly happy in, the raised
area of the marsh garden. Smaller-growing
than the weeping willow, it nevertheless
shares its larger relative's grace.

*Sparganium erectum*                    Europe to
SPARGANIACEAE                    Central Siberia
🌢 900 mm ☼
Thriving in full sun and preferring water about
300 mm deep, this large aquatic is useful for
planting effect and can add a different dimension of height and form, particularly to the
informal pool. In nature, its sword-shaped
leaves have been known to grow some 2 m
long, but in Australia they seldom exceed 1.5
m, and are usually between 600 mm and 900
mm. Propagate from the rhizomatous rootstock, which increases rapidly whenever the
plants become too crowded.

*Thalia dealbata*                    Southern United States
MARANTACEAE
🌢 1,4 m ☼ 🌢
One of the best aquatics for effect, this
species is distinguished by its scapes of
canna-like foliage up to 1.4 m or more tall. It
bears erect panicles of small violet flowers.
Group in a clump near the pool edge, in
450-600 mm of water. Propagate in spring by
division.

*Tradescantia virginiana*                    Eastern
COMMELINACEAE                    United States
🌢 25 mm 🌢 🌢
Another perennial subject for the raised zone
of the marsh garden, this creeping species
bears a succession of blue to purple flowers –
each lasting only one day – in terminal
umbels. The paired leaves are 150-350 mm
long. Propagate from cuttings in summer.

*Typha orientalis*                    Australia
TYPHACEAE
🌢 1-2 m ☼ 🌢
The common bullrush is a very useful and
decorative subject for a marsh garden. Often
referred to as the cumbungi, it grows to 3 m,
with long, slender leaves and the characteristic cylindrical, dark brown fruiting heads that
appear in summer. Propagate by division of
the rootstock at any time. Bullrushes may also
be grown from seed planted in submerged
pots.

*Wachendorfia thyrsiflora*                    South Africa
HAEMODORACEAE
🌢 1,25 m ☼ 🌢
The plicate leaves of this moisture-loving,
tuberous-rooted perennial are up to 1.25 m
long and create a fine focal point at the edge
of a marsh garden or in the surround of a
pool. Dense cylindrical panicles of bronze-
yellow flowers are borne from early spring to
early summer. Propagate by division of the
rootstock after flowering.

**Water Crinum:** see *Crinum campanulatum*

*Watsonia* spp.
IRIDACEAE
Most species of this interesting genus are

ideally suited to the fringe of the marsh garden or in clumps among the surround of an informal pool. See also page 114.

*Zantedeschia aethiopica*          Africa
ARACEAE
🌿 600 mm ☀ ☁
The spring-flowering arum lily is very much at home in the dampest raised section of the marsh garden and probably thrives better here than in any other part of the garden. Stalk-less leaves rise from the thick rhizomes to as much as 600 mm and fleshy stems a metre or more long bear the white spathes, creamy at the inner base, which are so much part of the spring scene in our winter-rainfall areas. Propagate both this species and *Z. oculata* by division or from offsets.

*Z. albomaculata*          Africa
This species grows to about 600 mm; its leaves are flecked with creamy colour and its flowers are white to pale pink. It is an ideal species for the marsh garden.

*Z. oculata*          Africa
🌿 600 mm ☀ ☁
The black-eyed arum is another species which thrives in a really damp situation, though it is more tolerant of drier conditions than *Z. aethiopica* and, used outside the water garden, is probably the better choice for less humid regions. Deciduous, its leaves are sparsely speckled and the spadix is short. The greenish-cream spathe has a large dark area on the inner side of its base.

*Typha orientalis*

Informal water garden with *Zantedeschia aethiopica* in foreground

# PLANNING AND BUILDING A POND OR MARSH GARDEN

Whether a pond is to be sunken or raised, built on the level or cut from a slope, its foundation must be completely firm so that, as a means of levelling, cut-and-fill should always be avoided. However well a filled portion – either in a dip or on a slope – is compacted, the soil will continue its consolidation for a long time and may eventually cause cracks in the floor of the pond. Water escaping through such cracks soon percolates the soil below, weakening its holding strength and allowing the cracks to widen. Should this happen, complete reconstruction is almost unavoidable.

If a pond is to be sited on a slope, it is wise to level its location in cut only, contouring the upper banks to accommodate a rock garden or suitably planted rocky outcrop. Such an approach is all to the good, as it will add to the informality of the pond.

Once the site is levelled and prepared to the chosen design, lay the floor in one day, remembering to extend it by a minimum of 150 mm all around the inner circumference, so providing an overlap on which the walls will be cast or built. Both the floor and the walls of the pond should be at least 150 mm thick, and the following specification should prove satisfactory for both: dry-mix two parts each of crushed stone (1,5-2 mm aggregate) and river sand with one part of cement; add enough water to mix the whole to a moist, workable consistency and lay the floor. Keep the surface moist – particularly where the walls are to join the floor – until the walls are built and the pond filled.

If concrete walls are to be cast, these should be thrown the following day and it is wise, therefore, to prepare the shuttering or formes in advance. The average pond will not require reinforcement. Ensure that the point of union between wall and floor is thoroughly moist before casting the concrete mix which must be tamped down well. The shuttering may be removed 24 hours later.

At this stage, to ensure an absolutely leak-proof pond, the inner cement surface should be treated with one of the new, self-curing water repellents which are available as powders and are non-toxic. Their waterproofing properties lie in reactions with cement-cured surfaces so that they may not be used over previously painted surfaces.

Alternatively, the walls of the pond may be built of brick – the main advantage here lying in the fact that no shuttering is needed – using a mortar comprising four parts of sand and one of cement. If water repellents are to be used, the brickwork will require plastering inside. Use a mixture of three parts sand to one part cement for the plaster, which should be at least 2 mm thick. The water repellent should be added to the mixture according to the makers' instructions.

All but the smallest ponds should have a drainage outlet in the concrete floor (see illustration opposite) leading to a suitable drainage point, and this should be set in place before the floor or walls are built. Fit the end of the outlet with a detachable handled tap, so that the unwitting act of a child, or deliberate vandalism, cannot drain the pond. Cover the interior outlet with a piece of brass gauze or perforated zinc to prevent materials blocking the outlet pipe. When the pond is drained – whether for cleaning or re-planting – remove and clean the gauze. Throughout the life of the pond it is important that, after draining, it should never be left dry for more than two or three hours. If re-planting, therefore, have all your plants and your new planting medium ready, so avoiding unnecessary delay.

## MARSH GARDENS
Whether the marsh garden is an extension of an informal pond, or a feature in itself, the principles underlying its construction are the same. Excavate the site to the required shape and about 700 mm deep, using the same methods of construction as for an ordinary pond but providing two outlets – one set in the floor and the other about 150 mm below the eventual surface level of the water. A perforated pipe, extending the length of the marsh and about 150 mm below the surface, provides an independent water lead, even when the marsh garden adjoins the informal aquatic pond. Providing two outlets ensures that surplus or stagnant water drains off reasonably rapidly – they

A simple, small, informal pond is easily built in firm level ground, with the use of heavy-duty plastic sheeting. Excavate the shape of the pond, remembering to leave a shelf at the side for shallower-growing plants. Remove any stones or protruding roots which might puncture the sheeting, then lay it loosely in place, holding the edges in position with bricks on the surface of the soil. Fill the 'pool' with water, whose weight will mould the plastic to the contours of your excavation. The plastic may then be cut to shape, leaving a wide flange which can be held down and covered with paving stones or slabs. Plants in this type of pool are best kept in pots.

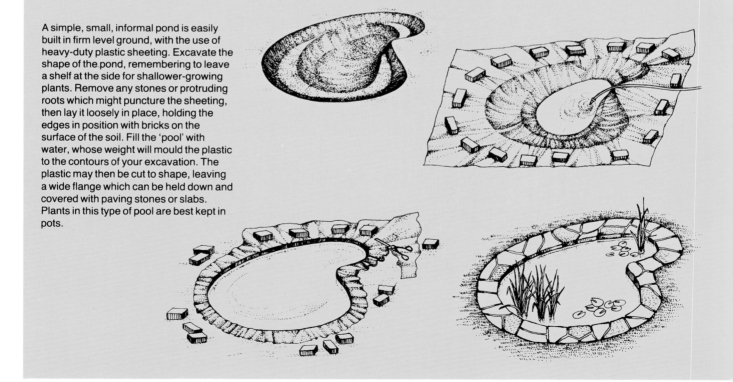

are more likely to be needed during the colder months than when there is active, lively growth of water plants. Flat-topped rocks or fabricated stepping-stones should be placed into position immediately after the floor is laid, making sure that their upper surfaces will be level with, or slightly above, the finished surface.

Cover the bottom 200 mm of the marsh garden with a layer of gravel, which will facilitate run-off of surplus water from the lower outlet. Over this, place a 250 mm-deep layer of a mixture of two parts of good topsoil to one part each of coarse sand and fibrous material such as coarse compost. Bring the growing medium to the desired level with a further layer consisting of equal parts of good topsoil, coarse river sand, coarse fibrous compost and well-prepared compost in which fresh animal manure was an ingredient. Have these planting materials and gravel ready so that two days after construction they can be placed in position and the water let in.

## PLANTING OF PONDS

Aquatic pond plants are grown mostly in containers, and require a soil medium which differs considerably from that recommended for the marsh garden. For the lower 160 mm layer, mix six parts of good loam to one part of well-rotted cow manure, or if the latter is not available, use good compost to which a heaped tablespoon of bone meal has been added. Over this, place a 150 mm layer of three parts of loam mixed well with one part of coarse, fibrous compost.

At this stage plant the subjects, firming them down and covering the surface with a 40 mm layer of coarse sand, to prevent the soil and compost mixture from floating to the surface. Water well and lower the potted plants into the pond to a depth where the foliage is just above the water level. Stand the container on bricks to adjust it to the correct level and, as the leaves grow, remove the bricks to lower it.

This, more elaborate, water garden has a cast concrete base with specially constructed troughs along one side and a drainage pipe which may be connected to a reticulating pump. The pot for lilies rests on stones so that it can be lowered or raised according to the plants' growing needs. Below: A typical marsh garden in which the surrounding land slopes gently into the precision of the pond itself.

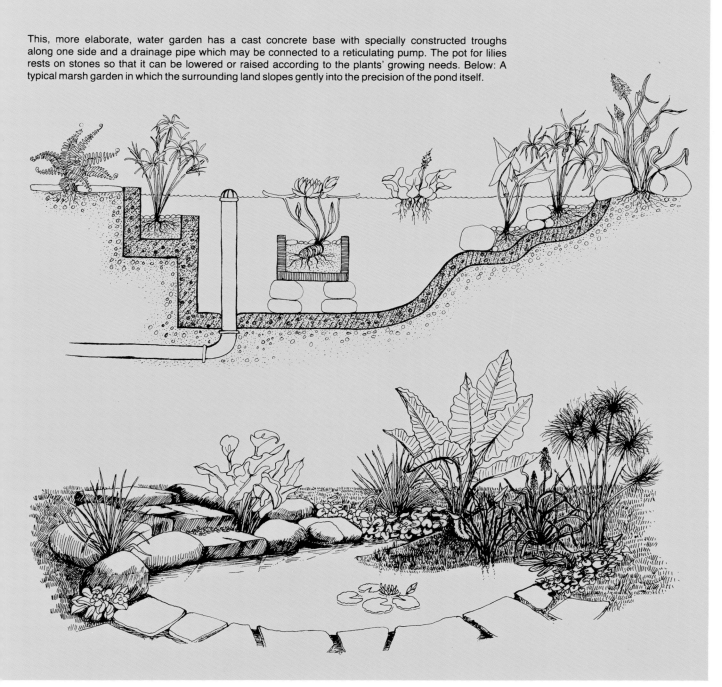

# CACTI AND *16* SUCCULENTS

## THE CAMELS OF THE PLANT KINGDOM

The arid semi-desert and desert areas of much of our interior provide ideal conditions for the growth of a botanical wonderland of succulents. These fleshy-leaved or leafless plants are marvellously adapted to storing moisture against long periods of drought, while their reduced and often waxy surface keeps loss through transpiration to a minimum. They belong to the family Cactaceae and, contrary to popular belief, occur in a wide variety of habitats, ranging from barren desert to high alpine ridges and forested, humid gorges. Many genera and species inhabiting arid regions have so thoroughly adapted to desert condi-tions that, with evolution, their leaves have modified to become thorns − thus reducing the surface area through which the plants could lose moisture.

With a few exceptions, cacti are indigenous only to the Americas, being found mostly in Mexico, parts of California and certain areas of South America, particu-larly Argentina, Chile and Peru. Strangely, although they come from such widely divergent climatic and geographic zones, the majority of cacti do extremely well under Australian conditions. By and large, they will tolerate a good deal of frost, the exceptions being the semi-climbing *Epiphyllum* and *Cereus* species which require a warmer, more moist situation. Although cacti may be cultivated in pots or containers, they grow much more freely when planted out and should then have a position entirely to themselves, for they do not mix happily with other plants.

Cacti are the only living plants possessing an areole, usually woolly − a miniature cushion which appears on the ribs or at the top of tubercles; and it is from these areoles that the thorns, offshoots and flowers appear. The thick epidermal layers of many cacti have a waxy coating and this, together with the absence of leaves, and the relatively brief lives of the flowers − they may bloom profusely, but individual flowers do not last long − helps conserve moisture. These physical characteristics help point the way to the correct cultivation of certain species. For instance, those with an obviously tough skin, or epidermis, many thorns and abundant hairy wool will almost certainly stand a good deal of direct sunlight. Those with a rather green appearance and sparse thorns will

probably prefer some shade during the hottest part of the day.

Irrespective of genus or species, all cacti and most other succulents not only enjoy, but demand, perfect drainage. If grown in a pot or other container, the standard mixture described on page 293 will satisfy most. Grown in the open, a well-drained site such as a scree in the rock garden, and where the surface is covered with a layer of small broken stone chips to a depth of about 25 mm, is ideal.

A few well-placed large rocks will provide all the shade that the cacti require. They also need ample light − although it need not be direct sunlight − free movement of air and protection from rain, if it is likely to fall for any length of time.

A well-drained rock garden, whether it is planned only as a home for succulents or for other plants, should appear as natural as possible. Rocks and stones should be placed in such a way that they seem to follow a natural formation of strata. If the stone work is laid in a higgledy-piggledy man-ner, not only will it be unsightly, but it may create drainage problems.

◀ The beauty of this *Borzicactus* flower belies the spines which guard the plant

## PROPAGATION OF CACTI AND SUCCULENTS

The best way to propagate cacti is from seed, though cultivars must be propagated vegetatively, as well as any species which do not set seed easily in your area, or which produce offsets so freely that sowing is unnecessary. For seeds use a mixture of three parts of washed river sand to one part of peat moss. Do not cover the seed: after sowing (in standard plastic seed trays) water from the base by holding the tray in a container of water until the surface darkens with moisture. Stand it in a semi-shaded position and cover with paper until the first signs of germination are apparent. Remove the paper at once and place the tray in a position where it receives full light, but no direct sunlight. In such a mixture the disease known as damping off should not occur; if it does, you have done something basically wrong, and no amount of spraying or watering with this or that will halt its progress.

Transplant seedlings when their spines are well advanced and don't be in too much of a hurry, because the original mixture in which they are growing is conducive to maximum root development. The seedlings should be transplanted 30 mm apart into trays containing the standard mixture. Do not plant them deeper than the soil line indicates.

Propagation from offsets is an immediate and rewarding way of increase: the young plants, severed by a sharp knife, may already possess roots, but whether they do or not, rooting is very quick in the mixture of washed river sand and peat moss mentioned earlier.

Most succulents can be grown from seed or leaf or stem cuttings. Unless otherwise indicated in the individual entries which follow, either seed or cuttings may be used for propagation.

*Adenium obesum* 'multiflorum'　　　　Africa
APOCYNACEAE
🌦 0,5-1,5 m ☼ ⊕ 🄵
One of the few succulents in the Apocynaceae family, the winter-flowering desert rose occurs in a wide variety of habitats, its natural range extending from the Arabian Peninsula south through Kenya and Mozambique to Namibia. The plant is leafless while in bloom, so that its masses of star-shaped flowers, each edged with pillar-box red, are shown off without detraction. Though in nature the flower stems may reach a height of 3 m, the cultivated desert rose is usually from 500 mm to 1.5 m tall. It is propagated easily from cuttings, demands perfect drainage and will tolerate neither frost nor prolonged cold.

*Adromischus cooperi*　　　　Southern Africa
CRASSULACEAE
🌦 250 mm ☼ to ◑ ⊕
The light green, club-shaped leaves of this succulent are speckled with purplish spots, which have earned it the name 'plover's eggs' among enthusiasts in Europe and the United States. Closely related to the genus *Cotyledon*, in which it was classified until recently, in summer and autumn this species bears papillose flowers which are purplish-red and whose stems, some 250 mm tall, rise well above the leaves. Propagate from offsets or by 'planting' a leaf in porous, sandy soil.

*Aloe* spp.　　　　Africa, Madagascar
LILIACEAE
Though there are more than 250 species to choose from, and most are indigenous to South Africa and Namibia, only some 20 species of *Aloe* are widely cultivated by gardeners. Specialists, particularly overseas, have bred a splendidly wide range of cultivars and hybrids which are richly coloured and invaluable for their garden impact. These are becoming available gradually and it is worth-while consulting your local nurseryman or specialist as to what choice he can offer.

In general, aloes do not lend themselves to a flat or formal situation. In a garden which lacks rocks, or even a bank, against which these plants are seen to best advantage, mass the aloes in one area where their difference in habits and colourings will create a special atmosphere of its own. A practical advantage of such a move is that most aloes enjoy similar conditions – well-drained, good soil, little water and ample sun – so that their management is simplified.

Following is a list of the most suitable and popular of our aloes for garden planting – inevitably it is limited, and the home gardener, no doubt, will have his or her own particular favourites.

*A. arborescens*
This species forms a large, imposing clump two to three metres high. It flowers freely throughout May and June, bearing red, conical spikes of blooms.

*A. cooperi*
A grassland species which flowers for much of the summer, this aloe does not form stems and the salmon pink, green-tipped blooms nestle among the serrated leaves. These form a clump little more than 300 mm high.

*A. cryptopoda*
A showy species 1.5 to 2 m high, this bears single or bi-coloured spikes of orange to scarlet flowers, in branched inflorescences. It is very similar to *A. wickensii* which also blooms in early summer.

*A. ferox*
This tall-stemmed species, two to three metres high, bears showy, candelabra-like inflorescences of red summer flowers. There is also a very beautiful, but rare, pure white form. Except when in flower, this species might easily be confused with *A. marlotii*, but the flowers of the latter are produced on horizontal branches, whereas those of *A. ferox* are borne erect. Both species are

*Adenium obesum* (Desert Rose)

characterized by persistent dry dead leaves which give them a ragged, untidy appearance if not removed.

### A. fosteri
In late summer and early autumn this low, clumped species bears yellow and red flowers on a much-branched, erect flowering stem up to a metre and more high. Occasionally both colours are mixed on the same plant.

### A. globuligemma
In May and June the metre-high flowering stem of this clumped species bears red buds and ivory yellow flowers along the upper margins of its sub-horizontal branchlets.

### A. microstigma
This low-growing, clumped species has spotted foliage and bears simple, metre-high spikes of orange to scarlet flowers in June. It is very attractive and showy.

Aloe striata

Aloe saponaria

Aloe cryptopoda

Aloe hybrids

*Argyroderma aureum*

*Carpobrotus edulis*

*Cephalocereus senilis* (Old Man Cactus)

### A. mudenensis
With its short (250 mm) stem and attractive spotted leaves, this is a splendid species for any garden. Showy orange to scarlet flowers are borne in July on metre-long spikes.

### A. saponaria
A stemless species, this aloe has spotted leaves and bears branched inflorescences up to one metre tall. Orange to red flowers of this widely-distributed succulent are borne in winter.

### A. striata
The procumbent coral aloe is also stemless and its leaves have a pink edge and no teeth. Pendulous, coral red flowers are borne in August and September on much-branched inflorescences nearly a metre tall.

### A. variegata
Usually stemless, and with many offsets, the partridge breast has attractive, spotted leaves. Yellow flowers are borne on un-branched stems about 300 mm high, in August and September.

**Argyroderma testiculare**      South Africa
AIZOACEAE
⊛ 250 mm ☼ to ☽ ⊕
When, some time ago, the genus *Mesembryanthemum* was divided and reclassified, this was one of the many species whose botanical name was changed – though, to the gardener, it will remain a typical 'mesem'. Its succulent, greenish-grey leaves form prostrate clumps, which in spring and summer are almost smothered in brilliant yellow or purple flowers.

*Cactus intortus*: see *Melocactus intortus*

**Carpobrotus edulis**      South Africa
MESEMBRYANTHEMACEAE
⊛ 200 mm ☼ ⊕
The giant pigface, or Hottentot fig, with its triangular trailing stems, bears yellow, pink or purple flowers followed by edible fruits which make a very good jam. The succulent spreads rapidly and is probably better suited as a cover for steep banks, or as a ground cover (see also page 52) than in the rock garden.

**Carrion Flower:** see *Orbea variegata*

**Cephalocereus senilis**      West Indies
CACTACEAE
⊛ 2 m ☼ ⊕ Ⓕ
This is a tallish cactus, reaching 2 m under Australian conditions but 10 m or more in its natural habitat. Its stems are densely clothed in white hairs, which give it its common name of old man cactus. Nocturnal, funnel-shaped, cream flowers arise from the cephalium, or

*Cheiridopsis* species

*Chamaecereus silvestri*, another popular cactus

*Cereus hexagonus* typifies the flowers of the genus

*Crassula coccinea* and, below, its flower

apex, and are slightly pink at first. Usually columnar, this species is also often much branched from about ground level.

*Cephalophyllum alstonii*          South Africa
AIZOACEAE
🌱 300 mm ☼ ☽
A trailing succulent with angular leaves, this species bears brilliant crimson-scarlet flowers, on stems up to 300 mm tall.

*Cereus peruvianus*          South America
CACTACEAE
🌱 3 m ☼ ☽ **F**
A fast-growing, tall-branched cactus, this species flowers at night. It has six to nine notched and rounded ribs from which slender, brown to black spines protrude. The large, creamy-white flowers are thickly trumpet shaped, and when in bloom make a rare sight on a summer evening. The flowers appear from the base to the top of the stems.

*Cheiridopsis cigarettifera*          South Africa
AIZOACEAE
🌱 150 m ☼ ☽
A stemless, clumpy plant, this succulent has greyish-green foliage with a white 'cigarette paper' covering part of each leaf. Golden yellow flowers are borne in spring and summer.

**Coral Aloe:** see *Aloe striata*

*Coryphantha pallida*          Mexico
CACTACEAE
🌱 120 mm ☼ ☽ **F**
This is one of the smaller-growing cacti, handsome in its globular shape and bearing close clusters of short, white radial spines. The large, pale buttercup yellow flowers are borne somewhat spasmodically.

**Crab Cactus:** see *Schlumbergera truncata*

*Crassula coccinea*          South Africa
CRASSULACEAE
🌱 450 mm ☼ ☽
This succulent perennial gem bears pseudo-umbels of rich brick scarlet flowers and is frequently grown in a pot to decorate a sunny indoor position. In the garden it is fabulous for a dry wall or pocket of rock filled with dry,

chippy soil. The startling brilliance of the spring and summer flowers has to be seen to be believed. *C. coccinea* is easily propagated from ripe seed, cuttings, and even leaf cuttings inserted in washed river sand in summer.

*C. falcata*          South Africa
🌱 450 mm ☼ ☽
The erect, thick fleshy stems of this species bear curved, thick, grey leaves 70-100 mm long. Brilliant scarlet flowers are borne in flat, terminal corymbs up to 100 mm across. These succulents are seen at their best against a rock face, their roots jammed between two abutting rocks. *C. perfoliata* is not as tall (250 mm) as its relative and has narrow, grey leaves set in pairs at right angles to the stem. Its flowers are variable, but usually red, though sometimes whitish, and are also borne in terminal corymbs. Propagate both these species from seed sown in September.

*Dorotheanthus bellidiformis* typifies the genus

*Drosanthemum speciosum*

**Crown of Thorns:** see *Euphorbia milii*

*Disocactus biformis*          Honduras
CACTACEAE
🌱 2 m ☼ ☽ **F**
Often used as a pot plant, this cactus is similar in many respects to the *Epiphyllum*.

Drosanthemum striatum

Ferocactus setispinus

Flowers of Echinocereus pentalophus

Cylindrical stems bear flattened, leaf-like branches which soon become pendulous, making this a good subject for the hanging basket. Numerous purplish flowers, some 50 mm across, appear spasmodically. This is not the easiest cactus to cultivate and, unless you possess a warm greenhouse, it is suited only to the warmly temperate to subtropical areas. Outdoors, hanging basket culture is probably wisest, providing the soil is very free-draining.

Dorotheanthus bellidiformis          South Africa
(Syn. Cleretum bellidiforme)
AIZOACEAE
⊛ 100 mm ☼ ⊛
The charming little succulent forms a much-branched clump with leaves about 50 mm long. A very showy annual, its spring flowers are borne in a brilliant range of colours – scarlet, orange, pink, cream, tangerine and purple. Propagate from seed sown in situ, in autumn.

Drosanthemum speciosum          South Africa
AIZOACEAE
⊛ 300-400 mm ☼ ⊛
The brilliant dew flower bears bright orange flowers with a dark central zone. It is bushy and must be raised annually from seed, as it is one of the varieties which cannot be propagated from cuttings.

Echeveria secunda 'glauca'          Mexico
CRASSULACEAE
⊛ 100-150 mm ☼ ⊛
This charming little succulent – one of the few from the New World – forms miniature rosettes, about 80 mm across, which produce numerous offsets. Brick red flowers with yellow tips are borne on stems 100-150 mm high. This species is often used as an edging to formal bedding schemes.

Echinocereus pentalophus          Texas
CACTACEAE
⊛ 120 mm ☼ ⊛ Ｆ
This species is probably the most widely grown of its genus. The dumpy stems are semi-procumbent, and the fine ribs are armed with white, radial spines which are dark tipped. It flowers frequently, bearing crimson-purple blooms up to 100 mm across.

Euphorbia caput-medusae          South Africa
EUPHORBIACEAE
⊛ 800 mm ☼ ⊛
From a stubby stem some 200 mm in

Nopalxochia ackermannii hybrid

diameter emerge numerous contorted and snake-like branches, often more than 600 mm long, to give this succulent its common name Medusa's head. Each year a new ring of branches is formed; these bear small, short-lived leaves and are tipped in spring by small white flowers. When the branches of this and the following species are broken they exude a poisonous, milky latex.

E. horrida          South Africa
⊛ 900 mm ☼ ⊛
A spiny, dull grey-green succulent which branches in clumps from the base in grotesque contortions, this species bears small green-yellow or brown flowers in spring. It is

Euphorbia caput-Medusae (Medusa's Head)

Euphorbia horrida

*Ferocactus* species

Miniature cacti make an attractive collection.

one of the slowest growing of the euphorbias and is a prized greenhouse plant in the United States, where it is popularly known as the African milk barrel.

*E. milii* Madagascar
1,5 m
The thin branches of the slow-growing crown of thorns are closely covered with dark spines and are tipped with a thin cluster of light green leaves. Flowers, borne throughout the year, comprise forked heads of brilliant scarlet bracts surrounding small, greenish-yellow blooms. These are carried on long, stick-like stalks arising from the leaf axils to create the 'crown' from which this succulent derives its common name.

*Faucaria tigrina* South Africa
AIZOACEAE
100 mm
The tiger's jaws, with toothed, greyish-green, succulent foliage, bears yellow or orange flowers.

*Ferocactus setispinus* Texas, Mexico
CACTACEAE
250 mm
This smaller-growing species conforms to everyone's idea of what a 'real' cactus should look like. It is squat, round, very spiny and bears the most gorgeous, buttercup yellow flowers. Sometimes these are marked with red centres. The strawberry cactus should convert the most ardent cactiphobe to enthusiasm.

*Gasteria verrucosa* South Africa
LILIACEAE
150-300 mm
This species is typical of a group of succulents closely allied to the aloe and mainly stemless. Their thickened leaves are usually arranged in two ranks, semi-spirally or in a rosette. The flowers are not showy, but the plants are interesting and accommodating subjects for the rock garden, imparting as

they do an indigenous atmosphere. All are propagated from seed.

*Glottiphyllum linguiforme* South Africa
AIZOACEAE
25 mm
A prostrate, stemless low-growing succulent, this species has glossy green foliage and bright yellow flowers.

*Hamatocactus setispinus:* see *Ferocactus setispinus*
*Haworthia margaritifera:* see *H. pumila*

*Haworthia pumila* South Africa
LILIACEAE
100 mm
Stemless rosettes from which offsets are produced mark all the haworthias. They are closely allied to the aloes, and at one time were included in that genus. Though their flowers have no particular floral merit, like the gasterias they are excellent plants for the rock garden where their unusual habit and mottled succulent leaves add to the interest and indigenous character of any rock garden. They are very much at home in a small crevice between two rocks, or some similar position. They are usually propagated from offsets.

*Lampranthus aureus* South Africa
AIZOACEAE
300 mm
A magnificent, bushy plant whose 450 mm flower-stems bear brilliant yellow blooms which are freely-produced and range between 50-80 mm across. One of the earliest ice flowers to bloom, *L. amoenus* is similar to *L. aureus*, but its triangular succulent leaves form more of a clump and its flowers are a brilliant purplish-red.

*Lithops lesliei* South Africa
AIZOACEAE
10-50 mm
The stone-plants form a large genus, mainly

*Lampranthus multiradiatus,* a typical plant

*Lampranthus blandus*

These *Lithops* spp. resemble pebbles

*Begonia X tuberhybrida*

**B. rex** Assam
⬆ 200-300 mm ◑ ⊛

This rhizomatous, hairy-leaved species is grown in all its many varieties and cultivars for the splendour of its foliage. The leaves of the king, or painted-leaf, begonia are 200-300 mm long and almost half as wide, are ovate and wavy, and are carried on fairly long stems. In the species the upper surface of the leaf is a rich metallic green with a 25 mm-wide zone of silver-grey, and with a reddish underside. It is impossible to describe the wide range of markings, zonal bands, and blotched or geometrically bi-coloured leaf effects of the numerous varieties and cultivars of this species. It is the principal parent in the creation of the hundreds of ornamental foliaged cultivars and hybrids, and, furthermore, these have been crossed with other hybrids, as well as being re-crossed with the species itself.

**B. X semperflorens-cultorum** Brazil
⬆ variable ☼ ⊛

An extremely variable hybrid species, the fibrous-rooted begonia has numerous varieties and superb cultivars. The latter range from the new, very compact, free-flowering forms in mixed or separate colours, to semi-compact and tall-growing bedding types. Though they are used almost exclusively for outdoor purposes (see page 322), they may also be cultivated for the indoor garden.

**B. X tuberhybrida** Garden origin
⬆ variable ◑ ⊛

Tuberous-rooted, this hybrid species embraces the wide range of cultivars, grouped into 13 different categories, which share a common leaf form and provide the bulk of the popular garden begonias. As far as indoor cultivation is concerned, these hybrids are best treated as annuals with tubers bought from a reputable nursery with a specialist begonia section. Named colours are often available, but a mixed lot will usually give all the colours one could wish for, from white

*Aechmea recurvata*

*Caladium bicolor*

through pink to deep reds, and pale cream through the yellows to old orange. They prefer medium light intensity and should be treated much the same as B. rex. Do not try and mix them, or B. rex, with other subjects in a trough unless you know that the other plants enjoy exactly the same conditions and treatment.

*Billbergia nutans* Brazil
BROMELIACEAE
⬆ 300 mm ☼ ⊛

The long, narrow leaves of the friendship plant form a rosette, not unlike that of a pineapple. Short, drooping or arched spikes

of flowers have large rosy bracts, with red sepals and yellow-green petals margined in blue. This popular and most attractive species is not particularly difficult to grow. Indoors it requires full light; if planted outside it should be in dappled shade. Ideal beside an ornamental pool.

**Bird's Nest Fern:** see *Asplenium nidus-avis*
*Bromelia nudicaulis:* see *Aechmea nudicaulis*

*Caladium bicolor* Tropical America
ARACEAE
⬆ 300-400 mm ◑ ⊛

Though the common varieties of this species

may be grown outdoors in fairly dense shade in the temperate regions, the sophisticated and delicately-marked cultivars and varieties are only at their best in conservatories or grown indoors with low light intensity. The spear-shaped or triangular-ovate leaves are either highly coloured or beautifully marked in white with a lacework or border of emerald green.

Caladiums require an open soil medium, which should be well drained, as cautious watering is required once the tuberous rhizomes have been started in early spring. A

Calathea makoyana (Peacock Plant)

potting mixture of equal parts of leaf mould, well-rotted manure or standard compost, and washed, coarse river sand is excellent. Feed regularly when growth is established, using a liquid fertilizer every ten days or so. Syringe freely on hot days, avoid draughts and, if used in a trough, combine it with other different varieties. Purchase young plants from a specialist, while the foliage is showing its true markings. Rest, keeping the rhizomes dry, during the winter off season.

### Calathea makoyana
MARANTACEAE                                    Brazil
🌢 300-400 mm ◐ 🤚
The peacock plant's lovely foliage borne on red stalks makes it an ideal choice for the indoor garden. Its broadly-oblong, obtuse and somewhat rounded leaves are olive green or creamy and marked from the mid-rib with outspreading blotches of pronounced dark, dark green in oval, pyriform or oblong shapes. It is shallow rooting, so grow it in a flower pot about 160 mm wide and 90 mm deep, re-potting it annually. It likes plenty of light but not direct sun and needs constant moisture during the active growing season.

### C. zebrina
                                              Brazil
🌢 400 mm ◐ 🤚
Common to most collections, the zebra plant has velvety green leaves whose upper surfaces are alternately barred in pale, yellow-green and dark green, with the undersides purple-red in maturity. Many colourful hybrids are available, some with highly coloured flowers in summer. All prefer low sun intensity and

Calceolaria crenatiflora

require warmth and moisture.

### Calceolaria crenatiflora
SCROPHULARIACEAE                                Chile
🌢 750 mm ◐ 🤚
A stout and popular indoor species, the slipper plant has large, ovate leaves which are coarsely toothed and, in the wide range of cultivars, variegated in many shades of green and brown. The flowers of the species, borne sporadically throughout the year, are yellow with a rash of brown spots on the lower lip. Again the plantsmen have been busy and the range of floral colours among the cultivars is magnificent. All Calceolaria species are easily propagated from ripe seed.

C. herbeohybrida: see C. crenatiflora

### Callisia elegans
COMMELINACEAE                        Southern Mexico
🌢 750 mm ☼ 🤚
An easily grown climber, the inch plant has beautifully marked ovate to broadly-lanceolate leaves about 70 mm long and half as wide. The foliage is dark green, striped silver-white above and with purplish undersides. It requires full sun intensity – but not direct rays – to maintain its leaf colours. This plant easily reverts to plain green and rapidly becomes an embarrassing weed in the warmer areas of Australia.

### Ceropegia woodii
ASCLEPIADACEAE                          South Africa
🌢 1 m ☼ to ◐ 🤚
A slender trailing plant from Natal, the necklace vine has ovate leaves which are variegated white with purple edges and undersides. It is happy in sun or shade, but must be kept moist in summer and rather on the dry side during winter. The trailing stems, which arise from the corm, are used to decorate kitchens and bathrooms, as well as being grown with other indoor plants. In other words, it is not at all choosey, but very, very attractive. A 100 mm flower pot, well drained, will provide it with ample growing space.

### Chamaedorea elegans
PALMAE                                       Mexico
🌢 1,5 m ☼ 🤚
Delightfully small for the indoor garden, even in nature the parlour palm is seldom more than 1.5 m high with its slender stem rarely more than 40 mm in diameter. A cluster of

Ceropegia woodii (Necklace Vine)

broadly lanceolate fronds comprising up to 14 leaflets crown the stem. This palm bears red-orange flowers but, because the sexes are on different plants, a single specimen will not fruit. Pot on as the plant grows, eventually finishing with a deep container some 250-300 mm in diameter. As with all palms, it requires good drainage, plenty of moisture and regular feedings with a good liquid fertilizer. A small application of blood and bone four times a year will prove beneficial.

**Chenille Plant:** see Acalypha hispida

### Chlorophytum comosum 'Variegatum'
   (Syn. C. capense)
LILIACEAE                               South Africa
🌢 300 mm ☼ 🤚
This species is indispensable for the indoor garden as its longitudinal, white leaf varia-

tions mix so beautifully with other plants. It is compact with *Dracaena*-like foliage, long, narrow and recurving, and bears white flowers in loose panicles. Rooted runners, similar to those of the strawberry, sprawl over the edge of its container. Avoid direct sun rays, though it requires full light intensity, copious water and regular feedings. Over-watering in cool weather causes leaf tips to brown badly.

*C. elatum:* see *C. comosum* 'Variegatum'

*Cissus discolor*                                    Java
VITACEAE
⊛ 2 m ◑ ⊛
An outstanding indoor climber, particularly when grown in a trellised trough, the trailing begonia has beautiful foliage. This is reddish-plum beneath, and velvet green above, fairly evenly splashed with silvery-white. The bristly, serrated leaves are oblong-ovate to cordate-ovate. It is easily cultivated, requires medium light intensity and climbs by slender tendrils. In the cultivar 'Mollis', the undersides of the leaves are blood red, while the velvet green upper surfaces are strongly veined, mainly in white. If strong growth is required, plant the cultivar in a trough as you would the species; however, it is quite happy in a 250 mm diameter flower pot.

*Clerodendrum thomsoniae*
VERBENACEAE            Tropical West Africa
⊛ 3 m ☼ to ◑ ⊛
This vigorous evergreen climber can be kept to compact, shrub-like dimensions by careful, persistent pinching out of the growing stems. Clusters of flowers, their pure white calyces later changing to pink, and crimson corollas, make a startling colour combination. This species needs careful cultivation; keep it moderately moist and protected from draughts. It flowers over a long period. Replace every other year, from semi-soft (nodal) cuttings taken in summer.

*Clivia miniata*                          South Africa
AMARYLLIDACEAE
⊛ 300-500 mm ◑ ⊛
This species is protected in South Africa and is a tender bulbous plant with dark green, strap-like leaves, and bearing an erect umbel of bright red flowers with yellow throats. In temperate areas pot up into 180 mm pots, feed well during the growing season and bring inside as soon as the flowering stems show. In colder regions, pot as above but keep indoors in low sun intensity. Keep moderately dry during the off season, when no extra food should be allowed. A wide colour range of hybrids is available and increases the interest, but do not overlook the species – it is a gem. (See also page 90.)

*Cocos weddelliana*                    Tropical Brazil
PALMAE
⊛ 1-1,5 m ☼ to ◑ ⊛
Recently reclassified as *Lytocaryum weddellianum,* this highly ornamental, slender palm is widely used as an indoor subject. Its stem, a mere 40 mm in diameter, bears graceful foliage. It is happy in the standard growing medium plus an extra part of purely

*Clivia miniata*

*Codiaeum variegatum* (Croton) cultivar

fibrous material. Most palms enjoy good drainage and plenty of moisture and food during active growth.

*Codiaeum variegatum* 'Pictum' Tropical Asia
EUPHORBIACEAE
⊛ 120 mm ☼ ⊛
The many varieties and cultivars of the croton are distinguished by their brilliantly coloured foliage and extremely variable leaf shapes – broad, narrow, lobed, sometimes corkscrew-like. They may be grown outside, in full light, in temperate to subtropical areas. Indoors or outdoors, they need constant moisture and will only attain the brilliance of colour for which they are noted, in full sunlight. If they are not to drop their leaves, sudden changes in temperature must be avoided. They appreciate frequent syringings and are good mixers in a trough with other subjects.

*Coleus* hybrids                          Hybrid origin
LAMIACEAE
⊛ 750 mm ☼ ⊛
The modern coleus hybrids or Joseph's coat are available in an astonishing array of colours and forms, most of which come true from seed. They are extensively grown outdoors as annuals (see page 65) but are valuable for indoor work as they mix so well with other subjects. Remember that when grown indoors they require a high light intensity, for their leaves last only a few days if set out in a dark corner. They are moisture-loving, but need perfect drainage.

*Colocasia esculenta* 'Fontanesii'
ARACEAE                    Sandwich Islands
⊛ 2 m ◉ ⊛
The taro, or elephant ear, are widely cultivated throughout the tropics for their edible tubers. The leaves of some are also eaten and the tubers are sometimes forced to produce tender edible shoots. This cultivar 'Fontanesii' is purple-stalked and is the common ornamental taro. Both species and variety are excellent for the indoor garden, requiring a highly moist atmosphere, frequent syringings, and an abundance of water when in active growth.

*Coleus* hybrid

*Columnea* X *banksii*

*Cordyline terminalis*

*Cryptanthus zonatus* (Zebra Plant)

Unless used in association with other subjects requiring similar conditions, grow them in individual pots and plunge them in the trough using the standard growing medium plus an extra part of fibrous material. These dramatic, but rank-growing subjects need to be kept in their place.

*Columnea* X *banksii*　　　　Garden origin
GESNERIACEAE
🌢 1 m ☼ to ◐ 🌢
This hybrid, derived from crossing *C. oerstediana* and *C. schiedeana*, has slender, hanging branchlets bearing greenish-bronze leaves, and russet-orange flowers. It requires high light intensity, but direct sunlight will scorch it. It is ideally suited to a hanging basket or a wall pot.

**Coralberry:** see *Ardisia crenata*

*Cordyline australis* 'Atropurpurea'
LILIACEAE　　　　　　　　　New Zealand
🌢 750 mm ☼ 🌢
This variety of the New Zealand cabbage tree will grow to 3 m or more outdoors but is unlikely to exceed 750 mm as an indoor subject. Preferably grow it as a specimen in an individual pot in the standard potting mixture. It requires high light intensity and moderate moisture at all times, as does the following species and its varieties and cultivars.

*C. terminalis*　　　　　　　East Indies
(Syn. *C. fruticosa, C. terminalis*)
🌢 1,5 m ☼ 🌢
There are many varieties and cultivars of this species which is itself strikingly handsome and relatively easy to grow. The species has long, narrow leaves, plum, with lovely red and pink variegations and suffusion towards the margins, one has broad green leaves with some pink and yellow stripes and diffusions,

*Crossandra infundibuliformis*

while another also has broad green leaves, but these are variegated a creamy-white when young, turning to rose and deep red with age. When these plants become too leggy, as they will eventually, make a cutting of the top, but do not throw away the bare stem. Carefully nurtured, this will produce axillary growths which, in turn, may be taken as cuttings when about 120 mm long. Some plants produce several variegated branches from the one stem.

*Crossandra fruticulosa*　　　Mocambique,
ACANTHACEAE　　　　Southern Africa
🌢 500 mm ☼ 🌢
In late summer, the attractively whorled leaves of this sub-shrub are topped by large spikes of long-lasting coral red flowers. It is happy in association with other plants which demand a hot, moist situation and medium sun intensity, or it may be grown as a specimen in standard potting mixture in a 120 mm flower pot. Both this and the following species are easily propagated from cuttings.

*C. infundibuliformis* Southern India, Sri Lanka
🌢 300 mm ◐ 🌢

*Cryptanthus bivittatus* has the same requirements as the zebra plant.

Dense, closely-bracted spikes of scarlet-orange flowers are borne on long stems almost continuously from late spring well into autumn. This species requires a warm, humid atmosphere and its dark green, ovate-acuminate leaves should be syringed frequently with tepid water. It is a thirsty plant during its growing and flowering period and should be cultivated in a trough with plants of similar requirements or as a single specimen in a 120 mm flower pot.

**Croton:** see *Codiaeum variegatum* 'Pictum'

*Cryptanthus zonatus*　　　　　Brazil
BROMELIACEAE
🌢 400 mm ◐ 🌢
Dark green leaves transversely banded with striking white bars, and crowded in a typical bromeliad rosette, give the zebra plant its appeal. The foliage is oblong-lanceolate, with undulate, sharply serrated margins. The white flowers are insignificant. This species prefers low light intensity and thrives in the standard growing medium to which an extra part of purely fibrous material such as that used in orchid cultivation, has been added.

*Cyclamen persicum* cultivar

*Cyclamen persicum* cultivar

*Cyclamen persicum* cultivar

*Cyclamen persicum*  Eastern Mediterranean
PRIMULACEAE
🌰 100 mm ☼ ⊛

The indoor gardener would be wise to obtain a good pot specimen, just in bud, plunging it in a trough along with other subjects requiring a high light intensity. A few plants in season – there are whites, pinks, salmons, reds and crimsons to choose from – will brighten the general effect just in the same way that one would also use the brilliant yellow and choco-late reds of gloxinias in their respective seasons. When flowering is over and the plant dies down, store the tuberous flat corms in a cool, dry place – watch carefully for renewed growth and then pot them immediately in a new growing medium – the standard mixture is quite suitable, given effective drainage.

*Dieffenbachia chelsoni*  Colombia
ARACEAE
🌰 750 mm ☼ to ◑ ⊛

Dumb cane is an excellent foliage plant, its dark satiny green leaves blotched yellow and with a grey-banded mid-rib. Keep it moist during active growth, holding back a little during the dormant months, except in tem-perate to subtropical areas where growth never really ceases, so that it needs a con-stant moist situation. In hot weather, syringe frequently. Failure to feed well and regularly with a liquid fertilizer or foliar feed will result in the leaves becoming a light anaemic green, instead of the normal healthy, dark green. If the plant becomes leggy, take a cutting of the terminal shoot, but maintain the old plant, as it produces axillary shoots which can also be used for propagation. Associate dumb cane in a trough with other plants with similar cultural needs and grow at least one or two specimens in individual flower pots. The acrid sap can cause sharp pain and, if it gets into your mouth, can cause temporary

*Dieffenbachia amoena*, similar to *D. chelsoni*

loss of speech. Cultivars with white markings are available and it is worth consulting your local nurseryman as to which of these he has.

*Dioscorea batatas*  East Asia
DIOSCOREACEAE
🌰 2-3 m ◑ ⊛

This is the yam whose large edible tubers up to a metre long are part of the staple diet in areas of the Far East. As an indoor plant, grown in a trough or large pot, it will put up a twining stem bearing glossy, deep green leaves which are heart-shaped at the base,

tapering to a slender point.

*D. elephantipes*  South Africa
🌰 3 m ☼ ⊛

If you have an indoor garden – or place on a protected patio – large enough to take a 1 m diameter tub, the elephant's foot or Hotten-tot's bread, could make quite a conversation piece. Not only was this plant the original source of cortisone, but more than half of the tuber – covered with woody facets – pro-trudes above the soil and sends up three or four woody climbing stems, which are covered in small, soft green, roundly-pointed leaves.

*Dizygotheca elegantissima*　New Caledonia
ARALIACEAE
🌑 1,5 m ☀ 🌑
An excellent and rather unusual subject, false aralia lends a new dimension to the indoor garden scene. At first glance, this species does not look at all like the Aralia tribe, but this is possibly because it is wearing its juvenile foliage – a characteristic it sticks to under indoor or conservatory conditions – like so many of the aralias do. So much so, in fact, that early botanists were wont to give separate species status to plants which were precisely the same species, one in juvenile clothing, the other with its entirely different adult foliage. This species possesses leaflets which are filiform, slightly pendulous, and deeply serrated. It requires high light intensity, no direct sunlight, copious waterings during active growth, and regular feedings.

*Dracaena ferrea*: see *Cordyline terminalis*

*Dracaena fragrans*　Guinea
LILIACEAE
🌑 2-3 m ◑ to ◉ 🌑
Though in its natural habitat this species reaches a height of 7 m or more with leaves up to a metre long, and bears panicles of fragrant yellow flowers, it is with its cultivars that the indoor gardener is concerned. These are smaller and grown for their attractive

*Dracaena fragrans*

*Dracaena deremensis* 'Warneckii'

foliage, their flowers being insignificant. 'Lindenii' has broadly-oblong to lanceolate, recurved leaves which are striped from the base to apex with striking, creamy-white bands. 'Massangeana' has longer leaves (up to 500 mm) with a broad yellow central stripe. Cultivation of all dracaenas is relatively easy, but remember that during the growing season they require lots of water and frequent, though restrained, syringings at room temperature. As with all indoor subjects, whatever their containers, perfect drainage is vital. The plant-lover will work on this question and make absolutely sure that surplus water drains away rapidly. Many plants are killed by the kindness of copious waterings, when the drainage system has broken down, thus excluding the free circulation of soil air. Plant all dracaenas with other plants of similar needs or as individual specimens. Propagate all from nodal cuttings at any time.

*D. godseffiana*: see *D. surculosa*

*D. goldieana*　Guinea
🌑 350 mm ◑ to ◉ 🌑
The glossy green foliage of this species is borne on a short stem and is prominently banded and spotted with white. Broadly-cordate, the leaves are 150-200 mm long and 100-140 mm wide. The young foliage is usually tinged with red. In subtropical parts this species also grows well outdoors in moderate shade.

*D. surculosa*　Tropical West Africa
🌑 750-900 mm ◑ to ◉ 🌑
A copious overlay of irregular white, pale gold, or cream spots gives the foliage of this species a particularly attractive charm. The leaves vary from lanceolate to oblong or ovate and are borne in sessile whorls. Small greenish-yellow flowers bloom spasmodically.

**Dumb Cane:** see *Dieffenbachia chelsoni*
**Elephant Ear:** see *Colocasia antiquorum*
 'Esculenta'
**Elephant's Foot:** see *Dioscorea elephantipes*

*Episcia reptans*　Guyana to Peru
GESNERIACEAE
🌑 120 rnm ◑ to ◉ 🌑
Though grown for its very attractive foliage, the small flame violet, which is creeping and much branched, bears pretty red-flushed flowers, whose 30 mm-long corolla tubes are hairy, pale red outside and soft, faintly-lined pink within. The ovate to elliptic leaves have wavy serrated margins and are variegated, dark green and sometimes greyish. They are lightly veined and hairy. It enjoys humid conditions and plenty of water during the active growth period.

*Eucharis grandiflora*　Andes
AMARYLLIDACEAE
🌑 600 mm ◑ 🌑
Though some gardeners claim that the Amazon, or eucharist, lily is difficult to grow, let alone to persuade it to flower, proper care will ensure than this bulbous species will flower regularly and regardless of the season. A

long flower-stalk, some 600 mm tall, rises above the broadly-tapering leaves and bears an umbel of three to six white, scented star-shaped blooms – each some 100 mm across. Pot bulbs in 150 mm-diameter containers, ensuring excellent drainage as when the plant really starts growing it requires copious waterings. Bone meal is a good feeding material to give it extra thrust. It resents direct sunlight and requires medium light intensity. When the lily has finished flowering, place the pot under a bench for a few weeks, making sure it does not dry out, and as soon as there are signs of regrowth, feed and water lightly, increasing this gradually. A new crop of flowers will soon appear. Older or pot-bound plants will flower more freely when well fed at the appropriate time.

*Exacum affine*　Socotra (Gulf of Aden)
GENTIANACEAE
🌑 400 mm ☀ 🌑
In summer, this small-leafed species throws up tall stems which bear bluish-lilac flowers with yellow throats in terminal racemes. The German violet is very greedy during the active growth period, but mixes well with other plants in the trough. Propagate from seed, as and when required.

*Episcia reptans* (Flame Violet)

**False Aralia:** see *Dizygotheca elegantissima*

*Ficus benjamina*　Malaysia
MORACEAE
🌑 1,5-2 m ☀ to ◑ 🌑
Thriving outdoors in the subtropical parts of Australia, its semi-weeping habit and ease of cultivation should make this species far more popular indoors than it actually is. It bears small, thin, leathery, elliptic leaves, which are a glossy dark green.

*F. elastica*　Tropical Asia
🌑 2 m ☀ 🌑
Universally known, the India rubber plant makes a stately indoor specimen, clean and imposing with large, alternate leaves on a single stem. These are a dark glossy green above with yellow or russet undersides. Though quite large-growing, it could take a few years to outgrow its home. Indoors it does not enjoy draughts. The first indication that it is not happy is a yellowing of the lower leaves. Should this occur there are a number of possibilities which must be examined at once: is it getting too much or too little water;

is there faulty drainage; is it in a draughty situation; or is it under-nourished? Though 'Variegata', with its yellow markings, is quite pleasing, as an indoor specimen the species takes some beating. When a specimen becomes too tall, as it inevitably must, take a terminal cutting 350 mm long. The cut portion will ooze a milky latex, and only when this has dried should the cutting be inserted in a well-drained mixture comprising at least 75% washed, coarse river sand. In a region sufficiently temperate to allow the old plant to grow in the open, do not plant it anywhere near the house, other structures, paths or near your neighbour's fence. The India rubber tree can make an enormous specimen, with the most destructive roots imaginable. Indoors the plant will appreciate fairly frequent syringings and, once a month, the leaves (which will collect dust) should be wiped off with a special leaf-cleaning substance, available commercially.

*Ficus benjamina*

*F. lyrata*                        Tropical Africa
🌱 2 m ☼ ☽
Another accommodating and easily grown species, the fiddle-leaf fig has large violin-shaped leaves. Where *F. benjamina* may be grown in association with other plants in a trough (though preferably in its own pot, otherwise its roots will fill the whole trough), both *F. lyrata* and *F. elastica* should be grown as individual specimens. The fiddle-leaf fig is easily reproduced from cuttings when it begins to outgrow its pot or trough.

**Fiddle-leaf Fig: see *Ficus lyrata***

*Fittonia argyroneura*                    Peru
ACANTHACEAE
🌱 100 mm ◒ to ◖ ☽
A dwarf, almost prostrate species, this is grown for its ovate foliage, 70 mm long and

beautifully netted with white veins. It is moisture-loving, needs frequent syringings with tepid water and requires warmth as well as a draught-free position. Because it is shallow rooting, plant it in a flower pot, 160 mm across and 60 mm deep. If a shallow pot is not available, place drainage material up to the requisite level. There is a species with rose pink veins.

**Flame Violet: see *Episcia reptans***
**Friendship Plant: see *Billbergia nutans***
**German Violet: see *Exacum affine***
*Gesneria cochlearis:* see *Sinningia cardinalis*

*Guzmania lingulata*          Tropical America
BROMELIACEAE
🌱 250 mm ☼ to ◖ ☽
Both the species and particularly its variety 'Cardinalis' have brilliant red bracts. Though both resent direct sunlight, they require high light intensity, are moisture- and humidity-loving and must have excellent drainage. To the standard growing medium add an extra part of purely fibrous material. If you are keen on the bromelias, this one is worth searching for. For details of propagation see page 355.

*Gynura aurantiaca*                        Java
ASTERACEAE
🌱 3 m ☼ ☽
The almost succulent stems of the very handsome royal velvet plant are covered with violet-purple hairs, while the large, soft, deeply-toothed ovate leaves are overlaid with iridescent purple. In temperate to subtropical parts it may be grown outdoors, where it makes a lovely splash of colour especially in summer, in a light, but shady position. Indoors, it needs high light intensity and regular feeding with a liquid fertilizer. It is easily propagated from cuttings.

*Hedera helix* 'Marginata'                Europe
ARALIACEAE
🌱 1-2 m ☼ to ◖ ☽
An excellent climber, either on a trellis or stick, variegated ivy succeeds well indoors, where frequent pinching out will induce a branched, shrubby habit. 'Marginata' has small ivy leaves, margined in white, cream or creamy-yellow, while 'Marginata-rubra' has a deep rosy-red margin, especially in autumn. (See also Chapter 10, 'Climbers', page 181.)

*Hoffmannia ghiesbreghtii*       South America
RUBIACEAE
🌱 1,5 m ☼ ☽
This magnificent foliage plant has oblong lanceolate-acuminate leaves up to 300 mm long. These are a dark, rich velvet green above, with dull purple and prominently veined undersides. The foliage effect is quite dramatic. Cultivate in a standard soil medium from which the compost has been omitted, since a rather poor soil condition increases leaf colouration. Replace from cuttings as the plants become leggy, which they undoubtedly will.

**Hottentot's Bread: see *Dioscorea elephantipes***

*Howea belmoreana*           Lord Howe Island
PALMAE
🌱 3 m ☼ ☽
This palm, along with the similar and perhaps better known *H. forsterana*, is indispensable for conservatory and indoor decoration, though the latter is probably better for indoor work or room decoration. For cultivation and further details, see page 220.

*Hoya bella*                            India
ASCLEPIADACEAE
🌱 750 mm ☼ ☽
Smaller-growing than *H. carnosa*, the miniature wax-flower, which thrives outdoors in temperate parts of the country, is a perfect plant for an indoor hanging basket. Feed and water well except immediately before its boat-shaped panicles of small violet flowers appear: vigorous growth at this stage prompts it to drop its buds. Grown indoors, it requires frequent syringings in hot, dry periods. Do not attempt to propagate either *Hoya* species from leaf cuttings; they will root certainly, but growth is very slow. Rather take a cutting with three nodes: one at the base, one at soil level and one with two leaves. Plant cuttings in washed river sand only.

*H. carnosa*                     Southern China
🌱 2-3 m ☼ ☽
This must be one of the most widely-cultivated greenhouse species in the world. Wherever you turn there seems to be a wax-flower. Indoors, this species does well in a trough with a trellis. Cultivate as you would *H. bella*, though *H. carnosa* will thrive outdoors only in the warmest parts.

*Hedera helix* 'Marginata'

*Hoya carnosa* (Wax-Flower) bloom and, plant

**Hypoestes phyllostachya** — Madagascar
ACANTHACEAE
⬥1 m ☼ ⊕
Though the polka-dot plant will thrive outdoors in temperate and subtropical areas, do not be tempted to plant it for it luxuriates and spreads like a weed and, once established, is difficult to eradicate. However, as an indoor foliage plant it is excellent for mixing with other pot-plants in a trough, and for filling gaps between stiffer species. Its long, thin, dark green leaves are enchantingly marked with lavender-pink spots. It is easily propagated from cuttings.

**India Rubber Plant:** see *Ficus elastica*
**Iron Cross Begonia:** see *Begonia masoniana*

*Ixora coccinea* — India
RUBIACEAE
⬥1 m ☼ ⊕
Grown almost exclusively outdoors in temperate and similar zones, the jungle geranium is a worthy indoor subject. It has shiny green leaves and bears umbellate corymbs of brick red flowers. Blooms in many other fascinating shades are available in the new cultivars. Indoors both species and cultivars require

high light intensity, but no direct sun. The plant's restricted root run means that it needs plenty of water and liquid fertilizer during the period of active growth.

**Joseph's Coat:** see *Coleus* hybrids
**Jungle Geranium:** see *Ixora coccinea*

*Justicia brandegeana* (syn. *Drejella guttata*)
ACANTHACEAE — Mexico
⬥800 mm ☼ ⊕
Though in temperate and subtropical climates the shrimp plant may be grown outdoors or on a balcony (see page 144) it also thrives as an indoor plant. It is extremely attractive in flower, having large overlapping, brownish brick red bracts which are freely produced. There is a very attractive yellow and white variety as well as a cultivar which has darker red bracts than the species. Indoors the shrimp plant is best grown as a specimen in a separate pot plunged, perhaps, into an ornamental container. Prune it frequently to maintain a short, well-branched form.

*Kalanchoe* spp. — Tropical Africa
CRASSULACEAE
⬥variable ☼ ⊕
This variable but highly ornamental and free-flowering group of succulents is summer blooming outdoors. However, indoors they may be raised from seed or cuttings for winter flowering, when they should be watered sparingly and grown in well-drained pots placed in a well-lit part of the room.

**King Begonia:** see *Begonia rex*

*Maranta leuconeura* — Brazil
MARANTACEAE
⬥300 mm ☼ to ◐ ⊕
This dwarf member of the genus and its

varieties are among the most popular of all indoor foliage plants. There are several other species with leaves anything up to 600 mm or so, but their cultivation is usually confined to conservatory work, or mass planting outdoors in the warm temperate to subtropical areas. At best, *M. leuconeura* grows some 300 mm high, with oblong or broadly-elliptic, green leaves which are banded or white-striped along the veins, and marked with darker green and purple undersides. The variety 'Kerchoveana' has larger oval leaves, which grow more or less horizontal to the stem and bear ten chocolate brown blotches on either side of the mid-rib, giving it the American common name of the Ten Commandment plant. 'Massangeana' is a smaller-leaved variety, nicely marked and with purple undersides.

Marantas prefer a shallow pot. Add an extra part of purely fibrous material to the standard growing mixture to ensure good drainage. These plants require a constantly moist situation, but will not tolerate standing water. In summer, syringe frequently with water at house temperature and feed regularly with diluted liquid manure or a balanced liquid fertilizer. Propagate by division of the crowns, in spring.

*Ixora chinensis*

*Kalanchoe* spp.

# BUSHHOUSE AND GLASSHOUSE MANAGEMENT

## MAKING THE MOST OF A CONTROLLED ENVIRONMENT

The advent of pre-cut and 'kit' type structures for the garden, has no doubt been responsible for making both the glasshouse and the bushhouse increase in popularity. Although winter climates in Australia are rarely as severe as those of Europe and the United States of America, either of these structures has many uses in Australia. In some cases, the bushhouse, with its covering of plastic mesh (no longer tea tree twigs as it used to be) is used to provide that cool and shady sitting-out place for entertaining on hot days, perhaps beside the swimming pool or the barbeque.

In other cases, the bushhouses act as weather proof and protective shelters for collections of favoured plants such as Australian native orchids, Fuchsias, African Violets and the like. There is no limit to their decoration, with hanging baskets, tree fern poles and even splashing fountains for refreshment. They create micro-climates of their own and make it easy for plants with similar needs to be grouped together for special cultural practice.

Glasshouses – or their equivalent in clear plastic covering – are becoming popular for advancing annuals and vegetables quickly to make the most of the usual long growing season in most regions. In some areas with cool winters, many plants may be over-wintered without harm and so considerably enlarge the range of plant species that can be grown in the area.

Material used in the basic frame also varies considerably, although treated timber is still regarded highly because of the harmonious blending with the landscape. Galvanised piping or strong wire mesh is used, coming in sections which are easily assembled by the gardener to make an almost instant structure. Even on unit balconies miniature versions of these are possible in which equally small versions of vegetables such as tomatoes, cucumbers and capsicums can be grown – both decorative and edible.

The following sections are some of the main factors which the home gardener can bear in mind when planning either a glasshouse or a bushhouse.

Although some will be a little too sophisticated for the average home situation, with a little common sense applied, they can be adapted to either structure no matter what materials are used in the rigid part of the frame or its covering.

Many of the plants listed can be grown in the open ground in most parts of this country and many from the previous chapter "Indoor & Balcony Plants" can be included or substituted for those in this chapter.

**BENCHES.** These may be built of a variety of materials, and their costs will vary accordingly. For instance, corrugated galvanised iron, properly supported and covered with a 50 mm layer of coarse sand is quite satisfactory. A reinforced concrete slab, with standards and angle irons will cost more, and last longer, but as far as growing is concerned, the plants won't know the difference. As opposed to a slatted timber bench, the concrete and corrugated iron types should be designed to allow a space of about 60 mm between the edge of the bench and the wall, to allow free circulation of air.

**DESIGN.** Unless the glasshouse is planned for a special purpose – for a group of plants which need extraordinary conditions – the first requirement in its design and erection is the admission of adequate sunlight. The second most important consideration is to be able to control the flow of air, admitting as much as may be necessary or circumstances demand. The size of the structure will be determined largely by the finance and space available, but in terms of controlling temperatures, the minimum size for a span roof – or free-standing bushhouse – should be in the vicinity of 3.75 m × 2.5 m. A span roof is always preferable as it admits light at all sides. Consensus of opinion suggests that it should run lengthwise, north and south.

**FLOOR.** This should be concrete or some other durable, smoothly paved surface which allows the floor to be flooded with water – damped down – either to cool the air or to raise the humidity, or both. Should the glasshouse have a bench (and it is wise to include one), surface the area beneath it with about 70 mm of gravel or cinders which will retain moisture. Modern forms of construction make great use of aluminium framing, which is strong and thin, and offers little obstruction to light. These are freely available, prefabricated, in different sizes. If you are building the house yourself, the rafters must be thin enough to allow maximum light.

◀ A splendid array of plants splashes this glasshouse with colour

**FRAMES.** Of all garden structures, the frame is certainly the most useful. And though it is not essential, neither is it a luxury, for it serves a multitude of purposes. Not only can a frame be one of the most efficient means to create a controlled 'climate' in which to germinate most seeds, but in colder parts of the country it may be used to over-winter such tender subjects as begonias and species of *Coleus*, as well as sheltering early seedlings of such plants as tomatoes, and peppers, in any part of the country, a frame can provide ideal conditions for propagation by cuttings.

The dimensions of a garden frame will be governed both by space and the home-owner's pocket. Ideally it should be 1.5 m wide and at least as long, with its rear wall about 500 mm and its front some 300 mm high. The slope of the glass or shade-cloth covering should be north facing, to catch the full sun. It may have a sliding cover of glass and timber fitted to a permanent brick-walled base, in which case the interior should be plastered, to eliminate any spaces between the brick courses in which insects can lodge. However, a perfectly adequate temporary structure may be made from loose bricks or timber, with an old glazed window as the 'cover'.

A permanent frame – again providing that space and the gardener's pocket permit – could be long enough to be equipped for part of its length, say 3 m, with soil-heating equipment and even a simple form of mist spray. This combination would allow the grower to propagate the most difficult of cuttings or germinate the most reluctant seed.

**HEATING.** Where heating is necessary during the cold months, the form and type will depend largely on two factors – the size of the house or unit, and how much heat is required, i.e. whether merely to sustain growth without cold damage, or to actively promote growth through to its logical conclusion, whether it be foliage, fruit or flower. Whatever the situation, bear in mind that badly constructed houses lose more heat than sound ones and that more heat will be lost on a cold, windy day than on a calm one. It is also easier to heat, and to maintain a predetermined temperature in a large house than in a small one. On the other hand, the growing requirements of the plant population of a small glasshouse are usually less complicated. In cold winter areas the home grower will see to it that his plants are such that they all enjoy more or less the minimum and maximum temperature which he can maintain. One or another of the many forms of electrical heating is probably the most efficient and convenient, but remember to have it installed by a qualified electrician. If the glasshouse is to be used to propagate cuttings, germinate seedlings, or otherwise actively promote growth, part or all of a bench may be equipped with soil warming cables. These are laid under 50 mm of sand and should be controlled by a thermostat located near to the bench. In discussing heating, I am not suggesting heating which virtually turns the glasshouse into a hot-house – this would be a horse of an entirely different colour. In the glasshouse, heating is introduced only to

While a free-standing glasshouse (above) is preferable, space may compel the gardener to settle for the lean-to type. This has the disadvantage of limiting light on one side. In either type, adequate methods of ventilation, as indicated, are essential.

prevent damage by very low temperatures, or to promote earlier than normal growth in early spring.

**LEAN-TO.** A 'lean-to' house may have the disadvantage of light being restricted to one side only, but it provides a highly practical and useful solution when a suitable north, north-east or north-west facing wall already exists. One or two benches may be accommodated, depending on the floor width.

**LOCATION.** When choosing a site, two primary requirements should be borne in mind – it must be protected from wind, especially a prevailing cold wind, and there should be no obstruction to light, such as the shade of trees or buildings. Since not all gardens can accommodate a structure of this sort without it looking out of place, many home gardeners like to locate their glasshouse adjacent to the vegetable garden.

**TUNNEL CULTIVATION:** see Special Spread, page 323

**VENTILATION.** All glasshouses require ventilation and it must be provided in such a way that it can be controlled according to the needs of the plants in any given set of climatic circumstances. The types of ventilation and their uses are illustrated opposite.

**Amazon Lily:** see *Eucharis grandiflora*

*Anthurium andraeanum*          Colombia
ARACEAE
🐌 800 mm ◐ ☀
The flamingo lily bears large arum-like spathes sometimes more than 120 mm long which are white or shades of pink and red. It is ideal in the cool glasshouse in temperate areas, though it will thrive outdoors in our subtropical regions (see page 84), and in colder areas may be raised in a warm glasshouse in winter to flower in mid-summer. Shade is essential and can be provided by other taller plants, or by using plastic shade cloth to provide 50% sunlight exclusion. The most suitable soil medium is very open and fibrous – two parts of fibrous loam, one part of peat moss, one part of coarse river sand, pieces of charcoal and one part of chopped sphagnum or peat moss. If grown with other plants which do not need the same high level of humidity, place the pot on a patch of sphagnum moss 250 mm × 250 mm and about 50 mm thick, keeping this moist on hot days.

*A. scherzerianum*          Costa Rica
🐌 300 mm ● ☀
This species is smaller, though otherwise similar in habit and requirements to its larger relative. Its spathes are more delicate, but are elegant in a colour range of white, white blushed pink, spotted pink and shades of red.

**Begonia:** see Special Spread, page 322
**Brazilian Lily:** see *Eucharis grandiflora*

*Caladium bicolor*
This species has been dealt with extensively

*Caladium bicolor*

in the previous chapter, 'Indoor and Balcony Plants' (see page 297). However they may also be cultivated as glasshouse specimens, and a word of warning is needed here. In a small glasshouse, where most of the plants enjoy lots of light and, in many cases, minimal protection from direct sunlight, there may be difficulty in reconciling these conditions with requirements of caladiums, particularly those with very delicately coloured leaves. Shading throughout their active growth is vital, as sun scorch will ruin the foliage. As the summer temperatures rise, so – by frequent damping down and occasional syringings – must the humidity be increased. Because their leaves are borne on long stalks, they cannot, like anthuriums, be pushed in amongst other taller-growing plants. One solution is to put the pots containing caladiums under the bench while direct sunshine is at its greatest, or use them in the indoor garden as soon as they have attained the necessary growth. Place the tuberous rhizomes in 130 mm pots, providing extra drainage as for anthuriums, and then pot on into 200 mm pots as soon as rooting is well advanced. During active growth, caladiums are gross feeders and require weekly doses of liquid fertilizer, or even straight liquid manure. Reduce watering as the foliage begins to fade in autumn. Unlike begonia tubers, *Caladium* rhizomes must not be allowed to dry out completely, or they will rot – just as they will also rot if given too much water. In very cold areas, do not allow the temperature to drop below 14°C. The following spring, shake out the rhizomes, clean and divide where necessary, then start them off again in fresh soil.

*Calceolaria crenatiflora*          Chile
SCROPHULARIACEAE
🐌 300 mm ◐ ☀
The popular annual glasshouse calceolarias are said to have arisen from a cross between

*Calceolaria crenatiflora*

this species and *C. corymbosa*, but it is probable that other species were also involved in the breeding of the lovely, colourful flowers we know today. Typical glasshouse plants, the winter/spring-flowering calceolarias are raised from seed sown in autumn. In warmly temperate to subtropical areas they are truly winter flowering, but in the cooler parts they will flower in spring through to late October. The seed is very fine (40 000 per gram) and should be mixed with fine, washed sand for sowing on the surface of an equal mixture of peat and washed river sand. Water only by immersion. Germination takes 8-12 days. When large enough to handle, prick the seedlings out into trays, setting them 60 mm apart in the same mixture. They need plenty of light, but not direct sunlight, especially in the hottest part of the day. As soon as the young plants are about 70 mm high, pot them into 60-70 mm-diameter containers, using the standard soil mixture for indoor plants (see page 293). Ensure a constant light and airy situation, damping the house down from time to time in hot weather to reduce temperature and provide slight humidity. As rooting activity demands, pot on into larger pots – 150-200 mm are ideal – in which the plants may be flowered.

*Chlidanthus fragrans*                   Andes
AMARYLLIDACEAE
🌱 250 mm ◐ ☀
Bearing trumpet-shaped, fragrant, golden yellow blooms some 80 mm long, the summer-flowering Peruvian daffodil may be grown outdoors in the warmer temperate and subtropical parts. In the cooler areas it should at least be started off under cover and if not flowered there, moved outdoors in its pot only in late spring. Bulbs are usually available commercially from July to September and should be planted immediately, 70 mm deep in 120 mm-diameter pots using the standard growing mixture. A little warmth will help early development, so, particularly on warm days, give them plenty of air and light shade. For a month or so before flowering give them regular light dressings of liquid fertilizer, but avoid spilling this on the dark green, linear leaves. After the plants have flowered and died down, keep the bulbs and soil fairly dry and pot up again the following late July, at the same time removing the many offsets which will be produced. These may also be potted up, placing several in a well-drained 150 mm pot for growing on for the following season.

*Clivia miniata*
Though this species, which has many popular cultivars and hybrids, has been dealt with in the previous chapter, 'Indoor and Balcony Plants' (see page 299), it requires special treatment in colder parts of the country and must have warmth in winter. Establish the fresh bulbous rhizomes in 180 mm pots of the standard growing mixture. After flowering, usually about September, the pots may be stored outside, in the shade of a tree. Keep them a little on the dry side until spring, when they may be watered freely and given dressings of liquid fertilizer, particularly in August and September. Leave them in these pots for a maximum of three years, when they must be

*Cyclamen persicum* cultivar

taken out and divided. This is not easy as their bases become intertwined and matted.

*Cyclamen persicum*   Eastern Mediterranean
PRIMULACEAE
🌱 200 mm ◐ ☀
The tremendous colour range of their sweetly-scented flowers and the equally varied tones and hues of their 120 mm-long cordate leaves, make cyclamens one of the most loved of all our garden plants. And today's wide range of cultivars, ideally suited to bushhouse cultivation, provides the owner of such a structure – or even a garden frame – with the challenge of producing this tuberous species from seed. The challenge is not particularly onerous, it is more a matter of having the right facilities and following a fairly rigid procedure.

If you have a glasshouse with even moderate heat, start off in mid-winter; if your glasshouse is unheated or you have a garden frame, sow the seed in early spring. Seed is expensive, but to sow, say, 50 use a standard plastic seed tray (about 240 × 170 × 50mm) filled with equal parts of washed river sand and peat, and firmed down with a firming board. Space the seeds out evenly and cover very lightly with the same mixture; water at all stages only by immersion. Cover the seed tray with paper and place it in a warm spot where the temperature will remain fairly even. From the eighth day keep a close watch for germination, removing the paper as soon as this occurs, giving the seedlings plenty of light but no direct sun.

When the seedlings are large enough to handle, or about 15 mm high, pot them off into 40 mm thumb pots containing the standard growing mixture. Only half cover the little corms. As soon as they are well rooted, pot on into 100 mm containers. Cyclamens are very sensitive both to over-potting and to either over-or-under-watering.

Potting into the final pot – 130 mm for the smallest corms and 150-160 mm for the most

vigorous – is usually in late summer, when every effort must be made to keep temperatures down and, while giving full light, exposure to the direct sunlight must be avoided. This situation is best achieved in a cool frame, with a 2 m-high, superstructure covered first with rainproof clear sheeting. This in turn, is covered with plastic shade cloth (giving about 30% sun exclusion) which covers not only the top but also encloses the sunny side to frame level to protect the plants from slanting sun rays.

Overseas, where winters are more severe and summers shorter and cooler than here, a cyclamen corm takes an average of 15 months to reach flowering maturity, so that plants grown from seed sown in August will start flowering in November of the following year. Here plants from seed sown in winter-spring will start flowering in May or June of the following year – taking about eight to ten months to bloom. Particularly from the stage when the young corms are potted on into 100 mm-diameter pots, extra feeding is necessary and may take the form of diluted liquid fertilizer or weekly doses of proprietary liquid fertilizer applied at the rate recommended by the manufacturer. Bottom feeding and watering is always preferable, but if top watering is unavoidable, try not to wet the foliage.

To flower old corms a second time, when flowering is finished continue watering as usual, gradually reducing this as the leaves begin to die. At this stage withhold water almost completely, but never allow the plants to become dry for any length of time. After this short rest, remove the corms, clean them carefully and re-pot into 70 mm pots. Though old corms flower freely, their flowers will be smaller than those produced by fresh, seedling corms. For the control of pests, see page 340.

*Endymion non-scriptus:* see Special Spread, page 320
**English Bluebell:** see *Endymion non-scriptus*, page 320

*Eucharis grandiflora*
The Amazon or eucharist lily, described in the previous chapter, 'Indoor and Balcony Plants' (see page 302), is also an excellent bushhouse plant. It requires no heating in temperate to subtropical areas but, in colder parts of the country, a warming system which will keep temperatures to a minimum of 7°C is needed. As the weather improves, a minimum temperature of 18°C will promote active growth. Water sparingly in winter, until active growth signals the need for more waterings, as well as a liquid fertilizer supplement every ten days or so. When the plants have become pot-bound allow them to flower once more before potting on into 250 mm containers, which is about the largest size one can reasonably handle. For protection against insect pests, see page 340.

*Eucomis comosa*                   South Africa
LILIACEAE
🌱 600-700 mm ☀ ☀
Although the bulbous pineapple flower may be grown outdoors in warmly temperate to

subtropical parts of the country, in less favoured areas it is a useful addition to the bushhouse population. Small, star-shaped fragrant flowers are usually produced at the height of summer and are greenish-white with a purple centre. They are borne on a 300 mm, many-flowered, cylindrical raceme, crowned with a tufted rosette of pineapple-like leaves. The lanceolate basal leaves are 300 mm long, and are an attractive, dark green above with mottled purple undersides. Pot up the bulbs in early autumn, in the standard potting medium and over-winter (giving little water) in a temperature not less than 7°C. They require lots of water during their period of active growth, and may be flowered in the bushhouse, placed indoors, or even plunged in their pots to flower outdoors. Propagate from offsets.

*Euphorbia pulcherrima*

Though the outdoor cultivation of poinsettias has been discussed in Chapter 8, 'Shrubs and Roses', page 135, these are also well worth growing in the bushhouse in areas of frost. Even in parts of the country where frosts are light and infrequent these may spoil the colourful bracts just as they reach their best in early spring. In really cold areas with heavy frosts, the glasshouse must be warmed if the plants are to survive without damage and *E. fulgens* will require more heat than the poinsettia. However, both species may be left outdoors in full sun during summer and early autumn. The dwarf cultivars of *E. pulcherrima*, which produce their crimson bracts when only 250 mm tall, and which have been treated with a substance to retard their growth, seem particularly popular as bushhouse specimens.

**Flamingo Lily:** see *Anthurium andraeanum*
*Freesia* hybrids: see Special Spread, page 320

*Fritillaria imperialis*          Western Himalayas
LILIACEAE
🌱 1 m ☀ 🌢

The crown imperial is probably among the best-known members of this large genus of approximately 80 different species and is one of the few occasionally available in Australia. Though *F. imperialis* will grow well in the open in coolly temperate and colder areas, I recommend pot culture. There are many cultivars but the type has a large bulb and stem upwards of one metre on which a terminal umbel of numerous roughly bell-shaped flowers are borne. These are pendulous, 50 mm long, and deep yellow or bronzy-yellow. In January-February plant the bulb in a 180 mm pot of standard potting mixture, covering it firmly with 100 mm of soil. Growth does not begin until early spring and the safest way to keep plants in good condition in the meantime, is to plunge them up to their necks in sand in a frame, fully exposed to the sun. Begin regular watering as soon as growth begins and bring them into the glasshouse when about 300 mm high, or earlier if the spring weather is unusually severe.

**Grape Hyacinth:** see *Muscari botryoides*
**Geranium:** see *Pelargonium* spp.

*Eucomis autumnalis*

*Hyacinthus orientalis*

Though hyacinths, tulips and narcissus species are dealt with and described in the special spread on bulbs on page 110, the bushhouse is the ideal place in which to cultivate them, though they may be plunged in the garden or flowered indoors once sufficiently developed. Acclimatized Australian grown bulbs of these species are usually available from commercial nurserymen

*Euphorbia pulcherrima* (Poinsettia)

*Hyacinthus orientalis* (Hyacinth)

between February and May and it is important to plant them as quickly after buying them as possible, for they bruise and damage very easily.

The best soil medium for hyacinths is peat moss. Plant the bulbs in shallow receptacles, bringing the top of the bulb level with the surface of the soil. The treated hyacinth does not depend on the soil medium for its sustenance, as it produces its flower by exhausting the food stored in its bulb; when it stops flowering, so is the bulb finished. Hyacinths require a light, warm situation, away from draughts and the direct rays of the sun.

**Jacobea Lily:** see *Sprekelia formosissima*, page 111.

*Muscari botryoides*                    Mediterranean
LILIACEAE
🌞 600 mm ☼ ☺
The grape hyacinth will thrive outdoors in loamy soil, enriched with compost or leaf mould, in the warmer temperate parts of the country, but is equally happy as a pot plant. In summer it bears a dense, short raceme of blue flowers with white 'teeth' on a firm stem which rises above the long, arching leaves. Cultivars include 'Album' with white flowers. This bulbous species is easily propagated from offsets, taken in autumn, or from ripe seed. Pot in the standard mixture, placing the top of the bulb some 30 mm below the soil's surface.

*Narcissus* spp.
Narcissus and tulips require a deeper receptacle than hyacinths (a standard 150 mm pot is ideal) and, since they produce feeding

# GIVING OUTDOOR BULBS A HEAD START

Many of the most beautiful winter/spring- and autumn/winter-flowering species of bulbous and cormous plants which are grown outdoors in many parts of the country, positively flourish in bushhouse conditions. Not only will they flower earlier than when grown outdoors, but their blooms are often larger.

Most of those which I list – and the gardener fortunate enough to have a bushhouse will have other favourites of his own – are relatively shallow-rooting, small bulbs and corms. These do best in containers which are wide rather than deep. Certainly most of the winter- and spring-flowering species fall into this category, as do the *Ixia* hybrids and *I. viridiflora*.

Among the species planted from February to April and which flower from July to September, my favourites for bushhouse cultivation include the various species and cultivars of *Lachenalia* (see page 99), the spring snowflake (*Leucojum vernum*), English bluebells (*Endymion nonscriptus*), grape hyacinth (*Muscari botryoides*), *Sparaxis grandiflora* and

*Tritonia crocata*. These and similar species of the gardener's choice should be started, in their containers, in an ordinary cold frame and they should be moved into the bushhouse when the really cold weather begins.

My choice of the bulbous and cormous species to be planted from July to September for summer and early autumn flowering would include the Jacobea lily (*Sprekelia formosissima*, see page 111), the tiger flower or one day lily (*Tigridia pavonia*, see page 113), *Nerine bowdenii* and *N. sarniensis* (see page 104), the *Freesia* and *Montbretia* hybrids and, of course, *Ixia viridiflora* and the *Ixia* hybrids (see page 99). These obviously benefit from the early, protected start which the bushhouse can provide.

By planting the smaller, shallow-rooting bulbs and corms in wider, flatter containers, a greater numbers of plants may be grown in each unit; equally they are easier to move when, at the flowering stage, they may be required somewhere other than in the bushhouse. Plastic or earthenware

containers with drainage holes are generally available and a unit with a diameter of 200 mm and about 100 mm deep is ideal for most of the species. Place broken crocks over the drainage holes and then cover to a depth of 30 mm with fibrous drainage material before filling with the standard growing mixture. Alternatively, standard 150 mm-deep pots may be used, increasing the drainage medium to 50 mm.

All of the species listed in the first group – with the exception of *Tritonia crocata* and *Sparaxis grandiflora* (five plants each to an 180 mm pot and planted 80 mm deep) – may be planted quite shallowly and about 50 mm apart, about 12 to a 200 mm diameter container. With the exception of the *Ixias*, the second group may be planted three to an 180 mm pot. Generally, all plants in both categories enjoy full sunlight at all stages of their growth, need copious waterings and light feedings during very active growth, and a gradual reduction of water as dormancy approaches.

roots, the standard growing mixture should be used, with special attention given to drainage before filling the pot. Plant both so that the tops of the bulbs are about 20 mm below the surface. Bear in mind that you are dealing with specially treated bulbs and all that is necessary is that the containers should be placed in a cool place until the growing tips appear above the soil. Once good growth is apparent, they should be given full light and normal waterings in a draught-free situation. (See page 110 for further treatment after flowering.)

**One Day Lily:** see *Tigridia pavonia*, page 113.

*Pelargonium* spp.
Though the wide range of geraniums have been dealt with extensively on page 106, in very cold parts of Australia they do need the winter protection of a glasshouse.

Most *Pelargonium* are excellent balcony and cool glasshouse plants and, providing they are correctly managed, do not dislike pot culture. However, even with careful pruning, designed to preserve their shape and provide a constant supply of young flowering wood, they do not last indefinitely and it is wise to take cuttings regularly, so ensuring a regular supply of young, vigorous plants. Start the rooted cuttings off in 100 mm pots, moving on to 150 mm containers when the plants mature and flower regularly. They require full light and a free air circulation and a happy plant is rarely bothered either by pest or disease. Watering is critical. Over-watering causes the plant to flower sparsely; thoroughly soak the pot and allow it to become almost bone-dry before soaking again. Trickle, trickle, trickle every day, and your geranium will soon die.

**Peruvian Daffodil:** see *Chlidanthus fragrans*
**Pineapple Flower:** see *Eucomis comosa*
**Tiger Flower:** see *Tigridia pavonia*, page 113.

*Tulipa* hybrids                    Garden origin
LILIACEAE
⚘ 300-600 mm ☼ ☻
Today's garden tulips have been bred and hybridized out of all recognition from *T. gesnerana*, the species from Asia Minor which was introduced to Europe from Turkey in the 16th century. There are splendid forms, in almost every imaginable colour, in the 15 classifications of tulip recognized by international horticulturists, though only three of these – Darwin, Darwin hybrid, and parrot tulips – have attained popularity among Australian gardeners. This is probably because only specially-treated bulbs do well – and these seldom excel after their first year's flowering (see also 'Cold Storage and Treatment of Bulbs', page 110). The hybrids and cultivars which Australian gardeners plant, do bloom encouragingly in their first year in all but the warmest parts of the country, though they are at their best – but again only for one flowering season – in the cooler areas. Tulips prefer rich, cool and moist soil and full sun, though in the warmer parts it is wise to provide some shade during the hottest hours

*Narcissus* 'King Alfred'

*Pelargonium inquinans*

of the day. Plant the bulbs in individual pots, or if they are to be grown outdoors, set them out 120-150 mm apart at a depth of 75 mm. The treated bulbs take nine or ten weeks to flower and should be planted in early winter in the warmer parts and late winter in colder areas for late winter/early spring and late spring flowering respectively. Cover the growing area with a good mulch and, in the summer-rainfall area particularly, ensure that the bulbs are watered regularly during the growing period.

# BEGONIAS

The origin of the modern, large-flowered, tuberous-rooted begonia hybrids is not so much confused as it is complicated. For more than a century hybridists have worked on some half dozen species, crossing and re-crossing them to produce the wealth of forms, varieties and colours which are freely available today. These may be grown from seed or from leaf cuttings (see page 355) but quite the best way for the amateur enthusiast to start is to purchase prepared tubers in spring, from a reputable nursery or seedsman. These will flower from January through to March.

Although dealt with generally in the previous chapter, 'Indoor and Balcony Plants', these hybrids, with *B. rex*, *B. masoniana* and *B.* X 'Gloire de Lorraine', are so essentially cool glasshouse subjects that their cultivation in this special environment merits additional comment.

Add an additional part of coarse fibrous material to the standard growing mixture to provide the open, quick drainage which these, and most other begonias, require. A well-developed tuber may be placed first in a 100 mm-diameter pot, re-potting it in a 150 mm container when rooting is well developed. The roots of these tubers are inclined to spread outwards rather than down, so it is wise to provide at least 70 mm of drainage material in the base of the container before adding the growing medium, which should be brought to within 30 mm of the rim. Try to maintain an even starting temperature of between 15 and 18°C. Place the filled container in the glasshouse a week or more before potting, so that its temperature is much the same as that of the environment; similarly, use water which is also at the same temperature as the surrounding air. Hollow the soil out slightly, place the tuber (hollow side up) in the centre of the pot and lightly cover the whole tuber with additional soil.

Some gardeners argue that the tuber should not be covered, but this theory is not supported by leading growers who usually cover them to a depth of 5-7 mm. The fact is that the tubers may also produce roots from their sides or even from their tops. If they are not covered, this potential feeding system is lost, as any exposed roots will wither.

For as long as practicable, water these begonias by immersing the container, removing it as soon as the soil surface darkens. Very little water is required during the early stages of development, and no fertilizer or other feeding material should be incorporated in the potting mixture. In fact, do not give the plants supplementary feeding until the first flowering buds form. When they do, add liquid fertilizer to the water every ten days. When potting on to the larger containers, provide a number of cut bamboo canes as

*Begonia* X *tuberhybrida*

*Begonia* X *tuberhybrida*

supports to which flowering stems may be tied. Buds appearing before, or immediately after potting, should be carefully nipped out as they are unlikely to produce good flowers.

Because these begonias require full light, but not direct sun, they should be protected with plastic shade cloth which may be rolled up or down, as the weather changes. *B. rex* and *B. masoniana* both require much the same treatment; but whereas the tuberous-rooted hybrids are dried off for the winter, these two species are kept growing, with the absolute minimum of water.

For good quality blooms, remove most of the female flowers as soon as they are large enough to handle. These are easy to recognize as they are produced on either side of the male flower and carry little seed pods at the back of the flower. After flowering, gradually reduce watering, though some water will be needed until the last leaf shrivels.

When the tubers show that they are dormant, cut the top foliage and any flowers back to within 200 mm of the tuber, knock the plants out of the pot and place them, undisturbed, on a tray under the glasshouse bench where water will not splash on them. The remaining stalks will fall off naturally and the tubers may then be cleaned and lightly dusted with fungicide. Store them in trays with bone-dry peat moss, in a place where the temperature will not fall below 13°C, nor exceed 20°C. Examine occasionally and remove any tubers which have not stored properly. Keep a very close watch from July onwards until new signs of growth.

# CULTIVATION IN TUNNELS

Though tunnel cultivation is a comparatively new form of horticulture and requires more management and a higher degree of expertise than most other fields of gardening, it holds many attractions for the home gardener. And though it was developed for intensive, mass-production cultivation, it is not the prerogative of the commercial grower. If a garden is large enough to accommodate a vegetable patch, even part of this should provide enough space for a small tunnel. Domestic kits are available at some of the larger nurseries; all the gardener has to do is to assemble tubular supports and spread the covering. But, provided he is something of a handyman, the average gardener should be able to construct his own tunnel relatively cheaply (see adjacent illustration). Remember, though, that no matter what length it is, a tunnel should be at least 3.5 m wide and 2.5 m high to allow not only free circulation of air, but provide ample space for control and cultivation activities.

Apart from the increased crops – whether of vegetables or flowers – which can be expected from this form of cultivation, it also allows the gardener to control temperatures and make the most beneficial use of water. And these aspects, coupled with the protection from the elements which tunnel growing affords, should make it possible for the home gardener to provide for most of, if not all, his family's vegetable requirements thoughout the year – particularly if a simple form of crop-rotation is practised – from a tunnel not more than 4-5 m long.

Though tomatoes, cucumbers and lettuce are the main crops grown commercially in tunnels, the enterprising gardener will also grow squashes, peas, beans and most of the *Brassicas* in his tunnel. And, because these are cultivated in plastic containers of growing medium, it is feasible for root crops to be grown in the soil 'floor' of half the tunnel. Thus half of the 'floor' would be covered in containers and the remainder open to normal cultivation. When these root crops have been harvested, compost and manure can be dug in and the soil allowed to lie fallow under the plastic containers which have been moved to this part of the tunnel, while their previous site is now 'open' and may be used to plant carrots, turnips, beetroot and even potatoes.

Plants such as tomatoes and cucumbers, which are heavy feeders, are usually grown in 10 litre plastic bags containing a medium of anything from prepared sawdust, bark, sand, gravel, peat, or combinations of these. Other vegetables may be grown in troughs formed of plastic sheeting. Water is fed to each container through

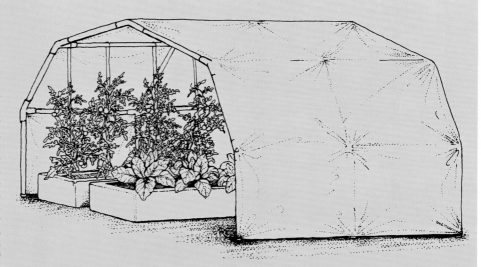

Tunnel cultivation is not the exclusive province of the commercial grower, and a small structure such as this can be accommodated in even a moderate-sized garden. The tunnel can be used to create a carefully controlled climate and is particularly suited to cultivating vegetables. It even allows the gardener to practice crop rotation.

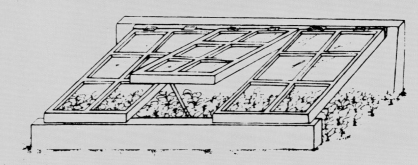

A garden frame is invaluable both for propagating seedlings and to over-winter tender plants.

a 20 mm plastic tube fitted to the main irrigation lead, and the flow may be controlled either manually or by means of an electrical timing device which may be set to deliver a given amount of water at predetermined intervals, depending on the crop, the time of the year and temperatures. Fertilizing is carried out by hand, by foliar feeding, or in solution through the irrigation system. In the latter case, the correct mixture of food nutrients may be prepared in a separate tank and fed though the irrigation systems merely by switching valves, when food is required. For the commercial grower a more sophisticated system, electrically controlled and fully automatic, will pass the necessary foods in correct proportions through to the plants, but such units are extremely expensive and not for the home gardener. (A good feeding formula is given in the special spread, 'Hydroponics', see page 260.) Many of the growing mediums may be used over and over again but before re-use it must be effectively sterilized, usually by treatment with methyl bromide.

The great advantages of tunnel cultivation – for both the commercial and the home grower – are rapid, uninterrupted growth and the possibility of complete protection against insect pests and fungus diseases. However, absolute attention to hygiene at all times is essential to success. Thus, not only must there be personal supervision on the part of the grower, but he also needs a sound working knowledge of basic plant management.

The main disadvantage – apart from the extra effort which the gardener will have to expend – lies in the wear and tear to greenhouse sheeting, which will probably need to be renewed every two years or so. Here, wind is the most limiting factor and the greater protection that a tunnel can be given the better. If a windbreak is necessary, establish it before putting up the tunnel (see Chapter 9, 'Hedges and Windbreaks') though 20% nylon, hail-guard netting may be used to effectively reduce wind strength.

A final word of warning. Do not try to convert a tunnel to a glasshouse, or vice-versa. Though both, in a way, serve similar purposes and create their own controllable micro-climates, their ventilation requirements are so different that the transition never seems to work.

# ORCHIDS 20

## EXOTIC BLOOMS WHICH ARE GAINING POPULARITY

Orchids have for so long symbolized the exotic and the expensive that an aura of mystique and myth still surrounds them in the minds of many gardeners. Orchids, even the terrestrial genera, are certainly different from any other form of plant life. Yet, once their needs and structure are understood, there are many species which are not difficult to grow, produce splendid flowers in a wide range of colours, and require none of the care that some of the more exotic members of the family ORCHIDACEAE demand.

There are almost 80 genera and over 600 species of orchids native to Australia. Particularly striking are the bulbophyllum, cymbidium, dendrobium, dipodium, sarcochilus and thelymitra genera.

Though the flowers of orchids may take many strange forms and shapes and range from the insignificant to the large and showy, all are resupinate (their flower heads are, in effect, upside down, see illustration page 329) with the pedicel or ovary usually twisted through 180°. Each bloom has three sepals which are usually narrow, often petal-like and in most, the central sepal is larger and of a different colour. Of the three petals, the lateral ones are usually alike while the middle petal, or lip, is of a different shape, often tri-lobed and its tip either recurved or its base ending in a spur or sac.

Of the thousands of species of orchids, all of the family ORCHIDACEAE – estimates of their genera range between 600 and 800 and of their species 17 000 and 30 000 – many are epiphytic, growing anchored to the bark of trees, but not drawing their sustenance from them. These are mainly the exotic blooms of the rain forests which extract nutrients from debris and mosses and absorb moisture from the humid air. The terrestrial species on the other hand are rooted in the earth and draw their nourishment from the soil. A few orchids are saprophytic: they do not possess the chlorophyll which allows most plants to convert sunlight into energy. Instead they depend on the small fungi which cover their roots to feed them by breaking down the debris of other plants. Though these bear some of the finest blooms, they are among the most difficult of all the orchids to cultivate. Ter-restrial, epiphytic and even saprophytic species of orchids may all be found in the same genera.

Much of the sucess of orchid growing lies in an understanding of the plant's natural habitat, its method of growth and feeding needs. For the beginner, a wise step would be to join a local orchid society – don't be afraid to ask questions, even the most expert grower started off with as little knowledge as you.

Establish which species do well in your particular area and then find out as much as possible about the orchid you would most like to cultivate. This need not be the easiest, for it is the interest which the grower shows and the understanding of the plant's needs, that are likely to gain the best results.

Depending on the locality's climate, some orchids or groups of orchids may be grown outdoors or, at least, with the minimum of shelter and protection. Others may demand high or low humidity, a temperature which must not fall below or rise above a certain degree, or even a changing miniclimate which echoes that of their natural home. In cool climates, the grower wanting to cultivate an orchid which requires year-round tropical conditions will need a greenhouse equipped to provide a hot, humid atmosphere in winter and a reduced heat but unchanged humidity in summer. This would probably involve the use of extractor fans – an additional expense.

In the same areas a different group of orchids, equally interesting and beautiful, may be grown in a simple shade house (see illustration, page 377) with some additional protection; and in the frost-free areas a more modified structure will prove adequate. Equally, in these warmer parts, the housing for orchids which need a constant tropical 'climate' will be much simpler and less costly than in areas of winter frost.

As far as potting mediums are concerned, the ideal is to provide as close a copy of the species' growing environment as possible. Thus, most indigenous and exotic terrestrial species require a fairly rich, fibrous soil, and special mixtures in which to grow these orchids are available commercially. However, if you wish to prepare your own, this mixture will prove satisfactory for the needs of most terrestrial species:

*Disa racemosa*

three parts of chopped fibrous loam, two parts each of washed river sand and leaf mould, and one part of imported sphagnum moss. Unless otherwise indicated, this mixture may be used for all of the terrestrial species which I have listed.

Most orchids produce pseudobulbs, thick, fleshy stems bearing one or more leaves which also act as water reserves, particularly for the epiphytes. These multiply either as clumps or by continuous growth at their tips, and division of these new growths is the simplest method of propagation, though the grower should ensure that the section of pseudobulb has at least one healthy leaf. The few species which do not have pseudobulbs are best propagated from stem cuttings or from the sucker-like offsets of those orchids which produce them. Propagate all orchids as soon as renewed active growth begins.

The following selection provides a wide range of orchid genera and species, and of sufficiently varied form and requirements to provide the beginner with a choice not only of blooms but also of varying degrees of challenge in terms of cultural requirements.

### Bulbophyllum weinthalii   Australia
🦋 ☼ 🌱

In its natural state this small epiphytic creeping orchid is found growing on the hoop pine *Araucaria cunninghamii,* from which it gets its common name of hoop pine orchid.

*Bulbophyllums* are mostly cultivated by orchid specialists, however, with a little care you can make these dainty and exquisite orchids a beautiful addition to your garden.

*B. weinthalii* has short creeping rhizomes with pear-shaped pseudobulbs that grow up to 150 mm high. Each pseudobulb produces a solitary leaf and flower, with the leaf stretching to 250 mm. Its flower is yellow with a green tinge and reddish blotches, and is about 10 mm in width.

In their natural state, *B. weinthalii* are shaded from the wind and sun by the trees they live on. Therefore, if cultivated they need to be protected from the hot sun and wind.

They require plenty of water, often daily. It is normal for the pseudobulbs to be wrinkled but if they begin to shrivel then they need more water. It is a good idea to let the mixture they are growing in dry out between waterings. A little liquid organic fertilizer should be given to the plant once a week during its growing period. They also need good air circulation and humid conditions as the roots absorb moisture and food from the air.

You can cultivate *Bulbophyllums* either in pots or on wooden slabs. Never grow these plants in soil as it will rot the roots. If you decide to pot them, then plant them in a mix of bark and plant fibre with polystyrene balls or a little moss to conserve moisture. If you decide to mount your plant, use a slab made from cork, polystyrene or a bark log, which you can easily attach to a tree or a large shaded rock. You will need to tie the plant firmly to the slab with a nylon thread, however, the plant will soon support itself as the roots develop quite quickly.

### Cattleya bowringiana  Central South America
🦋 750 mm ☼ 🌱

This purple-flowered species is a parent of, and typifies, one of the two distinct groups of magnificent epiphytes which are among the most popular of all cultivated orchids. It and its progeny produce large, individual flowers and fall into what is popularly called the 'labiata' section. This section is also characterized by having clavate pseudobulbs carrying a single, almost oval, leaf. The second group, characterized by *C. skinneri* and its descendants, is smaller but more profusely flowered and has pseudobulb-like, cylindrical stems, usually with two leaves. These are shorter than those of the 'labiata' group.

The hybridizing of these two groups and their re-crossing again with closely allied genera such as *Laelia, Epidendrum* and *Sophronitis* have created an amazing range of hybrids, all of which are very similar in their cultural requirements. Each has its own time of flowering, so providing a continuous succession of blooms, some large, some smaller, but often in profusion and in a mind-boggling range of colours.

Cattleyas are relatively simple to cultivate, but, because their mixed parentage results in a wide range of growth and flowering periods, the beginner should consult his local orchid society or a professional grower about the behaviour and needs of the specimen or specimens he intends to grow.

Most cattleyas will adjust to a winter temperature range of 14-18°C and a summer range of 21-32°C, and matured specimens can tolerate a drop to 10°C in a dry autumn – but there is danger if it becomes any colder. At the other end of the scale, summer temperatures of up to 38-40°C may be tolerated if the plants have adequate moisture and free ventilation. At such temperatures syringing in the morning and early afternoon is beneficial, but no moisture should remain in the green sheaths enclosing the young growths. These sheaths eventually clasp the pseudobulbs and give them winter protection; they should never be removed unless they are providing cover for insects.

In summer cattleyas need 70% shading, which should drop to 40% in winter. They will take more light intensity than most orchids. In summer, light green, as opposed to a dark, very healthy green foliage, serves as a reasonable indication that they have been exposed to sufficient light.

During active growth, water and feeding go hand in hand. Feeding is followed in a few days by a heavy watering to wash out any chemical excesses. Every two or three weeks during active growth, cattleyas should be dosed with a complete orchid fertilizer and should also be given an occasional proprietary feed based on seaweed emulsion or other specialized compounds. This feeding is followed by a short period of drying-out, though not to the extent that the pseudobulbs begin to wilt. Shrivelling of the pseudobulbs may result from too much drying-out during periods of active growth, or too much watering, especially in winter. When active growth really slows down, give only sufficient water to keep the pseudobulbs plump.

An important aspect of winter care is that watering and occasional feeding must be such that no surplus moisture remains on any part of the vegetable growths in the late afternoon and evening. Moisture combined with falling temperatures is sure to encourage harmful bacteria or fungi.

Re-potting is usually necessary only at the end of the second year or even later, and can present the beginner with quite a formidable task. It must be done in spring, immediately new root growth is observed. Once it starts, root growth is very rapid and, being brittle, the roots damage easily. Avoid excessive damage by soaking the whole container in water before removing the plant. Though removal from a plastic pot usually does not present a problem, sometimes the roots adhere tightly to the sides of a dry pot and a little surgery with a sharp, sterilized knife may be needed. Any damaged roots, or others extending around the surface of the pot, should be cut back cleanly to manageable size.

When propagating cattleyas do not cut the rhizomes into divisions containing less than two or three flowering leads and three or four healthy pseudobulbs. Choose a size of pot which will accommodate such a division for at least two years. In re-potting the original rhizome, place the cut portion against the

*Bulbophyllum* sp.

A 30-year-old White Diosma (*Coleonema album*) in semi-cascade style.

The sub-style 'struck-by-lightning', an informal upright *Olea europaea* subsp. *'africana'*.

## Suggested Subjects

**Trees** (Deciduous)
*Acmena smithii*
*A. sieberana* 'woodii'
*A. xanthophloea*
*Acer buergeranum*
*Banksia serrata*
*Bauhinia galpinii*
*B. purpurea*
*B. variegata*
*Bolusanthus speciosus*
*Cassia javanica*
*Celtis sinensis*
*Cercis siliquastrum*
*Crataegus laevigata*
*Elaeocarpus reticulatus*
*Erythrina caffra*
*Ficus benjamina*
*F. rubiginosa*
*Fraxinus americana*
*Ginkgo biloba*
*Gleditsia triacanthos*
*Jacaranda mimosifolia*
*Koelreuteria paniculata*
*Liquidambar styraciflua*
*Malus* X *atrosanguinea*
*Prunus cerasifera*
*P. cerasifera* 'atropurpurea'
*P. mume*
*P. triloba*
*Pyrus communis*
*Salix caprea*
*S. subserrata*
*Sophora japonica*
*Tabebuia chrysotricha*
*Tipuana speciosa*
*Ulmus parvifolia*

**Trees** (Evergreen)
*Acacia melanoxylon*
*Agonis flexuosa*
*Cedrus atlantica*
*Chamaecyparis lawsoniana*
*Cupressus macrocarpa*
*Juniperus chinensis* 'Glauca'
*J. chinensis* 'Japonica-aurea'
*J. chinensis* 'Pfitzerana aurea'
*J. horizontalis* 'Plumosa'
*J. sabina* 'tamariscifolia'
*J. virginiana*
*Pinus cembra*
*P. halepensis*
*P. radiata*
*P. sylvestris*
*Podocarpus falcatus*
*Quercus ilex*
*Q. palustris*
*Q. suber*
*Schinus terebinthifolius*
*Schotia brachypetala*
*Syzygium paniculatum*
*Taxodium distichum*
*Thuja plicata*
*Widdringtonia juniperoides*

**Shrubs** (Deciduous)
*Abelia schumannii*
*Berberis* X *stenophylla*
*B. thunbergii*
*B. thunbergii* 'atropurpurea'
*Bougainvillea* spp.
  (all except vigorous sorts)
*Caesalpinia gilliesii*
*Calliandra brevipes*

*Chaenomeles japonica*
*C.* X *superba*
*Cotoneaster franchetii*
*C. frigidus*
*C. pannosus*
*Forsythia* X *intermedia* 'Spectabilis'
*Hibiscus schizopetalus*
*Holmskioldia sanguinea*
*H. tettensis*
*Kolkwitzia amabilis*
*Ochna atropurpurea*
*Punica granatum*
*Tamarix aphylla*
*T. hispida*
*Wisteria sinensis*
*Woodfordia floribunda*

**Shrubs** (Evergreen)
*Abelia floribunda*
*A.* X *grandiflora*
*Arundinaria auricoma*
*Breynia disticha*
*B. disticha* 'Roseo-picta'
*Callistemon viminalis*
*Camellia saluenensis*
*C. sasanqua*
*Cantua buxifolia*
*Carissa macrocarpa*
*Coprosma repens*
*Cornus capitata*
*Cotoneaster horizontalis*
*C. lacteus*
*C. microphyllus*
*Cussonia paniculata*
*C. spicata*
*Elaeagnus pungens* 'Aurea'

*Escallonia* X *langleyensis*
*Feijoa sellowiana*
*Gardenia thunbergia*
*Ilex cornuta*
*Nandina domestica*
*Pyracantha coccinea*
*P. rogersiana*

# PESTS 22 AND DISEASES

## DISPELLING THE GARDENER'S NIGHTMARE

Mandibles at the ready and proboscises poised, an apparently endless host of creeping, crawling and flying creatures seem to pose a constant threat to the gardener's efforts. Unseen, an even greater army of plant viruses and the spores of fungi are also ever ready to attack should the climate or other conditions suit them. Yet, pesticide and fungicide advertisements notwithstanding, good husbandry and careful cultivation can not only diminish the threat, but also allow the gardener to maintain the upper hand.

Nor is the gardener entirely without natural support in his war against the blights and mildews of fungal onslaughts. Healthy, well cared for plants may emerge from such attacks unscathed; new, resistant strains of certain species are being developed by growers; and a sudden change in the weather may prove as detrimental to fungal growth as climatic conditions were beneficial to its inception.

But only in the most Utopian of gardens will there be no insect pests, snails, cutworms, blights or mildews; and there will be times when even the most conscientious horticulturalist must resort to the use of pesticides and fungicides to protect his plants. There is an increasing body of gardeners who shun today's chemical fertilizers and chemical control of plant pests and diseases, instead remaining faithful to time-honoured home remedies. But most of us resort to chemical control at some time, and in their use there are certain elementary safeguards which any gardener should apply.

## Security and Precautions
Always regard any pesticide or fungicide as potentially poisonous to man and household pets, whether through contact with the skin or as a result of being inhaled. If caution is exercised there should be no danger, but throughout any spraying operation – from mixing to application, and to the cleaning of the apparatus you have used – there is no room for carelessness.

Always store garden poisons – whether liquid, dusts or wettable powders – in a cool, locked cupboard or shed and ensure that the containers are securely closed. Most pesticide bottles have an inner plastic stopper beneath the screw-top and this must always be replaced to prevent fumes escaping. The lids of tins containing dust or wettable powders should be pressed firmly into place. And when such tins or bottles are empty, destroy them, so that there is no possibility of their being used to contain anything else.

Never spray or dust on a windy day, and, even if there is only a light breeze, operate from the windward side. It is wise to wear a protective dust-coat when applying pesticides or fungicides, and the coat should be washed regularly. Equally, after you have finished spraying or dusting, it is sensible to bathe and change your clothes.

Wear rubber gloves when measuring or mixing poisons, working in such a way that any fumes are not inhaled. Do not eat, drink or smoke during such operations, and should you require a break, wash your face and hands thoroughly.

Instructions about their use and the precautions which should be taken usually accompany all containers of toxic substances which the gardener may need, and these should be not only read, but followed. Most also indicate the compatibility of the particular agent – whether or not it may be mixed with other specific substances – and the 'safe' period, or the time which should elapse between application of the spray or dust and harvesting of edible fruits and vegetables.

To protect bees from the toxic effects of the insecticides, try to avoid spraying or dusting plants during their flowering period. Much the same protection will be achieved by application just before the petals open and after they fall – preferably the latter. And as a general rule, spray in the early morning or late evening when bees are least active.

## Insect pests
These fall into two main categories: the mandibulate or those which shred food with their jaws, and the sap feeders which puncture the plant's tissues with their proboscises, sucking out the sap. Caterpillars, beetles and cutworms are typical mandibulates while aphids,

◀ Though a delight to the eye, a caterpillar like this can wreak enormous damage.

thrips and scale insects are among the more common sap feeders.

The first group may be controlled by a stomach poison insecticide or a dual-purpose stomach-poison-cum-contact insecticide. The second group is mainly controlled by a contact poison or a systemic insecticide. When sprayed onto a plant the systemic insecticide is absorbed, making the sap toxic to certain insects. Particular care must be taken when using systemic insecticides as these poisons are also easily absorbed through the skin.

### Fungus diseases

Then there are the fungus diseases, such as black spot and powdery mildew. Though most fungicides are not as potentially dangerous as pesticides, they should be treated with the same respect.

Fungi fall into two broad groups – the saprophytic, such as mushrooms, which live on decaying vegetable matter, and the parasitic, which live on the growing cells of other plants. Both have two distinct stages of development – the vegetative and the reproductive.

The cap and stalk of the mushroom, for instance, are cleary visible above the ground, produce the spores, and are termed the fructification. Below ground are the vegetative parts consisting of millions of hair-like threads or hyphae, radiating from the base of the fructification and termed collectively, the mycelium.

The mushroom is an obvious example, but it should be understood that, say, powdery mildew on roses is not dissimilar, except that its fructification is minute, and its mycelium penetrates the living cells of the leaf to draw its nourishment.

At one time, because these fungi are so minute, they were not recognized as such and were called 'blights', as they were attributed to some supernatural agency beyond the control of man. Today, there are few fungus diseases which cannot be identified and treated with a fairly high degree of success.

For convenience of reference, I have listed the most commonly encountered plant pests and diseases separately. There are also many bacterial diseases – often of the gall type, such as crown gall – which may attack plants under certain conditions. However, their treatment is beyond the scope of the average gardener, and expert professional advice should be sought.

Woolly caterpillars, a garden pest which if left unchecked can rapidly destroy foliage.

# PESTS

**ANTS.** A wide range of ants, as they search for the honeydew excreted by soft-scale insects, encourage the spread of scale and aphids. But this should not be the signal for the wholesale destruction of ants. The only ants which should be destroyed, or even just thwarted in their activities, are those which are causing, directly or indirectly, damage to your plants. If hundreds of ants are running up and down a plant, you will know that they are up to something underhand and that they must be restrained. Control with Carbaryl or Malathion will be effective, Chlordane can be used however as it has a greater residual effect, use with caution where children and animals use the garden.

**APHID.** Possibly the most common garden insect pest, the aphid does enormous and two-fold damage – sucking the sap from the living cells and, indirectly, spreading diseases. These small, pear-shaped pests are black, brown or green, and live in colonies – sometimes so large that they cover an entire branch. Sucking the sap causes distortion in the leaf or stem as the cells collapse, and severe infestation often causes the leading stems to die back completely – in roses and citrus for instance. Control is not difficult and Malathion, Rogor or Lebaycid is usually sufficient to remove the aphids.

**BEETLES.** There are a huge number of beetles which do considerable damage to flower buds and to foliage. Their larvae often attack roots, seedlings or grass. Control by spraying with Carbaryl, Malathion, Thiodan or dusting with Derris.

**BUGS.** The stink-bugs, particularly, are sap feeders and often cause the leading tips of young stems to collapse. The Bagrada bug does extensive damage to cabbage and other cruciferous crops. The green stink-bug sucks the juice of fruits, causing depressions or scabby dry spots. All bugs are fairly easily controlled with Carbaryl, Malathion or Thiodan.

**CATERPILLARS.** Of the hundreds of different caterpillars – the larvae of moths or butterflies – some are large, some small, some appear naked, others hairy. But even small caterpillars can make short shrift of a cabbage, whilst larger ones eat with terrifying voracity, often ruining a plant before the damage is noticed.

While preventative spraying is essential in the case of vines, for instance, one does not wish to spray unnecessarily, particularly in the vegetable garden. It is better practice, from every point of view, to spray as soon as the presence of caterpillars is noticed, using a contact/stomach poison, which has immediate effect. Carbaryl, Malathion, Thiodan or Derris are ideal for ordinary use.

Aphids attack a stalk.

Aphids suck the sap of buds.

Bugs cluster on citrus leaves.

Beetles cause damage, but are often pollinators.

**CODLING MOTH.** While the moths themselves are no threat to the home gardener's fruit crops, their larvae can do enormous damage if not controlled. These are small, pale orange worms with dark brown heads which burrow through fruits, pushing out dark brown, crumbly excreta at the entrances to the tunnels they have made. Here preventative measures, before the larvae develop, are essential. Spray at petal-fall with Carbaryl or Lebaycid and continue at 14-day intervals. Discontinue spraying after fruit has been covered at least six times. Infested fruit should be removed and destroyed.

**CUT-WORM.** This is an 'under cover' caterpillar with powerful jaws, which eats young, and sometimes not so young, plants off immediately below ground level. Control by spraying the soil around the base of newly-planted seedlings with Carbaryl or Thiodan.

**EELWORM.** There are many genera and species of *Nematodes*, including several parasites which attack a variety of plants and may, if not controlled, cause damage of catastrophic proportions amongst such

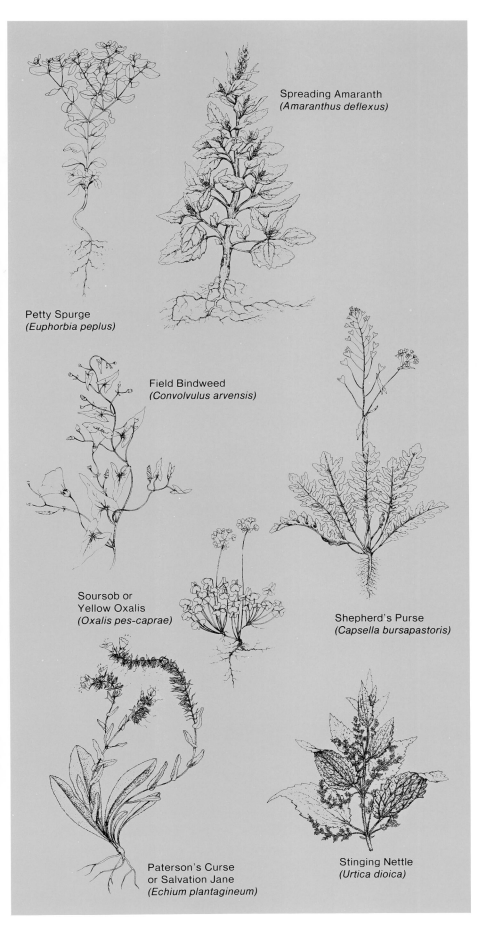

Petty Spurge
(Euphorbia peplus)

Spreading Amaranth
(Amaranthus deflexus)

Field Bindweed
(Convolvulus arvensis)

Soursob or
Yellow Oxalis
(Oxalis pes-caprae)

Shepherd's Purse
(Capsella bursapastoris)

Paterson's Curse
or Salvation Jane
(Echium plantagineum)

Stinging Nettle
(Urtica dioica)

**Sorrel, or Sheep Sorrel** (*Rumex acetosella*). Another unwanted North American visitor, this perennial, which reaches as much as 300 mm if allowed to grow, is pervasive. It not only has a quickly-spreading root-system, but is also self-seeding and will happily establish itself in cracks in paths, or patios as well as in lawns and pastures. Control by applying Roundup to actively growing plants when most have reached the early bud stage. This will provide seasonal suppression of Sorrel and partial reduction of plant numbers. Lawn Weeder will control it and so will Zero.

**Soursob, or Yellow Oxalis** (*Oxalis pes-caprae*). A perennial weed introduced from South Africa. Because its root swells into a whitish fleshy tuber producing numerous bulbils, and its flowers are followed by efficiently scattered seed, soursob has become a persistent weed in many areas. The attractive yellow five-petalled flowers are in bunches of 3-16 on a long stem held above a rosette of somewhat clover-like foliage. It can be controlled with Roundup applied from late July to early September, but before natural plant yellowing occurs. Soursob should be actively growing and not under stress of drought or water-logging when sprayed. Some oxalis species can be controlled with broadleaf selective herbicides.

**Spear Thistle** (*Cirsium vulgare*). This coarse, self-seeding biennial is another weed which puts down deep, powerful roots and, once established (full grown it reaches a height of some 1.5-2 m), can only be killed by chemical means. Young plants in cultivated beds are easily kept under control by hoeing, though this will not completely eradicate them. Ensure that their seeds do not spread, by attacking the plants before they flower. Control chemically with Zero or Roundup.

**Spreading Amaranth** (*Amaranthus deflexus*). This much-branched semi-prostrate annual weed has a stout fleshy tap root, broadly lanceolate, alternate leaves up to 35 mm long and shiny black seeds. Amaranth spp. can be controlled with Roundup.

**Spiny Emex** (*Emex australis*). The triangular 10 mm-long seeds of this common weed are tipped with strong spines which can cause considerable pain to bare feet and also injure the paws of animals. A semi-erect annual up to about 600 mm high, this deep-rooting weed with long ovate blades is best eliminated by hand. If it becomes severely established in a lawn – usually it is at its worst in neglected lawns or unkempt corners of the garden. Bindie or Zero will control this South African weed, chemically.

**Stinging Nettle** (*Urtica incisa*). It is mainly the coarse hairs of the stem of the weed which sting, though some of the hairs of the coarsely margined leaves may also have this effect. Thus it is not a weed to be uprooted by hand – unless the hand is gloved. Rather eradicate it by hoeing; the creeping rootstocks will die off eventually. Control with Lawn Weeder.

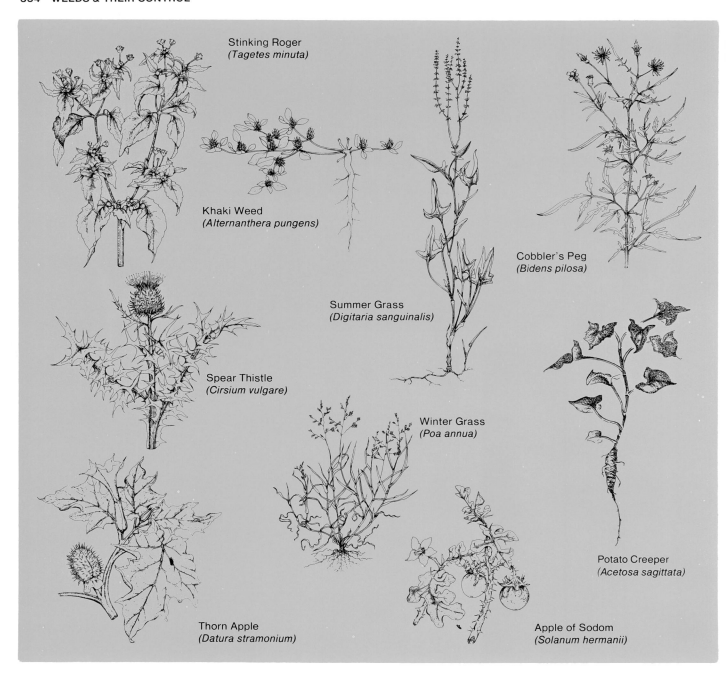

Stinking Roger
(*Tagetes minuta*)

Khaki Weed
(*Alternanthera pungens*)

Cobbler's Peg
(*Bidens pilosa*)

Summer Grass
(*Digitaria sanguinalis*)

Spear Thistle
(*Cirsium vulgare*)

Winter Grass
(*Poa annua*)

Potato Creeper
(*Acetosa sagittata*)

Thorn Apple
(*Datura stramonium*)

Apple of Sodom
(*Solanum hermanii*)

**Stinking Roger** (*Tagetes minuta*). This annual was introduced from America, and resembles a tall marigold, to which it is closely related. It grows to 2-3 m tall and produces extremely small but plentiful yellow flowers in summer. Stinking Roger should be pulled out before it goes to seed.

**Summer Grass** (*Digitaria sanguinalis*). Tall-growing (up to a metre) and rampant, this grass was once encouraged as fodder and it still provides good grazing in agricultural pasturage, though it is a noxious weed in the garden, appearing in lawns and paths. In both situations, uproot it by hand – the roots are shallow – or control with Kleen Lawn or Lawn Weeder.

**Wild Bindweed** (*Calystegia sepium*). Larger and more vigorous than the small bindweed, this weed is deciduous in the colder parts of the country, its stems dying back in early winter each year. It is a gross feeder and mainly reproduces itself by suckering and creeping both above and underground. Chemical treatment is the only certain method of eradication – and even then, the few seeds it produces may germinate several years after the wild bindweed appears to have been eradicated. Lawn Weeder and Bindie are registered for its chemical control.

**Winter Grass** (*Poa annua*). One of the most common annual weeds in gardens, this grass pervades beds and lawns with blithe impar-

tiality. It reaches its seeding stage particularly quickly, so that although it is easy to uproot by hand, there is a good chance that its very removal will broadcast seeds for the following spring. Similarly, on a lawn it is almost impossible to eradicate – hand weeding helps control it, but mowing spreads the seeds if every mature plant is not removed in time.

Winter Grass Killer from Hortico, is a selective pre- and post-emergence herbicide. This means it is effective against both emerging seedlings and established winter grass, but will not harm most established lawns. Endothal by Chemspray is a selective herbicide for post-emergence control of winter grass in turf. Winter grass can quickly take over a lawn during winter, only to leave ugly bare patches when it dies off in spring.

# PROPAGATION 24

## GETTING THE BEST FROM YOUR SEEDS AND CUTTINGS

Propagation, the art of whose success is at the core of all horticulture, is at once both the easiest and the most challenging, even difficult, of all the crafts that the gardener must master. It demands a basic understanding of the natural forces underlying plant growth which the gardener may utilize, encourage, but never oppose, whether he intends to increase the plant population by the relatively simple methods of sowing seed and division, or through more complicated processes such as layering and grafting.

Some plants, usually annuals, are propagated only by seed; others only by division or only from cuttings; but there are many genera and species which may be increased in several ways. And it is in these latter – and most frequent – instances, that the experienced gardener must bring his knowledge to bear and decide which method to follow.

Once the choice is made, propagation should be carried out in such a way that the natural processes of plant growth take place in the best possible environment. It is, after all, during its early development that the young plant is most susceptible to adverse condi-

tions, and for this reason factors which could interfere with or encourage the increase of plants must, as far as possible, be controlled by the gardener. These include the condition of the soil and its temperature, the amount of light and moisture available, and air circulation and temperature.

Simply, if a gardener were to take a handful of seeds and scatter them on the ground, even on prepared soil, he would be exposing them to several elemental factors over which he had no control – a sudden cold snap, a hot dry period, days of unexpected wind, heavy rain, drizzle and little or no sun. If, on the other hand, he takes the same quantity of seed, sows it in a correctly-prepared growing medium, in a situation where he has almost full control of light, moisture and temperature, and can provide protection from climatic extremes, his chances of successful propagation are enormously enhanced.

Explained below are the main methods of propagation which the home gardener may use and the basic equipment he will need to attain the best results.

**BUDDING.** This slightly sophisticated method of propagation is mainly important as a method of increasing roses, apples, cherries and most stone fruits. There are several approaches to budding but for most purposes, and certainly in the case of the beginner, the technique involving a T-shaped incision on the parent stock is probably the most satisfactory (see illustration, page 356). Where possible, this form of propagation should be carried out on overcast days, and it must be done with little delay. In principle, budding is similar to grafting and my later remarks concerning graft stocks apply equally to budding. Waxing is neither necessary nor advisable, but the bud should be carefully tied with the plastic bud tape which has largely superseded raffia. Subsequently, this must be examined frequently so that

over- or under-tying may be rectified.

**CUTTINGS.** In its three forms, this method is second in importance only to seed as a general means of plant increase and is probably the most widely used in the propagation of trees and shrubs. Some cultivars, particularly, will only grow true to type from cuttings. The three forms of cuttings are:

**Leaf cuttings,** which may be whole leaves or, in some species, portions of leaves. Certain succulents may be grown quite easily from a leaf broken off at the axil and then placed gently into washed river sand. Generally, however, the number of species which may be increased in this way is fairly limited. For certain *Begonia* and *Streptocarpus* species, leaf cuttings are the only really satisfactory

method of propagation.

The best container is a standard seed tray filled level with pure, washed river sand. Large leaves such as those of *Begonia rex* are laid flat on the sand and their veins severed at broad intervals with a very sharp knife. Use hairpins or bent paperclips to hold the leaf veins close against the sand's surface. Cover the leaf with a plate of glass (or cover the whole container with a large glass dome) and protect the cuttings from direct sunlight. Do not disturb or remove the glass until it is clear that little, complete plants have rooted and have become established.

**Root cuttings** are portions of growing roots, pencil thick and 40-60 mm long, and are usually taken during the dormant season. A sure indication of plants which may be propa-

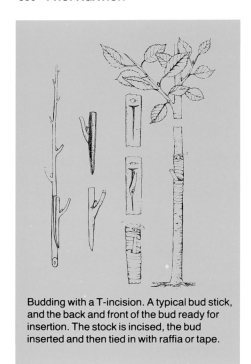

Budding with a T-incision. A typical bud stick, and the back and front of the bud ready for insertion. The stock is incised, the bud inserted and then tied in with raffia or tape.

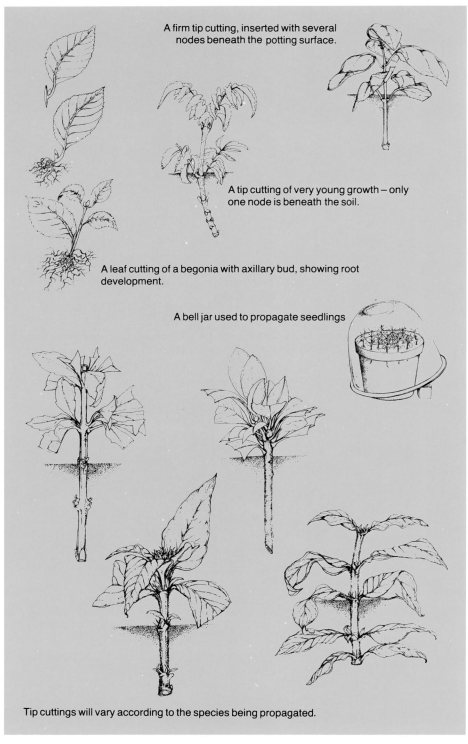

A firm tip cutting, inserted with several nodes beneath the potting surface.

A tip cutting of very young growth – only one node is beneath the soil.

A leaf cutting of a begonia with axillary bud, showing root development.

A bell jar used to propagate seedlings

Tip cuttings will vary according to the species being propagated.

gated this way is their facility to produce suckers when their roots are cut or disturbed – *Clematis*, bouvardias and oriental poppies are good examples.

Lay the cuttings horizontally in individual pots containing an equal mixture of pure, washed river sand and peat moss, and cover the root pieces to a depth of about 20 mm. Place the pots in a shaded section of the garden frame, or some other protected spot, and cover them lightly with straw or dry grass until the growing tips emerge. Root cuttings are placed in individual pots so that they can be left undisturbed until months after these tips have appeared and, in turn, become growing stems. The stem appears long before the cutting develops roots of its own and any disturbance before these are established almost certainly will result in failure. Wait until a few roots appear at the pot's drainage hole before moving the plant.

**Stem cuttings** are the most common method of propagation from cuttings, and comprise three distinct types – soft, semi-hard and hardwood. Softwood is the growing tip, 60-100 mm long, taken immediately beneath a node. These are usually taken in spring or early summer and should be placed, to a depth of half their length, in a container of washed river sand. They are usually encouraged to root early – it may take from five to 15 days – by the use of a mist spray unit or by being placed under the cover of a bell jar (see illustration opposite). If several cuttings are to be propagated, use a standard plastic seed tray; if only a single cutting is involved, a 60-100 mm-diameter flower pot will suffice. Test for rooting by pulling very gently on the stem of the cutting: when it is quite firmly lodged, rooting will have taken place. If a mist spray is not available, give the cuttings frequent light syringings of water.

Semi-hard cuttings are taken from early to late summer, from semi-matured wood which is part of the current season's growth. Nodal cuttings, 110-150 mm long, are placed either in a bed made up in the garden frame or into containers such as a standard seed tray or individual 130 mm-diameter flower pots, in pure, washed river sand. Depending on the species of plant, these will take from three to seven weeks to establish roots.

Hardwood cuttings are usually taken just before new growth begins and are of matured wood – anything from pencil thickness to about 25 mm in diameter – of the previous year's growth. They should be about 180 mm long. Place them in outdoor beds in an equal mixture of washed river sand and the soil in which the parent plant has grown. Rooting takes a few weeks and the new plants should be left to grow in situ until they are transplanted early in the following spring. Some species, such as the London plane (*Platanus* X *acerifolia*), may be cut during July, tied in bundles and buried 300 mm deep in light soil for as long as a month before being planted out. All hardwood cuttings should be so placed in the cutting bed that only 50 mm can be seen above ground. After planting, strew the bed with a light, loose layer of dry hay to protect the exposed stems from strong sunlight.

**DIVISION** is the simplest way to increase plants with fibrous or tuberous roots, and perennial asters and phlox as well as most chrysanthemums are propagated in this way. Some bulbous and cormous species, such as irises and paeonies, are easily increased by division but, whereas fibrous- and tuberous-rooted species are usually divided in spring, the bulbs and corms are divided after flowering – mostly in autumn. While fibrous-rooted plants are easily pulled apart, tuberous and rhizomatous rootstocks should be cut cleanly with a sharp knife. If the divided portion is large enough to have established roots of its own it may be planted in situ, but if only a small portion of crown and rootstock is taken, plant it in a pot or seed tray containing an equal mixture of washed river sand and peat moss and allow it to grow on until the new roots are established and fresh shoots appear.

**EQUIPMENT and STRUCTURES.** A garden frame (see 'Bush House and Greenhouse Management', page 323) is an invaluable aid to propagation, not only for the germination of seeds but for the rooting of cuttings as well. However, for the gardener who does not own or build a frame, an extremely useful but cheap protection for seedlings and cuttings can be provided by a tent-shaped cover. In small gardens this light structure will substitute ideally for a shade house, giving not only adequate shade but protection against heavy rains. Although the material is shade cloth, its steep pitch allows even the heaviest rains to run off and there is virtually no dripping onto the plant. In larger gardens, or where the home gardener wants to produce significant quantities of plant material, a permanent or semi-permanent shade house is needed. This may range from a simple construction using treated gum uprights with strands of No. 8 galvanized wire supporting the shade cloth, to a more elaborate design with a roof of treated poles and the shade cloth resting on lightly stretched chicken wire. (See illustration, page 377.)

Smaller items of equipment should include two sieves, one with a 10 mm mesh and the

other slightly larger. All newly-planted seed and seedlings should be watered with a very fine, light spray. When sowing very, very fine seed such as petunia and begonia (which is not covered), give initial water by holding the seed tray in a water container, removing it as soon as the upper surface darkens. (See also Chapter 3, 'Equipment and Tools', page 37.)

**FRENCH MOUND LAYERING,** which varies considerably from the usual form of 'tip' layering described below, enables the propagator to secure a large number of individual plants from a single branch. In early spring, just before growth begins, shoots of the previous season's growth are bent down from the stool and pegged parallel with, and about 150 mm above, the surface of the soil. When growth begins, all lateral shoots arising from the horizontal branch naturally grow upwards and at this stage it is pegged firmly to the soil. The main layering operation takes place as soon as the lateral shoots reach a height of about 150 mm. Soil is heaped up until the layer is covered to a depth of 80 mm, and this heaping up continues to a depth of about 180 mm as the lateral shoots lengthen. In early autumn the original layer lead should be

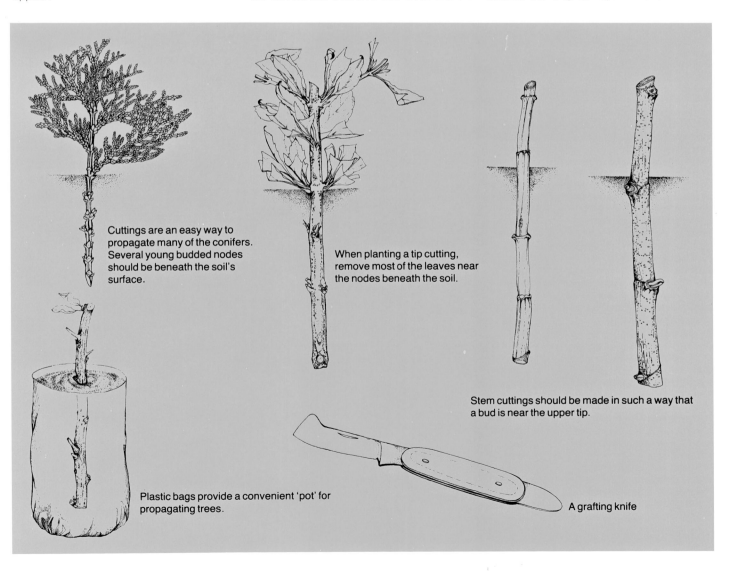

Cuttings are an easy way to propagate many of the conifers. Several young budded nodes should be beneath the soil's surface.

When planting a tip cutting, remove most of the leaves near the nodes beneath the soil.

Stem cuttings should be made in such a way that a bud is near the upper tip.

Plastic bags provide a convenient 'pot' for propagating trees.

A grafting knife

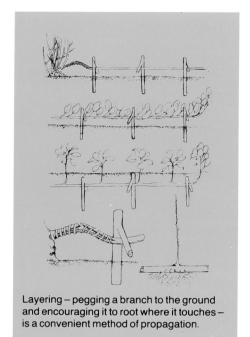

Layering – pegging a branch to the ground and encouraging it to root where it touches – is a convenient method of propagation.

partly severed and bound, so encouraging the production of roots along its entire length. The rooted branch is then cut into sections, each of which supports a new plant – the former lateral shoots. *Prunus glandulosa* and *Cotinus coggygria* 'atropurpurea' are particularly successfully propagated in this way.

**GRAFTING.** Modern techniques in propagation from cuttings have led to a decline in the practice of grafting, though there are still many species which are best increased in this way. This is chiefly practised on trees and shrubs where superior flowering or fruiting qualities of hybrid plants are to be combined with the more vigorous root system or disease resistance of the rootstock or to produce dwarf specimens. Usually the stock and scion (the previous year's wood of another plant) are of closely related species.

Fundamentally grafting is the fusion of the cambium layers of the two cut surfaces of stock and scion. The cambium is a thin green layer of tissue between the bark and wood and it is essential that these layers are placed in direct contact with each other to fuse and become one when growth commences.

Grafting is usually performed at any time when the stocks are in a dormant state, although a veneer graft can be carried out whenever scions are available. Outdoor grafting is usually done in early spring, and it is vital to have the stock slightly more advanced, or active, than the scion. To accomplish this it is usually necessary to cut scion wood – in longer lengths than the actual grafting size – and lay it under the soil in a cool place for a week or so. The graft must be firmly bound with raffia and then completely waxed over, as shown in the illustration of a *Fraxinus* graft on this page.

There are many methods of grafting, some very elaborate. The simpler and most successful methods are illustrated on this and the following pages. It is essential that the

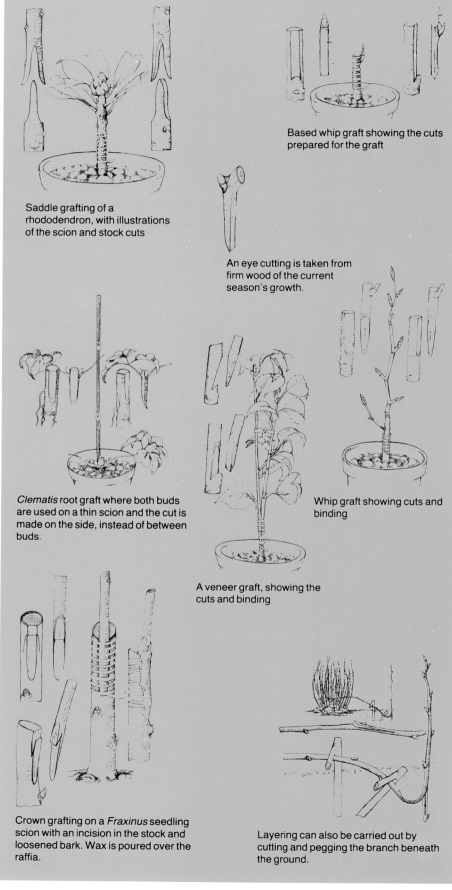

Saddle grafting of a rhododendron, with illustrations of the scion and stock cuts

Based whip graft showing the cuts prepared for the graft

An eye cutting is taken from firm wood of the current season's growth.

*Clematis* root graft where both buds are used on a thin scion and the cut is made on the side, instead of between buds.

Whip graft showing cuts and binding

A veneer graft, showing the cuts and binding

Crown grafting on a *Fraxinus* seedling scion with an incision in the stock and loosened bark. Wax is poured over the raffia.

Layering can also be carried out by cutting and pegging the branch beneath the ground.

stock be well rooted before being worked, and also free of pests and diseases. Protection from disease and drying out is essential during the healing over process.

**LAYERING.** Propagation by layers is a simple method of producing new plants that are true to the parent from established trees and shrubs. It is a suitable method for camellias, clematis, daphne, azaleas and rhododendrons. The illustration on page 358 indicates the type of wood to be used and the correct way of preparing the layer.

Most plants suited to layering will send up a young, strong growth from near the base of the parent plant. Rooting is encouraged when a bed of peat and sand is placed in the hole. To hasten root formation a slanting cut is made on the underpart of the stem and this portion is pegged firmly into the soil. Layering is usually carried out in autumn. The layers should not be cut from the parent plant until a good root system has formed – usually a couple of months. Some shrubs, such as rhododendrons may take a year or more before roots are sufficiently developed.

**PRICKING OUT:** see TRANSPLANTING

**SEED.** More plants are propagated by seed than by any other means; in fact the only reasons for not growing a plant from seed are that viable, or fertile, seed is not produced, or the plant will not grow true to type from seed. One of the reasons for the high cost of some seed is that plant breeders are involved in great expense in breeding them to grow true to type – the seed you buy will grow true, but seed saved from the flowers produced almost certainly will not. So, for success with annuals and vegetables from seed, it is wise to buy only from a reputable seed-house.

True species of long-lived trees are increased from seed and most are usually available from nurserymen or the Forestry Commission. On the other hand, seed of many of our indigenous species, whether herbaceous, sub-shrub, shrub or tree, is not so readily available and may have to be collected.

Pick pod fruits, such as legumes, broom and wattles, when they are dry. Store them in non-plastic bags until they are thoroughly dry – or until they explode. Capsular fruits, such as those of the eucalypts, bottle brushes and so on, should be picked when their colour changes from green to a greyish-brown. Store in dry paper and shake out the seed when the capsules shrink. Winged seeds, such as those of maple, ash and elm, should be collected when paper-dry, immediately before they fall, and sown at once. Palm seed should not be allowed to dry, but should be sown immediately there are indications that it will soon fall. The cones of most conifers ripen in autumn and should be collected as soon as the cone scales become dry and show signs of opening. Place on paper in a light, airy room, shake out when dry and store in brown paper bags, left open at the top and suspended from the ceiling. Sow in early spring.

Many native plants produce seeds with a hard outer shell which requires treatment by soaking in hot water. These include *Acacia*,

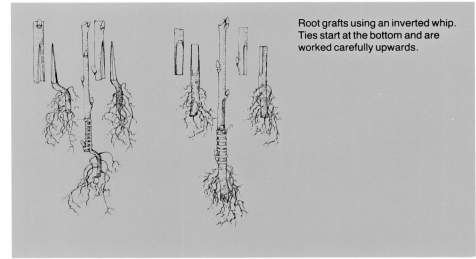

Root grafts using an inverted whip. Ties start at the bottom and are worked carefully upwards.

*Cassia, Hardenbergia, Hovea* and *Kennedia*. Immerse the seeds in almost boiling water and allow to soak for a few hours or overnight before sowing. Most banksias only release their seeds, from their thick woody cones, after a bushfire. Cones can be placed on a metal tray and gently heated in a slow oven for about an hour. The seed should then easily be tapped from the cone.

**Soil medium for seeds.** Ideally, seed should not be sown in soil at all. Fine seed such as that of petunias, begonias and primulas should be pre-mixed with fine washed sand. Sow fine and the expensive seeds of special F1 Hybrid/annuals in an equal mixture of peat moss and washed river sand. Place this in a plastic seed tray and firm down with a surfacing board. Pour about 10 mm of fine sand into an ordinary test tube, empty the packet of seed on top and, holding the thumb over the top, agitate the tube to mix thoroughly. Spread this mixture evenly over the surface of the firmed down growing medium. Water by immersing the lower part of the seed tray in a container of water. Cover with ordinary newspaper and keep a close watch from the fourth day onwards, removing the paper as soon as germination is apparent. The tray, suitably

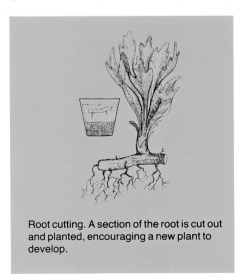

Root cutting. A section of the root is cut out and planted, encouraging a new plant to develop.

protected, should then be placed in a garden frame. After germination and during initial growth, a 40% shade cloth covering at frame height gives ideal protection. It is wise to sow all seed in trays rather than open beds, as trays allow better control and protection in terms of temperature and changes in the weather.

For ordinary or coarse seed, a good sowing medium is equal parts by volume of washed river sand, top soil put through a 10 mm-mesh sieve, and peat moss. A good general rule is to cover the seed to a depth equalling its diameter; thus a sweet pea seed will have about three times the cover of, say, a marigold. Water thoroughly with a fine spray, cover with a light layer of dried hay, keep a close watch and remove the covering as soon as germination begins. Dried hay is an excellent covering as it allows a free circulation of air and yet keeps the upper soil layer moist. If more watering is necessary before germination, water through the hay covering to avoid disturbing the surface soil.

**TRANSPLANTING.** To avoid the legginess which comes from overcrowding young plants, it is wise to 'prick out' all annual and vegetable seedlings when they are about 20 mm high. Seedlings of plants such as cabbages, tomatoes, peppers and aubergines do much better when transplanted into separate, 40 mm-diameter pots or even divided trays.

Easily transplanted seedlings, such as those of marigolds, calendulas, salvias, lobelias, zinnias and so on, may be set out 20-30 to each standard seed tray and finally planted out in the garden when they are about 50-80 mm high. Seedlings which do not transplant so readily, such as lupins, sweet peas and nasturtiums, when not planted in situ, should be sown individually, either in pots or divided trays.

Species of trees and shrubs raised from seed should be transplanted 15 to a standard seed tray when they are 40-60 mm high, and then put into medium-sized plastic bags when they reach a height of 150 mm. They may be transplanted after two or three months.

# PRUNING 25
## CORRECTLY CARING FOR YOUR TREES AND SHRUBS

The ardent pruning 'expert' whose actions ape those of a berserk lumberjack, though a figure of fun is none the less real. At the first hint of autumn, he or she emerges from the toolshed armed to the teeth with axe, saw and secateurs, and lays about the roses, shrubs and trees with reckless abandon. Irrespective of purpose or plan, nothing is spared until, exhausted but firm in the knowledge that 'pruning is done', he or she packs the butchering equipment away for another year.

At the other end of the scale, but no less real, is the timid sentimentalist who emerges each season with secateurs and a guilty conscience, makes a few tentative passes at the roses and shrubs before slinking away, fearful of the damage which he or she has done.

The reality of pruning lies somewhere between these two extremes – in the practice of an art which, done well, brings order and improvement to the garden and leaves its practitioner with a sense of satisfaction and pleasure. Pruning is the methodical and intentional removal of any part of a plant whether it be stems, branches, shoots or even roots, and its objective is the regulation of the plant to its most effective production of flower, fruit and foliage. Proper pruning encourages the fruit tree to bear fruit, the flowering plant to be as floriferous as possible and the ornamental shrub to be truly so – not scraggly and mis-shapen.

In all her functions, Nature tends to discard everything that is unnecessary, and in the garden man aids this process by removing all dead wood and any diseased or broken growth. Careful thinning of crowded growth allows more light and air to reach the plant, and here it is the weak, semi-dead and the most closely-crowded branches or twigs that the pruner removes first. Some healthy growth may also need to be removed – but only to achieve the gardener's objective.

Different plants have widely varying needs as far as pruning is concerned. Deciduous and evergreen shrubs and trees often require a widely different approach; though hedges may require regular clipping – in itself a form of pruning – to keep them to shape, they may require more drastic surgery at times; pruning roses and vines is an art in itself; and fruit trees differ enormously in their pruning needs.

But remember that in any pruning operation, the equipment used should be sharp and provide a clean cut. Jagged, bruised cuts encourage disease, attract insect pests and may sometimes prove far worse than no pruning at all. Where signs of disease are found, it is essential not only to prune away the infected growth, but to destroy it immediately to prevent spread of disease.

Following are the main requirements to be borne in mind when pruning particular plants:

**APPLE and PEAR TREES.** For any tree to fruit well there must be a reasonable balance between the size of its top and the extent of its root growth. If there is excessive root growth it is probable that too much food will be produced, leading to abnormal vegetative growth – generating leaf buds rather than fruit buds. This condition is apparent in healthy top growth though the tree shows no inclination to fruit. It can usually be corrected by root pruning, or shortening back the more vigorous main roots, which should be exposed and then cleanly cut. Root pruning should be carried out in autumn, about two months before the normal winter pruning season. This treatment usually is needed only for apples

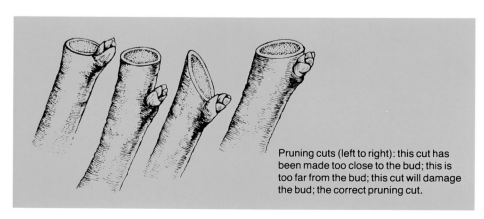

Pruning cuts (left to right): this cut has been made too close to the bud; this is too far from the bud; this cut will damage the bud; the correct pruning cut.

and pears. The need for such pruning decreases gradually and the balance between root and top growth usually levels out.

In winter pruning of the trees themselves, unwanted growths are cut back to two buds; in some cultivars these form fruit spurs close to the main stems. Once balanced growth is achieved, pruning is aimed at increasing fruit production and can only be determined by experience of the particular type of tree. Observation will soon establish the type and length of wood which will produce fruit. However, no matter the tree's age, the traditional open frame (see illustration, page 362) must dictate the general annual pruning pattern. And though the main pruning of apple and pear trees is in mid-winter, apple trees should also be pruned in summer after flowering, particularly to shape the tree and remove unwanted growths. (See also 'General Hints on Fruit Trees'.)

**BLACK CURRANTS.** These bear their fruit almost entirely on young wood so that there is no need to build up a framework. Cut new bushes to within two or three buds from the ground. In later years leave a few younger shoots unpruned, but in winter cut most of the shoots almost to ground level.

**CLEMATIS.** Pruning is most important to the development of strong, healthy clematis, and can be summarized as follows. The 'Florida', 'Patens' and 'Montana' groups, which flower only on the previous year's wood, should be thinned occasionally after flowering, cutting back strong growths here and there to induce low breaking, or strong basal growths.

The 'Lanuginosa', 'Jackmanii' and 'Viticella' groups should be pruned back annually to within 150 mm from the base of the previous year's growth and immediately above a bud joint.

**HEDGES.** If a hedge is to be well-furnished and thick at the base, the gardener should not be in too great a hurry for it to reach the desired height. If a hedge is allowed to become leggy at the base, it is almost impossible to make it thicken up. Plants 450 mm high should be shortened back to about 300-400 mm when active growth has started, and may then be left alone for the rest of the year, only shortening back if they do not fill out properly at the base. Each spring, prune back to about half the preceding season's increase of height. This will ensure a thick, well-furnished hedge from the base upwards and one which is unlikely to become leggy in later years.

If the hedge is to be a boundary windbreak of conifers, such as *Pinus halepensis*, do not remove the growing tips until the saplings have reached the total height. Never let them go beyond it, with the intention of shortening back at a later stage; though this may not prove fatal, the eventual condition of the hedge will not be as good as it could be.

**HYDRANGEAS.** There is considerable confusion among gardeners – as well as strong opinions – about pruning hydrangeas. Some

say: prune them to within three buds from the ground (about 250-300 mm) while others argue that they should be left alone! In fact the answer lies halfway between these schools of thought. Stems which have flowered should be pruned to within three buds from the ground. Those which have not flowered should be left alone, and any which are weak and straggly should be cut out altogether. Those of you who enjoy success and hold strong opinions on the subject – stick to them; those who don't know can follow these suggestions and know they won't go very far wrong.

**NATIVE PLANTS.** Most native shrubs benefit from pruning which will encourage bushier growth and more flowers the following season. When the plant is small pinch out the soft tips of the branches to stimulate side shoots. It is best to lightly prune bushes immediately after flowering, before too much growth has formed. After pruning water well.

**NECTARINES:** see Peach and Nectarine Trees

**PEACH and NECTARINE TREES.** Both of these fruit on young wood, so that any growth more than two years old is merely unproductive framework. When winter pruning, cut back the branches which have fruited to young shoots near their bases, so that there is always a succession of these developing each summer for fruiting the following year. Unless this succession is maintained, a tree can quickly become unproductive.

**PLUM and APRICOT TREES.** Until these trees begin to bear normally, annual pruning consists of shortening back the leaders by about a third to strengthen the frame, and removing badly-placed, crossing or weak shoots. After about three years growth settles down and usually it is necessary only to thin out crowded shoots, remove dead wood and slightly shorten extreme growths. Sometimes a plum tree will continue putting on enormous, lanky and unfruitful growth. There is little one can do about this; eventually the tree will settle down when natural balance has been achieved between top and root development. In the meantime, keep crowded growths thinned out, eliminate cross growths which threaten the symmetry of the tree, and only lightly shorten back leaders. Under these circumstances heavy pruning will only result in renewed lanky growth. However, water-shoots should be removed.

**POLLARDING** is the practice of removing the trunk of a tree down to a desired height and then allowing a wealth of new growth from this point. Conifers cannot be pollarded because they usually die when the main trunk is cut back below existing side branches. Flowering gums and other eucalypts, as well as poplars, may have their height restricted in this way, but though trees such as oaks and jacarandas will survive such treatment, they should never be pollarded, for much of their beauty lies in their characteristic shapes.

When pruning away a large branch, make the cuts in stages to avoid cracking and possible damage to the trunk

**RASPBERRIES, LOGANBERRIES and BOYSENBERRIES** all bear fruit on the laterals on the cane of the previous season's growth. Prune raspberries to eliminate old canes that have fruited, doing so as soon as possible after the crop has been gathered. Leave the strongest canes and shorten these back in the following mid-August to encourage lateral fruiting growths. Loganberries and boysenberries should also be pruned back in mid-August, taking as much as 600 mm-1.2 m off the canes, depending on their relative vigour.

**RED and WHITE CURRANTS, GOOSEBERRIES.** During the first two or three years no pruning is needed, except the removal of broken or borer infested canes. When pruning older plants remove the weaker canes, leaving equal numbers of the first, second and third year canes to ensure continuity of fruiting.

**ROSES.** See Special Spread, Chapter 8, pages 163-167.

**SEALANTS.** If a pruning cut is properly made, there should be no need for sealants to protect it from disease. However, in humid areas or when high rainfall accompanies heat at the time of pruning, if may be wise to apply a proprietary sealant to any pruning cuts more than 15 mm in diameter. Bordeaux mixture or a white oil paint will also serve this purpose admirably.

**SHRUBS.** Most gardens today contain plants from many parts of the world; some of these behave as they would in their natural habitat, others attain only a smaller stature, and still others may grow to twice their natural size. Variations in climate and soil also have an effect, so that one can never be certain that the nurseryman's catalogue specifications are going to be right. If shrubs threaten to grow too large for their allotted space they must be pruned regularly. (See also Chapter 8, 'Shrubs and Roses', page 117.)

**Evergreen shrubs.** Most evergreen shrubs grown in Australia – *Viburnum tinus*, *Feijoa sellowiana*, *Photina villosa*, *Protea* spp. and the ericas are typical – usually do not require systematic or regular pruning. Any pruning is merely to keep them to their allotted space, or to induce the shape which suits their particular position, or which the gardener decides they should assume. Such pruning should be done as soon as the shrub has finished flowering. Any hard pruning which becomes necessary should be done in the early spring to allow the shrub ample time during the growing season to become well-furnished and shapely again. Autumn-flowering evergreens are also best pruned in spring, immediately in front of the previous season's growth, to ensure that the plant retains its shape and does not become unduly lanky.

**Deciduous Shrubs.** Bearing in mind that most shrubs require little pruning, there are two moderately well-distinguished deciduous groups: those which flower on the current season's growth, and those which flower on that of the previous season. The first comparatively small, group is typified by *Spiraea japonica* and most *Ceanothus, Abutilon,* and *Buddleia* species. These are pruned in winter or spring and their flowering is the natural culmination of the shoots of the full growing season. In the second group, flowering buds are formed during the season's growth and lie dormant throughout winter, bursting forth in the late spring, or during the growing season. A few members of this second group, such as cherries and forsythias which flower in very early spring, should be pruned in much the same way as the first group, but immediately after flowering, to allow ample time for new growth before the season's growth is complete. Thus, if the second group is to be pruned at all, this should be done immediately after flowering, enabling the plant to produce adequate flowering wood for the next season. Some shrubs, such as *Ceratostigma* spp. and *Abutilon thompsonii* can be cut hard back just before spring growth starts; this not only ensures ample flowering wood for the new season, but also provides a good opportunity to restrict their size.

**TREES.** Any large, growing tree is pruned almost solely to maintain its shape, taking out cross-growing branches and dead wood. Occasionally a strongly growing side-shoot may threaten the symmetry of the tree, or prejudice the growth of the leader; this should be shortened back. Such pruning can be carried out at any time, preferably as soon as the fault or the need for action is seen. When young, conifers such as golden cypress (*Chamaecyparis lawsoniana* 'aurea') should be lightly trimmed in late spring, to induce a shapely, close foliage. Jacarandas should never be heavily pruned, even to restrict their size, as they immediately put on a tremendous rush of growth, which not only results in them becoming larger than ever, but spoils for ever their characteristic and rather attractive shape.

**General Hints on Fruit Trees.** Be it an apple, a pear, a peach or an apricot, when obtaining a young fruit tree straight from the nursery, examine its roots and cleanly remove any damaged parts. If there is only one stem, cut this back to within 400 mm of the ground before planting. If there are more than three leaders starting evenly 300-400 mm from the ground, select the best three, well placed symmetrically, and cut them back to a bud pointing outwards away from the central axis, about 150-220 mm away from the 'break'.

In the case of the 'maiden' or single-stemmed plant, select the best of three or five leaders after the plant has sent up a number of growths, removing all other shoots. In either case, a young plant with from three to five, fairly equally-spaced main leaders, should remain to form a natural 'cup shape' (see illustration). All inward-growing shoots should be removed as they appear, and during the following winter pruning, these main leaders can again be shortened back, this time again to an outward-growing bud about 150-300 mm from the base of the previous season's new growth — or about two-thirds of its length. The following year shorten back only lateral growths, leaving only the best placed and strongest; at leaf fall these should be pruned back to half their length. The first three or four years of pruning is directed towards building the cup-shaped frame of a tree with strong branches that will bear the weight of a good crop, produce a constant supply of fruiting wood and be open to the sun so that it can reach the centre of the tree to ripen and colour the inner fruit. Once a proper framework has been built up, pruning will vary according to the type of fruit tree.

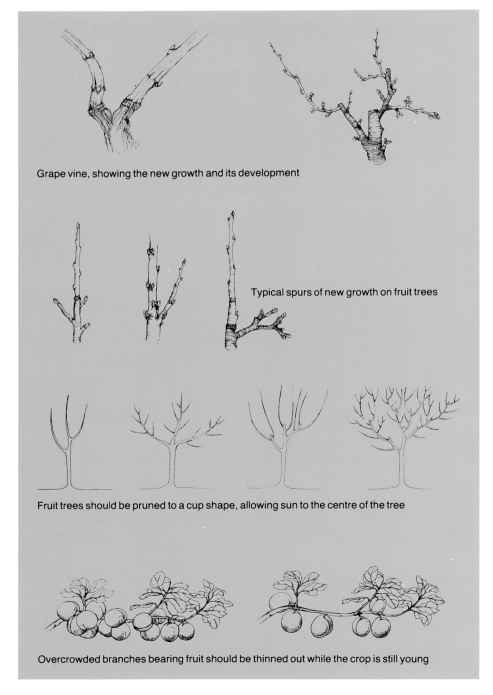

Grape vine, showing the new growth and its development

Typical spurs of new growth on fruit trees

Fruit trees should be pruned to a cup shape, allowing sun to the centre of the tree

Overcrowded branches bearing fruit should be thinned out while the crop is still young

# THE GARDEN ALMANAC

## JANUARY

**FLOWERS**

**Sow the following:**

alyssum, anemone, antirrhinum, aquilegia, aubrieta, bellis-perennis, calendula, calliopsis, cineraria, cornflower, delphinium, fox-glove, freesia, geum, gypsophila, Iceland poppy, larkspur, mignonette, nemesia, pansy, primula malacoides, polyanthus, ranunculus, schizanthus, scabiosa, sweet-pea, sweet william, stock, viola, wall-flower.

**Plant these seedlings:**

ageratum, amaranthus, aster, balsam, bedding begonias, carnation, celosia, cleome, coleus, cosmos, dianthus, hollyhock, lupin, marigold, petunia, phlox, portulaca, rudbeckia, salvia, statica, thochia, verbena, zinnia.

**Plant the following bulbs:**

coleus, felicia, fuchsia, ivies, indoor plants, magnolia, rhododendron, virburnum.

**Strike cuttings from these:**

bella-donna, clivea, crinum, iris rhizomes, lycoris, vallota, sternbergia, watsonia.

**VEGETABLES**

**Sow the following:**

beetroot, brussels sprouts, cabbage, cauliflower, capsicum, celery, cucumber, endive, leek, lettuce, onion, salsify, silver-beet, sweet corn, zucchini.

**Plant these seeds now:**

beans, beetroot, broccoli, brussels sprouts, carrot, cabbage, cauliflower, celeriac, cress, kohl rabi, lettuce, onion, parsnip, radish, peas, parsley, silver-beet, spinach, swede, turnip.

**FRUIT**

Bud fruit trees this month.

**LAWNS**

Keep lawns well watered during the summer months.

# FEBRUARY

## FLOWERS

**Sow the following:**

ageratum, alyssum, antirrhinum, aquilegia, bellis perennis, calendula, candytuft, campanula, carnation, clarkia, cyclamen, delphinium, gerbera, geum, godetia, honesty, Iceland poppy, larkspur, mignonette, mimulus, pansy, penstemon, primula malacoides, ranunculus, rudbeckia, russell lupin, scabiosa, schizanthus, statice, stock, sweet-pea, sweet william, verbena, virginian stock, viola, wall-flower.

**Plant these seedlings:**

ageratum, aquilegia, aster, canterbury bells, carnation, cineraria, cosmos, dianthus, fox-glove, gerbera, heuchera, holly-hock, Iceland poppy, kinnia, marigold, penstemon, polyanthus, sweet william, verbena.

**Plant the following bulbs:**

anemone, babiana, clivea, convallaria, daffodil, dutch iris, hippeastrum, hyacinth, jonquil, ixia, lachenalia, muscari, ranunculus, scilla, snow-drop, sparaxis, sprekelia, tritelia, tuberose, watsonia.

**Strike cuttings from these:**

abutilon, aucuba, azalea, camellia, carnation, cuphea, daphne, fuchsia, hebe, lavender, magnolia, native plants,  indoor plants, penstemon, pelargonium, photinia, rhododendron, viburnum.

## VEGETABLES

**Sow the following:**

beans, beetroot, carrots, kohl-rabi, onion, peas, silver-beet, spinach, swede, turnips.

**Plant these seeds now:**

beetroot, broccoli, brussels sprouts, cabbage, cauliflower, celery, celeriac, capsicum, cress, endive, leek, lettuce, onions, salsify, silver-beet, spinach.

## FRUIT

Remove spent raspberries, loganberries, and youngberries.

## LAWNS

Water thoroughly during the summer months.

# MARCH

---

## FLOWERS

**Sow the following:**

ageratum, anemone, antirrhinum, bellis perennis, calendula, canterbury bells, clarkia, cornflower, cyclamen, forget-me-not, freesia, gaillardia, godetia, gazania, helichrysum, ornamental kale, ranunculus, russell lupin, scabiosa, statice, stock, virginian stock, viola.

**Plant these seedlings:**

anemone, antirrhinum, aquilegia, calendula, cineraria, cornflower, fox-glove, gerbera, gerum, gypsophila, Iceland poppy, mignonette, pansy, primula malacoides, polyanthus, ranunculus, scabiosa, sweet-pea, sweet william, stock, viola, wall-flower.

**Plant the following bulbs:**

anemone, crocus, daffodil, dutch iris, freesia, galta, hyacinth, ixia, jonquil, lachenalia, lily-of-the-valley, lilium, muscari, ranunculus, scilla, snow-drop, sparaxis, tritelia, tritonia, tuberose, watsonia.

**Strike cuttings from these:**

abelia, azalea, banksia, buddleia, camellia, callistemon, carnation, conifer, cotoneaster, correa, forsythia, fuchsia, grevillea, hydrangea, leptospermum, magnolia, pelargonium, photinia, pittosporum, prostanthera, rhododendron, weigela.

---

## VEGETABLES

**Sow the following:**

broad-beans, carrot, cress, kohl-rabi, leek, onion, radish, swede-turnip.

**Plant these seeds now:**

beetroot, broccoli, brussels sprouts, cabbage, cauliflower, celeriac, celery, cress, chives, lettuce, onion, parsley, shallots, silver-beet, spinach.

---

## FRUIT

Check citrus fruit for collar rot.

---

## LAWNS

As for February.

---

# APRIL

---

## FLOWERS

**Sow the following:** alyssum, antirrhinum, bellis perennis, calendula, candytuft, clarkia, cornflower, cyclamen, forget-me-not, gazania, linaria, nemesia, pansy, polyanthus, russell lupin, scabiosa, statice, viola, wall-flower.

**Plant these seedlings:** antirrhinum, aquilegia, bellis perennis, candytuft, calendula, carnation, cineraria, cornflower, delphinium, dianthus, fox-glove, gazania, gerbera, gypsophila, hollyhock, Iceland poppy, larkspur, mignonette, mimulus, pansy, penstemon, polyanthus, primula malacoides, russell lupin, ranunculus, rudbeckia, statice, stock, sweet william, verbena, viola, wall-flower.

**Plant the following bulbs:** Calla lily, crocus, daffodil, dutch iris, freesia, hippeastrum, hyacinth, lilium, lily-of-the-valley, scilla, tritonia, tuberose, tulip.

**Strike cuttings from these:** abelia, aucuba, azalea, buddleia, buxus, browallia, carnation, conifer, cotoneaster, cuphea, cydonia, fuchsia, grevillea, hebe, photinia, perennials, penstemon.

---

## VEGETABLES

**Sow the following:** beetroot, broccoli, brussels sprouts, cabbage, cauliflower, endive, lettuce, onion, parsley, shallots, silver-beet, spinach, shallots.

**Plant these seeds now:** broad-beans, cress, herbs, leek, onion, swede-turnip.

---

## FRUIT

Plant berry fruits this month.

---

## LAWNS

Bent grass can be sown this month.

---

# MAY

---

## FLOWERS

**Sow the following:** aquilegia, calendula, clarkia, carnation, calendula, forget-me-not, gaillardia, godetia, larkspur, nemesia, nigella, polyanthus, scabiosa, statice, rudbeckia.

**Plant these seedlings:** antirrhinum, calendula, candytuft, clarkia, delphinium, forget-me-not, gaillardia, gazania, larkspur, mimulus, mignonette, ornamental kale, pansy, penstemon, primula malacoides, polyanthus, ranunculus, russell lupin, statice, stock, verbena, viola, wall-flower.

**Plant the following bulbs:** calla-lilly, eucomis, freesia, lilium, peony, sprekelia, tuberose, tulip.

**Strike cuttings from these:** berberis, cydonia, forsythia, hydrangea, kerria, ribes, viburnum, weigela, willow.

---

## VEGETABLES

**Sow the following:** artichoke crowns, asparagus crowns, cabbage, cauliflower, cress, endive, garlic cloves, horseradish pieces, onion, rhubarb crowns, spinach.

**Plant these seeds now:** broad-beans, cabbage, cress, herbs, leek, mustard, onion.

---

# JUNE

### FLOWERS

**Sow the following:**
alyssum, gaillardia, lobelia, rudbeckia, scabiosa, statice, verbena.

**Plant these seedlings:**
alyssum, antirrhinum, aquilegia, bellis perennis, calendula, dianthus, forget-me-not, larkspur, mimulus, pansy, polyanthus, russell lupin, stock, viola, wall-flower.

**Strike cuttings from these:**
abelia, abutilon, berberis, buddleia, cydonia, forsythia, fuchsia, hydrangea, kerri lantana, philadelphus, ribes, spiraea, tamarix, viburnum, weigela.

**Divide the following perennials this month:**
achillea, aster, astilbe, canna, campanula, delphinium, dicentra, gypsophila, helianthus, heuchera, hosta lily, paeonies, phlox, rudbeckia, violets.

### VEGETABLES

**Sow the following:**
artichoke tubers, asparagus crowns, cabbage, herbs, horseradish roots, rhubarb crowns.

**Plant these seeds now:**
broad-beans, onion.

### FRUIT

Prune early flowering stone fruits, apples and pears. Plums may require light pruning.

# JULY

## FLOWERS

**Sow the following:**  antherium, godetia, larkspur, linaria, mesembry, nasturtium.

**Plant these seedlings:**  antirrhinum, aquilegia, calendula, canterbury bells, fox-glove, gaillardia, godetia, hollyhock, larkspur, polyanthus, rudbeckia, russell lupin, scabiosa, statice.

## VEGETABLES

**Sow the following:**  artichoke tubers, asparagus crowns, cabbage, cress, herbs, horseradish roots, leek, onion, rhubarb crowns.

**Plant these seeds now:**  broad-beans, lettuce, onion.

## FRUIT

Spray affected fruit trees for curly leaf. Prune early flowering stone fruits.

# AUGUST

## FLOWERS

**Sow the following:** amaranthus, aster, carnation, celosia, coleus, cosmos, dianthus, larkspur, linaris, marigold, petunia, phlox, portulaca, rudbeckia, salvia, statice, verbena, zinnia.

**Plant these seedlings:** alyssum, bellis perennis, candytuft, delphinium, dianthus, gaillardia, lobelia, polyanthus, rudbeckia, stock, sweet william, scabiosa, verbena.

## VEGETABLES

**Sow the following:** artichoke tubers, asparagus crowns, cabbage, horseradish roots, leek, onion, spinach, rhubarb crowns.

**Plant these seeds now:** lettuce, peas, potatoes, rhubarb, silver-beet, tomato.

## FRUIT

Plant citrus trees. Remove spent canes of loganberries. Mulch strawberry plants.

## LAWNS

Spray now to rid your lawn of bindi or Jo-Jo.

# SEPTEMBER

**FLOWERS**

**Sow the following:**

amaranthus, aster, balsam, bedding begonias, carnation, celosia, cleome, cosmos, dahlia, kochia, marigold, petunia, phlox, portulaca, salvia, streptocarpus, sunflower, zinnia.

**Plant these seedlings:**

antirrhinum, carnation, cornflower, delphinium, dianthus, godetia, gypsophila, linaria, lobelia, marigold, mesembry-amthemum, nasturtium, statice, sweet william.

**VEGETABLES**

**Sow the following:**

cabbage, lettuce, onion, silver-beet.

**Plant these seeds now:**

butternut, capsicum, celery, cucumber, endive, herbs, lettuce, onion, peas, potato, pumpkin, radish, rhubarb, silver-beet, tomato, zucchini.

**FRUIT**

Feed lemon trees: Prune and feed passionfruit vines. Apples, pears, and quinces will require spraying against codling moth.

**LAWNS**

New lawns can be planted this month.

# OCTOBER

## FLOWERS

**Sow the following:**

aster, balsam, bedding begonia, browallia, cleome, coleus, cosmos, celosia, kochia, marigold, petunia, portulaca, salvia, sunflower. zinnia.

**Plant these seedlings:**

amaranthus, aster, carnation, celosia, delphinium, gazania, larkspur, petunia, phlox, portulaca, salvia, stock, zinnia.

## VEGETABLES

**Sow the following:**

beans, beetroot, butternut, capsicum, carrot, celery, cucumber, egg-plant, kohl-rabi, lettuce, onion, peas, potato, pumpkin, radish, silver-beet, sweet corn, tomato, zucchini.

**Plant these seeds now:**

capsicum, celery, cucumber, herbs, lettuce, onion, rhubarb, silver-beet, tomato, zucchini.

## FRUIT

Plant citrus trees, passionfruit and other climbing plants.
Fruit fly control will be required in affected areas.

## LAWNS

Sow kikuyu grass seed this month and November.

# NOVEMBER

**FLOWERS**

**Sow the following:** aster, balsam, bedding begonia, celosia, cleome, coleus, cosmos, kochia, marigold, petunia, portulaca, salvia, zinnia.

**Plant these seedlings:** ageratum, amaranthus, aster, balsam, carnation, celosia, cleome, cosmos, kochia, marigold, petunia, phlox, portulaca, salvia, zinnia.

**VEGETABLES**

**Sow the following:** beetroot, capsicum, celery, cucumber, endive, herbs, lettuce, onion, pumpkin, silver-beet, tomato, zucchini.

**Plant these seeds now:** beans, beetroot, cabbage, cauliflower, capsicum, carrot, celery, celeriac, cucumber, endive, kohl-rabi, lettuce, onion, parsnip, peas, pumpkin, radish, salsify, sweet corn, silver-beet, zucchini.

**FRUIT**

Keep citrus trees well watered during the summer months.

**LAWNS**

New lawns can be cut this month but do not set mower too low.

# DECEMBER

---

**FLOWERS**

**Sow the following:**
aster, canterbury bells, cosmos, cineraria, foxglove, hollyhock, Iceland poppy, penstemon, polyanthus, sweet william, tithonia, zinnia.

**Plant these seedlings:**
ageratum, amaranthus, aster, balsam, bedding begonia, browallia, celosia, cleome, coleus, cosmos, dahlia, dianthus, gaillardia, marigold, petunia, phlox, rudbeckia, salvia, thochia, zinnia.

**Strike cuttings from these:**
bouvardia, browallia, cistus, cuphea, daphne, fuchsia, hydrangea, indoor plants, magnolia, poinsettia.

---

**VEGETABLES**

**Sow the following:**
beetroot, cabbage, capsicum, cauliflower, celery, celeriac, cucumber, endive, lettuce, onion, pumpkin, salsify, silver-beet, sweet corn, zucchini.

**Plant these seedlings:**
beans, beetroot, broccoli, brussels sprouts, cabbage, carrot, cauliflower, celery, kohl-rabi, lettuce, onion, parsnip, peas, radish, silver-beet, swede-turnip.

---

**FRUIT**

Spray affected citrus trees for white wax scale.
Feed citrus trees with a good complete fertilizer and keep well watered.
Fruit fly control will be required in affected areas.

---

**LAWNS**

Cut lawns with mower setting high the summer months.

---

# A GUIDE TO CLIMATIC ZONES

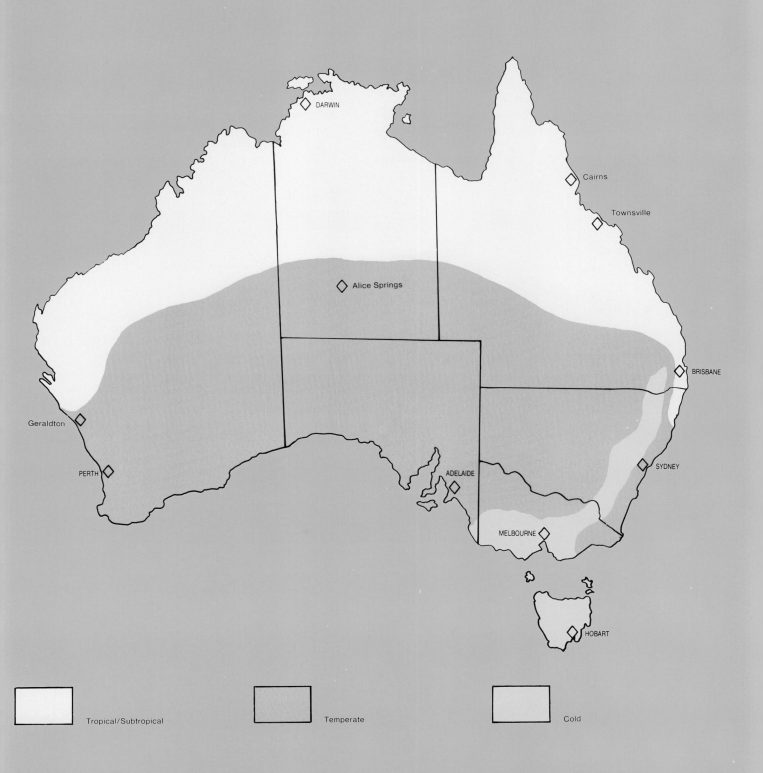

DARWIN

Cairns

Townsville

Alice Springs

BRISBANE

Geraldton

PERTH

ADELAIDE

SYDNEY

MELBOURNE

HOBART

Tropical/Subtropical          Temperate          Cold

# THE GARDENER'S GLOSSARY

**Balling:** a method of protecting the root system of an evergreen tree or shrub while it is being moved. The soil mass surrounding the roots is wrapped carefully in hessian or some similar material to eliminate risk of damage.

**Broadcast:** to scatter seed or fertilizer over the soil surface by hand.

**Broad-leafed Weed:** any plant in a lawn which is not grass.

**Chlorosis:** a yellowing of the leaves, usually the result of a nutritional imbalance – particularly a lack of iron. Such a condition is described as chlorotic.

**Conifer:** plants, mostly evergreen, such as cedars, junipers, pines, or the deciduous swamp cypress, which bear their seeds in cones or similar modified structures.

**Damping off:** a disease in the soil/air which attacks young seedlings particularly, causing them to rot, wilt and die.

**Defoliation:** an unnatural loss of a plant's leaves, affecting its health. Defoliation may be caused by high winds (which strip foliage away), drought or, more commonly, attack by insect pest or fungal disease.

**Die-back:** a situation in which the stem starts dying back from its apex. This may be caused by inadequate water, nutrient deficiency or more usually, attack by boring or sucking insects.

**Dripline:** the outer circumference of a tree's branches where the greatest drip concentra-tion occurs during rain. The plant's roots are most active along this line and fertilizers and/or water should be fed here.

**Ex containers, ex open ground:** plants, usually trees, which are allowed to grow in such situations for a year, or more, before being transplanted.

**Eye:** that part of a tuber such as a potato or dahlia which, when planted, will produce new growths; in terms of 'cut above an eye', this refers to a bud, usually lying in a leaf axil.

**Fallow:** soil which lies unplanted or idle to regain its strength, or so that successive growths of weeds may be destroyed.

**Fasciation:** the fusion of two or more stems or flowers.

**Fastigiate:** a strictly upright habit of growth.

**Feathering:** the practice of leaving growths on the stem of a developing standard tree or shrub. Though these growths are shortened back from time to time, they are only removed when the main stem has reached its desired thickness.

**Firming Board:** any piece of firm material with a flat surface, cut to fit the surface of a seed tray and used to level and press down the soil in the tray.

**Fogging:** the application of a super-fine mist spray.

**Forcing:** the process of hastening a plant's maturity of flower, foliage or fruit, in or out of season. This may be achieved by such varied means as controlled heat, unnatural humidity, shade and even pre-freezing – as in the case of bulbs.

**Ground Bark:** bark, usually but not neces-sarily of pine trees, which is ground up for use as a mulch or in potting compounds.

**Harden off:** before planting outdoors, plants grown under glass house, shade house or similar sheltered conditions are gradually hardened off by controlled, but increasing, exposure to the elements.

**Half-hardy:** describes plants which will toler-ate some slight cold or frost or will recover again after being damaged by severe frost.

**Hardy:** describes plants which will tolerate a considerable degree of exposure to frost, or other cold conditions.

**Heading back:** the process of cutting back the main leader or other shoots in order to promote a more compact growth.

**Heavy Soil:** a loose description of clay soil or soil comprising very fine, closely-packed par-ticles.

**Heeling-in:** the practice of making a shallow trench in which the bare roots of plants are placed and covered with damp soil until the gardener is ready to plant them.

**Honeydew Drip:** many sucking insects excrete a sticky substance called honeydew which is eaten by other insects, primarily ants. Cars parked under trees which are favoured by aphids often become covered with this messy substance – which is not always easy to remove.

**Humus:** animal or vegetable material in an advanced stage of decomposition.

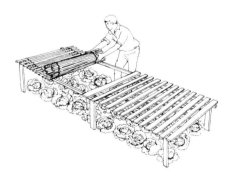

**Lath:** an overhead protective structure con-sisting of spaced laths designed to reduce sun intensity on the plants beneath.

**Leaching:** the process in which water dis-solves and washes away the various soil salts. Hence the need for regular applications of fertilizer, organic substances and so on.

**Leader:** the central upward-growing shoot of a tree or shrub, which must be retained for the sake of shape or form in such trees as oak, liquidambar, plane and ash.

**Leaf Mould:** partially decomposed leaves, particularly those of deciduous species.

**Leaf Scar:** the (usually) crescent-shaped scar on a stem showing where a leaf was attached.

**Mulch:** any loosely-packed animal or vegetable material placed in a thick layer over the soil surface between plants to cool the soil, reduce unwanted vegetative growth and conserve the soil moisture.

**Naturalize:** an informal planting out of plants, bulbs and so on, in an area where they are encouraged to establish themselves permanently by spreading or re-seeding.

**Offset:** short basal stems sent out by some perennial plants and sub-shrubs and which make new plants.

**Organic Matter:** any material of organic origin such as ground bark, partially decomposed pine needles, sawdust, waste, milled sisal fibre, compost, manure and so on which can be dug into the soil to improve its texture and fertility.

**Peat Moss:** a highly moisture-retentive substance formed from a variety of semi-decomposed mosses. It is sterile, with a slightly acid reaction.

**Pinching back:** the practice of pruning soft-wooded plants, such as fuchsias, by pinching out the growing tips so as to increase side growths and give the plant a more compact habit,

**Pot-bound:** this condition arises when a plant has been grown too long in a pot and its roots have become matted and tangled. This may also happen with a tree, or other subjects grown for too long in a container – in which case the condition is termed 'root-bound'.

Potting on

**Potting-on:** the process of transferring a plant from a small to larger container, to facilitate its growth.

**Pricking out:** relates to the removal of seedlings from a tray or bed to another site where they are set out further apart, to allow uninhibited growth.

**Root Run:** the area of soil exploited by the roots of an individual plant.

**Rootstock:** the root and the stem of a plant which furnishes the stock on which a graft or bud is made. (See illustration, page 358.)

**Runner:** a very loose term commonly adopted to describe a slender stem sent out from the parent plant and along which roots are formed. Most commonly applied to grasses.

**Self:** any flower of a single colour.

**Self-branching:** any plant, annual, shrub or tree (but particularly an annual) which branches freely without having to be headed back or pinched out to promote a compact habit.

**Setting out:** placing semi-grown plants, seedlings or bulbs in the situation in which they are finally to mature.

**Shade-house, shading:** a structure which provides protection from the sun but allows enough light through the covering to encourage growth.

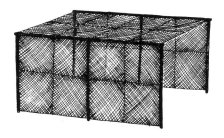

**Sphagnum:** various live mosses – such as sphagnum – native to bogs are collected and packaged for planting certain genera of orchids.

**Standard:** a plant that does not normally assume tree form, treated in such a way that a single stem develops, bearing a rounded crown of foliage. (See illustration, page 191.)

**Sub-shrub:** a woody plant with a maximum height of 600 mm.

**Sucker:** an adventitious growth which springs from part of a plant below the budded portion, or from the rootstock of any budded or grafted plant; suckers are sent out by poplars and many other plants when sections of the roots have been damaged or severed.

**Surface Sow:** see Broadcast.

**Tamping:** the use of a piece of wood, or similar implement, to gently but firmly settle the soil around the roots of a transplanted subject.

**Tender:** though there are degrees of tenderness, the term applies particularly to those plants which cannot accept any frost, or even prolonged cold weather in frost-free areas.

**Thinning out:** in pruning terms this means the removal of excess branches to give the plant a more open, balanced structure. In terms of seedlings, thinning out means removing little seedlings so that adequate room is left for the remainder to develop. The 'thinned out' material may or may not be re-planted in another position.

**Top Dress:** the application of soil, fertilizer, compost and similar material to the surfaces of lawn or beds.

**Topiary:** the craft of shaping plants – trees or shrubs – into various geometrical or informal shapes.

**Wrenching:** the practice of cutting the roots of a tree or shrub growing in the open ground to encourage increased rooting so that safe transplantation is possible. Wrenching is carried out during the plant's dormant season.

# BOTANICAL TERMS AND THEIR MEANINGS

**Acicular:** needle-like
**Acuminate:** drawn out, tapering point
**Acute:** sharply pointed, abrupt
**Adventitious:** arising from other than a usual place, e.g. roots growing from a stem or a leaf
**Alternate:** (leaves) arising at different levels
**Annual:** a plant that completes its life cycle within one year and then dies
**Anther:** pollen-bearing portion of stamen
**Areole:** confined to cacti; cushion-like structure, from which branches, flowers and spines may arise
**Aril:** an accessory seed covering formed by an outgrowth at the base of the ovule, e.g. in *Taxus*

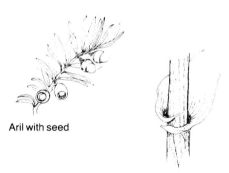

Aril with seed

Auricles on monocotyledon leaf

**Asexual:** reproduction without seeds
**Auriculate:** having basal ears
**Autotrophic:** a plant that manufactures its own food (See: heterotrophic, parasite, saprophyte)
**Axil:** angle of junction between leaf and stem
**Bark:** the external group of tissues, from the cambium outward, of a woody stem or root
**Biennial:** a plant that requires two years to complete its life cycle. Flowering is normally delayed until the second year
**Bifurcate:** forked, two-pronged
**Bipinnate:** twice pinnate, having separate leaflets on both primary and secondary divisions
**Bisexual:** hermaphrodite; stamens and pistil in same flower
**Bract:** modified leaves, similar to flower, often coloured

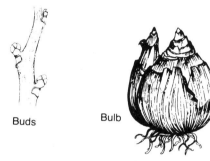

Buds          Bulb

**Bud:** an undeveloped shoot, e.g. over-wintering buds
**Bulb:** a short, underground stem with many fleshy scale-leaves filled with stored food

Carpels

**Calyx:** outer whorl of floral parts; usually green
**Campanulate:** bell-shaped flower, broadly based
**Carpel:** a floral leaf, part of the ovary, bearing ovules along the margins
**Caruncle:** a spongy outgrowth of the seed coat, prominent in castor bean seed
**Ciliate:** fringed with fine hairs

Coalescence

Compound leaf

**Coalescence:** a condition in which there is a union of separate parts of any one whorl of flower parts; synonyms are connation and cohesion
**Complete flower:** a flower having four whorls of floral parts (leaves): sepals, petals, stamens and carpels
**Compound leaf:** a leaf whose blade is divided into several distinct leaflets
**Cone:** a fruiting structure composed of modified leaves or branches, which bear pollen sacs or ovules, e.g. a pine cone
**Convex:** umbrella-like
**Cordate:** heart-shaped
**Corm:** similar to a bulb, but solid fleshed (gladiolus)
**Corolla:** inner circle of petals, usually conspicuously coloured
**Corymb:** a flat-headed inflorescence, opening from outside first
**Cotyledon:** a seed leaf, two in dicotyledons and one in monocotyledons

**Crenate:** with rounded or convex teeth
**Culm:** the hollow stem or straw of grasses, bamboo
**Cultigen:** a species which has evolved on its own, under domestication but not through cultivation
**Cultriformis:** shaped like a knife blade
**Cuneate:** triangular, wedge-shaped
**Cyme:** usually flat-topped inflorescence, but opening from inside first
**Decumbent:** prostrate, but with extremity ascending
**Deltoid:** triangular
**Dentate:** toothed, teeth directed outwards
**Dioecious:** unisexual; male and female organs on different plants
**Ecology:** the study of life in relation to environment
**Edaphic:** pertaining to soil conditions that influence plant growth
**Elliptical:** longer than wide, widest point at centre
**Elongate:** long, drawn out
**Emarginate:** indented at end
**Endosperm:** the nutritive tissue in many seeds
**Entire:** leaf margin smooth, without indentation

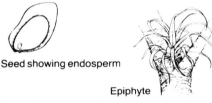
Seed showing endosperm

Epiphyte

**Epiphyte:** a plant which uses another for support, but takes no food from it
**Farinose:** covered with a mealy or powdery substance
**Filament:** fine stalk of an anther
**Filiform:** slender, thread-shaped
**Frond:** a synonym for a large divided leaf, especially for a fern leaf

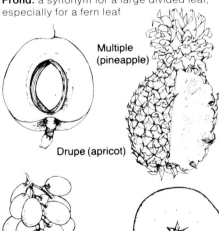
Multiple (pineapple)
Drupe (apricot)

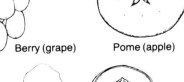
Berry (grape)
Pome (apple)

A peach developing from a flower

**Fruit:** a matured ovary
**Glabrous:** smooth, not hairy
**Glaucous:** bluish-grey, sometimes with a waxy bloom
**Glutinous:** sticky
**Hastate:** halberd- or spear-shaped
**Herb:** classically, a plant whose head above ground does not become woody and persistent – as opposed to a shrub
**Herbaceous:** non-woody
**Heterotrophic:** a plant obtaining nourishment from outside sources
**Hirsute:** coarsely haired
**Hybrid:** the offspring formed by mating two plants that differ genetically
**Incomplete flower:** a flower lacking one or more of the four kinds of flower parts

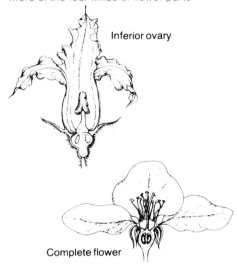
Inferior ovary
Complete flower

**Inferior ovary:** an ovary more or less (sometimes completely) attached to the calyx and corolla
**Inflorescence:** the arrangement of the flowering portion of a plant; a flower cluster
**Insectivorous:** plants which derive nourishment from insect life
**Internode:** the section of a stem between successive nodes, or joints
**Involucre:** ring or rings of bracts surrounding a flower cluster or umbel
**Laciniate:** jagged, cut into unequal lobes
**Lanceolate:** lance-shaped, tapering

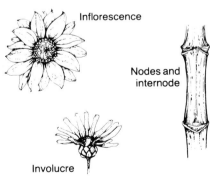
Inflorescence
Nodes and internode
Involucre

**Lateral:** from the sides
**Linear:** narrow, sides parallel
**Lobed:** leaf cut, or deeply indented, nearly to mid-rib or base
**Metabolism:** overall set of chemical reactions in the living plant

**Monoecious:** male and female organs in separate flowers but on same plant
**Mutant:** form derived from sudden change in plant or part of plant
**Mutation:** a sudden, heritable change appearing in an individual as the result of a change in genes or chromosomes
**Node:** slightly enlarged portion of the stem where leaves and buds arise and where branches originate
**Obcordate:** notched at apex, inversely heart-shaped
**Oblanceolate:** broad-ended, tapering towards base
**Obovate:** ovate, but with the broader end uppermost
**Obtuse:** blunt, rounded at the end
**Orbicular:** circular, ring-like
**Organic:** referring to compounds that contain both carbon and hydrogen; the material products of living organisms
**Ovary:** basal part of pistil, which becomes the fruit and contains the seed
**Ovate:** broad-based, egg-shaped
**Ovule:** rudimentary seed

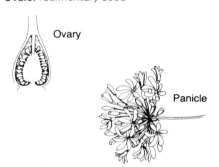
Ovary
Panicle

**Palmate:** leaflets radiating from apex of petiole
**Palmately compound:** as above but with more than three leaflets
**Panicle:** an open, branched inflorescence
**Papillose:** bearing small, pimple-like bumps
**Panduriform:** rounded at both ends, with a narrow middle; fiddle-shaped
**Parasite:** a plant or organism deriving its nourishment from another
**Pedicel:** the stalk of a single flower
**Peduncle:** primary flower stalk
**Peltate:** shield-shaped, petiole attached to leaf within the margin
**Perennial:** a plant that lives from year to year
**Perfect flower:** a flower having both stamens and pistils
**Perianth:** calyx, corolla, or both
**Petiole:** leaf stem
**Pinnate:** having leaves arranged on either side of leaf stalk
**Pinnatisect:** pinnately divided to the mid-rib but with leaflets unseparated
**Pistil:** female organ of the flower including ovary, style and stigma
**Pollination:** the transfer of pollen from the anther of a plant to fertilize the stigma
**Pubescent:** downy with short, soft hairs
**Raceme:** inflorescence in which stalked flowers are arranged along an elongated stem
**Regular flower:** a flower in which the corolla is made up of similarly shaped petals equally spaced and radiating from the centre of the flower

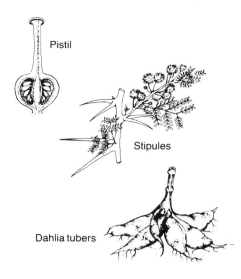

Pistil

Stipules

Dahlia tubers

**Reniform:** kidney-shaped
**Resupinate:** inverted, turned upside down, as in the flowers of most orchids
**Rhizome:** a creeping rootstock (stem), usually swollen, mostly underground, capable of sending up shoots
**Rosette:** a circular cluster of leaves, usually close to the ground
**Runner:** a stem that grows horizontally along the ground surface

**Sagittate:** arrow-shaped
**Saprophyte:** a plant deriving its food from dead organic matter
**Scabrous:** rough to the touch
**Scandent:** more scrambling than climbing
**Scape:** a leafless peduncle rising from the ground

**Seed:** a matured ovule without accessory parts
**Sepal:** segments of a calyx
**Serrate:** saw-toothed
**Sessile:** stalkless, close to stem
**Sinuate:** curved, deep wavy margin
**Spadix:** a fleshy spike, usually bearing large numbers of small flowers, but variable
**Spathe:** a bract-like structure partly surrounding an inflorescence, often showy
**Spatulate:** narrow-based oblong, broadly rounded at tip
**Spike:** unstalked flowers on an elongated stem
**Stamen:** pollen-bearing, male organ made up of an anther and a filament
**Stellate:** star form
**Stigma:** that portion of the pistil which receives the pollen
**Stipule:** a leaf-like structure at base of petiole
**Stolon:** a shoot which hugs the ground, taking root and so creating new plants
**Stoloniferous:** having underground, or surface rooting stems
**Style:** connecting stalk between the ovary and the stigma
**Succulent:** a plant with fleshy, water-storing parts
**Superior ovary:** an ovary completely separate and free from the calyx
**Synonym:** a superseded name
**Terrestrial:** a plant growing in the ground
**Tomentose:** being covered with matted down or wool
**Trichome:** a cellular outgrowth or a short filament of cells
**Trifoliate:** three-leafed
**Truncate:** appearing cut off at the end
**Tuber:** an underground stem, usually much swollen, with eyes
**Umbel:** a stalked inflorescence with flowers arising from a single point
**Undulate:** wavy margined
**Unisexual:** of one sex only
**Venation:** arrangement of veins in a leaf blade
**Viable:** capable of living or germinating
**Vitamins:** naturally occurring organic substances, akin to enzymes, necessary in small amounts for normal metabolism
**Viviparous:** producing seeds which germinate on the plant
**Whorled:** leaves in whorl around stem
**Xerophytic:** capable of living with minimal moisture

**SEED TYPES**

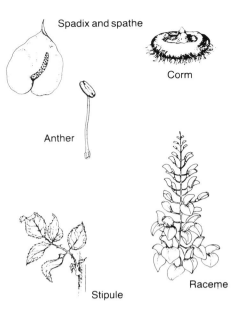

Spadix and spathe

Anther

Corm

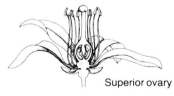

Stipule

Raceme

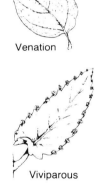

Superior ovary

Venation

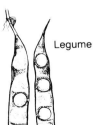

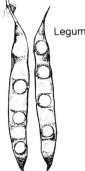

Viviparous

Umbel

Winged seeds

Legume

Achene (sunflower)

Capsule (poppy)

Follicle (*Grevillea robusta*)

Nut (acorn)

Schizocarp (dubbeltjie)

Silique (Cleome)

# THE ORIGINS OF PLANT NAMES

The origins of the generic and specific names of many plants have a charm and fascination that at times almost equals those of the plants themselves. Nor are these origins of interest to the linguist or botanist alone, for, though some names have an almost 'Alice in Wonderland' quality – others describe more mundane aspects such as the plant's shape, habitat, or the uses for which its leaves, sap, roots or flowers were widely known. Other names commemorate botanists who recorded a genus or species for the first time – or patrons, or fellow botanists, whom they wished to honour. Thus the genus *Tradescantia* is named after the English royal gardener John Tradescant, who died in 1638; *Nicotiana* has little connection with nicotine, but takes its name from the 16th century French traveller, Jean Nicot; and *Strelitzia* was named after Queen Charlotte, wife of George III, whose family name was Mecklenburg-Strelitz.

Except in the case of cultivars the convention of Latinizing botanical names, established by Linnaeus, continues to this day, but plants can derive their names not only from Latin, but from such widely varied tongues as Greek and Japanese, English and Arabic, Dutch and Hebrew – even Maori (*Hoheria*) and Egyptian (*Cichorium*).

Most of the early botanists were classical scholars – in Europe a knowledge of Latin and Greek was considered essential for any 'educated' man – and this facet of learning was frequently reflected in their choice of generic names. They often turned to the classical myths and gods in their search for appropriate 'surnames' for new plants. Linnaeus – who is himself commemorated in a single-species genus – named the spectacular *Protea* after the sea god Proteus; *Amaryllis* was given its name from that of a fictitious countrywoman in the writings of Virgil, and *Tagetes* from an Etruscan god.

Early nomenclature is sometimes misleading, for Linnaeus and others based their descriptive Latin classification of most 'exotic' plants on specimens which had often taken several months to reach their destination. A flower-head might have travelled half a year or more, deteriorating all the while, and so bore little resemblance to its natural state by the time it was named. In other instances species were classified on the basis of inaccurate sketches, so that references – particularly to their habit – were often misleading. Yet, because of the conventions of nomenclature, the specific name first given to a plant is retained; even if modern botanical science has led to a plant being reclassified, that specific name usually accompanies it on its move through the botanical lexicon. (The process of reclassification is on-going and – save in the case of certain indigenous genera and species, where local botanical nomenclature has been preferred – we have opted for *Hortus III* as the final arbiter where authorities differ in their naming of plants.)

Some of the more common – and most fascinating – generic and specific names and their meanings (or origins) are listed below. Descriptive specific names derived from Latin are given as direct translations, as explanations are generally unnecessary.

*Acacia:* from the Greek 'akanthos', meaning a thorn.
*acaulis:* without a stem.
*anthos:* a flower.
*arborescens:* like a tree.
*australis:* from the south – not from Australia.
*barbatus:* not barbed, but bearded – usually referring to a covering of fine hairs on the flower.
*berberis:* from the Arabic word for 'desert'.
*calceolaria:* from the Latin word 'calceolus', meaning a slipper

*Callistemon:* from the Greek 'kallistos' (most beautiful) and Latin 'stemon' (stamen).
*Callistephos:* from the Greek 'kallistos' and 'stephos' (crown). In this case referring to the seed.
*calluna:* from the Greek 'kallunein', 'to sweep', indicating the plant's use.
*campanula:* from the Latin 'campana' (a little bell) referring to the flower shape.
*campestris:* from the Latin meaning 'of the plains', and indicating habitat.
*cordatus:* shaped like a heart.

*darwinii:* named after Charles Darwin, the renowned English scientist.
*dendron:* a suffix from the Greek word for face – as in rhododendron ('rhodos' meaning rose).
*denticulatus:* finely-toothed, usually referring to the leaves of a species.
*digitalis:* from the Latin 'digitus', a finger.
*Gypsophila:* a lover of chalk, indicating the plant's preferred habitat.
*helios:* the Greek word for the sun – hence *helianthos*, or sunflower.

*hemerocallis:* from the Greek 'hemera' (day) and 'kallos' (beauty).

*hirsutus:* hairy.

*Hydrangea:* compounded from the Greek – 'hydor' (water) and 'aggeion' (vessel), in this case referring to the seed-vessel of the plant.

*incanus:* from the Latin, meaning hoary or grey.

*insignis:* meaning prominent or noticeable, despite its similarity to 'insignificant', which has quite the opposite meaning.

*Lavandula:* from the Latin word 'lavare', to wash. This refers to the plant's early use as a cleansing agent – which is reflected today in the continued use of lavender sprigs to 'sweeten' the air of linen cupboards and chests.

*littoralis:* derived from the Latin word for shore, and indicating habitat.

*Lychnis:* derived from 'lychnos', or a lamp, and referring to the fact that both the Greeks and the Romans used the leaves of plants in this genus to make wicks for their lamps.

*maritimus:* from the Latin, meaning 'of the sea' and indicating a plant's coastal habitat.

*meconopsis:* indicates the flower's similarity ('opsis') to that of a poppy – 'mekon' in Greek.

*Melaleuca:* reflects the two extremes of colour – black and white – and refers to the bark of the first recorded species in this genus. 'Melas' is Greek for black.

*Nigella:* from the Latin 'niger', meaning black.

*nudicaulis:* bare-stemmed.

*occidentalis* and *orientalis:* from the Latin meaning respectively 'from the west' and 'from the east'.

*officinalis:* indicative of medicinal or still-room use.

*pallustris:* from the Latin and meaning 'of the marshes'.

*Pelargonium:* one of the most evocative generic names. It refers to the plant's seed-vessels, which look remarkably like the bill of a stork (pelargos).

*Penstemon:* refers to the five (pente) stamens (stemon).

*pratensis:* from the Latin meaning 'of the meadows'.

*procumbens:* trailing, or of sprawling habit.

*Salvia:* from the Latin 'salveo' – I heal – and referring to the properties attributed to the plant in early medicine.

*saxatilis:* refers in Latin to a plant's rocky habitat.

*silvestris:* Latin reference to a woodland setting.

*Syringa:* takes its generic name from 'syrinx', a Latinized version of the Turkish word for a pipe. Pipes were carved from the wood during the early days of smoking in the Middle East.

*tomentosus:* with a felt-like covering, usually referring to plant leaves.

*Tropaeolum:* The ancient Greeks considered the flower and leaf to resemble a warrior's helmet and shield – hence 'tropaion', or a trophy, the symbol of victory.

# INDEX

hybrid 'Mrs. Rundle', *137*
hybrid 'Winston Churchill', *137*
*magellanica*, **136**
*procumbens*, 136
X *hybrida*, **136**
Fungicide Table, **347**
Fungus diseases, grouping of, **340**
*Funkia subcordata:* see *Hosta plantaginea*

*Gaillardia pulchella* (Ann.), **68-69**, *68*
Garden frames, **20**, *323*
Gardener's Glossary, **376-377**
Gardener and the Law, **27**
*Gardenia* (Shr.)
  *augusta*, **136**
  *globosa:* see *Rothmannia globosa*
  *jasminoides:* see *G. augusta*
  *thunbergia*, **136**, *137*
Garingboom: see *Agave americana*
Garland Flower: see *Hedychium coccineum*
Garland Spiraea: see *Spiraea* X *arguta*
Garlic, **264**, *264*
*Garrya elliptica* (Shr.), **137**
*Gasteria verrucosa*, **285**
Gay Feather: see *Liatris pycnostachya*
*Gazania*
  X hybrid (G.C.), **54**
  hybrids, **92**, *93*
  *krebsiana*, *5*; (G.C.), **54**
*Gelsemium sempervirens* (Cl.), **180**, *181*
Gem Squash: see Pumpkins
*Genista monosperma* (Shr.), **137**
Geraldton Wax-flower: see *Chamelaucium uncinatum*
Geranium: see *Pelargonium* spp. and *P. zonale*
*Geranium incanum* (Per.), **92**
*Gerbera* (Per.)
  *jamesonii*, **92-93**
  *jamesonii* hybrid, *93*
German Violet: see *Exacum affine*
Germination of seeds, **59**
*Gesneria cochlearis:* see *Sinningia cardinalis*
Giant Granadilla: see *Passiflora quadrangularis*
Giant Honeysuckle: see *Lonicera hildebrandiana*
Giant Protea: see *Protea cynaroides*
Giant Thuja: see *Thuja plicata*
Gidgee: see *Acacia cambegai*
*Gingko biloba* (Tr.), **210**, *216*
Glabrous, see Botanical Terms and their Meanings, **378**
*Gladiolus* (Per.)
  *alatus*, *93*, **94**
  *cardinalis*, **95**
  garden hybrids, *14*, *95*
  hybrids, Special Spread, **95**
  infections, *95*
  *natalensis*, **94**
  *primulinus*, **94**
  *psittacinus*, *95*
  storage of corms, **95**
  see also: Rust, *347*
Glaucous, see Botanical Terms and their Meanings, **378**
*Gleditsia triacanthos* (Tr.), **210**
Globe Amaranth: see *Gomphrena*

*globosa*
*Gloriosa* (Per.)
  *rothschildiana*, **94**
  *superba*, **94**, *94*
Glory Tree: see *Clerodendrum philippinum*
*Glottiphyllum linguiforme*, **285**
Gloxinia: see *Sinningia speciosa*
*Glycine max:* see Soya Beans
Goat's Beard: see *Astilbe japonica*
*Godetia amoena:* see *Clarkia elegans*
Gold Tips: see *Leucodendron salignum*
Golden Bell: see *Forsythia suspensa*
Golden Candles: see *Pachystachys lutea*
Golden Cypress: see *Chamaecyparis lawsoniana* 'Lutea'
Golden Elder: see *Sambucus nigra* 'Aurea'
Golden Feather: see *Chrysanthemum parthenium* 'Aureum'
Golden Japanese Honeysuckle: see *Lonicera japonica*
Golden Marguerite: see *Anthemis tinctoria*
Golden Privet: see *Ligustrum oralifolium* 'Aureo-variegatum'
Golden-rayed Lily of Japan: see *Lilium auratum*
Golden Rod: see *Solidago canadensis*
Golden Tuft: see *Aurinia saxatilis*
Golden Vine: see *Stigmaphyllon ciliatum*
Golden Wattle: see *Acacia pycnantha*
*Golden Weeping Willow:* see *Salix alba* 'vitellina' 'Pendula'
*Gomphrena globosa* (Ann.), **69**, *69*
Gooseberry, English, **244**
  pruning, *361*
  spray programme, **250**
Grafting, **358**
  crown grafting, *358*
  grafting knife, *357*
  roof graft, *359*
  saddle grafting, *358*
  veneer graft, *358*
  whip graft, *358*
  *Clematis* hybrids, *358*
  *Fraxinus* spp., *358*, *358*
Grape, **244**
  downy mildew on vine leaves, *345*
  powdery mildew on grapes, *347*
  pruning, *362*
  spray programme, **250**
Grape Hyacinth: see *Muscari botryoides*
Grapefruit, **244**
  spray programme, **250**
Grass cutting equipment, **37-38**
  choosing mowers, **38**
  electric mowers, **37**, *38*
  hand mower, *38*
  lawn edgers, **38**, *38*
  motor mowers, **37-38**, *38*
Grass Pink: see *Dianthus plumarius*
Green Stink-bug: see Bugs
Greenhouse
  benches, **315**
  design, **315**, *316*
  floor, **425**
  frames, **316**, *323*
  heating, **316-317**

lean-to, **317**, *316*
location, **317**
planning and management, **315-317**
plants, *314*
raising of outdoor bulbs, **320**
tunnel cultivation: see Special Spread, **323**, *323*
ventilation, **317**, *316*
Greenhouse and frames in garden planning, **20**
*Grevillea* (Shr.), *138*
  *alpina* (Shr.), **137**
  *banksii* (Shr.), **137**; (Tr.), *217*
  *baueri* (Shr.), **137**
  *caleyi* (Shr.), **137**
  X *gaudichaudii* (G.C.), **54**, *216*
  *gaudi-chaudii* (Tr.), *216*
  *juniperina* (Shr.), **137**, *138*
  'Mason's Hybrid' (Tr.), *216*
  *robusta* (Tr.), **214**, *214*
  'Robyn Gordon' (Shr.), **138**, *138*
  *rosmarinifolia* (Shr.), **138**
  *sericea* (Shr.), **138**
  *speciosa (Shr.)*, **138**
  *victoriae* (Shr.), **138**
Ground covers concealing manholes and drains, *51*
Guava, **244**
  spray programme, **250**
  see also: Fruit fly, *342*
Guernsey Lily: see *Nerine sarniensis*
*Gunnera manicata* (Per.), **272**
*Guzmania lingulata* (Per. ind.), **303**
*Gynura aurantiaca* (Per. ind.), **303**
*Gypsophila elegans* (Ann.), **69**

*Haemanthus*
  *katharinae:* see *Scadoxus multiflorus* 'Katharinae'
  *magnificus:* see *Scadoxus puniceus*
*Hakea*
  *corymbosa* (Shr.), **138-139**
  *laurina* (Tr.), **214**
  *nodosa* (Shr.), **139**
  *purpurea* (Shr.), **139**
  *salicifolia* (Tr.), **173**
  *sericea* (Shr.), **139**
*Hamatocactus setispinus:* see *Ferocactus setispinus*
Hand Forks, **38**, *40*
Hand Trowels, **38**, *40*
Hand Weeders, **38**, *40*
Happy Wanderer: see *Hardenbergia violacea*
*Hardenbergia* (Cl.)
  *comptoniana*, **180**
  *violacea*, **180**
Hare's Foot Fern: see *Davallia fijeensis*
Hare's Tail, **351**, *350*
Harola: see Fungicide Table
Hastate: see Botanical Terms and their Meanings, **378**
*Haworthia*
  *margaritifera:* see *H. pumila*
  *pumila*, **285**
Hawthorn: see *Crataegus* spp.
Heath: see Ericas, Special Spread
*Hebe* (Shr.)
  *speciosa*, **139**
  *speciosa* 'Purple Queen', *139*
*Hedera helix* (Per.)

(G.C.), **54**, *55*; (Cl.), **181**, *181*
  'Marginata', (Cl. ind.), **303**, *303*
Hedge Clippers, **38-39**, *38*
Hedgehog Cactus: see *Echinocereus pentalophus*
Hedges
  preparation and planting, **169**
  pruning, *361*
  see also: Fences, hedges and walls, **19-20**
*Hedychium* (Per.)
  *coccineum*, **94**, *94*
  *flavum*, 94
*Helenium autumnale* (Per.), **94**
*Helianthemum nummularium* (Shr.) **139**
*Helianthus*
  *angustifolius* (Per.), **94**
  *annuus* (Ann.), **69**, *69*, *289*, *290*
*Helichrysum*, *55*, **69**, *69*
  *apiculatum* (G.C.), **54**
  *bracteatum* (Ann.), *68*
*Heliconia*
  *brasiliensis*, **272**, *272*
  *latispatha*, *272*
*Heliopsis helianthoides* (Per.), **94**, *96*
*Heliotropium* (Shr.)
  *arborescens*, **139**
  *peruvianum:* see *H. arborescens*
*Helipterum manglesii* (Ann.), **70**
*Hemerocallis* (Per.)
  *fulva*, *96*
  *lilioasphodelus* **96**, *96*
Herald's Trumpet: see *Beaumontia grandiflora*
Herbaceous Border: see Semi-herbaceous Border
Herbs, cultivation and containers, **263**, *265*, *266*
  see also: Ch 17. Children's Gardens, **289**
*Heuchera sanguinea* (Per.), **96**
*Hibbertia*
  *dentata* (Cl.), **181**
  *procumbens* (G.C.), **54**
*Hibiscus* (Shr.)
  *moscheutos* (Per.), **96**
  *mutabilis*, **139**
  *rosa-sinensis*, **139**, *139*
  *rosa-sinensis*, 'Princess Marina', *140*
  *rosa-sinensis* 'White Wings', *140*
  *schizopetalus*, **139**, *140*
  *syriacus*, **139**, *173*
Hiccup Nut: see *Combretum bracteosum*
Himalayan Honeysuckle: see *Leycesteria formosa*
*Hippeastrum* (Per.)
  hybrid, **96**, *97*
Hirsute: see Botanical Terms and their Meanings, **378**
Hoes, common garden and Dutch, **39**, *39*
*Hoffmannia ghiesbreghtii* (Per. ind.), **303**
Hog Weed, *352*
Holly Fern: see *Cyrtomium falcatum*
*Holmskioldia sanguinea* (Shr.), **143**

**HOME-GROWN VEGETABLES**
**253-261**
  Aubergine: see Egg Plant
  Beans
    cultivation and deep-freezing, **254**, *254*
  Beetroot
    black spot on leaves, *344*

**Photographs** by T. Barrett, R. Bock, S. Brandt, K. Broadribb, O. Chunnett, G. Cubitt, B. Fey, N. Gardiner, J. Gillies, D. Greig, Hadeco, A. G. Kunne, Prof. Matthee, S. Macoboy, M. Monfries, J. Onderstall, Prof. K. Pienaar, P. Polglase, H. Potgieter, E. Rohe, C. H. Rostance, P. Sargeant, F. Stacey, Tamerlane, J. Watchman, P. Whitfield, M. Woods.